An East End Life

By Derek Martin

With Christine An Poster

Splendid
BOOKS

Published in 2010 by Splendid Books Limited

Written by Derek Martin with Christine An Poster

Copyright © 2010 Splendid Books Limited

Splendid Books Limited
The Old Hambledon Racecourse Centre
Sheardley Lane
Droxford
Hampshire
SO32 3QY

www.splendidbooks.co.uk

British Library Cataloguing in Publication Data is available from The British Library

ISBN: 9780955891632

Designed by Design Image Ltd.
www.design-image.co.uk

Printed and bound in the UK by CPI Mackays, Chatham ME5 8TD

Every effort has been made to fulfil requirements with regard to reproducing copyright material. The writers and publisher will be glad to rectify any omissions at the earliest opportunity.

Photo credits:
Derek Martin's own collection except mono plate section page 7 (top)
Graham Tonks www.grahamtonksphotographer.co.uk and page 8 (top)
Rex Features and colour plate section page 1 © Radio Times, page 3 (top) and page 6 (top) © FremantleMedia and pages 7 (bottom) and 8 © BBC Photo Library

Contents

Introduction

On the set of *EastEnders* one afternoon in early 2009, some of the younger cast members and I were chatting over lunch, when Lacey Turner asked me how I'd got into showbusiness. So I told them about the time I stood trial at the Old Bailey, which is where my acting story really begins. When I'd finished, someone said "You should write a book Derek!" This wasn't the first time I'd heard that said, so when it was suggested seriously to me a few weeks later, that I should write my autobiography, I have to confess to being more than a little embarrassed by the idea. After all, why would anyone want to know about my life? To me, there didn't seem much that was outstanding – I hadn't climbed Everest or been around the world in a hot air balloon, so what was so interesting about me that would captivate a reading audience?

Initially, I said I would think about it over the following week. I was told to write a few things down, starting with my early youth, and see how I felt. This I did. Once I got going, I began by reminiscing about the early years, growing up in London's East

End. Before I knew it, I'd written about two pages of scribblings, but hadn't got further than my fifth birthday! Then the thought occurred to me, since life in the East End of my childhood days was so very different from that of other walks of life, that it might be interesting to other people.

As I delved deeper and deeper, I began to feel quite proud of myself – looking back to the dreary housing; lack of proper amenities; little money and hardly any luxuries, I realised that the 'the boy done good' - I'd managed to build an altogether better life for myself through a lot of hard work, true grit and determination; coupled with an in-built sense of worth, terrific good humour and the ability not to take myself too seriously.

Over the last 10 years, with the ever increasing popularity of *EastEnders*, I had started to build quite a fan base, and I got to thinking about the huge leap from my early upbringing to my present lifestyle. It all started to make sense. Was it possible that I could open a lot of people's minds to the opportunities that are out there, and which they might have felt were unavailable to them? There was my answer. My thoughts kept returning to my early youth. Then, of course, there was no stopping me. I couldn't stem the flow now, not until it was all down on paper!

So, I hope you enjoy my story and don't think me too arrogant in wanting to put my colourful life, albeit tinged with some shaded grey, into words.

CHAPTER ONE

Evacuation

It was a bitterly cold, murky-grey, late November day. 1940: the year of the Blitz. This was the start of a mass exodus of women and children from London, but more especially, the East End, which had taken the full brunt of Hitler's merciless bombardment.

Earliest memories of my childhood are based around World War Two, the most significant being evacuation, so this would seem a good place to start my story.

I can picture myself now, even after so many years have passed, as the dreaded day came to fruition. Feeling sad and forlorn as I stood in the middle of the platform, my whole body shivered uncontrollably from top to bottom. A mixture of cold and fright no doubt. With my prominent, knobbly knees protruding beneath a pair of over-sized, hand-me-down flannel shorts, I must have looked every inch a child of the times.

Just one more tiny, faceless statistic amid hordes of equally nondescript citizens, gathered like tiny ants beneath the vast expanse of austere space which marked out a defining territory between the roof and platform of Paddington Station. Another skinny little seven year old.

That morning, I'd been reduced to slitting my shoes in order to make more room. My toes had been pushed, agonizingly, to their limit. There was hardly a child in sight who wouldn't have stirred the emotions of all who observed these harrowing scenes of evacuation.

The meagre ration books hardly afforded our parents the luxury of keeping up with their growing offspring. It didn't matter though, because we were all in the same boat. A uniform so to speak, distinguishing the hoi polloi from the upper classes.

Warm, steamy vapours floated in front of my face from quickened, nervous breath. A droplet formed precariously on the tip of my nose. I tried to reach it with my tongue but gave up and wiped it on the back of my hand instead. Not a friend in sight; I scoured the crowd for a recognisable face. No luck - I was on my own, except for Mum.

An uncertain destiny lay ahead.

There was a sinking, chewed-up feeling in the pit of my stomach. Surely my heartbeat was audible. Could Mum hear? It was pounding away under the Fair Isle sweater that Nan had knitted for my seventh birthday earlier that year. Certainly I could hear it. Gripping Mum's gloved hand tightly, I clenched my teeth in a pitiful attempt not to cry, still hoping somehow that I could will her into taking me home when the time came. I nuzzled my face into her hand to sniff the leather.

"Knee 'igh to a grass'opper," Mum used to describe me to people.

A dog-end caught my eye and I tried, unsuccessfully, to roll it over with my shoe. "Stop fidge'ing!" Mum had snapped. "Jus' stan' still - won' be long now." She smiled down guiltily, sorry for her short-tempered outburst. Everyone was on edge.

I was born in Bow, east London, on April 11 1933. Within the sound of Bow Bells. Therefore, I am a true, bona fide East Ender. That same year, Hitler came into power and 'Hyperion' won The Derby. Both events would prove to be significant. The latter only becoming apparent later on, when gambling became a dark force in my life.

Christened Derek William Rapp, I remained an only child for Bill and Christina, who were a devoted couple. Although they were poor, I was brought up in a secure and loving environment. Even though I was proud of my roots and my parents, I still spent most of my youth wishing I could escape from my ties with the East End. I think I'd seen too many films about how the other half lived and always hankered after things I didn't have. Mainly material things, like a large house with a swimming pool; sports cars, nice clothes and that sort of thing.

Dad had a really open and kind face with a strong, masculine jawline and bright, sparkling blue eyes. He was quite tall and powerfully built, with exceptionally strong arms, from years of working as a docker. Everybody loved my Dad, and people used to tell me what a great bloke he was all through my childhood. For all this though, it wasn't a good idea to cross swords with him because he could turn very quickly. He had the same deep streak of violence in him that is inbred in east London men. Mum, on the other hand was tiny – about five feet two inches. She had pretty features and thick, curly, dark brown hair which she wore fairly short. Her eyes were a very expressive dark brown, and could tell you what was going on in her head with one short glance. I always knew if she was cross with me by her eyes, whereas Dad's gave nothing away. Most of my chastising would come from Mum. In common with the times, men felt it was the mother's job to bring up the children when it came to daily do's and don'ts. My punishment came in the form of several hidings, usually using her slipper or a belt when I'd done something seriously naughty, or a slap for minor disobediences. She was always very fair, and throughout my life she made no bones about telling me if she thought I was wrong, and the other person right, in any form of dispute. On the other hand, if anyone did anything bad towards me, she'd let them suffer the full brunt of her wrath verbally, and if more serious action was required, she'd let Dad deal with it.

There was something about the East End though, for all its bleakness and austerity that gave a real sense of belonging. Locals were referred to affectionately as "the salt of the earth" by other

Londoners because they respected them for their hard labour, staunch loyalty to one another and unpretentious behaviour. Well known for its history of unlawful pursuits, the East End of pre-war years was ruled from within, by a handful of rival gangs who saw to it that order was maintained through a series of unwritten laws that everyone understood and obeyed. Theft from their own kind was rare and outlawed by most self-respecting villains. It was these codes that have shaped my thoughts and actions throughout my life.

Dad had shown me precisely how to use the gas mask, neatly housed in a square, cardboard box, which now hung carelessly over the left shoulder of my navy-blue Mackintosh. I loved the distinctive smell of the lining.

From out of nowhere, a deafening, thundering rumble stunned the crowd into silence as the steam-train rolled into view. Great puffs of smoke engulfed the domed space as the familiar, sickly-sweet clouds, choked their way into my lungs. This calmed me for a moment as I remembered the times I'd hung over the railway bridge with Dad, eagerly awaiting the arrival of the Flying Scotsman as it whizzed below, full speed to Edinburgh. The pavement used to shudder under my feet, as if hit by a mini-earthquake. In its wake, a vortex of bulbous, nebula cloud would envelop me as I struggled to find Dad through the haze.

The train came to a slow, piercing halt, with a final screech of breaks, just inches short of the buffer.

"Please Mum! I don' wanna go, I don' wanna go!" Sobbing violently, I had tried to free myself and run away. Mum just squeezed harder. With a tiny canvas suitcase tucked under her arm and into her ribcage in a vice-like grip, she grabbed my sleeve for extra security with her free hand. Nudging forward, we jostled, inch by inch, towards the compartment doors.

At this point, I heard Mum let out a yelp as one of the metal corner-pieces of her case cut into her right breast painfully. Perhaps she felt too numb to care. She said nothing.

Women of all ages and sizes clung onto their few, miserable possessions, held close to their bosoms, whilst still managing to hang on to their charges. They assumed, in a strange way, the role of prisoners-of-war, as they poured, snake-like, into the elongated carriages. How long this enforced exile would last, none of us knew.

"Dad! Dad! - I wan' me Dad!" I bellowed, at the top of my voice, until I was hoarse.

Pangs of fear continued to rage through my body and my steps faltered. My legs almost gave way, but I managed to clamber up into the gloomy carriage. It stank of stale tobacco and sweat. Mum found herself a seat and patted her bare knee to indicate where I should sit.

On either side sat two voluptuously over-weight women. It was going to be a long journey, so they offered to roll up their coats and make me a seat on top of their cases, which formed a neat line between themselves and the passengers opposite. Perched on the edge of the strongest one, facing Mum, I asked, "Where are we goin' Ma?"

"To the coun'ry, son. 'Ereford." She tried to sound calm and reassuring as she explained what would happen at the other end. Scared and alone she was none too sure of what to expect, but at that age I can be forgiven for not knowing any of this. Mum had received only the briefest instruction from one of the officials who'd informed her that we'd be living with a designated family who would meet us at the station. That was as much as he knew himself.

Green fields spread for miles, as far as the eye could see. This was a new experience for me. The unfamiliar sights held my thoughts captive for most of the journey. What was the countryside, after all, to a city boy like me? In my imagination I'd conjured up visions of weirdly dressed yokels with bits of straw sticking out of their hair, just as I'd seen in photos. Muck-spreaders we called them at school.

The only one still awake, I day-dreamed to my heart's content. The women were swaying from side to side in rhythm with the carriages' roll and it made me laugh out loud. Probably weary from emotional exhaustion, they slept for most of the three hours it took to get to our destination.

"Over there!" An official pointed in our direction as we stood on the platform. A friendly-looking couple smiled and stepped forward anxiously, pushing their way through the crowd towards Mum and me. "Is it just the two of 'ee?" enquired the woman. "Yes," came a faltering reply.

The house was welcoming enough, and although nothing untoward happened during my stay there, I hated everything about the place. I detested the rural atmosphere, the smell of silage and compost, as well as the classmates who used funny dialogue I didn't understand, failing in my innocence, to realise that they probably had the same trouble with my cockney accent. They were the foreigners - not me. I don't remember the couple's names but they had two children; a boy about the same age as me and a girl of about 12 or 13. Mum got a job in a factory in Hereford and I went to the local school with the boy, but he was never friendly towards me. Not once did he let me share any of his toys at home, and, bearing in mind children who were evacuated couldn't take any away with them, I thought him a mean and nasty boy. At school, he used to encourage his friends to gang up on me, bullying me and calling me, "Mummy's boy!" Several times I ran away from school during the day, and hung around the town until it was time to catch the bus home with Mum, who met me at the bus stop every day.

At the house, I had tantrums and screamed a lot, out of frustration I suppose. I used my temper as a means of releasing my pent-up anger. I told Mum I'd rather put up with the bombs than stay here. After just a few months, I made such a fuss and created enough of a hullabaloo to warrant a speedy return home. Mum agreed with me because I don't think she was happy at all either, although she would have hidden this from me at the time. Many years later, she confessed to me that we only stayed there as long as we did for my sake, and she hadn't needed much persuasion from me to return home. Apart from anything, she missed Dad, and couldn't wait to write to him with the good news to say we'd be back soon. Dad met us at the station and I was so happy to see him that I sobbed tears of joy as he scooped me up into his arms. Needless to say, we never kept in touch with that family. We were glad and relieved to be back in familiar surroundings.

The war was never far away and when the sirens sounded, I'd snuggle up in a make-shift sleeping bag, nestling under one of Dad's huge, powerful biceps. Just the three of us. Myself, Mum and Dad, huddled together against the rear tin wall of our Anderson shelter which had been placed at the bottom of the garden in Loxley Street. The house had two storeys, a basement, an outside lavvy, but no bathroom. Instead, a tin bath hung on a long hook in the kitchen, next to the fire.

Lit only by a tiny candle, placed carefully in a corner near the entrance, the shelter had become a comforting second home. As soon as our eyes became accustomed to the dark, Mum would snuff it out. Nothing should be wasted. I could never enjoy candle-light again because of this association, and loathe the smell of candles to this day.

"'Ere son. Chop suey an' noodles." Dad would chuck a brown paper bag at me.

Before proper Chinese take-away had been introduced, small cafes littered the West India Dock Road, close-by the docks, run by Chinese immigrants for the benefit of Oriental seamen. It wasn't long though, before the local workforce developed a taste for the new food.

Dad was a fireman and on duty every night at the fire station, but on rare occasions, if there was a lull in the bombing, he'd sneak back home, just minutes away, for a quick bite with the family. When I'd eaten my new, favourite food, Dad would settle me down by re-living the day's events. It was the nearest thing to a bed-time story.

So-and-so's house had been bombed out; a child had been rescued from a blazing shop; but by far the best stories were the ones about people who'd been found alive, beneath piles of rubble. In my eyes, my Dad was, undoubtedly, the bravest fireman alive. In fact, later he received the British Empire Medal for his outstanding bravery in the Fire Service.

On those nights the sirens sounded, all around we heard chitter-chatter and clanging tin cups, as shared flasks of tea passed among the gatherings. Gradually, I'd drift off to sleep until the 'all clear' sounded.

Before the war, Dad had grafted long and hard as a docker until joining up for the Fire Service. It was a sad and sorry sight to see his territory taking such a hammering. He tried not to dwell on it and focused, instead, on the job in hand. Sometimes, on Saturdays, he'd take me down to the dockside to see the huge cargo ships. If the coast was clear, we'd sneak below, into the hold and along to the engine room.

Being an only child I was used to getting my own way and friends learnt quickly that when I wanted to play the 'German' during our war games, there wouldn't be any arguments. By not having siblings, I had missed out on learning the art of sharing and used to wish, with all my heart, that I might have a brother to play with one day. Throughout my childhood I was lonely. My Mother's younger sister, Aunt Gladdie, was only five years older than me, so I looked upon her as the sister I never had. Gladdie lived with my grandparents still, just around the corner in Endive Place, so we would get together now and again. Mainly, we'd play games in the street outside my house and she was terrific fun to be with. During the latter part of the war, our favourite scam was to pinch woollens from her Mum's bedroom drawers, and even off the neighbours' washing lines, to sell to the rag and bone man. Wool was at a premium during the war so we got a few coppers for them, which we'd spend on going to the cinema.

Every summer we would go on a family holiday, either to Ramsgate or Camber Sands, for one week. There'd be Mum, Dad and me, with Dolly and George and later their son, known to all as Young Georgie, plus any other children who could come. Usually

Gladdie would tag along because her parents were working. We'd spend every day on the beach, making sandcastles or burying each other up to our necks in the sand. In the evenings, the men would go for a pint maybe, to one of the local pubs, while the women stayed behind playing games with us in the guests' lounge. There was never much money to spend, but all I remember was having fun every day. As we grew to our teens Gladdie and I drifted apart slightly for a while. She was very pretty, as were all Mum's sisters, and it wasn't long before she met a nice young boy, also called Bill.

When I was about nine, I had to be rushed to hospital from my school in Mile End. During morning playtime, a friend and I were wrestling on the ground. He was on top of me. While I was screaming for him to get off, a penny fell out of his top shirt pocket and into my mouth. I swallowed it accidentally, so they carted me off to the London Hospital in Mile End, where an X-ray showed it had gone into my stomach luckily, and not my windpipe. I had to stay in for three days, having several further X-rays, to track its progress through my digestive tract. Every time I went to the toilet, in a bedpan, one of the nurses had the tedious and most unpleasant task of sifting through the contents to look for it. Eventually it turned up on the Friday and the nurse came running in to show me the coin. It had turned black from stomach acids but they scrubbed it clean and sterilised it, and of course, I couldn't wait to show my souvenir to friends at school the following week. Mum and Dad came to fetch me at lunchtime on the Saturday and took me to the pictures, as a treat, to see Clark Gable in *The China Seas*.

Bomb sites formed terrific playgrounds for young boys. My friends and I were inseparable and we'd spend hours, re-enacting dog-fights and collecting memorabilia. Discarded bullets, spent shells, dented and misshapen helmets, tin mugs and shrapnel; forming the basis of a motley mishmash of paraphernalia that we'd hide somewhere safe, until the next time. Always assuming that the stashed booty would remain and not fall victim to yet another bomb.

During the black-out I'd sneak into the street to listen out for the distinct sounds of Junkers or Dorniers as they flew low, dropping their destructive cargo. It's a good job Mum and Dad were unaware of this caper, having promised faithfully to dive for cover or run to the nearest shelter when the sirens went. Like most of my contemporaries though, the lure of war was just too exciting. It held me spellbound for the full six years.

Miraculously, odd scraps of wood loomed up at me and my mates, from strange hidey holes in each new ruin, forming convenient shapes that could be imagined easily into rifles or Sten guns.

"Paa! Paa! Pop, pop, neeow, kaboom, kaboom! ....Hah! Gottcha! Gottcha!"

I'd oblige my friends convincingly, by feigning a slow, miserable and painful death. Clutching my chest with both hands, one atop the other over my heart, I'd drop to one knee slowly and laboriously. "Aaaaaaaah…………, I've bi'n sho'!" Ending with an over-acted, grand finale of body rolls. Talk about acting!

Tufts of grass had sprung up brazenly amid the rubbish, dotted here and there. By the magic of nature, seeds had an innate ability to settle in the most unlikely places. After the war, entrepreneurs such as Jim Gregory (who later became Director of QPR football club), would take over these barren wastes, turning them into second-hand car lots or markets and such like.

What was once an interior wall, all too soon became another's exterior, as one by one, streets were thinned out. A fitting stage backdrop or film set. Each tread of the staircase clearly stamped and silhouetted against a wall, spiralled skywards, like a scene from a Lewis Carroll novel. Perfectly-hung wallpaper unfurled slowly as rain became trapped behind the glue. Miraculously, whole fireplaces held firm, while odd mahogany or pine shelving hung, precariously, by a single nail or two.

New homes formed for daffodils, wild flowers and weeds, looking for all the world as if a bowl of freshly-picked flowers had been placed, painstakingly, on the mantle by its mistress.

I was number one to my parents and I was spoilt, but not in a material way; quite simply, their life revolved around me. As I said, Mum was strict and didn't stand for any nonsense. Dad, on the other hand, thought the sun shone from my arse and I could do no wrong. He let me get away with just about anything. The East

End mentality was such that the wrongs or rights of a situation had little bearing on the case when it came to family. Bill Rapp was no exception, and he would have killed, if necessary, to protect Mum or me.

My Aunt Alice lived in a big house a few streets away. One afternoon, not long after Mum and I had returned from Hereford, she'd called round for a visit. It got to about six o'clock when the sirens started. "C'mon - let's make a run fer it te my place. I feel safer there." Alice was edgy, and hated being away from the security of her domestic surroundings.

Mum grabbed a few things for the two of us, shoving them haphazardly into an overnight bag and made for the door. As soon as we were in the street, the anti-aircraft guns could be heard, making their usual deafening racket. With the bombs blasting away, great gusts of acrid smoke billowed towards us and I remember screaming with fright.

"No, I'm no' going - I'm no' going!" I yelled, kicking Aunt Alice on the shin as I hung onto the front door, continuing, "I wanna go in ours mum, please, please!"

"'E's too 'eavy fer me te carry," Mum had shouted to her sister-in-law, "We'll 'ave to stay 'ere. Quick, follow me!"

The three of us made the customary dash across the garden. Daft really, to call it a shelter, when in truth it offered little protection. Lots of people opted not to use them at all for this reason and preferred to make up their own somewhere in the house instead.

Typical hide-outs were under kitchen tables, cellars or cupboards.

Once inside, Mum would close the gap with a sheet of corrugated metal. This left a space of about two feet still open. I loved to watch, mesmerized, as the skies took on a new life in the dark. The whole country was under enforced black-out which gave an eerie feel to the outdoors. If an incendiary bomb came down, great shafts of light would fill the darkness, high above the rooftops, as building after building caught fire. Through the beams, darting shells could be picked out like fireflies, headed upward in quick succession as a barrage poured from the anti-aircraft guns. Like a grand firework display, London returned the compliment.

One thing I hated about the early mornings, as we left the shelter, was the smell of gas. It seemed to linger everywhere as supplies were cut into, through the bombing. I suppose it reminded me of my very earliest memory – that of having a gas mask fitted over my face, as a small four year old boy. I had to have my tonsils out and spent about five days at the Queen's Hospital for Children in Bethnal Green – subsequently bombed in 1941. It was a terrifying experience for any child, as the smell of gas hit you. I tried to fight it off with all my strength but of course the next thing I remember was waking up on a ward. Unlike modern trends, in those days, mothers were discouraged from staying with their children and I felt abandoned. Maybe that's why I was so reluctant to be evacuated; it must have instilled a deep fear in me.

During the night Dad must have come home for a few hours

because I woke up to find myself sandwiched between him and Mum. At around eight o'clock, Alice decided it was time to go home. As she turned into her street, it was clear that the house had been hit. Still standing, but not looking right somehow. The window sills weren't aligned properly and huge cracks cut deep into the brickwork. She raced back to get Bill. Mum, who wasn't much taller than me at that age, followed on, running as fast as her legs would allow. This was my first lucky escape! Dad opened the front door to make sure it was safe to enter. Both women were too numb to speak so he broke the silence first.

"Wait 'ere, I'm gonna look out the back." Of course I disobeyed and followed on quietly. The door was missing, and we could see, instantly, that the shelter had taken a direct hit. All that was visible was a smouldering crater; the size of which could have housed four double-decker buses. As we cast our eyes over the new landscape, it transpired that the hole had taken in both neighbouring gardens.

There weren't any signs of life, so without stopping to look further, we returned to the house. Alice and Mum were rummaging in the kitchen. It was imperative to salvage as much as possible. Dad drew me to his side. One step at a time, he proceeded gingerly to the staircase, checking to see if his weight would hold, before moving on. Up we went, past the bedrooms, and onto the second floor landing. What Dad saw next froze him to the spot. He pushed me aside. "Close yer eyes an' don' look!" Of course, true to type,

I did what all children do - exactly the opposite.

A headless torso hung, like a scene from the crucifixion, in the framework of the rear sash window, suspended and wedged inbetween the broken panes of glass. Charred, crumpled edges of red and white stripy material, the remnants of a pyjama top perhaps, were splattered with dried blood. I stopped in my tracks, riveted to the floor, as this bewildering picture sunk in. Under normal circumstances I'm sure this episode would have affected me badly, but most children who grew up during the Blitz became desensitised and unperturbed by such horrors because we were exposed to such things on a daily basis. By some miracle, the bed, dressing table and wardrobe had hardly moved. Half the ceiling was down and I could see a patch of clear blue sky through a gaping hole in the roof.

"Is it the lodger, Dad?" No answer followed.

Dad couldn't contemplate such a thought at this stage. He liked the bloke a lot. A musician who played the accordion. They'd spent many an evening round at Alice's having a good old sing-song. He beckoned me to follow him downstairs and into the front bedroom, which belonged to Alice. Once again, Dad was circumspect. Small, precise steps. He'd been doing this for long enough and had seen dozens of his fellow workmates injured through rushing, headlong, into blazing buildings, to know the importance of remaining vigilant.

Alice shouted up to us to bring any bedding we could from

her chest of drawers.

I obliged, and opened the bottom drawer carefully. A bloody hand came into view, lying on top of a neat pile of linen. A left hand. How on earth did it get there? This was a mystery that no one could fathom out, not even the police who'd been called in to oversee the proceedings.

When she heard about our find, Alice came upstairs to identify the hand. "Yeah, it's 'is," she stated blandly. She knew this, because, on the little finger was the signet ring her lodger wore. They never found out who the torso had belonged to. Once foul-play had been eliminated, there wasn't time for such formalities, considering the thousands of dead bodies there were at the time. The lodger was never seen again, but he might just as easily have come a cropper in the shelter. Missing, presumed dead, was how it had been left.

These images left a lasting impression on me, but luckily I didn't suffer nightmares. Like a cat with nine lives, this was only one of many brushes with death that I encountered throughout my life. An eternal optimist, I had a sixth sense that my number wasn't going to be up for a long time to come.

A fascination for the German Forces stemmed back to my childhood. Often I'd heard family members discussing our links with Germany, believing they were of Arian descent because of strong resemblances to a photograph Dad possessed of General Rapp. Napoleon's Aide de Campe was, in truth, from Alsace on the borders, but it suited my fertile imagination to pretend he was

German and a distant relative.

Sometime, towards the end of 1941, we were bombed out of Loxley Street. Mum and Dad must have grown increasingly worried about my welfare and safety. Mum worked all day in the laundry and Dad was hardly ever around. That left me to fend for myself too much. Hitler had new, ever more lethal weapons as each year passed. The V.1, or doodlebug, as it was commonly known, was one of them.

This bomb was so dangerous because no one ever knew where it would strike. It could be heard coming from quite a distance away - an intermittent droning sound. No sooner had it come into view, than it's engine would cut out. Without further ado, it would fall from the skies. Boom! No chance to run or take cover. My parents fretted over this, knowing that I came home from school alone. Suppose I couldn't hide? It didn't bear thinking. Their minds were made up, and I was sent to live with Nan in Ashford, Middlesex. She was Dad's mum.

Nan went without in order to do her best for me. Once a week I'd have fillet steak, bought on the black market of course, and didn't suffer any further hardship in that way again. St. Anne's Junior School in Long Lane, Stanwell, was only a short bus ride away although, truth be told, I often pocketed my bus fare and walked instead. I looked forward to getting back to some semblance of normality.

Once again though, I was the odd one out with my marked

accent and was bullied from the off. When Nan saw how dishevelled I used to look every time I came home; torn shirt-sleeves or ripped shorts, she decided to teach me a few tricks of defence - only hers didn't come from the Marquis of Queensbury's rule book!

After one such home-coming, and looking particularly the worse for wear, Nan sat me down for a stern talking-to. "Now look 'ere sonny," she said, shaking her index finger at me. "You ain't no good a' figh'in', so you gotta hi' back dirty, see. Wai' 'till they turn 'round an' then kick 'em in the spine!" Her eyes had taken on a gleeful slant and the corners of her mouth were fixed, as she spelled out her own vicious guidelines. She was the sort of woman you wouldn't want to cross.

Before her husband had been killed, Nan had been the victim of physical abuse. Customary drinking binges invariably led to violence. She'd end up with a good hiding and retaliate by throwing his dinner against the kitchen wall. This wound him up even more, and so it went on, week after week and year after year.

Dad had suffered the same fate as a growing lad, but vowed never to lay a finger on any wife or child of his. I don't remember a time when he lifted a hand to me in anger. Not that he was soft or anything, far from it in fact. Nan's old man had died during the early part of the war, while lying ill in hospital. He'd been in a ward on the top floor when it took a direct hit.

"Good job!" Nan had said.

My chance to show that I could look out for myself came

soon enough. A boy had hit me across the shoulder, full pelt with a cricket bat, after a game one afternoon. Wasting no time, I removed my trouser-belt and proceeded to whack the guy to the ground, using the buckle. What followed was pretty grim.

Once down, I sat astride the boy and continued striking his skull incessantly. By the time the teachers had been called, or seen the commotion, the poor lad's skin had been torn wide open, revealing the frontal bone. This, too, was damaged with a hairline crack already visible. Someone restrained me, and I was carted off in a police car later.

Too young to be prosecuted, I received only a severe warning. Thus, I gained a new nickname; 'Mad Rappy', and a commanding reputation. No one dared to cross me again. Power and fear are great levellers and armed with a leather strap for defence, kept in my pocket at all times, the other boys soon looked to me for protection. The injured boy returned to school, with his head stitched, and nothing more was said.

Sport became a good outlet for my pent up aggression. When school sports day came around, I won several events such as throwing a cricket ball the furthest, swimming and running. Parents didn't attend very often in those days and I never really had much encouragement while mine were away. Nan certainly didn't come. Football was my passion and I became a pretty good player. As my aggressive reputation grew, the teachers suggested I should take up boxing, in the hope it might rid me of some of my anger. I joined the school boxing club and loved it, and it wasn't long before I'd won through to the local championships. As the title fight drew closer, my headmaster took me to one side to tell me I'd been dropped from our team. He explained that because my style was very vicious – I had a killer instinct, like my all time favourite boxer Rocky Marciano - and local dignitaries including the Mayor were attending the event, he didn't want any upsets on the evening. Once I knew I could win a fight, I'd stop at nothing to complete the task, so to be fair I can see his point now. At the time though, I felt it was an unfair thing to do to me, so I gave up from then on and never boxed again.

On alternate weekends and holidays my parents would come and visit. Once, Mum told the story of a narrow escape. Soon after being bombed out, they'd gone to nearby Clemence Street, and, seeing what looked like an empty house, Dad kicked the door down. Not a soul had lived there for ages. Her sister and brother-in-law, Dolly and George, lived at number two, Alice had moved into number 30 since becoming homeless, and this was number 10. Now we were all reunited as a family, in one row, on the same side of the street.

Mum continued: while returning home from work one evening, towards the latter part of 1944, she had heard the dreaded sound of a doodlebug overhead and so dived into the baker's doorway for refuge. Meanwhile, Dad had been standing on the roof of the fire station, which acted as a useful look-out post. He'd spend hours up there, watching for the next influx of bombers. He butted in to finish the story: on this particular day he'd seen the same 'bug come over, followed in quick succession by more, dropping roughly where he thought our house was. Hearing the explosions, he'd shouted out to the others, "I'm off! That's me 'ouse, I'm sure of it!"

He rounded the corner and stopped short. The entire street had been wiped out. In a panic, and feeling sick to his stomach, Dad had composed himself. He knew his mates would be following shortly with the fire hoses.

Before the war, The National Fire Service had commandeered over 2000 Austin taxi-cabs to haul equipment through the streets. Not built for such heavy work, they didn't last more than a year or two and were finally abandoned, in favour of new wagons, based on the Austin K2 chassis. These were painted a dull, dark grey with a white circle on the sides housing the letters NFS. The driver's door held the Royal coat-of-arms, picked out in gold, and inscribed - G V1 R. My Dad loved them and drove at maximum speed whenever he was called out.

At one point, he thought he heard a movement under some debris, so started clawing at the slabs of rubble in a desperate attempt to find Mum. By coincidence, or perhaps by instinct, he'd looked up at the very moment his treasured wife came into view. They ran into each other's arms, crying and laughing at one and the same time. Another miraculous escape. Nan and I had sobbed throughout the story as the thought of it was too much.

When war had been declared in 1939, Nan had moved to the Ashford area to be near her sisters. This meant that for the first time in my life I had cousins to play with, the same age as me. Lenny and Ernie Ladlow and Teddy Debuse became constant companions. New friends, George and Harry, joined later to form a proper gang for the rest of our school days.

Heathrow airport didn't exist then, being mainly farmland. Every summer my new pals and I would work on the farms, potato-picking. The first runway was built, subsequently, where once there had been a river. Most of my spare time was spent either swimming or fishing in it.

Every family has its black sheep or skeleton in the cupboard and ours was no exception. Another of Dad's sisters, Aunt Joyce, had become a member of Moseley's Army or Black Shirts as they were known. She was a real fascist and drifted away from all of us so it never became necessary to disown her, at least I don't remember that being the case. Years later she came to her senses and rejoined the family.

War ended in 1945 and Dad needed a break from London, so he and Mum joined me and Nan at 57 Ravensbourne Avenue. He got a job at Ashford General Hospital as Transport Manager while she worked in the front shop of the Springfield Laundry.

Having thrived in this environment I was the only one of my group to pass the 11-plus exam. I never told my parents though.

When the results came, I lied, telling everyone that I'd failed, because I thought the grammar school might be a bit snooty and wanted to remain with my friends at the secondary modern. This wasn't one of my better decisions and later I regretted it.

CHAPTER TWO

Scams & Fiddles

The seed had been sown, years before, when Mum took me to films. Going to the cinema had been a special treat during the war years and had added a bit of light relief to an otherwise hum-drum life. I fancied myself as a John Wayne cowboy and would day-dream that one day I might be a film star, but then I imagine most kids do. As a young man though, aged around 20, the theatre and film world became more of an obsession. I, and my best friend Frankie Palmer, travelled all over London to see whatever films we could. Three or four times a week in the evenings and then off to the music halls on Saturdays.

The Empire group of theatres were dotted all over London. This was where we'd see the big stars of the day. People like Nat King Cole, Billy Eckstine, Al Martino and Billy Daniels. We were always on time for any performance, paying respect to the supporting acts which took up the first half; mainly chorus girls and comedians. Today, as then, I have little patience with anyone who turns up late for a performance.

Cinema has always been my church; my place of worship. The screen is the altar and the stars are the Gods - James Cagney as the High Priest, followed by Humphrey Bogart, John Wayne and James Stewart, to name but a few - all there to be revered from on high. The only difference being the congregation. If possible, there would be just one pew, reserved for my disciples - friends who know how to behave. As the lights are dimmed and the curtains part, a silent hush should follow. Absolutely no talking from now on. No sweets. No popcorn. A black room. Not a murmur please, from the second the film starts to the last credit. I think it's terrible that most people pay very little attention to the credits, but then I'm biased. Many a time I would get up from my seat in the cinema and shout: "Quiet please, I didn't come here to listen to you lot!"

Frankie and I had become pals during knock-about football at an old bomb site, three streets away from my home. We followed the Continental theatre circuit. Memorable films from that period were *Rififi*, *Wages of War, La Ronde* and *La Strada* which were shown at our favourite theatres: the Academy in Oxford Street, the Continental in Tottenham Court Road, the Paris Pullman in Chelsea and the Poly in Upper Regent Street.

Laurel and Hardy's last performance in England was at the Chiswick Empire; something I'll never forget. Other great live performances included Max Miller and Jimmy James.

After Clemence Street had been wiped out, Mum and Dad found what was to become their permanent home for the next 30-odd years. Taking up squatters' rights was a normal part of life in those days and Dad reported their new address at the local council offices the next day: 24 Baythorne Street, Mile End. He was given a rent book and charged 10 shillings a week for the privilege.

The whole family had been made homeless overnight so Dolly and George moved in. They had the top two floors while Mum and Dad had the ground floor. The small back bedroom on the middle landing was mine and I lived there most of the time until I was 38, the only drawback being that access to the outside lavvy was through the downstairs kitchen. From now on privacy could not be expected, but this never became a problem because we all lived happily together, grateful for the simple luxury of a roof over our heads.

Most of our belongings had been stored in the front room while we lived in Ashford, so Dolly and George enjoyed having the house to themselves for the next five years.

Having left school at 15, without any qualifications, I became an apprentice surveyor for Gale and Power Estate Agents in Staines, sticking it out for about a year and a half, but the pay was lousy; only 25 shillings a week. All my mates were earning three times as much so I quit and joined them at a wood yard in Stanwell as an unskilled worker, for the princely sum of five pounds a week.

A serious family split came about after Nan had an almighty

fight with Mum. She'd been kicked forcefully in the stomach and punched in the face. So severe was the hiding that she'd been hospitalised. Jealousy had been the root cause of this explosion from Nan. She could never get used to the fact that Mum was treated like a princess. She was also very pretty and Dad gave her gifts whenever he could. Nan apologised and begged to be forgiven saying, "It'll never 'appen again!" Enough was enough though and Dad had heard it all before so wasn't taking any chances. The family left and that was the last time we saw her.

The three of us came home to Baythorne Street in 1950.

For the year before signing up for National Service as every young man did in those days, I kicked my heels a bit, drifting from one thing to another. This included a short stint at John Wright's furniture factory, as a lathe cutter, where, by coincidence, Mum had worked for a while after evacuation, on the Mosquito plane.

A brief spell at R. White's drinks factory followed, doing a round with the advertising manager. In my spare time, I teamed up with Frankie to do a spot of business. We borrowed a horse and cart from another friend and became 'rag and bone' men. Calling out in the streets for "Any ol' iron! Rags an' lumbar! Any ol' iron!" In exchange, we'd hand out cups and saucers as payment; usually given to us by customers while on our rounds. Not exactly bone china I can assure you. At the close of business we'd take our haul down to the local depot to be sorted into different piles. Any extra cash came in handy. One thing I hated though, was having to collect the manure whenever the horse dumped its load onto the road. We had to shovel it into a bucket and take it back to the owner, who, I believe, then sold it on to gardeners.

July 1951, and it was off to RAF Padgate in Warrington, Lancashire, for the start of my two years of National Service. A shock to my system would be an understatement as I admit I was spoilt, and apart from the short spell as an evacuee, had never been away from Mum before. Certainly, I didn't know how to make a bed, darn a sock or iron a shirt. Everyone had waited on me hand and foot up until now, but a rude awakening lay ahead as I camped down for my first night in the barracks.

Thirty other young men shared this hut, from all over Britain and I could hear a few muffled sniffles here and there, from under the covers at lights out. Not used to undressing in front of strangers and always having been a bit of a loner, I found this difficult to get used to.

Getting kitted out with uniform, rucksack and the like, took a week and when asked if I had any preferences for work, without hesitation I replied, "Air crew, please Sir!" All through my childhood I'd wanted to be a pilot, and with my background, the only hope of receiving any training was through the RAF.

Then I was sent to Hornchurch in Essex for a five-day ability test and medical check. Sadly, I didn't perform well in maths. Algebra and geometry hadn't been taught in my class and for the first time I regretted bitterly not taking the place at grammar school.

Three officers sat on the enrolment board. One looked straight at me.

"Sorry, son, you haven't made the grade for air crew," he said kindly, going on to make a time-worn speech. "But your marks were nonetheless excellent. Had this been wartime son, you'd have been up in eight weeks and more than likely dead in 12. With the new fighter jets - Vampires and Gloucester Meteors - we need tip-top, skilled men. We can afford to be more selective now. Sorry, but you may choose any other section from the full list available." Standing to attention, I saluted. "Thank you, sir! Police, sir! Please, sir!"

I was dismissed and returned to Padgate to complete the standard eight-week square-bashing programme. 'Mummy's boy' became more disciplined and independent with each passing day.

The routine and drills were hard. At six o'clock every morning the sergeant would shout the alarm and, without allowing us a second to come round, the lads would be expected to march to the wash room. What little fluff I had for a beard got shaved off and rinsed in icy-cold water. It was freezing. Although exhilarating later on, when marching to time in the yard, the showers were the worst. A drill sergeant's orders help to warm the body temperature pretty quickly though.

"Left, right, left right, hup, hup, - 'bout turn! Left........ left.........left!"

If we didn't march in unison, "You'll carry on 'till yer get it right!" It was that simple. Cross-country runs were great and I became extremely fit, building hitherto unseen muscles. The RAF made a boy into a man; of that there is little doubt, and the training stood me in good stead for the rest of my life.

Home leave came next. Only one week though, before being sent to the RAF Police Training School at Netheravon in Wiltshire. This completed, the next 18 months were spent at RAF Hemswell, Lincolnshire, in Bomber Command. Most of my time was taken up with guard duties and it was here that I chummed up with Doug McKeown, who became a lifelong friend. We were drawn to each other through a mutual love of films. All RAF camp cinemas were called the Astra. Programmes changed every two days with further showings on Saturdays. Doug and I made sure we were always off-duty when the film-shows operated.

I yearned to become airborne still and would never miss an opportunity to join the squadron on a training flight. These usually consisted of a sortie over peace-time Germany to take aerial photographs, sitting up front in what was jokingly called 'the bubble'. The only career that could ever have come close to acting would have been that of airline pilot.

Favourite night time escapades gave me a raison d'etre to get through my time at camp. Under the cloak of guard duty, I'd sneak down to the Motor Transport section and take out buses, cranes, lorries or fire trucks - even the CO's car on occasion, for a fast spin around the camp tracks and roads. This gained me the 'Forces' nickname of 'cab-happy-Rappy'. Luckily I escaped detection or I'd have been court martialed. These 'games' helped later on when I became a stunt driver. If I could handle a tank round an obstacle course, I could handle anything on the road.

A new man came home to Baythorne Street in the summer of 1953 when my National Service came to an end. Strong and self assured. It was great to be reunited with old pals, especially Frankie. After a fortnight's holiday at Butlins in Clacton, I got down to the task of sorting out a career. Billy Butlin was a pioneer of those times with his ever expanding leisure business; providing cheap, safe holidays for all generations. It was also a magnet for young lads wanting to flee the nest and a natural choice for Frankie and me. Chalets had two double bunk beds and it was common to share with strangers, so Frankie and I, being the first to arrive, bagged the two lower ones. We soon got pally with the other two blokes who joined later and set about organising our first Saturday night out on the town. Let's face it, there was only one thing on our minds – girls. I spent ages getting ready; greasing my hair into a Tony Curtis quiff. Never a great follower of fashion, I did however, buy some Levi's 501 jeans from an American chap at Hemswell, to which I added a polo neck shirt and black leather jacket. I think I was quite a good looking bloke and I don't remember worrying about my looks in any way. Off we went to a dance hall on the seafront and it wasn't long before we spotted some local 'chicks' -

which was the common word we'd picked up, from the American soldiers of course. When most of the evening had passed me by, finally, I plucked up the courage to ask a very attractive brunette to dance, for the last couple of slow smooches. We liked each other, and I found out she came from Stamford Hill, but she said her parents would be furious if they found out about me because she was Jewish. Norma Levy came from a religious background, although not Orthodox, and she told me her parents would never allow us to date. She was staying with friends in the town but we made a decision to enjoy the week and worry about what to do later. Every day we'd meet somewhere in the town and stroll around, hand in hand, hoping none of her friends would spot us. The only other form of entertainment was cinema. Back row of course, which is where all the heavy petting happened. It sounds so old fashioned now, but at the time it was hot stuff. Frankie didn't mind because he'd found a nice girl too so we made up a four for most of the time. In the end it turned into a bit of a holiday romance and we arranged to continue seeing each other in secret. The commute was easy from Bow to Stamford and we spent some happy times together. About three months later it fizzled out and we parted amicably.

My Dad suggested I try the Port of London Authority Police for an opening. It was an obvious choice, considering he now worked for the PLA as a foreman and I had my RAF training. "They'd welcome you with open arms son," he'd said without hesitation.

Trouble was brewing ahead though. After spending three months training me at their headquarters in the Royal Docks, and at great expense, I asked to leave just 16 weeks later. The bosses were furious and I received a right bollocking! Sooner or later they'd have seen that I wasn't taking the job seriously anyway since my mates and I had set up a dice school, in the courthouse of all places.

I was convinced that I'd either end up very rich from the many scams to be found at every turn - stolen cargo, smuggled alcohol or cigarettes to name but three - or be doing a 10-year stretch. I didn't tell them that of course. Instead, I made some feeble excuse about not liking the job, and left.

My social scene, such as it was, consisted of Fridays and Saturdays spent drinking at the Blind Beggar in Mile End Road, or other pubs along there. That is, if I wasn't at the films with Frankie. Dad hated me frequenting those places as he knew the sort of company his son would come up against. Favourite haunts of the infamous Ronnie and Reggie Kray. Funnily enough though, it was the twins' older brother, Charlie, who befriended me and he would always have time for a chat with me at the bar. I knew the twins worked out at a boxing club in Brady Street so avoided going there as I didn't want to risk becoming too heavily involved in that scene. I'd heard the stories and they weren't pleasant.

Invariably, if you lived in the East End, you would socialise and mix with villains. It was unavoidable and when deciding to write this book I made the decision to tell the whole story - warts 'n all. So there are things I've done that I'm ashamed of but then hindsight is a great thing is it not? More of that later.

Apparently, my mate Frankie was an outstanding footballer and had been invited for trials at Spurs but for some reason didn't follow through. He would have been appreciated as a cultured player now. Instead, we became Chelsea fans and joined the Supporters' Club team later on. I don't really know why I chose to support Chelsea since most of my mates back home went to West Ham.

Favourite players in the 1950s and early 1960s were Len Shackleton, Jimmy Greaves and my all-time hero, John 'The King' Charles – in my opinion, the greatest British footballer ever.

A season ticket cost six guineas each, including reserve matches, and we saw as many games as possible from the corner wooden stand. A programme cost three pence (in old money). Ted Drake was manager then and we won the league in 1955 but had to wait another 50 years before Jose Mourinho came along to do it again. Our own team played every Sunday morning on Mitcham Common in Surrey. We would travel right across London; north-east to south-west. Winding through traffic precariously, on Frankie's old motorbike, I rode pillion on his 125cc BSA Bantam, come wind, rain or shine. They were lovely days.

It's probably clear to you, the reader, that I have enormous pride in both my parents. There's a framed, guilt-edged photo on my desk as I write this; of Mum and me with Dad, posing in front of Buckingham Palace the day he got his B.E.M. from King George VI.

I can remember clearly during the war how, on one of Dad's rare nights off, he kept darting outside to listen to what was going on. Even though he loved to be with us, he could never relax properly if he thought his mates were in danger. This particular evening he heard a massive attack being launched on the docks and so decided to go down to Limehouse and see if the lads were all right.

Either Aberdeen or Dundee Wharf housed all the petrol tankers which were stored, fully loaded, ready for use. Good job Dad had gone, because six of them were alight. Without a moment's hesitation he drove them out, one by one, while the other firemen hosed the lorries down. If they'd been left in the warehouse to explode it doesn't bear thinking how much damage, or loss of life, could have ensued. Mad sod! Dad was fearless though and risked his life many times - he deserved that medal.

In a different way, I'm just as proud of my Mum. She was a real grafter – both at home and work. Her life revolved around the house, which she cleaned thoroughly every Saturday morning until it sparkled. Then she and Dad would go shopping in Mile End Road, stopping off at Billy Pike's, the butcher. Mum maintained he was the only butcher worth going to because he hung his meat properly and would give her certain cuts which she couldn't buy anywhere else – like an H bone of beef. She was a very good plain cook and her Sunday roasts were something of a legend within the family. Only downside being that, like many women of her generation, she overcooked the vegetablcs. The house would reek of stale cabbage from Sunday to Tuesday! Added to which, Aunt Dolly would be doing the same upstairs.

Another popular thing in those days was the theory that the same meal should be produced on a set day each week, so Mondays were bubble and squeak – fried, with left-over meat juices and gravy added for extra flavour; Tuesdays were some form of meat pie or suet pudding – mince or steak and kidney; Wednesdays were pork or lamb chops; Thursdays were meat or chicken stews or casseroles and Fridays were fried fish and chips, of which Mum's were simply the best, and finally, on Saturdays we had Chinese take-away – which I still do to this day. Old habits die hard I suppose. We always had a pudding, often just tinned fruit and custard with a trifle or apple pie on Sundays.

Mum was in charge of all the money that she and Dad earned. He would give her his pay packet on a Friday and she'd hand him back a few bob as pocket money. She saved up any spare cash in a tin which she kept on the mantelpiece in our lounge, ready for any emergencies. If there weren't any that year, then she'd have a big spend up at Christmas. Once in a while they'd go to Southend for a day trip on the train.

After the war she worked for many years at a newsagent's in the City. The owners were a Jewish couple and it wasn't long before Mum started to enjoy the food, brought in by the wife. She liked it so much that she bought her own Jewish cookbook and started experimenting at home. After a while she changed or adapted many dishes. For example, we always had fried fish on Fridays which was now dipped in matzo meal instead of the typical English greasy batter we were used to. We also learnt to enjoy gefilte fish and salt beef, which she soaked in brine for a few hours, according to the traditional recipe, using a joint of brisket and a dish called cholent, which is left to cook overnight on a low heat in line with the rules of the Sabbath. Her Christmas cake was made from a Jewish fruit cake recipe – not very ethical I'm sure, but it was simply the best I've ever tasted. If any of us were ill, heading for a cold or something, she would make us her chicken soup, or Jewish penicillin, as it's known. We all laughed at this idea but it's been proven that chicken bones do have antibiotic enzymes in them, so not so daft after all. Of course there were many Jewish communities in east London at the time and we picked up many expressions which are still in use to this day, and have been adopted as cockney slang. Brick Lane was famous for its fabric and haberdashery shops and factories, then mostly run by immigrant Jews, and as far as I recall we all got on well. There was a mutual respect for each other's culture and although we didn't mix much, mainly due to the different religious laws and not for any other reasons, I don't remember anti Semitic behaviour as we began to see in later years. One thing we had in common was a true sense of family and loyalty which, sadly, although still prevalent in Jewish households, has diminished for the rest of us as modern life has taken over. I believe the newsagent was bought out by a large group and so for the last few years, before she retired, Mum got a job as tea lady in a firm of stockbrokers. She loved working there and was treated very well, but best of all was the Christmas bonus they paid out – as much as two or three thousand pounds; an enormous sum when you consider her wages were only about £18 a week in those days. Although my Mum was never demonstrative towards me, I knew she adored me and we used to joke with each other all the time. I never saw my parents kiss until the day Dad was hospitalised with his stroke. I guess it was just the way people were at the time and I never thought much about it.

Sometime after leaving the Port of London Authority, I decided to become a professional gambler. Of course no-one who gambles ever thinks they will become addicted. Since it is one of the most enjoyable pastimes for some people, it has the ability to creep up on you so slowly that you have no idea what's hit you until it's too late. Also, gamblers have a tendency to remember only their lucky wins and abandon the losses to forgetfulness.

Having worked out that winning £100 a week would be my ideal target; bearing in mind the average weekly wage then was £10 - equating to about £400 today - I set about studying form.

Maybe I got carried away because so many villains earned an average of £4,000 a week and the only honest way to do likewise was gambling of one sort or another. Horses, or the gee gees as I prefer to call them, were my thing. It's all about speed and skill, just as with racing cars and looking back, I can see why I loved it so much. Many of the most well known tracks were used for combined motor and horse race meetings so maybe that's what started me off, honestly I don't remember. Perhaps I caught the bug when I was 13.

Every week, Uncle Bob used to let me pick out a horse and put sixpence on, each way. He was a regular gambler and enjoyed teaching me all about the jockeys, trainers and form. Soon I began to understand the importance of 'turf' knowledge. Which horses preferred dry soil or wet, their best distances and the various blood lines. Most importantly, he taught me to have a feel for the horse and never to rule out gut instinct. I used to win the odd bob or two to spend on sweets.

As I got older of course, the stakes got higher. From memory, I don't think there were betting shops as such, not like today. Instead, an old lady used to knock on our door, carrying a large shopping bag. She'd collect the bets and always return the next day if we'd won anything. The woman must have been highly trusted, or maybe we were mugs? Who knows? Anyway, to get back to the

£100 a week plan. Each week I would pick a horse at odds that, depending on my stake, would return me a £100 win. Simple. For the first six months my plan worked really well and I wondered why I hadn't thought about doing this before. Such easy money; hardly any work involved; and loads of money to boot. Now and again I would deviate from horses and go to Walthamstow or White City Stadium to watch the dogs race, but I never enjoyed it as much.

My favourite horse racing venues were Epsom, Kempton Park, Newbury and Sandown because of their close proximity to London. Epsom is still one of my favourites, with its marvellous futuristic stand. Incidentally, this was used for filming the racing scenes in the James Bond movie *GoldenEye*. It seems to house a real melting pot of characters and invariably I bump into someone familiar whenever I attend.

Like all good things though, nothing lasts forever. This was true of my winning streak and heavy losses soon took over. More and more money went down the drain with each consecutive bet getting larger and larger, in a desperate attempt to recuperate funds. That's addiction for you. In the end, Mum would be called upon to get me out of trouble or to lend me the odd £20.

Eventually, sense prevailed and I restricted myself to Saturday betting only; allowing myself a set budget which I knew I could afford to lose. With an eye still on the big money though, later I enjoyed doing the ITV Seven. Each win would go onto the next race. Therefore, if you won the first six races it could amount to several thousand pounds going on the last race; depending on the odds of course. Psychologically, this thought helped me to wean myself off the heavy betting.

Not all my young days were spent at the cinema, playing football or gambling. There were girls around but I've never been very good at chatting them up. Probably because I was an only child and always felt uncomfortable and quite shy - still am to this day to be honest.

The Hammersmith Palais or The Royal at Tottenham were favourite haunts for most London lads at that time and I'd wait until the last slow smooch before plucking up courage to ask a girl to dance. Never having had a dance lesson in my life, it's something that has always terrified me so I certainly don't do jive, rock 'n roll, twist or funky chicken.

My first proper love, sadly, was for a second cousin of mine. We only kissed once, but the family put a stop to our relationship for obvious reasons, although at the time it was traumatic. Maybe because of seeing so many beautiful stars on the big screen, I have to confess that I've only ever been drawn to good lookers.

Most of my pals relied on me for transport if we went to films or dances because I was the only one with a car. I loved fast cars and my first was an Austin Healey Sprite or 'frogs' eyes' as it was known popularly – I was a lot thinner in those days. Some of my pals from our football team had been to a holiday camp where they chummed up with a Mr. and Mrs. Fowler, who were there with their two sons. On returning home, one of the sons, who was having a birthday party in Chiswick, invited them all to join him. Naturally, I tagged along. Here, I was introduced to a young and very beautiful 17 year-old girl. We got talking and I asked her for a date. Yes, it was love at first sight! I was smitten from the start. When parents started arriving to collect their various party goers, I asked Gloria's father permission to take her to see *South Pacific* at the Dominion in Tottenham Court Road. That was the start of a three-year romance.

Gloria was stunning and looked very much like the film star Eunice Gayson; a real English beauty who starred subsequently as James Bond's girlfriend in *Dr. No* and *From Russia With Love*. Everywhere we went Gloria turned heads. Although I felt proud it also gave me nightmares because I feared I might lose her. Maybe this was due to my abandonment as a child during the war, I don't know. Slim and petite, at around five feet six inches, she also had a lovely pair of legs. I confess I'm a bit of a legs man in truth. Actually, she had it all and everyone loved her.

Long courtships were common in those days but it wore me out commuting between Smithfield, where I worked at the time, and Chiswick, since we saw each other at least three or four times a week. Sometimes I'd pick her up en route, from Swan and Edgar in Piccadilly Circus, where she worked at one of the cosmetics counters.

Also around this time I was travelling up to Norfolk every

weekend for lessons at The Jim Russell School of Motor Racing in Snetterton where I'd been told I had a promising career ahead. I drove mostly Formula Junior cars; the Cooper V111 which was Jim's favourite, and later the Cooper Mk 1X and Mk X. Jim had been a very successful Formula Two and Three driver, competing against all the big stars of the day such as Stirling Moss and Jim Clark, winning many races in his class at all the major tracks of the era. He raced at Brand's Hatch, Silverstone, Aintree and Goodwood and on his home patch where he could work on, and build, his own cars in the garage he'd acquired earlier. By 1956 he'd started his famous Racing School. Drivers such as Emerson Fittipaldi, who later became World Champion, and Danny Sullivan were influenced by Jim and many even launched their careers from his school.

Much later on, in 1966, Jim was responsible for training James Garner and Yves Montand on the film *Grand Prix*. Racing was in my blood so to speak because I had appeared at almost every magistrate's court in the City and West End of London for speeding offences. Thankfully, there weren't penalty points in those days and it's a good job some of my speeds went undetected or I'd have lost my licence for sure. The best speeding places were the old A3 from Kingston to Portsmouth, or any open road in fact, where an opportunity arose to drive flat-out. Fear never came into the equation since I've always had nerves of steel.

With so much going on at one and the same time, Gloria and

I pushed forward with a date for our wedding. The two Mums did the usual fussing over arrangements alongside Mrs Fowler who felt very much involved, since she had hosted the party where we'd met. Naturally she took all the credit and responsibility for our union, having played cupid that night.

We tied the knot at Turnham Green Church in May 1960. The day went according to plan without a single hitch. Gloria took my breath away as I turned to watch her come down the aisle. She wore a short, white, silk dress which came just below the knee, with a short veil covering her beautiful face. I was bursting with pride I can tell you. Like most grooms, I paled into insignificance next to my bride, but I think I did look good; wearing a smart, new, mid-grey suit bought specially for the occasion. Her parents did us proud and put on a great feast which was held in the nearby church hall; decorated with lots of bouquets and balloons. I think there were about 100 guests for a proper sit-down lunch, with all the trimmings. No doubt a few of the men got drunk but all I remember was Gloria and me, happy as larks – or so I thought. Afterwards we honeymooned in Paris – my mates said it was like 'taking coals to Newcastle'. Finally I left home and we moved into a small flat in Chiswick. Things went well at first and Gloria got a job at the Heinz factory in nearby Harlesden.

All my life I've found it hard not to be possessive over my women and, because I was so besotted, I didn't give Gloria any space. About seven months later I discovered she was seeing the younger of Mrs Fowler's two sons. Adding insult to injury, the relationship had been encouraged by Mrs Fower herself.

To say I was devastated would be an understatement. I felt powerless and helpless so I suppose I used threats to try and hang on to Gloria. Most villains I knew used the most evil threats to get what they wanted, but hardly any of the lesser types actually carried them out, and I used the same methods over the years for all sorts of situations. Of course, that kind of behaviour doesn't get you anywhere, and deep down I knew it. Part of my upbringing had left a marked violent streak in me and although I've never hit a woman, I lashed out with any other means I could – mainly verbal abuse. I tried everything I could to get even with Fowler. I threw bottles at his bedroom window at night; one missed and went through the lounge window instead. I chased him by car every time he left the house; I even had a punch-up with old man Fowler when I went round to confront him about the situation. Things got a bit heated when Mrs Fowler started hitting me on the head with an umbrella, in the street, outside their front door. I wanted an explanation desperately, as to why they had encouraged the relationship between their son and Gloria. I never got one though. I went ballistic and chased the pair of them everywhere, to the extent they were so terrified by my threats that they ran into Chiswick Police Station for refuge. I was warned to stay away or charges would be brought.

Eventually I gave up all hope of salvaging our marriage and

accepted that divorce was inevitable. It took a long time before I would trust another woman. I have never been lucky in love I'm sad to say. Instead of winning Gloria back, all that happened is the wedge between us became deeper. She refused to have anything to do with me from then on. About 40 years later, I saw Gloria at a family funeral. We said "Hello," but nothing more. Now of course, as with many other incidents in my life, I do regret deeply my appalling behaviour.

Unfortunately, by this time motor sport had become very big business, with heavily sponsored Works Teams. People like me didn't stand a chance and so I gave up all thoughts that racing would become my full time career. I lost touch with some of my mates once I got married and I went through a very dark and lonely period. I didn't think about it at the time but I must have been quite depressed because I stopped going out for a while, preferring to stay home and watch telly with Mum and Dad. They were devastated by our divorce and I had to prevent Dad from going to the Fowlers' house because I'm sure he would have done some real damage. He wouldn't speak about Gloria, without cursing her under his breath, for the rest of his life.

Back in the East End once more with my parents, I started mixing with members of some of the old gangs. The Richardsons were a south London crew, fast coming up through the ranks as rivals to the Krays, but I never mixed with them. They were nicknamed 'The Torture Gang' because their favourite form of torture included pinning their victims to the floor, using six inch nails, while removing their toes with bolt cutters. Not very nice people. Something I'm truly ashamed of is an escapade that a few friends and I used to get up to. We'd go into the West End and treat ourselves to a slap up meal, where my mates would consume copious amounts of alcohol. Then one of us would go to the gents' toilet and smash the fire alarm glass. Amid all the commotion, we'd beat a hasty retreat without paying the bill. Since I wasn't a drinker, after a while I got fed up and bored with it all and stopped joining them. I met Charlie Richardson and his younger brother Eddie once or twice but that's all. Johnny Bindon was a notorious actor-cum-villain in the early '60s and I knocked around with him for a while. Deep down I worried about mixing with this crowd because I knew my Dad would never forgive me if I got into serious trouble with the police.

Acting was a legitimate form of work and also suited many villains because they could hide their otherwise lucrative scams under a cloak of respectability. Since acting jobs were scarce this meant the lads were free to do a spot of villainy in their free time so to speak. John was great fun to be around but I'm very glad I didn't become a member of one of those gangs. Also known as 'Big John' due to the size of his private parts, 'The Guv'nor' but I'm not sure why, and 'Biffo' because he was always in fights. He'd been discovered by Ken Loach who thought he'd be ideal for a part in *Poor Cow*. Since the stories and gossip that surround Johnny have been well documented over the years I shan't elaborate further. Suffice to say that most of them are true.

One evening I got a call from Charlie Kray asking me to drive to Crockford's Casino in the West End and park a short distance from the club because there were two plain-clothes policemen sitting in an unmarked car just outside the main entrance. He told me to meet him in the gents' toilet downstairs. I didn't ask questions, well, you just didn't. So I did as I was told and sure enough Charlie was waiting for me. The receptionist let me in even though I wasn't a member because Charlie must have told her to expect me. No-one argued with a Kray.

He handed me two guns and said, "Stick these in your pocket, wait 15 minutes and then go straight home." Checking to see there was no-one behind, he whispered in my ear, "I'll come and collect them tomorrow." I tucked each gun into the belt loops of my trousers so they were hidden by my jacket and carried out his instructions to the letter, but I must admit to feeling very nervous. I'd never handled a gun outside of being in the army and I was terrified in case the police stopped me outside. That's guilt for you. I wasn't a known face so the police didn't pay me any attention as I strolled nonchalantly past their car. Apparently, I'd done him such a big favour that he told me the next day, "Any time you need me, I'll do the same for you." Luckily, I didn't need to ask.

After a while, I began to accept that doing the odd bit of fiddling here and there was part of normal life. If you could get away with it of course. Needless to say that I did my fair share of petty wheeling and dealing, but nothing too awful or violent. Mainly it consisted of buying stuff that had 'fallen off the back of a lorry or two' from some of the well known burglars who'd come up to me in the pubs or clubs. Landlords were well aware what went on and it was an accepted part of East End life then; it probably still is. I did, on occasion, help someone out by storing the odd parcel but I never asked questions, so I couldn't be sure if they were stolen or not, could I? Throughout my time at Smithfield I had known it was a hotbed of petty crime and I settled down for the long haul.

CHAPTER THREE

The Old Bailey

Meat came off rationing in 1954 and in that same year, I got a job as a porter at Smithfield Market through one of my mates. My job was to carry the meat to and from the shops and lorries. If it was a single side of beef I'd carry it on my back or we used trolleys for larger orders. It was heavy work but I enjoyed my time there until I got myself into a serious spot of bother - but more of that later. The market buzzed with a vibrancy that's hard to explain; maybe the history and sheer space had something to do with it, I don't know. Tall arched walkways had once allowed the passage of livestock, on their way to the slaughter-house. Now they were filled to capacity with buyers and sellers alike, with lots of 'ducking and diving' as various deals were struck.

Mainly used by hoteliers and restaurateurs, Smithfield had been built originally to enable only the freshest meat to be supplied for the trade in the capital. Next to the railway, it meant animals could be brought from all over Britain, killed on site and prepared, ready for sale the same day. With the advent of fridges and freezers, this process has evolved, and the space adapted, so that refrigerated lorries can now park right in the market for deliveries. The work was hard labour I can tell you, and extremely physical, but I became very fit, especially building a strong upper torso. One of the main reasons why the market was a male dominated environment, and still is to this day, was because I doubt a woman would have the sheer strength to lift a side of beef onto her shoulder. Many top boxers of the day worked at Smithfield. People like the brothers Nosher and Dinny Powell, whom I met up with years later when we became stuntmen. Others were Ron Barton, who became British Light Heavyweight Champion; Terry Allen, European and World Flyweight Champion and Terry Spinks, also a British Champion, who won an Olympic Gold Medal in 1956. So you can see how good this work was for upper body muscle-building. We were up at the crack of dawn and in the cold of winter, I'd stop off for a full English breakfast in a nearby cafe. There were lots of cafes, packed full of workers, either reading the paper, chatting or joking with one another. Some pubs had all night licences but I rarely went to any of them. We lived in a world which co-existed with the rest of London, but hardly anyone knew about us.

This job was the longest I'd stuck at anything so far. I suspect the scope for fiddles could have been one of the main attractions holding my attention, and I earned a nice few bob on the side over the years. Thieving was rife, throughout the market, and in all quarters. Meat went missing on a regular basis; bribes were handed out frequently and I doubt any workers' families ever bought meat in a high street butcher's shop. We also bartered our goods with other traders. For example, over the period I got to know lots of delivery drivers in the cafe. Bread, milk, vegetables and groceries were swapped in the car parks or lay-bys. Let's just say I was never short of a few bob. Most likely I'd have stayed on for life if it hadn't been for a rather unfortunate incident which happened not long after my split with Gloria.

Three of my fellow workers and I had noticed, over a period of several weeks, that one of the shops within the market had a special delivery of Scottish loins of beef once a week. By the side of this shop was a small avenue which allowed vehicular access for dropping off purposes. Although we called them shops they were in fact wholesalers to the trade. The meat was always stacked neatly in a pile ready for the shop porters to collect. We reckoned they were worth several thousand pounds, and were just asking to be nicked.

The four of us planned how to go about it for a few weeks; deciding how, when, and who with. Another friend had a cafe close by, and a van, which we asked to borrow. He didn't want to be involved but agreed to lend us his motor. Our plan was for him to leave it by the stack of meat at 5am on the chosen day and disappear into the crowds back in the market, so we could continue with the theft. If caught, we'd simply say it was pinched without his knowledge. Of course getting caught wasn't an option we cared to dwell on.

On the due day we started loading up the meat when I noticed a small glow, as if someone was drawing on a cigarette, right at the end of the shop which had, until now, been bathed in total darkness. Immediately, I told the others we were being watched and that the police might have been called already. Now, my three mates were all married with children, but I was single again at that time. Quick as a flash, I made the decision. "You lot, scarper! I'll carry on loading. Leave it to me!" I shouted to them.

Within a few minutes the police arrived as expected. Surrounding me, one officer grabbed my arm, gripping it tightly, while he placed a pair of handcuffs on my wrists. "What are you doing?" he asked. "Loading meat, Sir!" Came my swift and slightly sarcastic reply. "Who told you to?" By now a note of irritability had crept into his voice. "A man in a white coat and flat cap gave me £5 to load it for him, Sir." After all, I had a genuine porter's licence so I hoped my story would ring true. Already a crowd had gathered at the scene and I thought I spotted my boss. Either way, I knew my number was up as far as this job was concerned.

Without further ado I was bundled into their car and taken to Snow Hill Police station in Holborn. After removing all my personal belongings the duty officer escorted me to a cell. I tried to keep calm and work on my story. A short while later I was transferred to an interview room. Throughout the rest of the day different police officers came in to question me. They all smoked and every part of the station had that unmistakeable stench of stale tobacco. Ceilings, walls and curtains were impregnated with brownish, yellow stains such as you see in pubs. I kept coughing as the fumes hit my nostrils. I stuck to my story but they kept telling me that my mates were in another room, singing from a different song sheet, and had confessed already. Over the years I'd learnt from various gang members how the police always try that line so I continued repeating myself, "I'm telling the truth. What friends? I don't know who you're talking about, Sir!"

Eventually I was released on bail under my own surety, having been charged with Larceny and Receiving, and told to report the following week at Guildhall Magistrates Court. The next day I went back to work as normal and made an appointment to see the Union solicitor. I kept my head down because I knew the bosses would be watching my every move. Word travels fast in a place like Smithfield, but they couldn't sack me unless I was found guilty.

A week later I arrived at court. Standing in the dock for the first time is a scary experience for anyone. With my friend, the van owner, next to me, it was established quickly that he had a cast-iron alibi and they released him. He winked at me as he passed in front, mouthing the words, "Good luck mate!"

My solicitor (or brief as we call them) asked the Magistrate if he could have five minutes with me. We went into a side room where I was informed that this particular Magistrate detested market workers and would, odds-on, find me guilty. Since it was my first offence, more than likely he'd be giving me the minimum stretch, so it was put to me that I should elect to go for trial by jury. Duly granted, a date was set for the Old Bailey, Court Number One, in four months time. Even though I had a clean record, and still have today, I knew I'd be looking at a two-year sentence if I was found guilty. Otherwise known affectionately as the Murder Room, Court One trials tended to evoke a condemnation of the accused, contrary to common law, as being guilty unless proven otherwise.

Dad came with me to the trial. I drove my Austin Healey, but handed the keys to him when we arrived as a precaution. The building has an atmosphere all of its own, starting with the famous gilded statue of Justice, depicted by a sword and scales, towering above the domed roof. Marble walls line the entrance and corridors but there's an eerie sense of prevailing doom everywhere. The swish of black gowns, as barristers and judges alike go about their duties; negotiating deals in hushed tones, while claiming odd spaces along the passage-ways and corners as imaginary, temporary offices. Furtive glances every few seconds lest someone overhear their conversations. Even the hardest of criminals, knowing they were guilty, would relinquish all hope in this place.

Surrendering my bail, and officially in custody, I descended the famous staircase to a cell below. Secretly, I was terrified, but in a perverse way it was exciting to be appearing on such a grand stage; it was all very theatrical. I'd seen many a courtroom scene enacted on the big screen. Not long before, I'd seen *To Kill a Mockingbird* starring Gregory Peck and earlier, in the late '50s, *Twelve Angry Men* with James Stewart.

Little did I know at the time that this was to become the turning point in my life and the start of my own acting career.

An officer escorted me to the raised dock. To my surprise the courtroom seemed a lot smaller than I'd imagined. The judge's bench was raised to about the same height as the dock and immediately in front of me on the opposite side; the jury to my right; barristers and solicitors below; the public gallery above and behind. There was a brass rail around the dock so I gripped it firmly to steady myself. Austere and bleak, the room was built to be intimidating.

"All rise," called the clerk. This was it. A reality. Yes, I was at the Old Bailey. Not too many people you meet can claim that one. How many men and women, before me, had stood in this very spot waiting to be found guilty or not guilty? Good job I didn't know the answer to these questions at the time, but I know now. In this same spot, Doctor Crippen and Ruth Ellis had stood, awaiting their sentences, "To be hanged by the neck until you are dead." Black cap over his grey wig, the judge would make the announcement in sombre mode. More recently, the Yorkshire Ripper Peter Sutcliffe had received his sentence here; and for the lesser crime of perjury,

Jeffrey Archer and Jonathan Aitken. It made my plight pale into insignificance. Nonetheless, my legs turned to jelly and I hoped Dad couldn't see the nerves.

Judge Carl Douglas Aarvold arrived, with all the pomp and ceremony as befitted his stature; clad in full ceremonial scarlet splendour, to take his place on the bench. Behind him, on the wall to his right, hung an impressive golden sword of justice. All the legal bodies present bowed to him in respect. Aarvold, who had only recently been instated as senior judge, was knighted in 1968. He had played rugby for England and The British Lions and was renowned for being fair. How could I have known then, that he would preside over the Krays' trial just three years later? To this day, I've never understood why my case came before this court. After all, mine was a petty crime in comparison. It's always intrigued me. Still, I do enjoy the fact that I have appeared at this most famous of all courts, alongside such infamous names.

Luckily for me, I've always looked a lot younger than my age and my barrister said it might act in my favour. Dressed in a smart navy blue blazer, white shirt and stripy, blue and white tie, I looked 17 although by now I was almost 26. My hairstyle had the typical Elvis Presley 'teddy boy' quiff but I'd slicked it down, especially for my court appearance. Next, the jurors filed in, one by one, and sat down in their pews. One of the women wore a vivid green dress and had striking red hair. In her late 40s, I reckoned. She caught my eye and I began to notice that every time I glanced in the direction of the jury she seemed to be looking straight at me. This continued throughout the trial.

That first morning was taken up doing all the preliminary stuff, with both sides putting their case to the judge. Most of the dialogue comprised legal-speak which was impossible for me to understand, nonetheless, I managed to follow the gist of what was going on. Lunchtime arrived and I moved towards Dad, thinking we could go for a bite to eat. No such luck. I was reminded that my bail had been surrendered and I would be in custody for the whole day. Instead, someone escorted me back to a shared cell where three other men, all on trial for murder, looked at the floor and said nothing. A short while later, one of the wardens came to fetch me and I was put in a cell on my own. They obviously realised I didn't belong with that mob. Lunch consisted of filleted fish, mashed potato and haricot beans served on a tray; with plastic utensils. It's funny, the small details you remember. Even though I was feeling quite stressed, nothing puts me off my food, as my waistband can testify, so I tucked in.

The afternoon passed smoothly, with questioning and cross-questioning. At four o'clock, the judge adjourned until the following day and I was released on bail once more. This time the surety had been set at £5,000. My barrister thought the day had gone well and reassured me. Next day was much of the same, with the usual glances at the red-head. The third day was all about the judge's summing up, offering guidance to the jurors. What he said absolutely slaughtered me. I couldn't believe what I was hearing and dared not look at Dad. His words, more or less, were; "If you believe that cock and bull story; about the man in a white coat and flat cap, then think again!" My barrister looked up at me and shook his head. "That's it," I thought, "I'm going down."

The jury retired to consider their verdict while I was escorted below to wait with a warden. After about an hour I asked him, "They're taking a long time, aren't they?" With a wry smile he said, "The longer they take, the better for you, son." Two hours later we heard rumblings from above and I was called upstairs. Back in the dock, I gripped the rail with a clammy hand. My head was swimming and my eardrums buzzed. I took a sip of water because my mouth was so dry my tongue was stuck to the palate. All I could do now was wait.

As the jurors came in, the red-head looked straight at me and I tried to decipher her expression. She moved her head slightly, first to the left, then the right. My mind raced. Did this mean 'not guilty' or 'you poor sod, you're going to jail?' The foreman of the jury stood up as the charges were read out.

"On the charge of Larceny, do you find the defendant guilty or not guilty?" The judge asked him. What seemed an eternity later, he replied. "NOT GUILTY!" Phew, I sighed with relief. "How do you find the defendant on the charge of Receiving?" Again. "NOT GUILTY!"

My release was announced; without blemish on my character.

I shook hands with my barrister and thanked him. Then I hugged Dad, who had turned very pale. Good job Mum hadn't attended for she'd have been a wreck.

Outside, we descended the Old Bailey steps and bumped straight into the red-headed juror. She smiled. "We voted seven for, and five against, but decided to give you the benefit of the doubt. You're a born actor! Now go away and be a good boy!"

After this first performance at the Old Bailey I decided to do something about becoming a proper actor.

Gossip in the pubs spread around, about how many petty criminals became 'extras' or 'walk-ons' to give them a reason for not being in a nine to five job. One of the first questions the police ask, when raiding villains' homes or interviewing them down at the station is, "Where did you get this money?" or "How do you support yourself?" Being part of the vague and mysterious world of theatre stopped police from asking too many questions about their whereabouts and also gave them an alibi. Anyone can claim they've been to an audition but were unsuccessful. Not easy for coppers to investigate those situations because not all casting sessions include taking names and addresses of those actors who are not chosen; not in those days anyway. Don't get me wrong here, I'm not suggesting for one minute, that it works in reverse: not all extras are villains!

Act One Scene One was a cafe in Soho and a favourite place to hang out for actors. Mainly out of work, it meant they could find out who was casting what, both for films and television, as well as the theatre. You met all sorts of characters there. Sometimes a singer or musician started to play, hoping a passing talent scout might pop in and 'discover' them. Yeah, in their dreams.

I went one morning, on my own, and settled down to glean as much information as possible. Eavesdropping was what everyone did and if you heard something worthwhile you either initiated a conversation or, if an audition was on somewhere nearby, left quickly to get there before too many others heard about it. Becoming a face or regular meant that you were in people's minds continually and it wasn't long before I frequented the place several times a week. The atmosphere was great and you could hang around for hours without any hassle.

Popular programmes at that time were *Z Cars, Adam Adamant* and *Compact*. When I overheard some of the lads talking about how these shows all used lots of extras, I butted in to find out more. What I really needed to know was how to find an agent. In the end it seemed that one of the most popular and well respected ones was Terry Denton de Gray, so that's where I went.

Terry had had a long career in theatre and starred as the 'Marlborough Man' on cigarette posters worldwide. With an amazing physique, good looks and plenty of charm it was easy to see why he'd become so popular. It was mainly through his connections to showbiz stars like Benny Hill that he found extras for all the shows. I think the agency had just sprung up unintentionally.

Outside the cafe I found a phone box and looked up the number. No time to waste now, so I rang for an appointment. Both nervous and excited, I wondered what Terry would be like. A secretary answered, giving me a time to come on that same Friday, and informing me to dress, "Smart-casual, and bring some photos."

Back at home I sorted out several pictures. One of me in RAF uniform which I hoped might impress; some of me in racing gear and, of course, one at the wheel of my beloved Healey. Little did I realise when she said 'photos' that she meant professional ones. Oh, well. Just goes to show how green I was. Come the day, I arrived suitably attired, clutching an A4 envelop. I didn't have to wait long before being ushered into Mr de Gray's office. He was a very handsome man, just as everyone told me. He put me at ease and I began to relax. "Have you ever acted before?" he queried. "Only in RAF theatre productions, just for fun." I told him truthfully. He asked to see my photos but didn't embarrass me by mentioning how amateurish they were. Instead, he suggested I visit his good friend Michael Barrington-Martin who had a studio, just around the corner.

Michael said my surname was all wrong and lacked a certain ring to it. Ok, no problem. I changed it to Martin as soon as my first portfolio was completed. Not very original of me, I admit, but it stood me in good stead for the next 45 years and it had worked for the likes of Dean Martin, Dick Martin, Tony Martin and Strother

Martin! Terry booked me to work the following week in my first ever part, as an extra (nowadays called supporting artists) in *Z Cars*. That was it. I was on my own, in at the deep end.

Full of apprehension and uncertainty, I arrived at the rehearsal rooms which were housed at a Boys Club in west London. Up until now, I had no idea about this arrangement, thinking everything happened in the main studios. Nine o'clock on the dot, I turned up for work. A young girl, called a third assistant, explained what was happening and directed me to where all the other extras had congregated. We were expected to provide our own costumes unless a uniform was required. To my relief, when I realised how much hanging about there was, in-between takes, I knew I'd be able to learn the ropes from the sidelines by observation. First scene was in a pub. James Ellis was one of the leading actors and my role started off at the bar. I had to down my pint, drink up, turn around and leave. Dead easy. What a doddle.

Two days later we took the episode back to Studio One, Red Assembly, at BBC Television Centre in Wood Lane. When I left, in the dark of that first evening, it dawned on me that for the first time in my life I hadn't noticed the time. No lunch or tea break. Enthralled with all the goings on; I'd been watching the cameramen, electricians and lighting guys (or 'sparks' as we call them) and every scene that followed mine, in order to glean as much as possible about backstage action. Nothing else mattered to me now. Even my pangs about Gloria began to wane as I drank in the atmosphere. To this day, I still get emotional when I remember that time.

This was it. Acting would be all I ever wanted from now on. Three guineas a day, three days' work, but the fee was irrelevant for I no longer cared about the money. If I had won a fortune back then, I'd have done it all for nothing just to be a part of that family, known as 'The Business.' This might sound a bit pathetic, but anyone who has ever found a career that fulfils them in such a way will understand what I mean. It was a far cry from the 'high on the hog' career at Smithfield. My lifelong journey into television was about to unfold.

In those early days, the theory was that you could only become an actor if you'd been to drama school. Whether or not it still exists today, I'm not sure. For theatre it possibly does, but television and films are different. Series like *Compact* and *Z Cars* used the same group of extras time and time again. In one scene you'd be a member of the public in a bar somewhere, or a passerby in a bank shoot-out in the next, maybe even a copper in the station in a third scene. You'd be surprised how unnoticeable we could make ourselves. The camaraderie among us all was great and I think I enjoyed it particularly because it was similar to the atmosphere of Smithfield.

One day I was called to the Elstree Studios in Hertfordshire for a small part as a waiter on *The Lena Horne Show*. Now here was one sexy lady, and my favourite singer to this day. I had to stand behind a bar while she greeted me with, "Evening Pierre!" She lingered on the word "Pierre," suggestively, and my knees went a bit wobbly. During our lunch break, she rehearsed in the empty studio with her husband, the pianist Lennie Hayton, while I sat in a corner, out of view, to enjoy my private concert.

Regular work came in, on all sorts of programmes, and I started to build a bit of a reputation for being reliable, punctual and ready to try anything. Central Casting was another excellent agency and now that I was learning the ropes I discovered early on that most of the other artists were on several agents' books at the same time.

I appeared on *The Morecambe and Wise Show* often. Eric was so funny during rehearsals it was hard to keep a straight face. Both Eric and Ernie were down to earth characters and very friendly. Whenever I met them on other occasions, such as award ceremonies, they would remember me. BBC Television Centre became my second home in the '60s. The place was a hive of activity, with plays, comedy and drama series. It seemed as if I was there all the time. On reflection, work flourished at ITV as well and most actors found small parts almost all of the time. Nowadays, with the popularity of so many reality shows on the box, it must be much harder for aspiring actors. I have a bit of a thing about this, always have, even when it comes to animated commercials, in that I feel real actors should be used, thereby ensuring a continuous flow of work. It saddens me when I look back at just how many series, plays, drama and variety shows there were before this modern obsession took over. There are exceptions, such as the celebrity reality shows, because, even though I don't like them personally, at least the celebrities get paid for competing. Thank goodness for soap operas, that's all I can say.

The Benny Hill Show soon became one of my favourite programmes to watch and I used to hear from other actors that it was great fun working for him. I hoped he would use me but for some reason never did – maybe I wasn't pretty enough! However, I chummed up with several dolly birds who did work for him - lovingly called 'The Benny Hill Girls' or 'Hills' Angels.' Another beautiful extra that I met, while filming a Hammer Production, *The Evil of Frankenstein*, was Heidi Lane, but we were never in a relationship. At the time, she was married but even later, when she divorced and remarried, we still stayed "just good friends" as they say, and she has remained a lifelong friend.

Now Heidi was a real laugh. She came from south London but had Irish origins. Her twin brothers also worked in television and she introduced me to lots of people. Dolly Reed was a Playboy Bunny and another friend, Valerie Stanton who was a 'Benny Hill Girl' joined what we called our 'gang'. Valerie was like a blond version of Sophia Loren and I had a real crush on her but didn't let on and never took things further. She lives with her husband in Los Angeles now. The three of us went to films, parties and generally hung around the studios and sets together. I loved going out with them, as any normal red-blooded male would, because they were all stunning lookers and I could feel the green envy emanating from other blokes wherever we went.

As a trio, Dolly, Val and I used to seek out astrologers, palm readers, clairvoyants and even tea-leaf readers to find out if fame and fortune would come our way. Dolly became a centre-fold 'Playmate of the Month' in 1966, eventually going to live in America where she married Dick Martin, of *Rowan and Martin's Laugh-In*, remaining with him until his death in 2008. Not just one trophy on my arm, but two. How greedy was I? No-one ever believed me when I explained we were all just friends. I suppose it did seem a bit implausible. Not least, explaining this phenomenon to future girlfriends, one of whom would become my second wife.

For the past 30-odd years, Heidi and Dolly have kept me up to date with all the Hollywood gossip; dinner parties with Dean Martin and Frank Sinatra and much more besides, but I'd better stop there or this book will never get finished.

Heidi soon remarried. A location manager called Robert Simmonds, who later worked on *Superman* and *Star Wars*. Bob taught me all about fine dining. Not only was he a fantastic cook but he used to invite me to join them at all the most exclusive restaurants such as L'ecu de France, The Caprice and Mirabelle. He failed to indoctrinate me where wine was concerned though because, as he put it, I was a philistine and preferred a cup of tea to alcohol. Now picture the scene. Bob had been educated at Westminster, a top public school, and his father was a Harley Street surgeon. By contrast Heidi came from a council house in Clapham and her mother was a domestic help. I call it 'fink 'n fought' versus 'la de da.'

Over the years I've watched the three children, Carl, Ingrid and Nicholas grow up and we still keep in regular contact. That brings to mind some of the times when Heidi was pregnant. Queuing is an abomination to me and if ever I fancied going to one of the big West End cinemas such as the Carlton or Paris Pullman, I'd take Heidi, with Bob's permission of course, so we could jump the queue. Other times when she wasn't pregnant, I'd encourage her to stuff a pillow down her trousers and pretend she was my wife. We ought to have been ashamed of ourselves.

Bob got a job as production manager on a TV series called *Ski Boy* which was being shot 1,300 feet up in the mountains of Switzerland. At the end of filming he had to fly to Morocco where he was due to start a film called *The Message* starring Anthony Quinn and Irene Papas. I think he was expected to be out there for about six months but he needed someone to drive his new Range Rover back to England, which was full of his equipment. I had nothing on at that time so agreed readily; glad of a few days break. I flew to Geneva first class, courtesy of the film company, and caught a train for the two-hour journey to meet Bob. After an overnight stop, I followed Bob in the company Volkswagen to the mountain foothills. We said our goodbyes and off I drove, crossing the border into France somewhere near Macon, and proceeding along the motorway towards Fontainbleau, on the outskirts of Paris.

About 75 miles into my trip, there was an almighty bang which sent the car careering all over the road. Luckily my driving skills got me out of trouble, and there wasn't much traffic, so I managed to pull over onto the hard shoulder. I discovered the rear nearside tyre had shredded, so I proceeded to unload the boot to get to the spare wheel. To my horror, the spare tyre was devoid of any tread and completely bald, so I changed it anyway because at least it did have air in it. Almost two hours later I repacked the car and continued.

My mind was on the tyre the whole time because I was terribly worried that I'd get another puncture. When I'd got to within 40 miles of Calais, tiredness got the better of me so I stopped at a services motel ready for a fresh start the following morning. All I could do, after checking the tyre was still sound, was to pray I'd get as far as England when I knew I could call for assistance if need be. Well, although I made it across the channel, my luck ran out in south London; Streatham to be precise. Sure enough, the AA came to my rescue and fitted a new inner tube, which we'd had to wait three hours to purchase. I was relieved to get home in one piece I can tell you but much of this adventurous journey had been lovely, including the scenery along the entire route. Driving a 4 x

4 was a new experience as they weren't as common in those days, and mainly used by farmers, so the feeling of sitting up high was great – it didn't cost me a penny as all expenses were covered; plus Bob had given me some extra cash for my trouble.

The ITV Studios were in Elstree (now owned by BBC and used for filming *EastEnders*) where I was working on a play. Right in the middle of a scene, the director interrupted to tell us the shocking news that President Kennedy had been assassinated. It's true what they say, we all remember exactly where we were on that fateful day.

I really enjoyed my work, every part of it; the early morning shoots, sometimes starting at 5am, the freezing cold days while on outside broadcasts, where we'd have to put up with thermal underwear; being dunked in ice-cold water enacting fight scenes in rivers and the like. The list is endless. You have to love it that's all I can say. I'm not alone in my feelings, as I've met dozens of actors over the years who agree. Once acting has got into your blood, whether theatrical, film or television, it's nigh on impossible to shake off.

So many lovely actors and actresses, as well as all the thousands of unsung heroes who work off-camera, have helped shape my career and given me a great deal of happiness. Colin Clews, the producer of the legendary *Morecambe and Wise Show*, used me quite a lot. My agent received a call from him one time regarding *Sunday Night at the Palladium Live* and *The Charlie*

Drake Show. These were rehearsed and filmed on the Sunday and we'd be there from the crack of dawn until the end of the show, at about 10 o'clock. During the rest of that week, Frank Ifield was the star turn. Can you imagine how I felt when I was given his dressing room to share? At the side of this famous stage there is a brass strip separating it from the wings. My part was right at the beginning of the show. While Charlie was being lowered from above, onto the stage, in a space ship, I had to come on in uniform and announce, "Welcome back Major!" My big moment; three words. During the time while I waited in the wings, I couldn't help but feel proud. Here was I, Derek from Bow, about to tread the same boards as all the top stars who had gone before.

During this period, commercials were a very lucrative added source of income, as long as you weren't under contract to the BBC. I had some funny experiences doing beer adverts. Worthington E was my first but I'm not a drinker. All through the 'takes' they used the real thing instead of coloured water, so by the end of the day I was drunk as a skunk and had to be sent home in a cab. The things you have to do to earn a living eh? Next it was the Guiness advert but I never made it past the first day as I threw up in the gents' loo, in the pub where we were filming. Still, I got a second day's filming out of it. One of my best known commercials was for Loctite super glue and I leave you to imagine some of the jokes I had to put up with over that.

Once I was teamed up with up with my old pal Terry Downes

for a Cadbury's chocolate commercial. We had to re-enact the scene from *On The Waterfront* where Marlon Brando and Rod Steiger are in the back of a cab. Terry played Brando and I played Steiger and we spoofed the lines for a Mother's Day slant, substituting the word 'chocolate' wherever possible. It was funny and I often think back with fond memories and a happy smile to those exciting, fun-filled times.

CHAPTER FOUR

Pulling Stunts

Throughout my early years as an extra many time I appeared on programmes that required some form of action such as riding, fencing or fight scenes. On the set of *Softly, Softly* one day, I met an actor-cum-stunt arranger called Derek Ware who also ran the Havoc Agency. He suggested I might have a future with stunt work. Market days as a porter had left me with a powerful physique and my looks were suited to all sorts of characters, although mainly villains and cops. Well, this appealed to my dare-devil nature straight away, so I didn't need any persuasion to join. Not long after, I began to build up a solid reputation, as I learnt more and more tricks of the trade from each stunt I did. I met up with my old pals from Smithfield, the brothers Nosher and Dinny Powell who had made a name for themselves also by now as stuntmen. Nosher was a real hard man. A professional boxer who had won the Southern Area Heavyweight Championship, as well as being a bouncer and stunt co-ordinator. It was easy to see why he became such a good all rounder and we often worked together. Nosher's two sons, Greg and Gary, are now top stunt directors who've worked on the James Bond and *Harry Potter* films.

I've always been a big boxing fan and have seen many fights over the years including Terry Downes' World Middleweight Title fight in 1961, when he defeated Paul Pender. He is most famous for beating Sugar Ray Robinson, but since Sugar Ray was 41 at the time it wasn't too difficult. I used to go to all the big fights when I lived in the East End; at the Mile End Arena, York Hall in Bethnal Green, Shoreditch Town Hall, Harringey and the Albert Hall. All the while I lived in east London, I'd keep fit by running in Victoria Park in the early mornings and usually I'd see some of the famous boxers doing the same - people like Sammy McCarthy and Joe Lucy - before going to the local Mile End Baths for a hot rub in a tub, followed by an icy cold dip in the plunge pool. Joe Lucy's son Tom is also now a stuntman and often appears on *EastEnders*. We all seem to follow each other around.

Eventually I became an accomplished horseman, but not before a few mishaps and accidents. Derek Ware was going out with a girl who worked at a riding centre and livery stables in Little Bushy and he took me there a few times but I only knew the rudiments and certainly couldn't class myself as an experienced horseman by any stretch of the imagination. I was called upon by Nosher to attend riding auditions at Pinewood Studios for the film *Carry on Cowboy*. I turned up very early in the morning to join the crowd, gathered in a field behind the studios. To my shock, I discovered that most of them were ex-jockeys, circus acts, and the crème de la crème of stunt riders. My task was to ride bare-back down the field, holding a rope reign, attached to the horse's headpiece; while firing a bow and arrow at a given target on the fence. Bearing in mind I had never ridden bare-back before and had only recently learnt to ride, this was a daunting prospect to say the least. Seeing the look of horror on my face, Nosher said, "Don't worry mate, it's a piece of cake!" Easy for him to say. Squeezing the girth with all the strength of my thighs, I set off. About 50 yards down the field I fired my arrow successfully and, when I reached the end, I turned to come back but began to slip sideways. I knew I'd gone past the point of no return. Legs in the air, I fell off, to the accompaniment of a loud ripping noise as my breeches split in half. Luckily, that time nothing but my pride was hurt. Needless to say, my fame as a stuntman spread more for my expertise behind a steering wheel.

Another difficult stunt comes to mind. I was doubling for an actor on the movie *The Rise and Rise of Michael Rimmer*, where he was supposed to fall backwards off the end of a pier, carrying a large rock-shaped nugget of gold. The fall wasn't that high, being about 20 feet. The mock pier was rigged up in a school playground somewhere in north London. As customary, I placed lots of boxes and mattresses around the area which would carry the brunt of my fall, and checked it two or three times. Although it wasn't a major stunt, as stunts go, it was nonetheless unnerving because I had to fall backwards, without being able to see the landing. Two takes later though and it was in the can as we say.

Further exploits included high speed chases with lots of crashes and pile-ups. Memorable programmes of that period include the *Doctor Who* series during Jon Pertwee's time in the early '70s when I did several stunts. He was a good man to work with and I respected him. He and I were dreadful pranksters, with each trying to outdo the other, but he beat me hands down. The exact details are a bit hazy here but sometime in the spring of 1973, I think we were filming the series of *Doctor Who – Frontier in Space*, near Rochester in Kent. The cast were all booked into a large hotel-cum-pub for a couple of days. I'd driven there in my lovely new silver 2.8 Jaguar, which I parked at the back. During filming the next day, somewhere nearby, word came through to us just as we finished lunch, that a silver Jag had been involved with one of the brewery delivery lorries back at the hotel. Apparently, several crates of beer had been dropped, and smashed accidentally onto the car. With a pang, I knew it must be my car. We weren't due to finish the shoot until five o'clock so there was nothing I could do but wait patiently. As each hour passed I became more and more worked up and agitated because someone had told me the driver had driven off, meaning I couldn't have the satisfaction of punching his lights out even.

Upon our return, I was first to get off the coach. My poor car was covered in a tarpaulin, with broken crates and bottles strewn all over the place. I pulled the sheet back, only to discover that there was nothing wrong with the car. A cry of, "April Fool!" rang out loud, from the crew and cast. As I turned round, I caught Jon doubled up with laughter, as he called out, "That'll teach you to play tricks on me!" It took me about an hour, and several cups of sweet tea, to get over the shock. The Master was played by Roger Delgado but I never got to know him well, even though our paths crossed many times.

Michael Bentine was one of the most amazing men I've ever met. It was a privilege to work on both series of *It's a Square World*. Michael had a presence about him; one which we all felt. Extremely intellectual, without being pompous, he was a kind and gentle man in every sense of the word. Whenever there was a break in rehearsals, he would sit down somewhere and within a few minutes a group would have gathered round him. A truly great raconteur, he would tell stories or discuss interesting topics. We'd be enthralled; like an adult version of children's story time. On one episode, we were all aboard a Chinese junk, moored on the river Thames, outside the Houses of Parliament; firing blanks from a cannon. Even though this wasn't the real thing it was still very loud. The 'bowler hat and briefcase brigade' as I call the office workers there, had gathered along the Embankment but just stared at us, with expressionless, vacant looks. Good job it wasn't for real. Still, that's typically British isn't it? The next day we realised a press photographer had taken photos, as we were splashed across several newspapers.

Boating is not for me and I get sea sick at the slightest movement on water. The credits and opening scenes for *It's a Square World* involved eight men in a rowing boat. It had a hut on it with a tiny chimney on top, out of which bellowed black smoke. All of us wore sou'westers and on film it looked pretty convincing; with the wind blowing gales (from wind machines), and so forth. Believe it or not, the whole scene was shot in a children's boating pond in Victoria Park, east London. In 18 inches of water, and with all our weight, the boat soon sank into the sand at the bottom. Even so, with only the slightest movement, I managed to be violently sick over the side.

The London to Brighton race was another hilarious sketch of Bentine's. It involved a pram race where lots of the regular extras dressed as nannies or babies. We'd run for a while, then get onto a coach for a few miles, until we'd filmed most of the route at short intervals, making it look authentic, right up until our arrival at Brighton Pier. Imagine what Nosher Powell looked like, in this uniform; ex heavyweight boxer and six foot six inches tall - plus stiletto heels! At the end of the series, Michael had a cast lead replica made of a television camera, complete with tripod and mounted on a wooden base, signed by all the cast. It sits on my office dresser and I count it as one of my most prized possessions.

Derek Ware called me one day to discuss a dangerously fast chase scene, using minis. His agency had been asked to supply stuntmen and I think he was stunt arranger. It was a new film which would be shot in Italy and would star Michael Caine. Lovely, I thought, never having been there before. Yes, you guessed right. It was none other than *The Italian Job*. He told me all about the now famous pursuit: under tunnels, through traffic, up and down steps etc. When the time came though, Derek told me I was needed up in Scotland to help arrange the action on a new series instead. If I'd known the impact of that film, as the classic it is today, I'd have found a way to get on it but that's life. In the end Derek got the part of Rozzer, one of the gang in the cliff-hanger which ended the film, literally.

I went up to The Trossachs in Scotland for a six-week stint on a TV series called *The Borderers* with Ian Cuthbertson as the lead and a very young Michael Gambon in a supporting role. Each episode would showcase a guest star, such as the late John Thaw. It was hard work, especially when dressed up as a villain, being chased by the good guys. Still, it was lots of fun and we enjoyed many after-shoot parties, round at our various guest houses. By the way, these landladies are unsung heroes too. Can you imagine what pranks we got up to; away for weeks at a time? Roy Street was with us as the stunt arranger. Earlier on, he had taught me how to pull a horse over and was, without a doubt, the best stunt rider in Britain at the time.

Around this time, the late Bryan Mosely, who played Alf Roberts in *Coronation Street*, became a good friend and I used to go up to Leeds to stay with the family. He had five kids and I often babysat for them. The kids called me Uncle Pineapple because I used to threaten to put the world to rights with a hand grenade, down at the set. Only joking of course. I used to tease them up North about our fish and chips in east London, so one day, Bryan said, "I'll show you a proper fish restaurant!" We ended up on the edge of Ilkley Moor at Harry Ramsden's and I have to admit he was right. A fantastic place. No pun intended.

Terry Wallis came from Braintree in Essex and started out about the same time as me. We met in the early '60s, at the very start of my career, in a modelling agency called the Gordon Eden-Wheen Agency. (Gordon was very camp and loved us because we were so butch!) Terry and I were very good friends back then, but sadly he died a few years ago. I'm godfather to his son Carl. After several years had passed, without his career progressing in the way he'd wanted, he and his wife Venetia bought a village general store in Essex. Close by were several American Airbases where Terry had chummed up with a few Master Sergeants, in charge of the PX's. These are like huge department stores which sell just about everything and most American airbases have one. Terry and I would meet up and I'd load a few crates of bourbon, gin and whisky to re-sell in London. Never one to miss out on an opportunity, this was yet another nice little sideline.

One of my favourite stunts was on the sitcom *Queenie's Castle*. It starred the legendary Diana Dors who, although past her prime, was still a sexy lady. She was very down to earth but loved all the trappings of stardom. She used to turn up at the studios in her Rolls Royce which we often sat in, sipping champagne, while listening to Frank Sinatra cassettes, in-between takes. She was a great laugh and had a bubbly personality; everyone loved working with her. My stunt involved driving a car at break-neck speed, up a sweeping set of stone steps which formed the entrance to one of Britain's largest council estates, Seacroft in Leeds. It was said that had Hitler invaded Britain successfully, this would have been the SS headquarters. Having missed out on *The Italian Job*, I viewed the stunt as a small compensation.

I hurt myself many times doing stunts, as is the nature of the job. But working on the TV series *Elizabeth R* really took the biscuit when it came to horse riding and stunts in general: episode six to be precise. The Queen, played by Glenda Jackson, has sent her troops to Ireland to quell the rebels. (This was filmed at Chobham Common in Surrey.) As ever, I head up a column of troops, all suitably attired in armour. A shot rings out and I'm supposed to fall off the horse, onto soft ground, which we'd prepared earlier. One of the rebels is to attack me from behind. The first shot was fine, but directors, bless them, always want the same scene from a different angle. So we went for the second take. Unfortunately, this time I caught my foot in the stirrup and headed for a nasty fall. I twisted my body, landing with full force on my shoulder, breaking my collar bone. As if that wasn't awful enough, the bad guys couldn't hear my screams above the commotion of gunfire and clanging armour, and so proceeded to punch me as planned.

Just as I was leaving to go to hospital, the director reminded me that I would be required at the studios, in three weeks' time, for dialogue. My part was horseman to Sir William Cecil (played by actor Robert Hines), so I had to deliver my lines with my arm in a sling. By this time my mind was pretty well made up to stop doing stunts, other than arranging them. I'd worked as a stuntman on nearly all episodes of *Elizabeth R*, forming good friendships with many behind the scenes people such as Elizabeth Waller, the costume designer. At that time she was one of the best in the business and she won an Emmy for this, as well as a BAFTA for *The Camomile Lawn*. A downside of our business is that because we work for so many productions, over a period of years, it remains difficult to keep up with all the thousands of acquaintances we meet. We keep in touch for a few years and then, somehow, circumstances change and we lose touch.

My biggest responsibility around this time was to arrange the action scenes for the *Paul Temple* series starring Francis Matthews and Ros Drinkwater. Ros and I went on a couple of dinner dates but nothing more. Also, I managed to get a regular character as Paddy Carson, sidekick to George Sewell. This was my first good speaking part and I had dialogue in almost every episode. Steve Emmerson had been a first-time extra on one of the shows a few years earlier when I'd taken him under my wing and shown him the ropes a bit. He too, progressed to stunt work and now often doubled for me, but had to dye his hair because it was a lot greyer than mine.

When the series ended, I approached the producer, Derek Sherwin to ask his advice, and explained how I felt. Really, I was getting a bit old for stunts now and wanted to become a legitimate actor. On the strength of my recent part, I thought this was the right time, and asked the best way to go about it. He recommended a friend of his at the James Garrod Agency.

For many years I'd hated the way 'posh' actors tried to speak cockney dialogue. Although many were marvellous actors, it sounded awkward and I felt embarrassed listening to them. Their whole demeanour was wrong; from the way they held a cigarette, to their walk and stance. Nowadays we'd say their body language wasn't right. Somewhere, I knew there was a suitable niche market for me, since I didn't aspire to playing Hamlet or any other grand theatrical roles. To this day, I've been asked many times to do a spot of theatre work, but my agent knows the answer is an emphatic "No!"

Don't get me wrong, there isn't anything the matter with theatre. It's me. I never feel comfortable playing to 'the Gods' and speaking in a loud voice. Instead, I love the intimacy of the camera and feel very much at home in front of it. Another reason is a lack of confidence in a world that is foreign to me. Remember, I never attended drama school and came up through the ranks so to speak.

Throughout my time as a stunt man, during the '60s, I continued to see many live performances. A great fan of jazz music, I frequented Ronnie Scott's Club where I saw all the greats; Ella Fitzgerald, Lena Horne, Sarah Vaughan, Count Basie, Buddy Rich, Johnny Dankworth - who has died during my time of writing this book and will be missed greatly by his fans, and of course, the wonderful Cleo Lane. Sadly, the big band sound was beginning to fade from popularity with the advent of the modern pop era, as groups like the Beatles, Rolling Stones, The Animals, and all those that followed, took over. *Little Red Rooster* was my favourite song of that time although I've never been much of a pop fan. I used to go to the Albert Hall to see the likes of Oscar Peterson, and I loved Stan Kenton, Jack Parnell and Ted Heath's bands. An era that's been lost forever, I feel very privileged to have been around at that time. In later years I used to frequent Quaglinos in Bury Street, where I saw lots of good singers – but not all of them became famous.

Just about this time, 1970, I met the girl who would become my second wife. I'd popped in, unannounced, to see Barbara, a friend from my Chiswick days, who ran a textile office in London's Golden Square. It's always refreshing to talk to someone who isn't in The Business. Anyway, one of her friends had the same idea. We were introduced, chatting about this and that as you do, and then I made an excuse to go, shocked at my reaction. A bolt of lightening had just struck me. Later that day I phoned Barbara to ask the low down on her friend. Who is she? What's her name? Is she single etc.? I found out her name was Christine and she, too, was doing small walk-on parts and a bit of modelling. At the same time, she worked part-time at the Penthouse Club in Shepherd's Market as a Penthouse Pet. (Pets were attractive girls who acted as cocktail waitresses to the club's wealthy clientele.) Her agent, it transpired, was an aunt who happened to own a theatrical agency called Alison's Entertainment Bureau based in Kilburn. This was an amazing coincidence, because I'd been on Alison's books myself, doing voice-overs, for a couple of years and, to cap it all, she had the office next door to Derek Ware's Havoc Agency, which is how we'd met.

At 10 o'clock the following day I called Alison to find out more and see if Christine might be filming at the BBC any time in the near future. Imagine my surprise when I discovered she had two days work on *Paul Temple* at the end of that same week. This was fate; no need to consult a clairvoyant this time. With an excuse to turn up at the studio, although not filming on those days, I couldn't wait to see her again. The day came and I waited for a suitable lull in filming to sneak up from behind, put my hands over her eyes, and say, "Guess who?" Of course, Christine had no idea. As the saying goes, the rest is history. I arranged our first date but had to wait a long time. Chrissie Rigg, as she was known then, was off on holiday to see her sister in Kenya and wouldn't be returning

Proud day at Buckingham Palace as Dad collects his BEM, with me, Mum and Nan.

'Digging for Victory' with Nan.

Just before being bombed out of Loxley Street in 1940.

After my 'performance' at the Old Bailey, my first composite shots to set me on my way as an actor.

Standing to attention at RAF Padgate in 1951.   Halt! Who goes there? Guard duty at RAF
Hemswell in 1952.

Sorry Stirling! Racing at Snetterton Race Track in 1958.

Cutting the cake.
My wedding to Gloria
in 1960.

Stunt rider in 1969.
Look at me go!

Stick 'em up! in *The Elusive Pimpernel* in 1969.

Looking mean and moody with Billy Orrigan in the drama series *The First Churchills* in 1969.

Teaching *Blue Peter*'s Peter Purves the art of screen swashbuckling, with my old agent and pal Derek Ware.

My evil 'Brando' look on *Law and Order*, my big break in 1977.

Yes he does have a large one! Pulling a stunt with the larger than life Johnny Bindon in *Jake's End* in 1982.

Caught bang to rights! With William Lucas in the popular TV series *Black Beauty* in 1973.

What a good looking fella! Robert Wagner doesn't look too bad either! Filming *Hart to Hart* in London in 1983.

for five weeks. Oh well, just my luck.

I busied myself and the time soon passed. Already I knew she was the one for me. One of the loveliest girls I'd ever seen. Seventeen years my junior, she'd won Britain's Super Girl competition and came fourth in Miss England. Long blonde hair hung half way down her back; big blue eyes, and the softest, most luscious lips, which I couldn't wait to kiss. Five weeks later, to the day, and I rang the doorbell to her rented flat in Turnham Green. Oh dear, back on Gloria's patch. Never mind, I tried not to think of it as an unlucky omen.

What a shock awaited me as she opened the front door. Short brown hair replaced the long blonde locks. Skinny Chrissie had also put on about two stone in weight. What was I to say to my friends? Everyone knew by now that I'd met this gorgeous bird, and couldn't wait to meet her. Never mind, I'm pleased to say she was just as lovely, only now there was more of her.

For our first date I took her to a little Italian restaurant called Rugantino's in Romilly Street in London's Soho. Call me sentimental but I saved the bottle of Chianti as a memento; empty of course. At the time, I still had my metallic silver 2.8 Jaguar; my pride and joy. Chrissie loved it too; the leather interior, burr walnut dashboard and wire wheels; plus the speed. After a few evenings out, bearing in mind I still lived at home with Mum and Dad, I became increasingly worried about where to take Chrissie later on, for coffee, if you get my drift. Derek Ware came to my rescue and lent me the keys to his flat which was situated conveniently in the centre of town.

About two weeks later I took her home to meet Mum and Dad. I was a little apprehensive in case she was put off by our humble abode, especially only having an outside loo. We came from opposite ends of the social spectrum where so-called class was concerned. She confessed to being nervous in case my parents didn't like her. Chris had an impeccable English accent and spoke beautifully – her mother taught English language and literature and came from an upper class background; her grandfather having been the first financial director of the De Havilland Aircraft Corporation at it's inception. Neither of us needed to have worried though because the introductions went really well, with lots of easy conversation. Chris loved them both from the start and felt at home immediately. Dolly and George waited upstairs for an appropriate moment to come down. Dolly shrieked with laughter, "Oh! You're white!" I'd told them Chris came from the "blackest parts of Africa" and she took this to mean she was black, when all I meant, jokingly, was that she'd been brought up in the East African bush, on a plantation. That first weekend, Chris slept in my small bedroom while I bedded down for a night on the couch; not that I slept much. I felt relieved, because Chris got the thumbs up from my whole family, as she met them all gradually, over the next few weeks. Although technically, Chris was the well-bred one, when her parents met me, her mother said she could see I'd been brought up very well, as I had impeccable manners. Dad had taught me how to treat a lady, that was true, and I would always hold doors open, walk on the outside of a pavement with the lady on the inside, and open the passenger door to my car, but I'd also been to many places, met affluent and influential people and learnt much through observation. I knew how to hold a knife and fork correctly, as well as which ones were for what course, in restaurants or at dinner parties. Through my work as an actor since, I've had many doors opened to me that, hitherto, would have been closed in days gone by.

By her own admission, Chris couldn't act. Work was never particularly plentiful so she changed her shifts at Penthouse to work full time. This meant being on duty in the Piano Bar for lunches until three o'clock and back again in the evening as a cocktail waitress, often not finishing until two or three in the morning. Not an easy way to start a relationship. Once again, I became terribly jealous and waited every night to take her home. Chris was a very flirtatious girl and often I'd be watching as she left the club, with several men obviously trying to chat her up. Sometimes they'd leave their telephone numbers on a drinks' mat which I'd find in her bag. I couldn't blame them, because she looked really cute and sexy in her Pet costume. These were skimpy little French maids' outfits, in different colours of velvet, shaped very tightly, and low cut, to show off every curve – the cups had specially designed pockets for the girls to stuff tissues into, adding extra cleavage. To finish the look, a frilly white 'pinny with a huge bow at the back and matching collar and cuffs. Under the skirt, which only just covered their bottoms, they wore a pair of frilly knickers, black fishnet tights and stiletto shoes. Chris had the only black velvet one, which she commissioned the seamstress to make for her. Truthfully, Bob Guccioni, who owned Penthouse magazine, had started the club as a rival to the Playboy in Park Lane. I hated it so much that I made her give it up. Eventually she became a student nurse at Middlesex Hospital in Isleworth and I was much happier. I never called her Chrissie, just Chris, although I had a couple of nicknames for her. One was "Doll Face" and the other "Bubbaloo" but don't ask me why as I've no idea. It soon caught on and most of my friends called her "Bubbaloo."

Chris still shared her flat with another Penthouse Pet. When the day came for her 21st birthday, we arranged a party. Trouble was, most of her friends were taking some form of illegal substance or another and when it got to around midnight I could see the flat was going to get trashed so I threw everyone out. Chris was furious with me but I was just looking out for her interests and, in truth, I wanted her to give up the old life and start afresh with me. Her flat mate moved out and I replaced her. While lying in bed one lazy Sunday morning we decided to get married and move away. Actually, I think she proposed to me this time, since I was never sure enough of her reply to ask her properly. Naturally, I was thrilled to bits because I couldn't bear the thought of losing her. I couldn't afford a proper diamond engagement ring but managed to rustle up enough money for a semi-precious stone garnet ring – Chris's birthstone, and set in 9 carat gold.

I had been going through a bit of a bad patch with not much work coming in, so there wasn't a lot of money to hand for a big do. The Register Office in Acton was booked for March 17 1971. Heidi and Barbara, who was heavily pregnant at the time, were our witnesses and afterwards they came home with us for a slap-up wedding breakfast, cooked by me. Not a very grand occasion was it? We were ecstatically happy though and started making plans for our future. Both sets of parents were upset that they hadn't attended but when we explained that, as it was a second marriage for me, and we didn't want any fuss, they accepted and forgave us.

Property prices at that time were going through the roof. Most houses were sold as soon as they came onto the market and could go up at a rate of £1,000 a week. At the start of our search the type of house we wanted averaged £4,000 but we ended up paying £7,500 only a few weeks later. We had to be quick. Chris spotted an advert for Number 4, Eve Road in Isleworth, being sold privately by the builder who had renovated it. Detached; two bedrooms; Edwardian etc. We arranged to meet at the house but he told us there were lots of other viewings that day. We were the first, but, not wanting to take any chances, we arrived an hour early and waited in the front porch. Several other couples parked up outside and when Mr. Walters arrived I heard Chris say, "We'll have it!" He laughed and said, "You'd better come in and see it first!"

We lived there for nearly 10 years, most of which were very happy. Mr Walters met us on the completion day, to hand over the keys. Mum and Dad also turned up to help us move in, along with the small removal van, so I forgot to carry Chris over the threshold. In truth, it would have been nicer if we could have spent a few hours alone, but we didn't want to hurt Mum and Dad's feelings as they were so excited for us.

DIY was all the rage back then and we loved it. Dad and I bought The Reader's Digest DIY Book and set about making a pine double bed for our first task. Chris was very good at decorating so I left that side to her. When I look back at the fashions of the day I shudder with embarrassment at the things we did. There was a fabulous marble fireplace in the through-lounge, which we painted over in white gloss. Walls were done in gunmetal-grey emulsion, a paler grey went on the ceiling, with the cornice and central rose picked out in white. A red and black stripy sofa completed the picture. At the dining room end we added a bright red suite consisting of a table, chairs and dresser bought from one of the new chain stores that were springing up everywhere. I think it might have come from Magnet. Adding insult to injury, we put in the latest aluminium windows to replace the original sash windows. Remember it was the '70s so I hope we may be forgiven. Sacrilege, I know, especially when all of us realise how important it is to preserve these features now. I sometimes wonder if it's been put back to its former glory.

I still had work but there wasn't enough to sustain us, and we relied heavily on Chris's income. Nursing wasn't for her so she trained to become a beauty therapist at the Delia Collins School in Knightsbridge, whilst working in the evenings at our doctor's surgery. Once qualified, she started her first salon above Novajon's hairdressers in Twickenham. This gave me the freedom to make a once and for all decision about my own career.

Mum and Dad kept nagging me to get "a proper job" now that I had responsibilities. Chris also thought I should give up all hope of getting a big break. One evening we went to BBC Television Centre in west London for a preview of something I'd done. As I opened the the doors to the main entrance I turned to Chris, with tears in my eyes I said, "And you want me to give all this up?" To be fair, she put up with a lot in those early years and worked hard to support me. Needless to say, she let me off the hook and I carried on, with hope in my heart. One of the main reasons for deciding to write my memoirs was to try and make people realise that, when faced with disappointment and adversity, whatever the work or career might be; through hard work and patience, it is possible to achieve your goals. It certainly worked for me.

James Garrod became my agent for the next 19 years and we became firm friends. Alison said he was the only other agent, apart from herself, she would trust but he was held in high esteem in the business generally. Before becoming an agent he had worked for RKO Radio in a managerial capacity. This was a very stressful job and James began to have heart problems. Heavy business lunches and too much booze hadn't helped. One day, he told me his story; one we could all learn from.

A change in lifestyle was required so he worked out how much he needed to live on. Once he began compiling a list of the things that gave him the most pleasure: two bottles a week of good Claret; his boat, which he moored at Shepperton, and the odd gourmet meal, he realised this cost but a 10th of his salary. His insurance policy, as he put it, was an immaculate pale blue Jaguar which he garaged, only to be taken out at weekends. I doubt it had more than 3,000 miles on the clock even though it was about 15 years old.

During his time at RKO he'd met hundreds of producers and casting directors so he set up an agency in Conduit Street. Twenty one artists was the maximum he'd represent at any one time. This meant he could devote all his efforts to getting them plenty of work, whereas other agents often took on hundreds of artists, all competing for a handful of jobs.

The first time Chris spoke to James over the phone she fell in love with him instantly. A rich voice; smooth as chocolate, with deep, husky tones. When she met him eventually, even James chuckled at her surprised look. He greeted her with, "You thought I'd be tall, dark and handsome, didn't you?" Whereas, he was only five feet three inches tall and not what you'd call traditionally handsome, although certainly he had a kind face. Most women reacted that way he explained and he was used to it.

Early on James made it clear that he wouldn't be sending me to auditions unless they were for speaking parts. Well, that meant a lot of waiting because producers had to get used to a new Derek. It was heartbreaking, to say the least, when I had to turn down a lot of lucrative stunt work.

Wherever I go, I seem to meet shady characters. Even Chris introduced me to a couple she'd met at Penthouse, who seemed really nice people on the surface. Bill and Kathy Evans used to be regular customers of hers. They became friends and eventually we started going out together for the odd meal. Bill always insisted on paying because, as he put it, "I need to get rid of cash!" We were often invited round to their home; a modest apartment in south London, where we'd meet up for a few drinks while waiting for his taxi. He used the same bloke for every trip so that he could drink freely. We often wondered what Bill did for a living. He appeared to have lots of money, but didn't seem to do much work. Once, when I asked him, he laughed and said, "You'll find out one day!"

Sure enough, I did find out when I read the headlines in the paper one morning. Littlewoods Football Pools had been the target of fraud by one of their most trusted senior staff members, in charge of the sorting office. As I read on, I saw the name Bill

Evans. Putting two and two together, I rang Kathy to check even though I was convinced it was him, as it all fell into place now. It's all a long time ago, but the gist of it was as follows: I found out he used to have false postal names and addresses. He'd put in winning coupons after the Saturday draw, so a cheque would be sent to these addresses. Apparently, as I found out later on, he made the mistake of including the taxi driver in one scheme; to let him earn some extra money. In a way, Bill had been very shrewd, until now that is, because he'd never told a living soul. Also, he made sure the wins were never too big, thereby not drawing too much attention. When it came to splitting the money, his friend wanted more of the cut. When he failed to get it, he grassed Bill to the police with an anonymous tip-off. Bill got a custodial sentence and Kathy kept her head down for a long time. I think she felt the police would be watching her every move. We lost touch; but I've often wondered what happened to them

CHAPTER FIVE

Law and Order

It took about a year before decent bit-parts came my way. Gradually, my agent managed to persuade casting directors to give me a chance with dialogue. To begin with, several weeks could go by when I had nothing to do, so I asked my next door neighbour Martin if I could help out on any building jobs, as his labourer. Martin's father had sold us our house after dividing a piece of land he owned into two, with building consent for a small detached house on the other plot. This he gave to his young son as a wedding gift.

Martin and Caroline lived in a caravan at the bottom of the garden while he built their house. This seemed to take forever because it had to be done at weekends and, being newly-weds, they wanted also to have a good time. They were terrific neighbours and even though very young, early 20s I think, we all got on really well. I enjoyed my work, thankful for the extra money, because, as an old fashioned sort of bloke I didn't like being supported by my wife. All credit to the guy though; eventually he built a superb, modern house. I seem to remember it took about six years. Rather astutely, he'd managed to make it water-tight and habitable so they could move in, without completing the roof. This meant they didn't have to pay rates on the property for a while because, technically, it wasn't finished.

With some gentle persuasion my parents moved closer to us because their old house in Mile End was destined for demolition, being part of several new housing programmes in the Hackney Borough. Everything came to a head when Dad was offered early retirement from the PLA, with a voluntary severance pay packet of £5,000. More money than he'd ever had in his life. It seemed a good idea to make a fresh start and so Chris and I tried to persuade them to buy their own house. We sorted out a few small terraced properties in and around Isleworth and Hounslow, because you could still pick up the odd bargain for about £5,000. Also, the ones we were showing them were pretty run down and would need a lot of money spent on renovation. Mum had lived in these types of old Victorian or Edwardian homes all her life and she was looking forward to something spic and span and brand new. I could understand this, but new properties carried much higher price tags. In the end, they settled into a brand new council development in Hounslow. I remember their excitement at having an indoor bathroom and the whole place being so pristine, with a proper fitted kitchen. Out of their savings, they bought all new carpets, curtains and furniture having paid to have everything back in Bow taken to the dump. They turned up with only their personal belongings but I'd never seen Mum look so happy. Dad took up gardening for a hobby as well as one or two paid jobs for neighbours in order to keep active, while Mum fussed around him, and I think they were very happy. Trouble was that he'd been a heavy smoker all his life, having started at about 14 years old, and although he'd given up in his 60s, it had left its mark. After suffering with hardening of the arteries for several years, he had a couple of minor strokes, not long after the move, so I was very pleased they now lived near me.

Generous to a fault would be understating the truth where my Dad was concerned. His hand would be in his pocket before you could finish asking for anything. Often he'd try to persuade us to let him buy things for our house but we were far too independent and always refused. With such a large sum in the bank, and knowing how much we were struggling, it bothered him a lot, so he decided to surprise us with a family holiday instead. Mum and Dad had never been abroad and he put it to us that they were too nervous to go without our help. Clever old chap. Only the best would do, so he booked a four star Thompson Winter Break in Tenerife. It was mine and Chris's first holiday together as a couple, and, since we hadn't had a honeymoon, we were very grateful.

On arrival at the hotel, Mum checked out the rooms, marvelling at the luxury. Coming out of the en-suite bathroom, Dad remarked, "What an amazing place, it's even got a gent's toilet!" Chris and I didn't have the heart to tell him it was a bidet so I expect he used it as a urinal for the full two weeks. We beat a hasty retreat back to our room next door, promptly bursting into fits of giggles, like naughty children. Most of us today, who have become accustomed to regular annual holidays abroad, can't comprehend how it must have seemed to people like Mum and Dad. I don't think they'd stayed in a proper hotel ever before.

It's a holiday I'll never forget. Mass tourism hadn't quite started yet, and the island was very beautiful, with its mixture of lush greenery contrasted by the black volcanic sands of the coastline. Mount Teide to the south looms up high, and can be seen from every angle; tall and majestic, as it looks down on all the little villages below. I seem to remember that Tenerife is also famous for its lace and we visited one of the island's factories. We were staying in Puerto de la Cruz, which is on the warmest side of the island, and it was the first time I had been somewhere hot enough to sunbathe in the middle of January. It took a bit of getting used to I can tell you, and I made a promise to myself, if I ever made the big time I'd buy a holiday home somewhere just like this.

Soon after our return I bumped into Ray Acton, an old friend from Butlin's holiday camp days, and whom I hadn't seen for years. He was backing out of an antiques shop, in Old Isleworth, carrying a table, just as I rounded the corner from my bank. "What the bloody hell are you doing?" I shouted, as he knocked me off balance, before realising who it was. We were so shocked at seeing each other again, after nearly 15 years of losing touch. He told me that this was his shop and although he called it an antique shop, it was more of an up-market bric-a-brac affair. Even more of a surprise came next when I was told to follow him home for a bite to eat and catch up on the past few years. As we drove into his turning I said, "I live in the next road!" Later on we went out to the back to look at his boat when it dawned on me that our two gardens backed onto each other, being separated only by a small river.

Meeting up with Ray again was a wonderful piece of good luck. He lived with Tricia, an ex-airline stewardess, who, , was training, coincidentally to be a beauty therapist. She was a real beauty herself and Chris said she reminded her of Elizabeth Taylor. The two girls got on really well, forming both a friendship and business partnership later on. Eventually, when Tricia qualified, she bought a share in Chris's salon. The four of us socialised quite a lot and on one occasion we booked to see Frank Sinatra at The London Palladium, on what turned out to be his last performance in England. Tickets cost a fortune and took up most of our savings, but it was worth it. When you hear people talk about an atmosphere being 'electric' I know what they mean. A heightened buzz could be felt as soon as the band started playing. None of us realised Sinatra was already on stage, with his back to the audience. Suddenly, the music stopped, as gusts of smoke pushed up through the floorboards. Out stepped the great crooner, singing *Come Fly with Me*, to a rapturous applause. Someone on the end of our row had started the foot tapping routine, which grew to a crescendo. Fantastic drama.

Most of Ray's shop was supplied with stock from auction rooms and house clearances. Help was often required for deliveries and collections, on an ad hoc basis, and so I stepped in whenever I was without acting work, or 'resting' as we thespians call it. This arrangement worked well for both of us as it meant Ray didn't have to employ anyone permanently and I could say yes or no, depending on my commitments. Ray, was a very honest bloke, as this next story will reveal. After being called to a house clearance not long after the owner had died, we were moving an old chest of drawers from the bedroom when a drawer started to fall open. It crashed to the bottom of the stairs and out streamed hundreds of bank notes. When we'd finished counting them, it came to just under ten £10,000, which Ray handed in to one of the daughters. I'm not too sure if I'd have done the same or not, I'm ashamed to admit. Around the corner from the shop was a commemorative plaque, on the wall of a wholesale food store; formerly the site of a family home; stating Vincent Van Gogh had lived there from 1876-80. Records show he'd gone to work in Old Isleworth as a teacher and lay preacher. In those days it was a just small village with a coaching inn and a massive convent.

Now I had a theory about this. Ray sometimes did small jobs, taking various items of value from the local convent to nearby auction rooms. It occurred to me that, since Vincent was penniless throughout most of his life, he might have gone to this convent for food and drink. What if the nuns had taken one or two sketches or paintings as recompense? The Catholic Church is renowned for its accumulation of art and I like to think that somewhere up in the attic there might be a few of Vincent's early works, hitherto not seen before. A bit fanciful of me maybe, but then I've always had a vivid imagination.

A short time later, Ray and Tricia married. It was my job to drive Tricia to the church but I recall she was annoyed with me for arriving too early – typical woman - so I drove around to pass some time before returning. It was a small family affair, with about 60 guests, followed by a reception at Richmond Hill Hotel. They wanted to start a family as well and, as it turned out, they succeeded in the latter before us. Jeremy came first, followed a couple of years later by Matthew. Naturally, the business needed full time staffing as it was really thriving by now, and so Tricia left to concentrate on bringing up the children. Chris employed a manageress to replace her, as well as several new therapists.

As I mentioned previously, I was a lot older than Chris and we had made the decision not to postpone having children. Now that we had our own home we wasted no time in trying for our first baby. It wasn't long before we knew something was up though because a year had gone by without any luck. At first we went to our GP who suggested various preliminary tests at the local hospital. In the end we registered at Chelsea Hospital for Women where we spent the next nine years, having every test and operation available at the time. Chris underwent four major operations but to no avail. Without dwelling on all the reasons why we were having problems, the bottom line, in the end, was that we were allergic to one another, with my sperm being killed off as soon as they reached their destination. I admit to feeling relieved that the fault wasn't mine. Most men can't bear to think they are less virile in that department just because they cannot sire a child. The fact that medically, it doesn't make any difference at all, is beside the point. Ask any man and he'll agree with me.

Psychologically, the more you try, the less likely a pregnancy becomes, because the tension is unbearable. As for sex, well, instead of being something you do spontaneously for pleasure, it becomes a job that has to be performed, at the right moment, on the appointed day of the menstrual cycle. That is, after douching in an alkaline solution of vinegar. I ask you, how unromantic is that? It put an enormous strain on our marriage. At the same time we were both working and Chris's business began to suffer. Each time we'd leave Chelsea, with our hopes high, only to be dashed the following month.

After about four years, a new consultant came to Chelsea Hospital. Mr. Harrison took a fresh view of our case, and it was through him we discovered the allergy problem. I can see him now,

. sitting across the desk from us as he announced cheerily, "Don't worry Christine, I'll get you pregnant, by hook or by crook!" Realising what he'd said, the three of us burst out laughing. True to his word, he did just that. Chris had gone for a post-coital test the following month, after taking a course of medication. This involved taking a swab of sperm from the vagina and looking at it under the microscope. Mr. Harrison called me over. "Quick Derek! Come and look at this, they're all swimming normally." Turning to Chris he added, "You know, this could be it."

Some people have the gift of instilling confidence, and he was one of them. We drove home on cloud nine, full of expectation and couldn't wait for the end of the month. To our great joy we discovered the pregnancy test was positive, just as Mr. Harrison had predicted.

My in-laws had moved recently to Thurso in the north of Scotland and we'd arranged to visit them at this time. Never having been before, we stopped off in Edinburgh to do some sightseeing en route. While on a tour of Holyrood Castle, Chris became doubled up in agony and started to bleed heavily. She was rushed to hospital but insisted on returning to London. Within an hour of our arrival at Chelsea Hospital she was being operated on for an ectopic pregnancy. At one stage I was summoned into Sister's office and told to expect the worst, because the surgical team had needed to resuscitate. Thankfully, the operation was successful and Chris returned to the ward. I've never been more pleased to see her in my life.

To say we were devastated would be an understatement and it took us a long time to recover. It would be almost impossible for Chris to conceive now, since she'd lost the only fallopian tube that had been any good. I caught Mr. Harrison, looking very sad, standing in the corridor outside the ward. He shook his head, making the usual commiserations. I think we both knew this was the end of the road. After a while, we went to thank him and say farewell. He suggested thinking about adoption but we weren't ready for that yet and hoped to get lucky in the future still. Time passed and I started to get more work. The salon was doing really well, so Chris was kept busy and life plodded along normally for a while.

James went on to get me work on nearly every TV show worth appearing in, including *Angels*, as an in-and-out character part playing Pauline Quirke's screen Dad. Some of the most popular shows during this period were *Sweeney*, *Minder*, *Dempsey and Makepeace* and *The Saint*, and I got small parts on all of them. At one stage I even auditioned for the part of Dennis Watts in the early *EastEnders*, getting down to the final six, but Leslie Grantham won, and played it very well. Julia Smith, the producer of *EastEnders*, told James at the time, "I love Derek, and his work, but he isn't quite right for the part." I was bitterly disappointed, and spent the next few years hoping I might get another opportunity, as most cockney actors do. Funnily enough, not long after, I was offered the part of Frank Butcher but I was required to start after three weeks, just when I'd signed another contract for a second series of *King and Castle*. That's the way the cookie crumbles in our business; either no work at all, or everything comes at once and you have to turn things down. In the end the role was given to my old pal, the late Mike Reid and, as it turned out, I think the part was made for him.

Les Blair was a bit of an avante guard director at the BBC and he asked me to do an improvised television play; about builders. I've maintained always that life and work experiences, such as labouring for Martin, helped me to build up my characters and this one was no exception. We spent a couple of weeks in the rehearsal rooms and then shot it on location. When it was all over, Les said to me, "I have something in mind for you next year. I'll be in touch." This is something you get a lot, from directors and producers alike, but more often than not, you never hear another word and so I paid little attention but thanked him politely anyway.

Towards the end of 1976 I was getting some decent parts which boosted my confidence a bit. James had decided to work from home and cut down a bit, so he chose a handful of artists to represent, and I'm glad to say, I was one of them.

The Duchess of Duke Street followed the success of *Upstairs Downstairs*. It was in fact, based on the true story of Rosa Lewis who, having started out as a servant, gradually worked her way up the ladder, becoming a renowned cook and working for all the stately home owners of the day, until purchasing the notable and very fashionable Cavendish Hotel in London. I played the part of Ben Smythe, a stall-holder in Covent Garden. The Duchess came to buy my quails and their eggs. Gemma Craven, who played the part, was a beauty and most of the men on set fancied her rotten - including me!

Some big stars began their careers in British 'sex and romp' farces. On the assumption that, like me, they needed the money, I don't mind admitting to my embarrassing film credit. I had a minor role in *Adventures of a Plumber's Mate* playing a motorcycle dealer, alongside Elaine Paige who made her acting debut as Daisy. When the film was completed, Chris and I went to the premiere. Elaine was sitting in the row in front of us, chatting to the girl next to her, and we couldn't help eavesdropping. She was very animated because she'd been told earlier that day that she was down to the last two for the part of Eva Peron in *Evita*. I heard her say she would know the result the following day. We got carried away on her excitement and couldn't wait to buy a paper to find out. To my mind, no-one has ever bettered her performance as Argentina's First Lady, Eva. Had Elaine known how her life would change after this role, I doubt she'd have accepted the part of Daisy, since she is even more ashamed of the film than I am!

Money worries had subsided so Chris and I went on our first holiday alone. It was 1976, and we chose the Mediterranean island of Kefalonia. We wanted a quiet, unspoilt place and that's exactly what we got. It was a sleepy holiday destination for Greeks from the mainland and, as yet, hadn't been discovered by any of the major tour operators. First, we flew to Athens for an overnight whistle-stop tour of all the main sights, before catching a flight to the island. We loved it and I think it was one of our happiest times together. It gave us a chance to relax, away from the pressures of hospital visits and our obsession with babies. A sub-tropical island and an oasis for those wanting to get away from it all. Little sandy coves dotted all over, surrounded by wonderful pine forests, giving up their heavenly scents which wafted across the island on gentle breezes every now and then. I've never been back, but friends tell me it's no longer like that, having succumbed to the demands of the tourist. It's gone the same way as some parts of Spain, like Torremolinos. One of our great joys was meandering along the back streets, to family-run restaurants, where customs dictated we go into the kitchen and choose whatever dish took our fancy. Of course, seafood was most popular, being caught by local fishermen daily and we managed to convey our wishes to the hosts using some fanciful hand gestures, since most of the islanders didn't speak English.

On our return, I realised it was time to say goodbye to my old Jag as it needed a lot of work to keep it road worthy. I bought a lovely second hand Ford Capri; chocolate brown with cream leather upholstery. Quite a fast, sporty little number but only really suitable for two people, even though there was a small seat in the back, you'd have to be a child or a minute adult to fit in!

True to his word, come spring the following year, my agent James got a call from Les Blair again, asking me to audition for a series of four, 80-minute films, called *Law and Order*. I was called to a church hall in Ladbroke Grove to meet the writer G.F. Newman and the producer Tony Garnett. Les Blair greeted me on arrival and introduced me to the others. Improvisation was a new concept at this time, and one of the other actors, Billy Dean, tried out a scene with me. My part involved playing a copper who is trying to coax a prisoner to plead guilty when he gets to court. Billy and I played around with dialogue for a while and it went well. The following week Les rang my agent to tell him they couldn't make up their minds whether I should play the prisoner or the detective. James asked him, "Which is the hardest?" Les replied "The copper." Job done. Although I didn't know it yet, this turned out to be my first ever leading role, as Detective Inspector Fred Pyall. Little did we realise at the time what a huge impact the programme would have.

Three floors of a new office building in Euston had to be taken over to create a police station. The set designer was granted permission to photograph every department of New Scotland Yard and reproduce them, ready for filming. Although we had scripts of a type, the whole innovative idea was to ad lib and improvise as much as possible, thereby making the scenes appear more authentic. None of us knew how big or small our parts were because of this, never having seen a synopsis of the plot even. Something similar had been tried a few years earlier with the ground-breaking film *Kes*, directed by Ken Loach. Each morning we'd be given a rough outline of a script and told to read it; learn as much as possible; then rehearse. Two advisers arrived on the set each day; a retired detective sergeant and a serving one. *The Detective's Tale* was to be the first film, followed by *The Villain's Tale*, *The Brief's Tale* and finally, *The Prisoner's Tale*. The gist of the plot was to produce a documentary-style drama series showing corruption within the police force. Fitting villains up; taking bribes; planting evidence etc. Plots like these are right up my street because, I'm afraid to admit, I believed most of the content of those tales. Cynical to a fault, that's me.

The trouble was, due to my past associations with the seedier side of life and the criminal underworld, I know for a fact that this sort of thing went on all the time. Having said that, from talking to various police officers over the years, if you look at it from a justice point of view, usually they admit only to fitting-up known criminals, who've managed to escape detention; on a technicality or some other point of law. Frustration sets in on their part as, time and time again, the villains are let off. This doesn't make it right, I know, but I'm merely putting both sides of the argument here and of course I'm not suggesting for a minute that it's normal practice across the board.

I had to portray D.I. Pyall as a sly and seedy character. In the first episode, I discover from an informant that one of the notable villains, Jack Lynn, Peter Dean's character, is about to stage an armed robbery of a supermarket. Apparently, I've been obsessed with booking this villain for quite some time but hitherto have been unsuccessful and I make it clear I'm out to get him this time around. Jack Lynn gets wind of this though and abandons the raid. Meanwhile, not long after, there is an armed robbery by another four known criminals. Three of them are nicked but the fourth member of the gang gets away. I seize the opportunity to fit-up Lynn by planting evidence and implicating him at the scene of the crime. There's a twist to the story though. In *The Brief's Tale*, we see the three guilty men acquitted, on a technicality, but the innocent Lynn is found guilty. Ken Campbell played his part brilliantly, as a fumbling, slightly dubious, if not bent, solicitor.

In my opinion, the final episode, *The Prisoner's Tale* is the most harrowing. Peter played it with great conviction, so much so that many people, myself included, wondered if he'd ever been in jail. We watched him enter the prison as a happy-go-lucky, petty criminal but, as the story unfolds, the guards take a dislike to him, due to their hatred of criminals who keep protesting their innocence. They beat him up frequently, put him into solitary confinement and abuse him in every possible way. He rebels against the establishment and immediately is prescribed drugs to keep him calm. Gradually, we watch him deteriorate into a fuddle-brained broken man. When all four films were completed, Chris and I went to the preview at the BAFTA cinema in Piccadilly. To see myself on the big screen was an eye opener in itself. At the end, Chris turned to me with great pride and said, "Del, you were the lead!" The first I knew about it.

The other three films were completed and the whole series shown in 1978. BBC telephone lines were jammed with complaints for hours after the first film showing. The public thought it was a real documentary and refused to believe that British policemen could be 'bent'. Detective Inspector Pyall was a nasty piece of work. I even had people shouting at me in the street for months afterwards, but just as many thought it was a fantastically true portrayal. It causes controversy to this day and the jury's 'still out' so to speak. Looking back, I can see why it upset so many people. After all, they were used to Jack Warner's honest face on *Dixon of Dock Green,* with his kind manner and community spirit.

My career really took off from here on, and it was the beginning of a very happy and bright episode in my working life. Chris and I decided to celebrate my new success with a holiday. Her sister lived in Nairobi, having moved there when the rest of her family returned home to England, and she's remained in Kenya ever since. I'd never been anywhere like it before and looked forward to planning visits to the game parks and having some time to relax at the coast in Mombasa. I'd heard so many stories from Chris, about life in East Africa, but nothing can prepare anyone for the true magic of such a continent – so different from our own culture.

Georgina and Marshall Muir ran a very successful catering business which included outside events as well as running a well known bar called The Dambusters on Wilson Airport and all food, served at the Nairobi Race Course – from the kiosks and restaurant to the Jockey Club. They had done the catering for several films, including *Born Free* as well as the TV series, *Edward and Mrs Simpson* and were an extremely popular family. This included seven children! It seems Georgie made up for the children Chris and I lacked. We booked for five weeks, staying in Nairobi for the first three so that we could visit several game parks. The ex-pat community is quite small and there's a free and easy lifestyle which is hard to explain. For example, when we'd go onto the veranda for breakfast, it was common to find two or three strangers tucking in to fruit and cereals before us. Of course they were family friends who simply introduced themselves and we'd carry on. The same would happen in the evening, with friends popping into the lounge bar and helping themselves to a drink. All the homes have an indoor bar – it's part of the tropical culture. The drinking is a way of life and let me say, my brother-in-law was a capable drinker and leave it at that. To give you an example: we arrived at Jomo Kenyatta Airport at six o'clock in the morning, after an eight-hour flight. Marshall greeted us by taking me straight to the bar for a glass of milk and whisky chaser. Bearing in mind I had neither met him before, nor did I drink, Chris kicked me on my shin to let me know I shouldn't refuse. I think I had about two or three drinks before he drove us home but, not surprisingly, I don't remember a thing because I fell asleep. Nairobi is about 6,000 feet above sea level so it takes a few days to adjust to the altitude at the best of times without adding alcohol to the equation. Instead of an introduction to Georgie and the rest of the family, I got out of the car and promptly laid down on the front lawn. The gardener had to help me to bed and Chris was left to make the explanations.

After recovering for a few days, we headed off on safari to several destinations. Our first route started with the Ngong Hills and out towards the Rift Valley - one of the seven wonders of the world, then climbing up to Mount Kenya Safari Club. It was owned at that time by the actor William Holden, who had fallen in love with the place while on an expedition. Throughout his ownership, and with the help of his partner, actress Stephanie Powers, they organised a conservation programme which had not been rivalled in East Africa, as well as adding a touch of Hollywood glitz to the old colonial charm. Early members included Lord Mountbatten and Winston Churchill, and many of the big stars came to visit. Nowadays I believe it covers more than 100 acres but has been taken over by a modern hotel consortium. Friends tell me it's lost a lot of the old charm, so I'm glad I saw it then.

We stayed for a night in one of the cottages that Holden had built; paid for as a treat from Georgie and Marshall. Our cottage had a makuti roof and was styled on the traditional rondavel dwellings – from a Dutch word meaning roundhouse. On entering, the first thing that surprised me was the warm glow emanating from an open fire, placed centrally in a sumptuous lounge, and furnished in typical African style. I hadn't realised how cold it gets at night. The next day we went to Aberdare National Park for our first trip. This is where the famous 'Treetops' hotel is, but we couldn't afford a night there. The views are unbelievable; with sweeping terrain to the foot of the mountain and a backdrop of snowy peaks. Dotted around the slopes lie the various plantations – mainly tea and coffee. Back to Nairobi, and then off on a long trek to the lakes of Naivasha and Nakuru with its sea of salmon-pink flamingos. Then we crossed over a painted line on the road, under an arch, depicting the Equator, as we headed towards the mountain township of Eldoret. If you've never been to Africa, please may I suggest you try to, because it's almost impossible to describe without taking up the rest of my book; so I'll do my best to whet your appetites by summarising the rest of the holiday in brief.

The main game parks en route to Mombasa are East and West Tsavo and Amboseli, where I saw all the 'big five' - elephant, lion, buffalo, rhino and leopard. To look at a lion which is strolling past the car nonchalantly, at about three feet distance, is something I'll never forget. The difference in their stature and sheer magnificence cannot compare to that of the lions we see in captivity. We stayed a night at Kilaguni Lodge where we put our names down for a wake-up call during the night should any of the big five come to the watering hole. Sure enough, around 2am we heard a gentle buzzing sound above our heads notifying us to get moving to the veranda. These are built on stilts; to prevent animals from invading our privacy; and overlook the water from a safe distance - two or three hundred feet away. The sounds of Africa at night are something special too, with bullfrogs and crickets in full song.

We continued down through the park towards Mombasa, heading north to Malindi, stopping off for a week at Ocean Sports Club in Watamu; a very modest and carefree hotel right on the sands, overlooking the Indian Ocean. Pure indulgent heaven that's all I can say. Snorkelling and coral diving were daily pursuits, as well as swimming in the warm turquoise waters to keep cool, drying naturally in the baking hot sun, with just the shade offered by palm trees. We soon gave up sunbathing under them though, when we heard about a German tourist who had been killed by a coconut falling on his head. Georgie and Marshall had a holiday home on the south side at Diani Beach so we met up with them for a few days. To reach it meant crossing over from Mombasa by ferry. This is not a trip for the faint hearted, since it carries hundreds of passengers, cars and lorries and appears to be sinking so low into the water that I felt sure we'd go under. Safety issues and loading weights are not taken into account, but I took the view that if everyone else does it regularly, it must be alright. We had to wait an hour to get on but I passed the time wandering outside, up and down all the little shanty huts that try to sell tourists anything from fruit to wood carvings. I bought some soapstone elephants and the customary salad servers, but one of the nicest things was the tea that is brewed by the roadside. They have a unique method of making it. Tea, milk and sugar are boiled together, in a pan on top of a small gas burner, such as we use for camping. It may sound awful, but trust me, it's delicious. Nothing like the tea we're used to back home though.

Heading back to Nairobi, we went a different route. By the foothills of Kilimanjaro in Tanzania, we crossed the eastern side of Amboseli and headed north to the Masai Mara. Georgie drove, but there had been some heavy rainstorms for a few days and we became stuck in deep mud. We were too scared to get out of the car because anyone who does is a fool. Luckily, from out of nowhere, there appeared a tribe of masai, dressed in native costume, who had come to our aid. Among them was a young chap of about 25 who spoke to Georgie in Swahili. He stood out because he was dressed in western clothes. In short, it transpired he was a co-driver on the East African Safari Rally. Talk about good luck! He took over from Georgie, who had straddled herself across the middle of the front seat, and manoeuvred us out of trouble. A few hours later we entered the Masai Mara where several herds of elephant, complete with babies, were clearly visible, albeit in the distance; so it had all been worth it in the end. An overnight stop, where we slept under canvas, ended our stay in style. A barbecue had been arranged for the guests and we had a great evening's entertainment given by a group of tribal dancers. I was sorry to leave the Muir home because we'd been spoilt and made so welcome by them and their friends. Africa is a wonderful continent but I've never been back, so maybe I'll return again one day.

Their business partner was a lovely chap called Charles Levy, and soon after our return he retired back home in England. He and his sister had a place in Chelsea, so we kept in touch regularly. Either we'd play golf or whenever Marshall and Georgie came back on home-leave, we'd all meet up at their home in Oakley Street.

Sadly, not long after our return, my personal happiness was marred by the sudden death of my father. It was just before the screening of *Law and Order,* so he never saw my success. If he had, more than likely he'd have carried a placard telling all and sundry who I was. Dad was extremely proud of me. He died following a massive stroke, on Boxing Day in 1977 aged just 68. When the ambulance had come to collect Dad, Mum went with him while Chris and I followed by car. As he was being admitted onto the intensive care ward, the charge nurse took all the details down from Mum; medical history, age, date and that sort of thing. Then he asked for their marriage date. Obviously Mum was in deep shock, but told him without hesitating. I was stunned to hear the words, "January 1933." Only three months before I was born! I never said anything at the time but afterwards I did question Mum. It's funny, but some things fell straight into place; as if I'd known subliminally. Like the fact that there weren't any wedding photos in the house, or among our photo albums; neither did they celebrate an anniversary, nor could I remember seeing any cards to each other. Mum laughed, a little bit embarrassed by the revelation. She said, "It wasn't sordid or anything – we loved each other and it just happened." Sex was a topic that had never been discussed in our household and I didn't even get the fatherly chat about the birds and bees. We never spoke about it again.

I spent the whole time during the days that followed Dad's stroke, by his bedside with Mum and Chris. Holding his hand, I kept imagining I could feel it move in an attempt to tell me something but I was wrong and they were just involuntary twitches. The intensive care nurses suggested we keep talking to him; about anything and everything, in the hope he might hear us. I told him how much I loved him and, at one point, I remember shaking his shoulders and shouting in his ear, "C'mon Dad. You can do it. C'mon!" Several times I thought he responded but sadly he passed away. We were all grief stricken.

My parents' house move had turned out to be a blessing in disguise because at least Mum could be comforted by us after Dad's death. She never really got over his loss though and lived an almost reclusive existence until her own death on April 23 1999, at 84 years old. Although she witnessed my early successes, sadly, she too, missed out on the real fame that would come my way much later, through *EastEnders*. Their presence is always with me and I like to think both look down on me, from somewhere out there.

Before Mum died, she'd had a long discussion with me about her funeral arrangements. Adamant that it was to be a simple affair, without any flowers, and a service to be held at the graveside and not in church, she made me promise not to go against her wishes. She wasn't religious and didn't wish to be hypocritical in any way. I think she knew I was broke at the time and must have realised the end was nearing and wanted to get this all off her chest. There was a small pension fund that she and Dad had paid into, for as long as I can remember, which was supposed to cover all costs. On the day of the funeral, the family members attended and everything was done just as Mum had asked, but I had a shock afterwards. As if the pain of losing Mum wasn't bad enough, her sister Gladdie came over, seconds after the service, to tell me she never wanted to see me again. It took a while for her words to sink in, and when I asked what was wrong she said she was disgusted at how simplistic the funeral had been, and thought I'd skimped on it. This really hurt me at the time but I knew it wasn't true and resolved to forget about the incident. There's one thing I'm not, and that is mean. Quite the opposite in fact, as all my friends and other family members can vouch for. Injustice is something that's difficult to bear when you feel helpless to do anything about it. I couldn't make her see reason and we've never spoken since.

Things went mad for me after *Law and Order*, with lots of guest cameo parts as well as some fantastic leads. I bumped into Diana Dors again on an episode of *Sweeney* followed by appearances in several episodes of *Minder* and *Taggart*. Robert Wagner and Stephanie Powers were very popular at the time, in a series called *Hart to Hart,* and filmed one episode entirely in England. Once again, I was a copper who had to arrest them. It was a very enjoyable job as they were nice people to work with.

Sometimes it made a pleasant change to work on radio and get out of the studios for a while. The BBC was putting on a new 90-minute play based on the novels by R.D. Wingfield. *A Touch of Frost* started out over the airwaves and I played none other than the loveable detective, Jack Frost. To quote Michael Cain, "Not a lot of people know that." I managed to solve six crimes in that short space of time. Following its success, I auditioned for the TV role but was unlucky. David Jason was hot property at the time, after his many triumphs, and was a household name. Del Boy Trotter to Jack Frost saw a terrific transformation of characters and he has earned his place in the hearts of the nation. Next I joined Robert Lindsay for six episodes of the comedy show *Arthur and Me*. Robert is great fun to work with and a true professional in every way. Although I enjoy a good joke on the set, I like to work with actors and actresses who turn up on time, knowing their lines and what's required of them.

My agent called me one morning to tell me he'd landed me a "nice little part" in a big production film which had taken over the whole of Shepperton Studios. Dino de Laurentis brought James

Cagney out of retirement, for a comeback after 20 years, on the film *Ragtime*. I knew nothing of this so asked James what my part was. "You're playing the Assistant to the New York Commissioner of Police," he told me. "And who's playing him?" I replied. Well, when he told me it would be James Cagney, no less, I nearly dropped the phone. My all time hero. Truth is, I'd have waved the fee just to appear with this great actor, but of course James said, "Be quiet Derek, I need the commission!" Why Shepperton, and not New York, I wondered? Apparently, there were major labour problems at the time and so England had been the natural choice.

I'll never forget the first day Cagney arrived on the set. The scenery department had built a replica facade of the Grand New York Museum, where a siege was about to commence. There must have been at least 200 extras as well as stuntmen on horseback, playing mounted police. A limousine pulled up, right in front of me, and out stepped The Man. Without any prompting, the whole place erupted in applause and cheering. The noise was deafening and tears of emotion rolled down the cheeks of even the toughest of men, including myself. This went on for about six or seven minutes until my hands hurt. Eventually, JC put up a hand in thanks, saying, "Ok folks; let's get on with the show!"

We filmed for about five weeks. Since all my scenes were with him, we often talked between shots. He spoke about *Angels With Dirty Faces* and *White Heat* and answered all my questions about other Hollywood stars. *Ragtime* would be his last film, and although he was old, his speech and twinkling blue eyes had lost none of their magic. Milos Foreman, of *One Flew Over the Cuckoo's Nest fame*, directed the film and I learnt a lot from the experience.

Not long after, the RAF wanted me to do a promotional film for them, to be shot on location at their air base in Belize. This would be a very new experience for me since I had never been to Central America before and certainly not in a jungle. When I arrived, it took a while to get used to the heat and humidity. My quarters were very basic but the Commanding Officer had seen to it that they were at least comfortable, and I settled down for the duration. What I hadn't realised was that the location would be in the heart of dense jungle which could only be reached by helicopter. We took off, for our first day, in a Puma and for a moment I felt I was in the midst of an episode of *M.A.S.H*, one of my all-time favourite series. I think I was there for about three weeks and enjoyed all the banter among the guys, taking me back to my own Service days I suppose, and I had a great time.

Upon my return home, I received an invitation; for the crew and cast to spend a day at RAF Wittering, to watch a Red Arrows display. We were shown around the camp, looking at various Harriers, Hawks and other fighter jets, followed later on by the thrilling display itself. The ground shook as the planes flew low, over our heads. The display team crew joined us for lunch later on in the Officers' Mess. It was fascinating listening to their explanations of some of the formations and I envied them.

Around this time, golf became a new hobby, when a friend requested my company for a day on the course. After a while I became reasonably good at the game and my old pal Steve Emmerson suggested I join the Charity Golf Circuit. Made up of several different groups, they do a tremendous amount for all sorts of charities. Lots of celebrities have signed up to it; mainly actors and sportsmen such as, Bernard Cribbins, Roger De Courcey, Tom O'Connor, and Kenny Lynch. The list is too long to put down here but there are many, many more. A great guy called Max Morgan organises the Sir Henry Cooper and Mike Reid Classic, held every year in Portugal, on behalf of Sony. The circuit has a huge fan base and most tournaments draw big crowds. We play all over the UK and Europe, although mostly in Spain and Portugal, and each of us tries to fit in as many events as possible around our own busy work schedules. For me, one of the nicest things about being a member is that I never know who I'm going to meet until I get to the destination.

I'll explain how it works. Large companies and corporations pay hefty sums of money to the charity involved on that day, in order to send three of their players to the tournament. Here, they're teamed up with a fourth member, from the celebrity group – chosen from a draw. There are usually about 20 companies signed in to each event. For their fee, they get a full breakfast on arrival, an allocated celebrity, a round of golf, and to finish off the day, a three-course dinner in the evening during which time an auction is held to raise even more money; mainly donated sports memorabilia; and finally, some form of entertainment such as a comedian or singer. Everybody goes away having had a marvellous time and I've kept in touch with lots of the company players over the years. These events raise huge sums of money for charities such as Born too Soon at Kingston Hospital and organised by The Stage Golf Society; SPARKS for children's diseases; The Guild of Great Britain Golf and Quiz nights and The Variety Club of Great Britain to name but a few.

Of course the celebrities don't get paid but we're always looked after very well; staying in lovely hotels and all travel expenses are covered. To be honest with you, the more I write, the more I realise how lucky I am because, since becoming an actor, there's hardly an aspect of my life that hasn't given me great pleasure and I've never considered any of it to be work.

CHAPTER SIX

Test-tube Babies

Although Chris and I had nigh on given up any thoughts of having a child of our own, we still held on to a glimmer of hope. One of the producers at the BBC knew about our problems and suggested we tag along to a film preview, about all the latest fertility treatments being offered at Hammersmith Hospital. Robert Winston (now Lord Winston) was a pioneering surgeon and headed the team. We were introduced to him at the theatre but for some reason never sought his help. I think it was because we'd gone privately to see Professor Ian Craft, another one of the leading men in this field, to discuss new options.

We had learned recently about the birth of the world's first test-tube baby, Louise Brown. Patrick Steptoe was ahead in the race, and although he was the first to be successful, there were other teams, in many countries, ready to start their own IVF programmes. Travelling up north to his clinic proved too difficult so we wasted no time, having heard that the treatment was available at Professor Craft's clinic in London.

On reflection, I don't know how Chris coped with the emotion of it all. I shan't go into the full details here but a summary is necessary, in order to understand the trauma involved. Several hormone injections were required before we could start, so that Chris's ovaries would produce multiple eggs. Apparently, the more that could be mixed with my sperm, to be fertilised in the laboratory ready for re-implantation, the higher our chances of success would be. Any woman without healthy fallopian tubes has to bypass them in this way, so that the fertilised sperm can attach to the uterine wall. This all sounds pretty straightforward now, writing it down, but the complications are many and varied. One of them being multiple births if, for any reason, all eggs were to be fertilised. Sperm, once implanted, are indiscriminate. Hence the quintuplet and sextuplet births we read about from time to time.

For a start, when I arrived at the clinic, a nurse would hand me a small sterile pot, about two inches in diameter, and then usher me into a tiny cubicle to perform my duty. It wasn't as funny as it sounds because, to cap it all, there were usually 20 or 30 other couples in the waiting room, all knowing exactly what I was about to do. My shyness had to be quashed but I could never look anyone in the eye when I passed them by. However macho a man might be, when he's on his own in this situation, it becomes quite difficult to get enthusiastic about sex and sometimes, believe it or not, it's difficult even to get an erection. Naturally, the hospital staff understood these problems, so there were lots of girlie magazines

– even some pornographic ones, on a shelf in the cubicle.

Luckily for me, I have a great sense of humour and am a big joke teller, but during this episode even I couldn't summon up much enthusiasm for gags. All these procedures have to be done with precision and even split-second timing on occasion. Once, I'd been filming up at Pebble Mill in Birmingham and had to return to the hospital at a given time for the fertilisation procedure. It was imperative to get the sperm there on time, while keeping it fresh. One of the doctors suggested I perform the deed on the train, in order not to waste valuable time. As the train pulled out of the station, I began to panic. What if I miss-judged the time of arrival at Euston? What if I did it too soon and it wasn't fresh enough? Please believe me when I tell you, all this trepidation is not conducive to performance. Having planned ahead, I chose a time to move towards the toilet. Luckily, the noise from the train's speed helped me switch off to my surroundings. Several times I heard the door catch move, as other passengers tried to use the facilities. Eventually, I managed it. I wonder what the taxi driver would have thought if he'd known what precious cargo I had in my top pocket. It had to be kept there, next to my heart, in order to keep it warm. No, not for any romanticism.

We were unsuccessful this time. IVF is terribly expensive and we couldn't afford a second attempt. Chelsea offered to put us on their programme, now up and running, but instead we went to see a counsellor there to discuss adoption. It's a funny thing, but once we knew all was lost, it came as quite a relief, and instead of being forlorn we were filled with a new kind of hope and excitement. The end of an era, nearly nine years had gone by. Was it worth all the pain and heartache? Who knows. What I do know is that, in hindsight, it probably wasn't because it had taken a terrible toll on our marriage.

A short time after the treatment, Chris had an affair with an ex-boyfriend. She told me she'd met him by accident in Regent Street while on a shopping spree in the West End. Maybe she thought some miracle would happen with someone else. I went crazy and begged Chris not to leave me, but she wouldn't listen. She moved out for a few weeks and rented a flat quite close by. This chap was a married man and hadn't left his wife the first time when he was with Chris, so I knew he would hurt her again. I was right, and after a few months he told Chris he would not be leaving home to set up with her. Although terribly hurt and angry about the affair, my love for her was all-encompassing and, being a soppy fool, I forgave her. Since the affair hadn't lasted long, and Chris wanted to stay with me, pleading to be taken back, I agreed. Love can do strange things to a person's character. By nature, I'm a real hard man and normally don't suffer any wrongdoings done to me by anyone. Where Chris was concerned though, I couldn't imagine life without her so I was left with little option but to carry on. Thankfully, neither of our parents found out and we carried on as if nothing had happened.

We went ahead with contacting the local adoption agency, and I suppose we thought that everything would settle down once a child was around. Lots of couples make that mistake, but it seemed alright to us at the time. Adopting a baby in the '70s was extremely difficult. Most girls had access to easy abortion through the NHS, coupled with the absence of old stigmas attached to single parenting, therefore many opted to keep their illegitimate babies. Very few came up for adoption and we were encouraged to consider older children, or those with some form of disability.

Our attitude to the whole thing had never altered, in that we wanted a family, no matter what. We were prepared to take on all sorts of children. Of course we'd have preferred to have a tiny baby that looked just like one of us; that's normal; but it wasn't the be all and end all, as with other couples. When the time came for filling in all the forms, I remember being horrified that having a squint was classed as a disability. For crying out loud, surely there's an element of risk with your own offspring isn't there? However, the adoption officer told us that many couples turn children down for the most minor abnormalities, and that they were unlikely to succeed with their application for those reasons, since it meant they were probably unsuitable to become adoptive parents.

Several months went by following our acceptance and we heard nothing further. Neither of us could include patience as one of our virtues but we managed, somehow, not to pester the agency for news. During the hot summer of 1978 Chris was kept so busy in the clinic with her clients, preparing for the beach and holiday, that she almost forgot about everything for a while.

Then, quite out of the blue, one Monday in the middle of August, we got a phone call at 8.30 in the morning. Chris answered it. Mrs Seager, the adoption officer who'd been dealing with our case, was on the line. "I hope you're sitting down," she chuckled, "I have some news for you. Would you be interested in twins?" Chris was numbed into silence for a few minutes while the enormity of what she'd heard sunk in. With a tremble in her voice, she replied, "Yes, yes, of course!" An appointment was made later on that day, for Mrs Seager to come round and fill us in on the details.

In all the excitement, Chris had forgotten to ask how old they were, or what sex, and we had to wait an eternity to find out. I think we just sat on the sofa until the time came, too shocked to move and wondering if they were delinquent teenagers or not. Chris was beside herself with joy and I must admit to feeling more than a little ecstatic myself. By a strange coincidence, Chris had a twin brother too. A few hurried calls were made to her manageress at the salon, to prepare her for taking over the running of the place, followed by calls to our families.

When 4 o'clock came, Mrs Seager arrived to give us the low down. First, she had to calm us because we were firing questions at her so fast, she didn't have time to answer. Slowly but surely, the facts were outlined: they were boys, only four weeks old, plus some family background to their parentage. "When can we see them?" I asked impatiently. "I'm going to take you now, if you'd like?" She replied, grinning from ear to ear. Silly question. Off we went to see our babies. It still hadn't sunk in, and I can only describe the feeling as being one of intoxication. Yes, we were drunk with excitement. That's the best way to put it, and I hope you can imagine how we felt and understand it.

Just a short distance away, the car pulled up in front of a very smart semi-detached house. The foster mother greeted us warmly, putting a finger up to her lips intimating she wanted us to be quiet. The babies had just dropped off to sleep after their feed, and we followed her into the lounge on tip toes. At either end of the couch was a tiny bundle, wrapped in a white shawl. Without a doubt this was love at first sight. Not one, but two beautiful boys. Whenever I visited friends, like Bob and Heidi, gazing down at their new-born child I used to wonder how I'd feel, and now I knew. There was lots of paper work involved and we had to wait a further three days before we could bring the boys home. Their natural mother had named the twins David and Jonathan and we decided to keep it that way, but added a middle name – David William, after Dad and Jonathan Derek, after me. We wanted to be able to tell the boys later on, that their natural mother had chosen their names. Mrs. Seager explained that, in her professional opinion, we should start mentioning the adoption to the boys when they were about two or three years old, so that it would never be too much of a shock. Opinions are divided on this subject, but Chris and I agreed with her.

Buying two of everything took up the whole time. Most parents have nine months to prepare and we turned up at Mothercare, cheque book in hand, ready to stock pile in mere hours. Two sterilising units, about 16 bottles; eight dozen nappies, 20 baby-grows plus lots of clothes, coats, mittens and bonnets. Since this wasn't really my domain, I don't recall it all now, but I know it took several hours. One of the women at the checkout commented to Chris that she'd got her figure back very quickly to which she just nodded, not knowing what to answer. Next we bought a twin pram, two cots, baby bouncers and so on. The spare room had to be organised the following day, redecorating and carpeting it in suitable colours. Although we bought two cots, we put the boys end to end in one of them, for the first few weeks, in our bedroom. Chris wouldn't let them out of her sight for a second.

Unbeknown to us at the time, social workers were on strike, and our case wouldn't go before the court to make the adoption official for another nine months. All that time we fretted over the chance their natural mother might change her mind and want them back. This didn't bear thinking about. When we brought the boys home that first time, there were several bouquets of flowers waiting for us on the doorstep, from friends and family. Just like an ordinary Mum and Dad, that's how it felt. Those early months were unimaginably exciting. Chris and I became very close, sharing all the parental duties equally. We would each feed one baby, every four hours, and then change over at subsequent feeds so that we could hold both babies in turn. Night time feeds were hysterical because the babies never woke up at the same time, neither did they need changing in unison! It became so exhausting after a while, that we would wake the sleeping one up to enable us to get a few hours rest in between. David was a guzzler and would down his bottle in a matter of minutes, while Jonathan took his time and would nod off every few seconds.

When the boys were tiny, they looked very alike but not so much that you couldn't tell them apart, so they are fraternal twins and not identical. David had been born first, and was the bigger of the two, weighing in at 5lbs 3oz, while Jonathan, who followed 10 minutes later, weighed 4lbs 13oz. We were given all this information by the foster mother who had taken them in when they were just four days old. As the months passed, the size difference became more marked as David shot ahead of Jonathan. Funnily enough, this is not the case now because, as adults, they are almost the same height and stature, although they no longer look alike – no more than any two brothers might.

The adoption was legalised nine months later and we became a proper family at last. We had David and Jonathan christened in the local church in Isleworth and settled down happily to parenthood while life returned to normal once more. Our wonderful neighbour Martin built us an extension to the side of the kitchen so that we could fit in the two high chairs and pram etc. and it also doubled as a play area. At this juncture, all I can tell you is that we loved them as much as any natural parent could love their own children and they have given us both endless joy and happiness ever since.

Not long afterwards, when the twins were about a year old, we realised it was time to move. With only two bedrooms, we'd simply outgrown the house. Although sad to see it go, I was making good money now, as was the salon, so we wanted to go up in the world. Eventually, after a lot of searching, and arguing, we settled on a pretty 1930s detached house with four bedrooms; 12 Cole Park Gardens in Twickenham. It had belonged to a doctor and his family, but needed quite a bit of doing up. Chris had set her heart on a complete renovation, so we started organising workmen, as both of us were far too busy to do any of it ourselves now. This time though, we were older and wiser, so none of the earlier garish colour schemes, and we managed to retain most of the original features. After a lifetime spent wishing I could live in a really nice house, such as I'd seen when visiting friends now that I lived in west London, this one was a bit of a dream come true for me. It had a small carriage driveway, double garage and lovely manicured gardens. Chris had fallen in love with another house in Hounslow, but I'd made a promise to myself when I left the East End finally, that I would live in a nice area one day and at the time, Hounslow was a bit down market, mainly, I suspect, because of its close proximity to Heathrow Airport.

The salon was very busy at this time, being run by a manageress with seven therapists, but Chris wanted to get back to work for a couple of days a week and so we decided to find a child minder for the boys. A wonderful woman called Sheila Scott answered our advert and after a short trial period, she settled in for the duration. We felt lucky to have found her because the boys loved her. She was extremely artistic, and set about transforming the smaller of the spare bedrooms into a playroom. On one entire wall she painted the most amazing mural, full of zoo animals and greenery, which she varnished over to make it washable. Then we put up a long workbench in front of it for the boys to do painting or craft work. On another wall we erected cupboards to hide all their clobber and mess. I've always loved big rooms and this house was certainly spacious. We kept the bathroom in its '30s style, complete with original wall and border tiles – all black and white with chrome taps. The kitchen had the original floor to wall cupboards with leaded light glass fronts at the top and base units - all hand built in dark oak; but we painted them chocolate brown gloss, and finished the theme off with antique brass handles. The floorboards were sanded down and stained in a dark oak to match, while the walls were painted in brilliant white emulsion. For the first time in my life I had a kitchen table big enough to seat six people as well as a formal dining room. Mum loved it and used to boast to friends and family how well I was doing.

Once all the decorating had been finished, we invested in a fully fitted bedroom suite. The room had a lovely bay window and from the bed I could see nothing but the trees tops which lined the road outside. This had been one of the deciding factors in choosing the house, and being the last one in a cul-de-sac we seemed to have more than most.

Around the time of our move we decided to buy some form of holiday home, as a bolt hole for weekends. Both of us were under pressure, especially me, since my work schedule was pretty heavy at the time. An apartment abroad was out of our financial reach so we'd been recommended to look at static caravans as an alternative. We soon found one at the Harleyford Estate, an idyllic spot next to the marina, and right on the Thames at Marlow, in Buckinghamshire. With its tranquil setting, it was the perfect escape.

The mobile home was much larger than anything I could have imagined, with a separate double bedroom for us, and a smaller one with bunk beds for the boys. They used to take it in turns for top bunk, on a rota system, each weekend. The views from our front lounge were magnificent, with various boats of all sizes floating past, and we couldn't wait for Fridays to come round, excitedly packing all afternoon. The journey didn't take long; about 45 minutes; because we'd leave after rush hour. It was also a great place for friends to come and visit every now and then. With a glass of wine in hand we'd watch the sun set, throwing it's reflection onto the water. Amazingly, Chris even managed to cook some superb meals in the tiny galley kitchen.

Where there's water, a boat yard will never be far away and

a couple of minutes walk down the tow path led to a very good one, complete with chandlery. Walks were plentiful and we used to go for long hikes with the buggy, sometimes taking a picnic with us. Since the boys' arrival, I'd had to sacrifice my lovely Capri in part-exchange for a Renault 4x4; a poor man's version of the Range Rover, to accommodate the mass of stuff that went with us on every trip but I didn't mind one bit. They were great days and life was good.

CHAPTER SEVEN

Murder and Mayhem

Life has a nasty habit of knocking the stuffing out of you every now and again, when it's least expected. Just when I thought things were plodding along nicely for Chris and me, I was about to enter one of the worst periods of all. Call me naïve, or green, but honestly I thought we were happy. Sadly, I was wrong.

Without wishing to sound like a pompous ass, I've always been a one-woman guy and never been unfaithful in a relationship, whether married or otherwise. It's simply the way I am. Naturally, I'm not stupid enough not to know that some men, and women for that matter, don't necessarily share my ethics, but now that we had the boys, I probably took Chris's fidelity for granted after her last indiscretion. More fool me. Here we were, with a beautiful new home that Chris had put lots of effort into creating; a thriving business; our wonderful little lads and the mobile home; coupled with my work which kept on flourishing month by month. Everything in the garden was rosy; or so I thought.

One evening, I was asked to baby-sit because Chris wanted to see a film with a friend. Perfectly harmless I thought, foolishly. I learned later that there were other people involved and she went to a party instead. Here, she was introduced to a man called Reg. Obviously there was an attraction because they began seeing each other on a regular basis, although I was kept in the dark for some time.

Chris asked me to move out for a while, saying she needed some space to sort out her feelings for me, so I rented a small flat in Twickenham, close to her salon. My friends were a great help and used to invite me round for the evenings but, as anyone who has suffered with depression knows only too well, sometimes you can't face people, even though you might be lonely. Because I thought Chris had a touch of depression I agreed, but still had no idea anyone else might be involved. Knowing my wife and boys were only a couple of miles away, was intolerable and I felt terribly lonely, sometimes driving up to the house so I could be near them. Christmas came a few short weeks later and Chris took the boys with her to stay with friends in Berkshire. I tried desperately hard to pull on Chris's heart strings. It's probably the nearest I got to begging her, but not knowing there was someone else in the equation, I simply couldn't understand why she didn't come home.

I became suspicious not long after though, when I realised she was going out quite a lot in the evenings, leaving the boys with our child minder. This drove me mad, so on one of these occasions, I started driving around all over town, like a demented fiend, to see if I could find her. Unless you've experienced pure jealous passion it will be impossible to imagine the strength of my anger. It took over my whole psyche, physical being and every waking moment. When I look back at all the years I carried on feeling this way it's a miracle I didn't have a nervous breakdown or become seriously ill in some way. My advice to any bloke of a similar disposition would be this: seek help immediately – from a counsellor, marriage guidance or any similar body of professionals. With hindsight, I should have found a good woman to take my mind off things and concentrated on starting a new life instead of wasting so much energy on my feelings of bitterness and hatred.

Chris had a very distinctive Fiat Panda; it had a black body with a huge white Panda bear depicted on each of the two front doors. It was a special edition so there weren't many about. By sheer chance I spotted it in a lay-by, on the North Circular Road. Parking on the opposite side, I waited, for what seemed like hours. Around about midnight, a car pulled up behind hers and I saw, instantly, that she was in the passenger seat, with a man next to her. Then they started kissing. By now I was sick with murderous rage and fit to kill. How I crossed the main road without getting run over remains a mystery, but I did. Opening the driver's door, I grabbed the guy by his throat, and tried to gouge his eyes out. Chris screamed in terror and started punching me to let go, so I released my grip and he got out.

"Go home Reg and let me handle things. I'll be fine," she told him in calm but firm tones. After much abusive language, and a few kicks to his groin, I let go and he left. Chris was in shock, saying she wasn't able to drive, and asked me to take her home. As we crossed over the road to where my car was parked, we waited for a couple of cars and tankers to pass by. I was raging mad and for a split second I almost pushed her under one of them, but the thought of our boys stopped me. Thank goodness.

Several times over the next few months I came dangerously close to murdering her. There was so much fury inside of me, I frightened myself even. How I didn't hit out at Chris or strangle her I'll never know; honestly I felt that bitter and angry. She knew obviously how I felt and didn't allow herself ever to be alone with me. I contemplated suicide once or twice and resorted to emotional blackmail on Chris. I recall phoning her one day, threatening to take the boys with me to Beachy Head and kill us all; another time I gave her a time and date when I would be doing it. I would scream and rant, all my hurt and anger pouring out of me. Obviously I never did any of those terrible things I threatened because the boys were always at the back of my mind, even in the darkest hours and I know I would never have harmed them; it was just yet one more panic method of trying to get Chris back. After a while I gave up and concentrated on work, but inside the pain ate away at me for a long time to come.

My world collapsed from that moment on but, being a professional, I carried on working and tried not to let it show. Normally, I hardly ever drink alcohol; just an odd glass of wine perhaps, but I vaguely recollect arriving on the set of *The Sweeney* one day, with a thumping hangover from the after effects of Pernod. I fell asleep in a director's chair, in-between takes, and one of the cameramen took a photo of me, looking ashen grey. The cast were concerned on my behalf as they'd never seen me in this state before. How I got through that day's filming I'll never know. By now I had moved back to the house and, as a temporary measure, Chris used two rooms at the back of her salon; one as a bedroom for the boys and the other a studio lounge for herself, until she had decided exactly what she wanted to do.

I had a big fight scene with Dennis Waterman at the end of *The Sweeney,* which Peter (Pebbles) Braham was arranging and Steve Emmerson was doubling for me. When Peter saw that I was in the scene, and knowing me from earlier stunt days, he asked the director if I could do my own. For two reasons it made sense. One, it would look more authentic and two, the director needn't cut the scene so much. For poor old Steve though, this would mean he'd lose a day's money, so I suggested he do the jump, off a low shed roof - while I do the fight. Everyone agreed. My chosen weapon was a shovel, while Dennis wielded a chain. The scene went well and no-one was hurt. Of course, Dennis won the fight, ending with my capture and his immortal catch phrase, "You're nicked!" I must say, it all looked very realistic, when I saw the clip later, on film.

Chris and I saw a counsellor for a while who had been recommended by the Court at our divorce, as part of the welfare team concerned with minimising the effects on the boys. Acting in conjunction with the liaison officer who had been assigned to us, she did her best to calm me down but sadly, it was too late. Ultimately, Chris went to live with Reg in Wood Green, taking the boys with her. This was the final straw for me, so I took revenge a short while later. Every last vestige of sensible rationality had gone, and I couldn't separate my own emotions from my behaviour as a father. Naturally I'm ashamed of myself now, but at the time, nothing and no-one could knock any sense into me. To be honest, I used the boys to get back at Chris, albeit unintentionally. One thing I was glad of – my father wasn't alive to see our breakup. For two reasons; firstly, he too would have been devastated, as was Mum, because Chris was looked upon as the daughter they would have loved but never had, and secondly, because I think he would have killed her for hurting me. The split affected the boys and I know that they used to cry for me. At such a young age it was understandable because they were too young to understand why I wasn't around anymore.

Fortunately, I continued to get regular work and when I was offered a role in a film called *Spaghetti House Siege*, I jumped at the opportunity as it meant filming in Italy. The movie is based on a true story about the managers of a chain of restaurants who meet up, at the end of each week, to collate their takings ready for banking. On this occasion, the takings amount to approximately £13,000. Three Nigerian gunmen, claiming to represent the Black Liberation Army, a Black Panther splinter group, plan an armed robbery but when it fails, they take nine Italian restaurant staff into the basement and hold them hostage. However, one of the waiters manages to escape, raising the alarm.

The gunmen demand an aircraft and a safe passage to Jamaica. I played the part of Superintendent Hutchinson of the Metropolitan Police, who tries to negotiate a deal. All requests are denied (as indeed they were in real life when the drama took place) and the siege continues for six days...

Even though the actual spaghetti house siege took place in London's Knightsbridge, because the film producer was Italian, the movie was shot on location in Rome. Cunningly, I told Chris that I wanted to take the boys on holiday but instead, my old mate Terry Wallis joined me, to act as child minder, while I worked during the day. One of only three hotels in the city with rooftop swimming pools, our accommodation couldn't have suited us better. (Apparently it had once been a high-class brothel in by-gone days!) We all had a great time. Unfortunately, the Sunday papers got hold of the story with a bold headline splashed across the page: 'DEREK MARTIN TAKES HIS BOYS TO WORK'. Chris found out the truth soon enough when she read the newspapers. We were away over three weeks in which time I didn't keep in contact with her at all. I wanted her to know what it felt like to miss seeing the boys. When we got back she was furious and took me to court. The judge reprimanded me and told me to return the boys to her immediately. I knew that if ever I pulled a stunt like that again I could jeopardise my access arrangements so I made a conscious effort to comply with the court rulings. Having just spent three whole weeks in Italy with me it must have been awful for the boys, as we returned to weekend visits only. It was all such a mess. While we were away, they kept asking me when mummy would be coming and I had to make up stories to satisfy their questioning.

While I was in Rome, I'd go sightseeing with the boys but they were a little too young to appreciate the beauty that surrounded us. I met some interesting stars too. Our producer, Fernando Ghia, took us to a smart restaurant one evening, where I was introduced to the late and legendary Anthony Quinn, another actor I admired very much and Franco Nero, who'd been heavily involved with Vanessa Redgrave. I believe they married and had a child.

Sooner or later I knew there would be an official custody hearing, but beforehand, a social worker had been allocated our case. Her job was to keep the two of us on an even keel, organise mutually acceptable access arrangements, and generally look out for the twins' welfare. Although they get a lot of bad press, I have to say that our liaison officer was excellent. She tried to make me see reason, almost succeeding, but each time I thought I'd cracked the calming down bit, a few days later I'd revert back to Mr. Angry.

Well-meaning friends suggested I resort to medication, such as Valium, but I didn't.

Dazed and bewildered, I have only slight recall to the day in court. I put forward what I considered to be a very good case for custody, but in my heart of hearts I knew the boys would be better off with their mother. The magistrates obviously thought so too because, although it's all a blur now, the only words I can remember are, "Joint custody, with care and control to the mother." My heart sank, but when I saw the relief on Chris's face, I felt happy for her in a perverse way. Thus, I joined the masses of poor sods in the same predicament, and entered into the role of part-time fatherhood.

In my mind, there is little doubt that divorce and separation cause untold long-term damage; not only to the children involved, but to the parents and extended families that join in along the way. Talking to others who have taken this path, often as not, they admit to wishing they had never left their partners; on the grounds that the grass isn't always as green as they thought it would be. Our parents, of course, knew this and didn't need university studies to tell them so. While Chris and I were engaged in the meetings with our social worker, I'm convinced that if only the rules were to change, making it impossible to get a divorce for at least six months after the decree nisi, and before the decree absolute, many couples would stay together. I don't remember anyone trying to help us to patch up our marriage. If it had been compulsory for couples to seek help, for at least six months before granting the decree absolute, then I'm sure Chris would have come round and given our marriage another chance.

Rightly or wrongly, my own belief is that parents should find a way, if at all possible, to remain together until the children are at least adults. When you talk to couples who have done just that, they will tell you that breaking up isn't worth the angst. Sticking it out and staying together forever is best, because by then, mostly, they've ironed out the creases and grown deeply fond of one another. Genuinely, in our case, it wasn't my decision to make.

I commenced with the ritual of having the twins every other weekend, with shared holiday periods, and tried to get on with my life. In reality though, I didn't calm down for another 20 years. The house became a very lonely place. One minute it had been filled with the joy and laughter of two happy little boys and now there was nothing but a ghostly silence. All the work to make it a lovely family home was wasted and I started to feel bitter and resentful. I also began to hate the place. I would telephone to speak to the boys but whenever Chris answered the phone I found it impossible to be civil to her. She would raise her voice and invariably the conversations were overheard by the boys.

When the boys were about three and a half, I got a part in a film on location in Iraq. Saddam Hussein had requested an historical documentary film to be made; about the 300 soldiers from the Manchester Regiment who were massacred near Hillah in 1920, during the Arab uprising against British rule. Several big stars were booked, including Oliver Reed who had left by the time I got there, and James Bolam.

Because Iraq was at war with Iran at this time, all civilian flights could only route down a narrow airspace corridor over Jordan, and were permitted only to land, or take off, between 2am and 4am. The last two hours of the journey were completed in total darkness; curtains drawn and no cabin lights. On arrival, our luggage was searched to ensure that we hadn't brought in any western newspapers, literature or alcohol. Needless to say, I heard later that Oliver Reed, who was a notorious boozer, had tried to smuggle a few bottles in but upon detection they were duly confiscated. I could tell you a few stories about Oliver, but most of them are unprintable, being suitable only for risque publications. For the duration of our stay, we were put up in a five star luxury hotel. We'd been warned before leaving England that the rooms would be bugged and strict instructions were handed to us not to talk about the war or the police and under no circumstances should we run down the Iraqi regime or we might be imprisoned.

Wake-up calls were 4.30am. After a light continental breakfast we were escorted to the desert in a convoy of Jeeps. By the time we arrived, the sun was just rising and I witnessed one of the most spectacular sights. The sands were covered in a thick, white frost which moved eerily, in a snake-like motion, as the rays hit; rather like those speeded-up films of clouds you see on TV sometimes.

Suave or what? *The Chinese Detective* with David Yip in 1981.

Happy days with ex-wife Chris.

Looking nervous, Chris and me at Acton Register Office in 1971.

With no help from Dad! My pride and joy, David and Jonathan in 1982.

With Nigel Planer in *King and Castle* in 1986.

But fellas, I can't swim! Filming *King and Castle* on London's Battersea Bridge.

After you m'lud. As Donald Campbell's butler in *Speed King* in 1979.

Si Signor! Alex Morris in the ill-fated *Eldorado* in 1993.

Check mate! With the boys in 1986.

As Private Gruber in *Private Schultz* in 1981.

A career highlight - working with Hollywood legend James Cagney on *Ragtime* in 1981.

As guest character George Talbot in *The Bill* with Billy Murray, as dodgy DS Don Beech.

As Gary Marshall in hit TV series *The Governor* with Janet McTeer in 1995.

She's the pretty one! With Fat Marjorie aka Matt Lucas on *Little Britain* in 2005.

Where to Guv'? Charlie Slater at work behind the wheel as a London cabbie.

Proud Dad Charlie on Kat and Alfie's colourful wedding day in 2003.

Celebrating in the Slaters' kitchen with Alfie, Kat and Mo in 2005.

Within 20 or so minutes all traces of frost had disappeared completely, giving way to scorching heat as the day wore on.

Apart from the Brits, there were lots of Arab cast members, mainly extras and bit-part actors. The Iraqi director carried a whip, which he used frequently on his crew. He didn't dare use it on any of us but we all found it distressing to witness, although we couldn't voice our opinions.

Cannons had been set up, ready for real ammunition (or so we were told) to be used during takes. None of us could figure out how they could be fired though, because we were only 50 miles from the Iranian border. Since I played the Gunnery Sergeant, I have to confess to being a little apprehensive, in case the Iranians thought we'd opened fire on them, and replied with the real stuff!

On my days off, I'd meander round the souks, usually alone, because my fellow actors were too nervous. To me, it was just like Petticoat Lane, only with a different language. We were allowed to make phone calls, although monitored of course, and about four weeks into the shoot, I called my solicitor for some reason. The news wasn't good. While away, the decree absolute of our divorce had come through. With no chance to argue or salvage my marriage, it hit me hard. I thought a conspiracy had taken place. Feeling shattered, I asked the English representative if I could return home on compassionate grounds. Again, tons more red tape; exit visa and papers, but in due course I managed to get back safely. I felt helpless to do anything, but worse still, was the realisation Chris would probably marry Reg.

Sure enough, their wedding took place, under a cloak of great secrecy, because all their friends and family were worried about what I might do to sabotage the event. They were right to be worried. I tried every ruse I could think of to find out details. Just as well I didn't succeed.

Unfortunately, I was my own worst enemy. Due to my irrational and abusive behaviour whenever I collected the boys for our weekends together, Chris and Reg decided to move far enough away to make it too difficult for me to pester them, yet without jeopardising my custody order. They moved to Wiltshire and my world collapsed once more.

It was a two hour journey each way. Still, it was my own fault I suppose. Sometimes I feel a bit guilty about the demands I made on the boys. As they got older, I'm sure they'd have preferred to stay at home with their friends. When they became teenagers I would be given excuses sometimes, for not coming on their next weekend because they had planned to do something else. No doubt lots of distant fathers feel this way, coping with inner conflicts. This arrangement carried on for a further 10 years; up and down the M3 and A303, which I got to know like the back of my hand and could have negotiated blindfold by the end. Holiday seasons were the worst; stuck behind campers and caravans, all heading for the West Country.

Throughout my life I've been extremely fortunate with friends, most of whom have stayed loyal to me through all my ups and downs. None more so than Rod Appleyard, whom I'd met through a friend of Chris's in the early '70s. He helped me to get over the worst stages of my divorce; trying to keep me calm and make me see reason. He still ranks as one of my best mates. Rod worked in his family business, selling wholesale fish, mainly to hotels and restaurants all over England. Sometimes I'd accompany him on a buying trip, to places like Grimsby or Hull. Also, he liked a bet on the horses and we'd go to Sandown or Kempton Park; only he bet quite heavily, whereas I'd learnt my lesson already on that score.

He's great fun to be with and an evening spent with him and his friends is good for me and my ego because none of them are in this business; they keep my feet firmly on the ground.

Lots of people have asked me over the 28 years since my divorce, why I never remarried. As all my friends know, I'm a real family man and it's a great pity, I admit, that I didn't settle down with someone. The boys have always come first with me and I wanted to make up for all the hurt they must have suffered through the break-up, without any selfish distractions, such as having another woman around. Quite simply, I've never been able to let go of my emotions for fear of repercussion. I could never risk going through that experience again. Don't feel sorry for me though, because I have a very happy, full and active life in spite of everything.

CHAPTER EIGHT

Cops and Robbers

After the success of *Law and Order* offers of work started to come in fast and furiously. The BBC was doing a new drama series called *The Chinese Detective* which gave a fresh slant to the usual recognisable detective shows of the day. David Yip played the lead, as Detective Sergeant Ho, with me as his boss, Detective Chief Inspector Berwick. It was unusual to see a Chinese actor playing the part of a detective and the public warmed to him straight away. The show became very popular, with 14 episodes screened over a two-year period.

Berwick was a bit of a racist to begin with, and didn't take kindly to ethnic minorities going to university, getting degrees, or earning promotion too quickly. He was of the old school, where men were expected to work hard, over many years, before gaining higher status. Added to which, Ho did nothing to ingratiate himself, by working in an unorthodox and bolshy fashion and ignoring normal police procedures. He got results though. As the series unfolded, we saw Berwick gradually, and begrudgingly, begin to respect Ho. We filmed on location mainly, all over the East End and Millwall, and David and I got on really well as a team.

Being the eternal joker on set, I made sure David didn't escape my pranks. All through the series, whenever we were heading off to a location or investigating a crime, David did the driving. I would wait until just before the director called "Action!" and nudge the gear-stick into neutral with my knee. He'd rev up but go nowhere. It was months before he cottoned on. I can never resist a good wind-up.

I gave David the nickname 'spring roll' which he accepted good humouredly. I don't think we ever fell out over anything and at the end of the second series, he gave me a gift. We were all congregated on the set, while the entire crew looked on. Intrigued, I started to open a large parcel, about two feet square, but when I opened the box, there was a smaller one inside. This went on until only a tiny one, about six by three inches, was left. Everyone burst out laughing when I revealed a real spring roll. He got me back nicely that time.

Several old friends would pop up in different episodes, some having had major roles in the past. Memorable cameo characters such as Ian Hendry who had starred in *The Avengers* and the film *Get Carter* with Michael Caine, George Sewell, best known for his portrayal of DCI Alan Craven in *Special Branch,* and Tony Caunter whom I'd worked with on *Queenie's Castle* and who starred later as Roy Evans in *EastEnders*. It was before my time unfortunately, as I'd have loved to be in the same cast as him. Also Pam St. Clement who now plays Pat in *EastEnders* appeared in another episode. I identified with the character because he spoke, and thought, like many police officers in the East End. It's true to say that prejudice was rife in those days. Even today, I'm sure there's still an undercurrent, even if it's been quashed superficially.

At one point, the BBC decided to do a short documentary on David and me, to satisfy public curiosity I suppose. Mainly about our backgrounds and origins, as well as how we'd become actors. First, David took me on a walk-about tour of Stratford East Theatre, explaining how and when he'd joined the famous Joan Littlewood company. The scene changed, and I reciprocated by taking him to Smithfield Market. After showing David around I turned to him, saying, "If you look over your left shoulder, you'll see the stage where I first appeared." Of course, it was none other than the Old Bailey and I had to explain what I meant to the viewers.

The series had been devised and written by Ian Kennedy Martin, one of the most prolific writers for both the small and big screen, and who had produced *The Sweeney* and *Juliet Bravo*. It's quite common practice, for writers and producers alike, to use the same actors for several different shows. Once a mutual respect has formed, I guess they relax, in the certain knowledge they'll get a reliable and good performance from you. Although I didn't know it at the time, Ian had written another series, with me in mind for the lead.

King and Castle was introduced first as a pilot film on Thames Television's Storyboard series. This was a very good place to try out ideas for new series, such as *Woodentop* the forerunner to *The Bill* and when Ian offered it, he had insisted that I play Detective Sergeant Ronald King. As a relatively new face on the lead scene so to speak, the bosses were reluctant to use me, but Ian threatened to take it elsewhere, so they decided to take a chance on me. King was a corrupt police officer who sails close to the wind; forced to quit the Metropolitan Police when his somewhat dubious activities threaten to catch up with him. By chance, he teams up with a more gentle, yet tough character called David Castle, an instructor in the Japanese martial art of Aikido; played by Nigel Planer. Although not everyone's idea of a perfect partnership, nonetheless, they decide to start a business together.

Setting up a debt collection agency, the pair go about their business in a rather precarious manner; managing to keep within the boundaries of the law but not always acting in the best interests of their clients. My screen office was in Harlesden where I had a secretary, played by Mary Healey. She had a great sense of humour and we still keep in touch. Penelope Wilton, the long suffering wife to Richard Briers in *Ever Decreasing Circles* appeared, as a potential girlfriend, but it didn't work out because she was far too classy a dame for Ronald King. The series ran for two years and once again, lots of marvellous guest performances by the likes of David Suchet, Andrew Cruickshank and the comedian Dave King.

Again, I bumped into Terry Downes on the set one day and was amazed to discover that we were in a fight scene together – only I had to knock him out, in a car park behind a pub.

Nigel was great to work with and a good bloke. I was Mister Noisy, always talking, while Nigel pottered about the set quietly. He's gone on to do really well for himself with many plays and films to his credit, notably as Neil in the hugely popular '80s TV series *The Young Ones* and in the West End show *Chicago*, as well as being the author of several books. After a couple of years Thames decided to devote more energy into *The Bill* which had taken over a bit from our viewing ratings, and, as it turned out, this proved to be a wise move as it ran for over 25 years.

Here I was, playing the same part again. Yes, I was type-cast, but with my accent and previous credits it was easy to see how this situation could come about. Many actors will turn down roles if they think this is going to happen to them, but I couldn't afford to, and took whatever was offered, glad to be working. I used to hope that one day, out of the blue, a script would land on my mat, with an entirely unique role. Romantic leads were out because either I was too old by now and not what is considered to be the traditional leading man, but I longed for a casting director to put me in something that would show my softer and kinder side. After all, many older people fall in love don't they? Then there are the family men and I would have loved to play a regular Dad. All in good time no doubt.

As you're aware by now, I'm a bit of a film buff. The '70s saw some great movies, as well as a new brigade of talented actors. All the old 'greats' were getting just that; old; and it was time for some new blood. People like Al Pacino, Robert de Niro, James Caan, Gene Hackman and Jack Nicholson rank among my favourites with some beautiful new leading ladies of the time such as, Candice Bergen, Katharine Ross, Ali MacGraw, Faye Dunaway and Meryl Streep. The following are my top 10 films of all time; *On The Waterfront*; *East of Eden; The Godfather; Suddenly Last Summer; White Heat; West Side Story; One Flew Over the Cuckoo's Nest; La Strada; Paths of Glory* and *Shane*. I wonder how many of you agree with that list? My two all time favourite actresses though are still Jeanne Moreau and Giulietta Masina – to me, the two sexiest women on the screen and none of the new brigade has ever matched them I'm afraid.

During the late '80s and early '90s I started getting letters, sent via my agent, from people I hadn't seen for years. For example, someone from my old National Service days requested my company for a reunion and asked if I would give the customary after-dinner speech. The thought of meeting up with all the old gang was great and so I agreed readily. Now Lincolnshire is not my favourite county, probably because my only memories are of bleak, flat plains. Since then I've realised that there are some beautiful areas though, not least of which are The Wolds, and the countryside from Stamford to Bourne and Grantham. Heading north, out of Hertfordshire on the A1, brought good thoughts to mind, as I reminisced about the old days. On arrival, I was greeted by my old mates Doug McKeown and Henry Hall and I scanned the crowd for other familiar faces, but it was difficult to recognise everyone after so much time had lapsed. Sadly, a few of the old gang were missing and prayers were said in remembrance of them. We had a great time and I try to attend as many reunions as possible. One chap reminded me of the Saturday nights, when I used to pinch a three-ton covered lorry and drive into Gainsborough, to pick up the lads after they'd been to a dance. I'd forgotten also, that every Tuesday I had to accompany an officer on the bank run. At the Armoury I had to draw a revolver, six rounds of ammunition, and even though I knew I wasn't supposed to load the gun, being me, I did. We collected about £15,000 and I used to hope we'd be robbed – seen too many films I think! Many years later, when reading about Michael Bentine, I learned he'd also been stationed at Hemswell, during the war. If only I'd known that when we worked together, we could have had some great chats about the good old days.

All of us have our flops, and I haven't managed to escape mine. The ill-fated *Eldorado* series came next. Conceived by Julia Smith and Tony Holland, the creators of *EastEnders*, it was meant to fill a gap in the TV market of British soaps. The BBC collaborated with an independent film company, Cinema Verity run by the late Verity Lambert whose earlier successes included the launching of *Doctor Who* back in 1963. I'd worked for her many times before. Following the success of *EastEnders*, the BBC had hoped *Eldorado* would bring some of the sunshine and glamour that Australian soaps, such as *Home and Away* and *Neighbours* had done.

I was cast as Alex Morris, the main villain in charge of running crime on the Costa del Sol in Spain. They flew me out a month before Christmas for one week's filming. On my return, I was surprised and delighted to learn that they wanted me back as a regular character, starting in the New Year.

The series was shot entirely on location, in Coin, a small town sitting on the edge of the main highway, midway between Marbella and Malaga, on the Costa del Sol. They had a purpose-built village with apartments, shops, bars and restaurants, some with roof terraces which overlooked some stunning scenery; toward the coast beyond. My journey to work every day was about as good as you can get. Fuengirola is a vibrant coastal resort just a few miles south and whenever I had spare time to visit I'd team up with a gang for some swimming or sunbathing. The programmes were meant to portray the everyday lives of the ex-pat, European community. In a nutshell, the series was plagued with problems from the off. Several of the lesser roles were played by amateurs, with phony accents, who didn't really have the required experience to handle a long-running soap of this type. For example, it was embarrassing listening to Scottish actors, playing Swedish characters, in English, only with a so-called Swedish accent. Confused? Well, we were! Sometimes, during a take, they'd forget themselves and lapse into broad Glaswegian in the middle of a sentence. Interspersed, dubbed dialogue would run alongside English when a scene required several different nationalities at one time. Viewers found it hilarious and to be honest, it was turning into a comedy of errors. Quite understandably, this started a chain reaction among the critics and the reviews got worse with each passing week.

Lots of ex-pats joined in as extras. None of them could speak a word of Spanish so I assumed they had only just arrived. To my amazement, soon I discovered that many of them had lived in Spain for 10 or 15 years! I get annoyed at this, because the British are very arrogant. If we live in a foreign country, we should at least learn the rudiments of their language, and it's no small wonder the Spanish people often refuse to talk to us in English.

We had lovely accommodation and I must say our lifestyles were pretty spectacular. At weekends, and a couple of evenings a week, there were barbecues or parties so there were plenty of sore heads at rehearsals the next day. I had a two-bedroomed villa with terrace and swimming pool, halfway between Fuengirola and Mijas. We worked at a fast and furious pace, filming each episode over four days. Soon after arriving I got friendly with the transport manager, persuading him to let me borrow a little car, so that on my days off I could explore the real Spain. I'd drive about 15 miles inland, where the terrain changed dramatically. It was like being in a third world country, with little villages, more like hamlets, dotted all over the hills and mountains. Olive groves spread for miles, and every now and then I'd spot an olive oil distillery.

Other times, I'd venture into the cities. I visited Cordoba, Granada, Cadiz and Seville. The cathedral there was magnificent; built around the time of St. Paul's and the Basilica, it's one of the largest in Europe. Inside the main entrance was an enormous tomb, supported and mounted on four carved statues of native Indians, standing about 12 feet high. It's reputed to contain the remains of Christopher Columbus but I believe DNA tests are now being carried out, to see if this is true or false.

We filmed all the outside broadcasts along the coast; from Gibraltar to Malaga, stopping at lots of little villages along the way. Well documented, this Spanish coastline was lovingly dubbed the 'Costa del Crime' and before long, I'd bumped into a few familiar faces from the underworld. I used to eat in all the good restaurants, especially those in Marbella, so unavoidably, I couldn't miss the true ex-pats - the villains.

Almost as if for real, my character, Alex Morris had a sort of lieutenant called Marcus, played by Jesse Birdsall, who ran things whenever he was away on business. In the script, Alex has a 50ft yacht, moored in the Marina and he decides to use it for his wedding to an old flame, Trish Valentine, played by Polly Perkins. He takes her out to sea for the ceremony. Unfortunately, my old sea-sickness problem reared its ugly head again. When Alex goes to kiss his bride, she very nearly gets splattered. Luckily I managed to hold back long enough to finish the shot, but I was very relieved to touch base again, on dry land.

Polly was also a singer and she knew all the clubs along the coast, having worked most of them. One was owned by Ronnie Knight, ex-husband of Barbara Windsor, who was on the run at that time from the British police. Wanted for his part in the six million pound robbery of the Security Express depot in Shoreditch, he escaped jail by joining all the other gangsters and villains in Spain. Ronnie, his girlfriend Sue, Polly and I, all met up in an Italian restaurant. It was a good night and I discovered Ronnie and I had a few mutual, nefarious acquaintances from the East End. Also, that he used to frequent The Royal at Tottenham the same time as me. Later, when we returned to his club in Fuengirola, a reporter from The Sun newspaper took a photo of us, sitting on a swing; Sue on my lap and Polly on Ronnie's. The next day, the headline read, "MR. BIG MEETS MR. BIG".

Most of the leading actors were excellent and it's a shame they were thwarted in this way. Increasingly, they found it hard to play a straight part, as each week saw a rapid deterioration of the show. Some of the reviews made painful reading. Since then, opportunities have been missed in my opinion. The idea is still a good one, and I'm sure it could have been a great soap if a bit of time, money and effort had gone into changing it. On a lighter note, at least the Spanish business people loved us because we spent lots of money in the shops and on entertainment, so we certainly can claim to have boosted the local economy.

Internal shots were done almost entirely in and around the villas, rather than using studios. The trouble with that though is the sound and acoustic quality is compromised. Even now, whenever there's a sound problem on any programme at the BBC, it's laughingly referred to as '*Eldorado*-sound.' Behind the scenes, arguments sprang up among the production team and Julia Smith was reported to have had a nervous breakdown. She left and Corinne Hollingworth stepped into her shoes, making several drastic changes. First, all the less experienced actors were sacked, as were many of the scriptwriters and she tried desperately hard to revive the show; but too late. Even though the quality did improve, when Alan Yentob took over, as Controller of BBC, he axed the programme.

Many of the regular stars had rented out their own properties back home, on two or three year contracts, because they'd been assured the series would have a long run. Just goes to show you what the downsides are to this business. When the show finally closed, there was a lot of bad feeling. For my part though, I still remember it as one of the best times I had ever.

Over the years I got used to my separations from the boys but it still hurt me to be away from them for any length of time. I'd come home regularly to see them and they came out to Spain a few times for holidays during the year it lasted. There were some beautiful villas for sale, especially inland, and I must admit I was sorely tempted to buy one. Security over the show made me hesitate, and what a blessing in disguise that turned out to be.

Back to normal life once more, I returned home to await my next role. Living a precarious life has two sides to it. On the one hand it's exciting not knowing what's around the corner, but the downside is insecurity. Most actors tend to be very careful when they're earning substantial amounts of money, saving it for a rainy day. Tempting as it is, to spend the spoils, we just never know how lean the 'resting' periods might be and it's a bad move to allow ourselves to get carried away. I had sold the house in Twickenham and downsized to a smaller, modern terrace in Hanworth, for this reason. It was easier to maintain, my mortgage payments reduced and I was much closer to the main road out of London so cutting my weekend journeys down by as much as half an hour. Coupled with this, many of the smaller villages en route were earmarked for bi-passes, to enable a much smoother and faster traffic flow along the A303. Towards the end of this access period in my life, I had cut my journey time from two hours, to just over one – sticking to the 70mph speed limits of course!

They say all good things must come to an end we know, and that included my special relationship with my agent James. I got a phone call to come to his home. I looked forward to these visits because we'd sit in his garden, with its gently sloping lawn, rolling down to the Thames. The time had come for his retirement and he wanted to give me plenty of notice to find another agent. With tears in my eyes, I offered him, and his wife Sylvie, my best wishes for a long and happy retirement. Truthfully, I was gutted, because we'd got on so well, for over 20 years, and the thought of starting again with someone new, unnerved me. James did one of the nicest things for me though. He wrote to every television and film company that I'd worked for, requesting they send all my repeat fees directly to me. This was a sweet and touching gesture.

As luck would have it, in 1995 I found my current agent, JLM (which stands for Janet Lyn Malone), Personal Management. She is now semi retired and living the good life on the Costa Brava, so her business partner, Sharon Henry, looks after me. The first part she secured for me was to be my only role for a long time to come. She and I get on really well, but it's a good thing we didn't know that work was going to dry up afterwards, or maybe she'd have changed her mind about accepting me onto her books!

Soon enough, I received that first call from Sharon, who told me I had an audition with Lynda la Plante Productions for a new series set within a prison and called *The Governor*. It was just for one episode, where my character had to escape in a helicopter. I'd been dying to work on something Lynda had written because she seems to get right to the nitty gritty of whatever the script is about. Her attention to detail is well documented and she is held in high esteem by all who work with her.

When I arrived, the receptionist ushered me in to meet the

casting director. Several people were there, including Lynda herself. The first thing she said to me was, "I'm a big fan of yours, from *Law and Order* days." I replied, "And I'm a big fan of yours, but I've never worked for you!" I read the part, but just as I was getting ready to leave, she said, "Would you mind reading this part for me?" She handed me the script again. When I'd finished, the casting director told me, "We'll be in touch." By now I'd heard that so many times, I paid little attention. Months later, Lynda told me that when I'd left the office that day, she had turned to the others saying, "I've cast the wrong character for the male lead! Derek is the one to play Gary Marshall." The other actor must have been paid off, but to this day I have no idea who he was, and I confess to feeling a little sorry for him.

To explain the plot: Helen Hewitt, is the first woman to be put in charge of Barfield, a maximum security prison; almost completely destroyed by recent riots. She receives a lot of animosity from both staff and inmates, but is determined to raise the prison's profile. I play her second in command.

I travelled regularly, back and forth from Heathrow to Dublin, where the series was shot, and along with the rest of the cast, stayed at a luxury hotel called The Westbury, in Grafton Street. I considered it an honour and a pleasure to work with the brilliant actress, Janet McTeer, in her role as the Governor. Our characters were very different, in that she was a university graduate who had been fast-tracked to her position, whereas I had worked my way up, from prison guard to Deputy Governor. Throughout the series it's clear I intend to be a governor one day, so I exhibit a bit of sour grapes towards her now and then. I'm glad to say that I didn't have any experience of prison, apart from my short stay in the cells of Snow Hill and the Old Bailey, but I'd heard plenty of stories from others I knew who had, so I tried to get a sense of the atmosphere for the script.

Several terrific actors appeared in the series, such as Eamon Walker as one of the prisoners. He'd played Marigold in *'Till Death Us Do Part, Othello* in the West End and starred in the successful television series *Oz.* Another well-known name is Craig Charles of *Coronation Street* and *Red Dwarf* who featured in two episodes, and Idris Elba in a supporting role, who later went on to star in many Hollywood movies and dramas including hugely successful *The Wire*.

Lynda often flew in to see how the production was coming along. One day, I was walking behind her with Liz Thorburn (her right-hand person), when I commented that, from the back, Lynda looked like Madame Defarge, with her long and curly, ginger hair. Lynda overheard me and said, "Don't forget Derek, I write the scripts. If you're not careful, I might turn you into a transvestite!" All good fun.

We worked hard but I enjoyed every minute of it. Dublin is, as the song says, 'a fair city', and the Irish are such warm-hearted and friendly people. Temple Bar was a favourite area, with an abundance of bars, clubs, restaurants and bistros. On one of my days off I went for a tour of the Guinness factory, where I saw the process from start to finish. This is Ireland's number one tourist attraction. From the original Storehouse, built around 1904, using steel and glass in the shape of an enormous pint glass, one of the first things that intrigued me was to see how huge the hop sacks were. There are seven floors where we were guided through every process of manufacturing the 'black stuff' or 'pint of plain' as it's referred to also. What surprised me most was that there are only four ingredients: Irish barley – some of which is roasted like coffee beans to produce the distinctive flavour and colour; hops – which give the bitter flavour and aroma; water – eight million litres per day which are pumped from the water of the Wicklow mountains in Dublin and finally, fresh yeast – according to our guide, still fermented from the original extracts used by Arthur Guinness himself, who was one of the first of the Master Brewers. The whole production process is a closely guarded secret, handed down from one generation to the other. Once the tour is over, the guide takes you through to where the barrels are housed and offers a taste, complete with thick, creamy, white froth on top. Finally, we were taken to the seventh floor restaurant where we were treated to a free pint. I tasted a sip, out of politeness, and gave the rest to a little Irishman standing next to me. He downed it in one, without so much as a gulp in between. Very impressive. The tour is tiring so the rest is most welcome and I tucked into some lunch while taking in the panoramic views over Dublin which are a joy to behold.

The attitude of the Irish is very laid back and I find it refreshing. A group of us went to Lansdown Road Stadium to see an Ireland versus England, Rugby Union game. England trounced the Irish, and on their home soil to boot, but there wasn't the usual moaning or nasty comments such as the English make after a match in which we've lost. Instead, a nearby crowd shouted out, "It's only a game! The drinks are on us!" Some of our football supporters could learn a thing or two from this. Friendly banter, in an atmosphere such as this, was a shining example of how things should be at any sporting event. After all, it's meant to fun isn't it? Once, for a little treat, I went to the races at Leopardstown but never won a cent; in spite of the fact several so called 'people in the know' gave me hundreds of 'dead cert' tips.

One time some of us went to County Cork for a weekend, to a little coastal town called Kinsale. It's full of world renowned fish restaurants, and many famous, wealthy customers fly in from the continent for gastronomic breaks and, true to its reputation, we enjoyed some fabulous meals too. Even though I'm not religious, someone on the set told me I couldn't leave Dublin without going to see The Book of Kells, an ancient Celtic manuscript of the four gospels. I'm very glad I went because it is magnificent to look at, housed in a glass cabinet, with vibrant pictures surrounding the text; mainly golds and reds.

On another occasion, the Governor of Mountjoy Prison, the largest jail in Dublin, invited me to visit. He said he'd be delighted to show me around to give me an insight into what a real prison was like from inside. I accepted readily, but honestly, it gave me the heebie-jeebies I can tell you; with the sound of clanging keys and electronic gates shutting behind us. How anyone can bear the thought of a return stay is beyond my comprehension. Most of the inmates' days are spent indoors, under strip lighting, with hardly a glimpse of proper daylight. I'd go stir crazy for sure and would mend my ways forever upon release. He took me up to where the cells were and I heard odd music coming from some cells where prisoners are obviously allowed to have radios, but many I passed had no sound at all. What a lonely existence I thought. We stood outside one particular cell door and he told me to look through the spy-hole. I saw a man sitting on the edge of his bed, reading a book. The Governor turned to me, "He's the chap who blew up Lord Mountbatten!"

Another thing I love about the Irish is their sense of humour which is very droll. For example, we went to a pub just outside Dublin one evening. It was in March and I asked the landlord, "When do you close?" To which he replied, "In October!" He wasn't joking either, he meant it. What can I say? Having vowed all my life that I'd never live anywhere but England, all I can tell you is that I changed my mind after filming there, and would happily live in Dublin. My only regret is that I never visited

Tipperary while in Ireland – as the saying goes, "Never put off 'til tomorrow......."

CHAPTER NINE

Lean and Mean

After *The Governor* work almost ground to a halt. This can happen to actors for no apparent reason. Maybe their faces no longer fit, or the style of programme for a particular era no longer suits them. Who knows, least of all the actors themselves? I've often wondered if, because my heart might have been so heavy, that the sparkle had been lost from my performance. It did return, but not before a couple of very lean years had gone by, as I explain later in this chapter.

Fortunately, I received regular income from repeats of my old shows still. Many of you might not know that every time a programme is shown again on TV, or sold abroad, we get a fee. Not the original one, but a percentage. Depending on the circumstances of the sale, the fees can be as little as 1% or as large as the full 100%. By now I had appeared in hundreds of episodes, on almost every show, for nearly 30 years, so I received plenty of small repeat fees which all add up. To this day, I still get them from the '70s for *Doctor Who,* and sometimes the cheque is for less than the cost of a stamp. Most actors elect to put these amounts back into the Equity charity fund.

Travelling to Wiltshire every time for my access weekends cost a fortune. Coupled with mortgage repayments and living expenses, my savings soon dwindled to zero, quicker than I could have thought possible. For about two years I let the bills pile up, too scared to open the envelopes, while I buried my head in the sand like an ostrich. Eventually, the building society threatened to repossess my house and I spent a long time trying to negotiate with them – interest-free periods and that sort of thing. It wasn't entirely my own fault. I'd misunderstood something my accountant had told me, a book-keeping issue, so when I received a tax demand for an extortionate amount of money, I was ill-prepared and certainly didn't have the funds to pay. The Inland Revenue accepted that a genuine mistake had been made, but nevertheless, I had to settle in full. They did allow me time to pay, but I never recovered from the shock. It's something that I still feel bitter about because I felt my accountant should have paid something towards the bill – and I know she had insurance, but wouldn't admit any liability. I can say this freely, since I no longer use that firm.

As you are aware by now, I had a few shady friends and acquaintances, and in times like these it's easy to fall back on old habits. Before becoming an actor I'd had many jobs, and classed myself as a bit of a 'Jack of all trades'. Not one to sit on my backside, waiting for the phone to ring, I set about calling all my old friends, to see what work might be available. Maybe some driving or taxi work would be nice, since I had a very smart, black Granada Scorpio. A Cosworth engine gave it a bit of poke, making it ideal for me take on mini-cab work. Equally, as a free agent, I could make myself available at the drop of a hat, for any television work, should I be required. That's one of the major problems facing actors; when times are lean, how can we take on a normal nine to five job?

John Harvey came to my rescue. An old pal of mine, who wasn't a hard-nosed villain, but did a bit of wheeling and dealing here and there. Having asked for his help, I heard nothing for a few days. Then he called me very early one morning, after about a week had gone by. "What are you doing tomorrow?" he asked. "Nothing, mate!" I said, relieved, sensing that some money would surely be coming my way, or he wouldn't be asking. "Meet me at 4am outside The Swallow Hotel in Harlow, exit Junction 26 on the M25." Then the phone went dead.

When I got to the car park at just before 4 o'clock, I saw John, sitting in his car, with another bloke in the passenger seat. It was freezing cold at that early hour of the morning and I remember asking myself what had possessed me to agree to this. They got out and came over. John introduced me, "This is Mick." That's all I knew about him. Continuing, he explained, "I want you to drive Mick to Dover. You have to get two, day return tickets for the ferry to Calais." No need to show passports that way. "When you get to France, Mick will tell you where to go. I'll see you all right when you get back, Del." I knew what he meant; I'd get paid in other words. I thought nothing more about this, assuming I was just doing Mick a favour, on behalf of John. Perhaps John couldn't help his friend because he was unable to leave the country. Not my place to ask prying questions.

I couldn't mention my horror of boats as I was too desperate for the money. Mick got into the back seat of my car and we travelled in silence. He had breakfast on the ferry, but I declined for obvious reasons. Upon our arrival at Calais, I turned to Mick, "Where to Guv?" He smiled, "Amsterdam; Schiphol Airport, please Del." Mick explained the reason; there wasn't a border control, so we could travel through France and Belgium to Holland, without any questions being asked. Nice and straightforward. By now I had begun to realise there was definitely something fishy about Mick. It rained all the way but I made good time. During the journey he relaxed a bit and opened up. All he offered, by way of explanation, was that he intended going to South America. No elaboration, no detail, and so I assumed he had taken his passport, but didn't ask.

Once safely at the airport, Mick passed me a rolled up wad of £100 in 20s. I refused, telling him that John would be paying me when I got back. He insisted though, so I took it. Adrenalin kicked in, and I began to feel a little apprehensive in case we'd been followed. All I wanted now was to get home as quickly as possible. Without resting, I refuelled, bought a sandwich and cup of tea; turning the car back towards Calais. When I got there, to my dismay, I watched a ferry pull out of harbour, just a few yards out to sea. Typical of my luck at that time. When the chips are down, everything seems to go wrong. So I put the seat into recline mode and caught up on some much needed sleep for a couple of hours.

Back at Dover, I was just pulling out of the terminal, when John rang me on my mobile. I could tell that genuinely, he didn't know where Mick had gone; I enlightened him and he sounded surprised. By now I was absolutely knackered and couldn't wait for my bed. John and I met up the next morning, when he handed me a brown envelope. I opened it in front of him. It contained £5,000. Not a bad wage for a day's work, eh? Looking back, I know it was silly of me to risk doing anything I thought might be suspicious, but I pretended nothing untoward took place because I was so desperate for money at the time. Honestly, I didn't think it was serious stuff because I knew John had lots of associates who were property developers or antique dealers.

I started doing all sorts of driving jobs for John. One included taking a large sum of money up north to Stockport. My instructions were very specific, "Put this in your glove compartment. Don't exceed 70mph all the way. Be outside the station at 11 o'clock and a man will contact you. Don't worry, he has your registration number."

Never one to be late, I arrived at the appointed hour as instructed.

After a short while, a man tapped on the nearside window. I let him in but he said nothing. Opening the compartment, he took out the envelope and departed, without a single word. Another lucrative little earner, and again, no questions asked.

A few months later, John asked if he could rent my garage at home for three months, at £100 a week; payable in advance. This was too good to refuse. My new house in Hanworth was a modest, but very nice, three storey town house on a small estate. Being a cul-de-sac meant it was always quiet. Most of the residents worked at Heathrow in some capacity, due to its close proximity. The garage was integral to the house, with a door leading into the utility room. John put extra locks on all the doors and secured it from my side with a large padlock. He explained that various people would come to deposit stuff, while others would come and remove things from time to time.

Since this was my home, I ventured to ask a few questions this time. "You're not storing drugs or anything, are you John?" I received an emphatic, "No!" He told me it was valuable antiques; hence all the added security. I believed him and said nothing more. The only other bit of information given was that I mustn't speak to anyone who came to the garage, under any circumstances. To this day I have no idea what went into it, but I don't think John would have lied to me.

Although I couldn't know how close I was to getting my next big break at the time, I took what was to be my last driving job for John. It entailed taking someone over to Paris. He was an enormously powerful looking guy, weighing about 22 stone, I reckoned. He had a middle European accent and a couple of deep scars on one cheek. Let me say, he wasn't the kind of man I'd want to cross swords with, and leave it at that. I was supposed to drop him off, at one of the best five star hotels in Paris, and return to England with him the next day. My intention was to find a small, cheap hotel for myself, but when we arrived he insisted I check in, saying he would pay. We parted company and I amused myself for the rest of the afternoon and evening. Being on my own in Paris brought back memories of my honeymoon with Gloria, so to cheer myself up I hailed a taxi and went to the Champs Elysees to mooch around the shops, and enjoy a slap-up meal. It would have been a waste to be in Paris without sampling its most famous cuisine. Returning to the hotel at around 11 o'clock, I settled into what was a very sumptuous suite, to watch TV. About midnight, there was a knock on my door. Thinking it would be my companion, I opened it. To my shock and surprise, a very beautiful, and sexy looking girl smiled at me. Her coat was open, revealing a stunning, and extremely curvaceous, scantily-clad figure. "I 'ave come to look after you!" she said suggestively, with a throaty, husky French accent. Not my scene, I'm afraid, so I sent her packing, although I do admit to being tempted for a moment. It's just not my kind of thing.

The next day, I discovered she'd been sent, courtesy of my

companion. He couldn't understand why I'd dismissed her, but we didn't discuss it further. We had a pleasant journey home and I have no idea what his business in Paris was about. The fee wasn't as much this time, about £1,000 I think, but I certainly wasn't complaining. At one point I asked simply if he'd had a good meeting, to which he replied, "Yes, thank you!" He didn't elaborate further and made it clear by his tone that the conversation was over.

The twins had grown into young men and life changed into a different pattern. Chris had split up with Reg and moved to London, after just 11 years; the same length of time as our marriage had lasted. In 1995, finally, she married the same ex-boyfriend she'd had the first affair with, and I knew I would have to learn to live with it somehow. You'd think I'd have calmed down by now, but I hadn't. One of the boys came to live with me for a time while the other went to university in London, staying with Chris. For this reason, I decided not to do any more work for John, since it was pretty clear by now, that he was heavily involved in something illegal and I couldn't take any more risks. I had begun to feel more and more apprehensive as the months went by. Some of the men who came to the garage looked a bit dodgy to say the least, and once, when I'd been out somewhere with John, he'd thrown his mobile phone out of the passenger window, into the Thames river. When I asked him why, he said, "I have to get a new mobile every week, so my calls can't be traced." Well, you don't do that sort of thing unless you're into something very illegal, do you?

As the boys were over 18 now, my official access days were over and since they no longer lived in Wiltshire, I had to try and get along with Chris, in order to keep the peace and be able to see my sons more easily. After all, they were adults now with busy lives of their own.

Chris rang me one day, out of the blue, saying she wanted to talk. It was New Year's Day 2000, the first day of the new millennium. After much deliberation, and deep questioning of her actions, the gist of the conversation was about how sorry she was for all the hurt and pain she'd caused me, and the boys, indirectly. She pleaded with me to forgive her and start afresh, as friends. Sadly, we'd always been very good friends, all the time we were married, and it was a great pity to have lost that side of our relationship. We both broke down, crying into the phone and I agreed. I asked her why it had taken her so long to do this. She told me it was simple. Her 50th birthday was coming up and, coupled with the arrival of the new Century, she had been thinking long and hard about all the pain and sorrow she'd caused – not just to me, but also to the boys.

It took all my willpower to turn up at their home in north London that first time. I had to shake hands with her new husband, whom I'd hated and resented for over 20 years; but I managed it. To say it was easy would be lying, but it wasn't as difficult as I'd envisaged. We sat in the garden, having tea and cake, as if nothing had ever happened, and I realised we had a lot in common. Sport is always a good ice-breaking topic, and we conversed about the merits of his team, Arsenal, and mine, Chelsea. One thing that really blew me away was Chris's garden. It was incredible, and when I commented on it she explained that she had just won the title Best Front Garden in the Barnet in Bloom competition. She certainly never did any gardening while we were together so it genuinely surprised me. Feeling very pleased with all the praise, she then produced a letter from the organisers of *Gardener's World Live* inviting her to stage a small garden at the Birmingham NEC. I must say, I was very impressed by her new hobby. Then she took me aside to give me a grand tour of the whole garden, explaining the layout as we went around. Divided into five separate 'rooms' according to the Chinese elements, fire, earth, water, wood and metal, Chris had planted everything in the colours that belong to each of those elements. I must say I was fascinated and saw a whole new side to her. If you ask me she missed her vocation in life, but when I said this to her she just laughed, "It's my hobby Del. If I did it for a living, I wouldn't enjoy it so much!" She checked to see how I was feeling about the meeting and I reassured her that all was well with me.

The boys said how much pressure had been lifted for them by this new relaxed lifestyle. No longer would they have to choose where to spend Christmas or birthdays, as by now, they were both pretty fed up with all the rows between their Mum and me. I came away, after that first visit, feeling as if a weight had been lifted from me too. Deep down, I still can't forgive completely, but I've managed to accept and I wish it could have been like this always.

On a lighter note, now that one of the boys was living with me, we decided to get a dog. I'd always wanted one, but with my precarious lifestyle it hadn't been possible. With two of us at home, we figured there would always be someone around to look after it. My son looked up Battersea Dogs Home on the internet and scrolled down to see what dogs were available. We turned up to look at several one Saturday, and found Giles. He seemed to be looking at us pleadingly, with big brown eyes which were saying, "Pick me please." He was a classy-looking mongrel so we called him Giles – we think he's half Staffordshire Bull terrier and half Labrador, but of course we can't be sure.

After the customary interview, to ensure we were suitable candidates to own a dog, they went on to explain that he'd been mistreated and needed very sympathetic handling. After that, we were allowed to take him home. Giles was only about a year old but of course no-one could be sure. He's been a loveable and marvellous companion ever since and we love him dearly. I try to support Battersea in any way I can, because they fulfil a great need in our society and do a grand job.

For the first time ever, Chris could come and visit me in my home if the boys were there. A lot of bridges had to be built, but gradually it became easier. On one such visit, she could see me looking very dejected and asked what was wrong. "I can't pay this month's mortgage, and I don't know how much longer I can stall them." It was a relief to tell her the truth and she listened intently. "Del, I can lend you the money, how much do you need?" Feeling embarrassed, I replied in hushed tones, so our son wouldn't hear, "Five hundred quid." True to her word, she wrote me out a cheque, there and then, saying I could pay her back any time when I could afford it.

Not long after, my agent Sharon rang me early one morning. I had become used to infrequent calls from her of late, so I got that twinge of excitement which comes with the certain knowledge that something good is about to happen. "Derek, I have been asked your availability for a part in *EastEnders*," she announced calmly. "Are you joking, Sharon?" I queried. Seriously, I thought this was a wind-up. She said, "I never joke about work." She'd been trying to get me onto *EastEnders* for months and she sounded really happy, but warned me not to get too excited yet. It took a few minutes for her to explain that I needed to go to the studios at Borehamwood the next day, to meet the casting director, Julia Crampsie. There were other actors going for the part, so unlike the last occasion, this time it wasn't a sure thing.

The meeting went well and Julia took some photographs, asking me if I'd mind coming in on the following Saturday for a screen test, because there were five other actors up for the part of Charlie Slater. She needed to see all of us with different members of the Slater family. Casting a whole family, especially with five daughters, I could appreciate how difficult it was going to be; getting resemblances to each other has to be absolutely right. The following Saturday I arrived at 8am and was told I'd be needed all day.

Some of the parts had already been allocated - four of the five daughters and Mo, the mother-in-law. That still left Zoe and Charlie. Various actresses for the part of Zoe, the youngest daughter, came in front of the camera with the other four actors, and me. Next, we each had to talk about our characters individually, on film, followed by several interactions with the other family members. There was a funny atmosphere among the actors during intervals, because none of us had any security about our parts, so I suppose it was natural that we found it difficult to relax with each other, off camera. When it was all over, John Yorke, the Executive Producer, thanked us all for a productive day. He added, "Don't worry, those of you who are not successful this time around, may well return as other characters, in the near future." Then, we were told to expect a call within a fortnight. I left, quite exhausted, yet exhilarated, feeling I'd done my very best. Now all I could do was wait.

I can't say that I felt confident because I thought we'd all been good on the day, so all I could was wait patiently. I busied myself around the house and garden for a while. Then I called Chris, who by now had become one of my best friends to call with news, both good and bad. "I'll come over next Tuesday if you like?" she suggested. Bearing in mind she lived the other side of London, it took her about an hour to get to my place.

When she arrived, I told her all about the film shoot, explaining the full storyline, about the part being that of a family man, whose wife had died two years earlier leaving him with five daughters to look after. Chris kept reassuring me, "You'll get it Del, I'm sure you will. Won't it be nice, having daughters for a change?" she joked. We had some lunch with our son, but around 3 o'clock, just as Chris was preparing to leave, the phone rang. My heart was leaping in my chest in case it was my agent; I had a sixth sense it would be her. Desperation is a terrible thing, and that's exactly what I was now. Boy, did I need this part.

CHAPTER TEN

Third Time Lucky

My hand shook as I lifted the receiver, "Hello Sharon. Well?" I answered. "The part's yours!" Genuinely sounding happy for me, she continued with, "I'll let you calm down and call you tomorrow with the details. OK?" If I could have done cartwheels down the road I would. Chris gave me a big congratulatory hug; by now our son David had joined in, guessing the news. The two of them were jumping up and down in excitement with Chris shouting, "I knew it! I knew it! I knew it!" A short while later, she left to return home and I tried to control my emotions, allowing everything to sink in. This was going to be a fantastic new chapter for me and I guessed the part would last at least a year. I knew also that it would be a make or break time in my career.

The next day Sharon called with the details as promised, explaining that I would be under contract for two years, with an option for a third. Little did I know then that I'd be on it still 10 years later, and counting! My first filming date was set for July 10 2000. What a marvellous start to the new millennium. I hadn't felt this happy for years. Once the shock had subsided, I concentrated on what I knew would be the busiest and best period of my entire acting career. I went to the studios for a day, to meet the full cast, many of whom I knew already. At long last I would be playing the family man I am, and had always wanted to play, and not the villain.

That first filming day, I stood outside number 23 Albert Square, for the Slaters' opening scene. I was first to be introduced to the viewers. Several council workers, played by extras, were finishing off some external renovations and decoration to the property that was to become our new home, making lots of dust and a terrible racket. My neighbour-to-be, Jim Branning (John Bardon), is standing outside his front door and says to me, "What a terrible noise!" To which I reply, "That's nothing. Wait till you meet my girls!" Or words to that effect. A couple of days later we filmed the rest of the family arriving, with all our furniture, in a removal van.

For the purpose of this chapter, the longest in my story so far, I shall introduce each member of my family using their character's name. The only time I use real names is when I'm talking about my personal relationship with them, off camera. This way, I'm hoping to avoid confusion. So here we were; Kat (Jessie Wallace); Lynne (Elaine Lordan); Little Mo (Kacey Ainsworth); Zoe (Michelle Ryan), Belinda (Leanne Lakey – but she doesn't appear until much later); Mo Harris (Laila Morse), my mother-in-law and finally,

Garry (Ricky Groves), my future son-in-law. The Slater girls soon became a big hit with the public. All very beautiful in different ways, and of course I loved them equally, as any father would!

We were an instant hit, I'm glad to say, but not everyone took to us straight away. Some viewers thought my girls were loud, brash and a bit common, especially when they pranced up and down Bridge Street, dressed brazenly in scanty outfits. It didn't take long though, before they warmed to us, and soon we were one of the main families on Albert Square. My girls were all established actresses except, perhaps, Michelle, who was only 16. It wasn't long before she made her mark though, going on to win many accolades and awards.

When you consider how many hours we spent together during the first few years, more than most real families, I'm glad to say I had a very good rapport with all the Slater members, and I don't remember any rows or angry moments. Jessie was down to earth and a bundle of laughs. Full of fun, and I think I had a bit of a crush on her, along with a few million male viewers; probably still have, but I'm far too old to contemplate such thoughts. Elaine was a lively girl, with her feet firmly on the ground, but sadly she had personal problems which affected her performance in the show later on. Kacey was the quiet one, engaged to Darren, a good man. We had one thing in common – both of us were dog mad, and we keep in touch still. We enjoyed working together and she too, became a future award winner. Then there was the baby of the family, Michelle, who was great fun to work with. Later on, as Zoe, she and Kat would enter the history book of soaps, with the immortal lines, "You can't tell me what to do, you ain't my Mother!" To which Kat replies, "Yes I am!" Leanne was lovely too, but I didn't really get to know her as well as the others because we would go for months without meeting. Her character, Belinda, has only been a guest role. In the storyline she has married an estate agent and moved up north. She becomes embarrassed by her roots, and is a bit of a stuck up cow, turning her nose up at the rest of us. We see her from time to time, but usually only for weddings or funerals.

As for the rest of my family members, Ricky and I got on really well. He's a good actor, and apparently, an excellent cook, although I've not had the pleasure of tasting his cuisine yet. We shared some memorable scenes together, and of course, as Garry, he later marries Charlie's daughter Lynne. Last but not least is Laila, although she prefers to be called Mo now, both on and off the set. We knew each other already from way back. We're good mates and get on well. In her character as Mo, we've had some good scripted scenes, mainly where she disapproves of any new relationship Charlie tries to form, because she feels he only belonged to her daughter Vivienne, who has died two years before the Slaters' move to Albert Square. She's always "sticking her oar in" as she puts it, just like the archetypal, interfering mother-in-law. Already a well known actress before *EastEnders*, Laila had starred in *Nil by Mouth*, directed by her brother Gary Oldman who is now a big Hollywood name.

The Slater family was the brainchild of our Executive Producer John Yorke, and Tony Jordan, a prolific lead writer and story consultant for the show. He'd lived in the East End and worked as a market trader so was well equipped to write for the series.

Although I had worked at the same studios in the early '60s and knew my way around, the sets for *EastEnders* were spread all over the place on different stages, so it took me a few days to work them out. Luckily, the interior of the Slaters' house was on stage one and quite near my dressing room. Also, home to the sets of the Queen Vic, cafe and launderette. All the exteriors are on what is known as 'the lot' which includes Albert Square and Bridge Street. I must say I have a lovely dressing room which consists of an en-suite shower room with WC and basin, where I keep a spare shaving kit and personal toiletries. My room has a comfy bed, desk, telephone, fridge and the all-important TV of course; which I supplied. Nice and cosy in the winter and cool in summer because there's also a huge wall fan. It's a fabulous place to sit quietly and go over my lines, ready to be called for the next scene. For all the cast members this comes in the form of a voice over the intercom, which happens to be situated in the corridor just outside my door, "Derek Martin – 10 minutes – stage one!" Followed by a five minute warning, but mostly they call me on my phone. I'm never late, but heaven help anyone who is!

My next door neighbours are June Brown (Dot Branning) to one side and Barbara Windsor (Peggy Mitchell) on the other, with Jake Wood (Max) and Jo Joyner (Tanya) along the way. I've nicknamed it Bishop's Avenue because it's so quiet. All the younger actors are further down the corridor where they can make more noise. Wardrobe and make-up departments are in close proximity too. Our little 'complex' also has a communal green room furnished with several really comfortable sofas, chairs and a huge TV. This is where we all congregate when we feel the need for some company. Sometimes one or two of us go off into a corner to rehearse a scene or we sit and talk. There's also a tea bar where we can purchase hot or cold drinks, snacks and hot food. The studios are, literally, our home from home and a much needed requirement for all actors. It's hard for the general public to understand the workings of such a massive industry, but if you consider how much dialogue there is to learn for a programme that is shown four days a week, and how little time we have to learn it all, coupled with extraordinarily long days that can go on for 12 hours at times, I think you'll appreciate that these little extras are not luxuries but necessities.

The Slater family worked non-stop for the first six months while our storylines integrated us into the local community. Each of us had specific individual stories so that our characters could be built up, becoming popular and well loved by our viewers. Kat was showcased first, gaining quite a reputation as a good time girl while Lynne was trying her best to get Garry nailed and up the aisle. Then we had all the trials and tribulations of Little Mo's relationship with Trevor while Zoe experienced the usual teenage problems. Mo, bless her, became established as a ducker and diver of dodgy deals, with a fertile and vivid imagination for thinking up lots of naughty scams at any opportunity.

Patrick Trueman (Rudolph Walker) and his sons came to live in the Square a while later, and again, it was lovely to meet up with Rudolph, as we hadn't seen each other since Italy where he appeared with me in *Spaghetti House Seige*. Not long after this new family's arrival, one of his sons, Anthony who is a doctor has an affair with Kat. Then, when they split up he moves in on Zoe. More sparks; from both families this time.

Now Rudolph is a big cricket fan and knows all the West Indian teams from way back. We're always discussing the merits of our respective country's teams and it does get a bit heated sometimes. He goes home to Trinidad from time to time and brings me back some delicious mangoes as a treat. Another highlight for me also came from Rudolph, but this time it included the whole cast and crew. Just before we'd break for the festive season, his wife made a gigantic Christmas cake, which took months to prepare. Naturally it was laced with lots of rum, spices and other spirits. Magnificent! Like eating pure alcohol. Five minutes later and it had all gone, as the vultures came in for the kill.

The late Wendy Richard, who played Pauline Fowler, shared her love of dogs with me. We were both daft over our own, and used to send cards from one to the other for a joke. One day she suggested I meet her at Earls Court for the annual charity event, The Alternative Dog Show, and I suppose that's how it all started. This is a great event; run as a spoof of Crufts for any breed of mongrel. Terrific fun, but taken very seriously by the dog owners of course. I've been tempted to enter Giles but haven't done so yet, although I suppose he's past his prime now.

One of the good things about *EastEnders* is that the scripts often pick up on difficult or taboo subjects and Charlie's daughters seemed to go through most of them; from rape to incest, homosexuality, prostitution, abortion, ethnicity and domestic violence – which is where I'll start my resume of the plots; for those of you that may not have watched the programme. The storyline about battered wives was the first major expose of life as it really is. Little Mo and Trevor have a rocky marriage, because he's a moody character, with a violent and unpredictable streak. Typical of such women's behaviour in real life, Little Mo forgives him after every beating. Things go from bad to worse and one day Trevor rapes her, to teach her a lesson for some small and insignificant misdemeanour. Kacey portrayed her character brilliantly, as the timid little mousy and downtrodden housewife.

Little Mo snaps, and attacks Trevor with an iron, thinking she's killed him. He doesn't die though and leaves the house somehow. Prosecuted for attempted murder she gets off because the Slaters do a deal with him, not to give evidence against her in exchange for Kat not reporting a violent attack he'd made on her earlier. Little Mo files for divorce after her release, but is taken hostage by an outraged Trevor, who imprisons her in the house, along with his baby son by Donna, with whom he'd a brief affair. Unfortunately, a fire breaks out but only Little Mo and her baby are rescued. Both Trevor and a fireman, Tom, die.

During those first few years the viewers continued to believe, quite naturally, that Zoe was Charlie's youngest daughter. Then a new character turns up out of the blue - Charlie's brother Harry, who lives in Spain supposedly. Played by a wonderful actor, the late Michael Elphick, who was a friend I'd known from *Private Schulz* days. Kat appears to be very hostile towards him, and when Charlie quizzes her about this, she reveals the truth. To his horror, he discovers that his own brother Harry had abused her sexually when she was young, making her pregnant at 13. Charlie and his late wife Vivienne were told the father was a boy at school but Kat was unwilling to name him at the time. She went away to have her baby and no-one else in the family knows the truth apart from Mo. Charlie ended up bringing up her child, Zoe, as his own.

Once Charlie has all the facts he goes after Harry, with the intention of killing him. Instead, he gives him a good thrashing and tells him never to set foot in England again. Of course the story gets more gripping each week, as Zoe finds out that Charlie's not her real father but that her Uncle Harry is. This storyline really captured the public's attention. I had some very emotional scenes with Kat. Instead of the usual horrible, loud-mouthed characters I'd played in the past, it was the best chance I've ever had to show this side to my acting ability. Forty years of pent-up anger and emotion were unleashed, with real tears and snot running from my nose. At the end of filming, I was drained emotionally and physically exhausted.

Zoe has a turbulent and emotional see-saw existence after discovering that Kat is her mother. First, she gets engaged to Dr. Anthony Trueman for a while when he's finished with Kat but that doesn't last long. Then she falls for the handsome heartthrob Dennis Rickman who is Dirty Den's son. Dennis is in love with Dirty Den's adopted daughter Sharon but she is infertile so can't have his child. In order to put a stop to what he considers is an incestuous affair, despite the fact that Sharon and Dennis aren't actually blood relations, Dirty Den concocts a plan to make Zoe pregnant and then claim the baby is Dennis's, in the hope that he'll marry her. Later, she is persuaded to have an abortion. I hope you're keeping up with all this - the plot goes on a bit more, but in the meantime Zoe leaves home and teams up with a prostitute who leads her astray. Eventually she returns home and begins to build a proper mother-daughter relationship with Kat.

Lynne spends all her time trying to get a reluctant Garry to the altar. He loves her but can't bear the thought of giving up his bachelor freedom. In the end she wears him down and he agrees finally. In the meantime, Lynne has been flirting with Beppe di

Marco and sleeps with him on the eve of her wedding. The marriage is not very successful, and Lynne has an affair when she meets her ex-fiance Jason, who had jilted her at their wedding. After much soul-searching she decides to stay with Garry, but a year later it's Garry who has an affair, but he fathers a child. This is too much for Lynne to bear, so the couple separate. A while later they get back together and Lynne falls pregnant, but a tragedy follows. While on a fairground ride, Lynne is crushed when it crashes down on top of her. Although she survives, the baby dies during a caesarean operation. Unable to forgive Garry for past infidelities, she leaves Walford to stay with an aunt.

When I'd been on *EastEnders* for about a year, it became obvious that it would be sensible to move nearer to the studios. The journey to work each day was taking a toll on my nerves. Unavoidably stuck in traffic on the M25 and A1 for hours at a time; both notorious roads for being congested most of the day, I'd resort to turning off at any opportunity. Trouble with that strategy, though, is that often I'd get stuck in yet another grid-lock, or worse still, get lost completely. Let's face it, where can you go these days without traffic jams? Friends suggested the area around St. Albans, since prices in north London, or anywhere inside the M25 Orbital for that matter, would be prohibitive. Although I earned good money, I still had no idea how long my storyline would last and couldn't risk over-spending just yet.

My old pal John Harvey had split up recently from his wife

and wanted to sell their house, downsizing to a smaller apartment. I'd admired his home for a while, which was very close to the studios, at Hatfield, and where I could pop round sometimes for a bite to eat, in-between filming. Our work schedules could be erratic. Often, we'd be called for a few hours in the morning and then back again in the evening, so it was never worth the hassle of travelling back to Hanworth. One of my first major decisions, after signing the contract with the BBC for *EastEnders*, was to ensure I never took any more risks, by doing favours for old friends or acquaintances. Never knowing truly what John was up to, and having explained my feelings to him, he accepted that I had to be squeaky clean. He was my friend though, and I wasn't prepared to dump him, especially since he'd been such a good pal to me when the chips were down, so I kept in touch as often as possible.

This was a chance not to be missed. Always needing to get rid of spare cash, John found the best way to do it was by spending money on the house. He'd built an enormous extension, adding double the space to the kitchen, utility and cloak rooms. No expense had been spared on internal décor either. This would be to my advantage, because the house was in a cul-de-sac of identical properties, so there was a ceiling to the asking price. In fact, the property was really worth about 25% more than the figure we settled on, but John wasn't fussed. He left me most of his furniture and all the fixtures and fittings. I reckoned the lights in the lounge were worth £1,000 alone, so make no mistake, I got the better part of this deal.

As luck would have it, I sold my home very quickly and the move went smoothly. Now I could get to the studios in about 20 minutes and I made lots of new friends. Giles was the only one who wasn't happy with his new surroundings. For the first week or so, whenever I spoke to him he'd glare at me, eyes down, and slink off to his basket. Like all dogs, he got over it soon enough.

To say I was a little apprehensive would be stating the obvious, but I'd lived in the west London suburbs for over 30 years and knew the area well. As an adult I had never lived in the countryside and it felt very strange at first. John gave me a few guided tours and within a short space of time I felt at home. He moved to Enfield with his youngest daughter, but we'd meet up from time to time, for a pub lunch or a round of golf. We caused a stir when we were out sometimes, because John was a dead ringer for David Jason in his role as Del Boy; in every way, not just facially, but also his voice, stature and demeanour. By association, members of the public would assume we were working on a programme together and once or twice, he even signed autographs for a laugh.

After a while I set about the task of redecorating the house to my taste. The lounge was very spacious and light, with an elegant stone fireplace, either side of which were two large recesses. This enabled me to indulge in a luxury I'd hankered after for many years – a Bang and Olufsen 40 inch TV. I paid an obscene amount of money for it, but I was nearly 70, and had been working for 55 years, so call it a well deserved bonus, from me to me. Honestly I don't have many vices; a non-smoker who hardly drinks alcohol from one week to the next. My one big hobby is watching films and I have a vast collection of DVDs - about 700 - so I don't feel it was too extravagant.

Years ago, I had a friend who was almost as big a film buff as me. You may remember him; the '60's pop singer Doug Sheldon, who had a hit single with *Run Around Sue*. We used to phone each other at odd times with trick questions such as, "Who played the part of C.W. Moss in *Bonnie and Clyde*?" Or, "What was the name of the summer residence in *Doctor Zhivago*?" We'd each try to out-do the other by picking the most obscure early roles of famous stars, before they became household names. All good fun. I was sorry to lose touch when he moved to Israel, although he did contact me once, after seeing me in a programme over there. By the way, the answers to those two questions are; Michael J. Pollard and 'Varykino'.

Back to *EastEnders* then and my screeen'family.' In 2002 we had the pleasure of Alfie Moon's (Shane Richie) company. He's a loveable rogue and it's inevitable from the outset that he and Kat will start a relationship. After much hoo ha surrounding his background, they decide to take things slowly and start an on-off relationship that spans about two years. Kat ends it though when she returns from New York engaged to a local gangster. Eventually they declare undying love for each other and get engaged. The wedding was scheduled for Christmas Day and expected to clean up as the soap 'wedding of the year'. However, in true soap storyline style, the path of true love is never easy and the arrangements become fraught with problems. With typical drama, it becomes apparent that Alfie isn't divorced from his first wife yet so he plots with a friend, to trick Kat by staging a bogus ceremony. Just as it's about to be cancelled, Alfie's solicitor turns up with the Decree Absolute and they get married for real.

The marriage is doomed from the start however and it's not long before they split up. Alfie targets Little Mo next but that relationship is a bit of a non-starter and fails soon after. Eventually, there's a happy ending as we see Kat and Alfie get back together. In 2005 we wave a sad farewell to the couple as they drive away from Walford, heading for a new life, we're led to believe, in America. The viewers were heartbroken to lose them both, but sensibly, the scriptwriters left the storyline open, for a return if need be. And as fans of the soap will know by now, both Shane Richie and Jessie Wallace have indeed just returned to Walford as Alfie and Kat.

Something dreadful happened in 2003. I received a call one evening, from John's daughter. "Is my Dad with you?" she asked. "No love, I haven't seen him for about a week." I reassured her, that if I heard from him I'd phone her. Apparently, he was supposed to meet her for dinner but hadn't shown up. John's life was such that I wasn't worried unduly. On the Friday she phoned me again, "Dad's turned up." I was pleased so I said, "That's good." Then she continued, "Yeah, only he's dead; been murdered." I was numbed into silence, while the enormity of what I'd just heard sank in.

It turned out that John had been shot in back of the head and his body set on fire. Later the full details of what had happened came to light. I found out he was owed a considerable sum of money by a man called Savvas Petri. It seems he'd gone to collect it, but a violent row ensued. At some point he was shot and his body was then wrapped in plastic and put into the boot of Petri's car. Later, possibly days after, Petri and his son Theodosi, drove up to Westhoughton in Lancashire, to pick up another business associate, Terence Cook, at his waste and recycling plant. The three men then had a meal at a pub near Cook's home - with John's body in the boot.

The three men then travelled to Cumbria where they dumped John's body behind a wall in a field close to a service station at Junction 37 of the M6 in the Cumbrian fells. Cook claimed in court that he only found out about the dead body in the boot an hour-and-a-half into the journey. During the trial Petri's son said his father had doused the body with petrol and set light to it. Later, a passer-by had spotted smoke and investigated further. Still smouldering when the police arrived, the body was so badly burned that it was unrecognisable. The police identified John by fingerprints taken from his burnt body.

It's a strange feeling talking about a close friend that has met with such a brutal death. I can only hope John really was dead before being burned. He may have been a bit of a villain, but he wasn't a violent man and certainly he didn't deserve that.

The task of identifying the body was difficult, because the police couldn't match John with that part of England. Thirty officers were assigned to the case and Operation Junction became the biggest murder hunt ever conducted by Cumbrian Police. Several detectives came down to London to interview all John's known acquaintances. Mobile phone records, coupled with motorway automatic number plate reading cameras, meant police were later able to piece together the movements of Petri and his son and Cook.

Savvas Petri was convicted of murder and sentenced to life imprisonment, with a recommendation he serve at least 20 years. The other two were cleared of murder but convicted of the offence of assisting an offender and given six years each. Good. At least the family felt that justice had been done and finally, could organise a proper funeral for John, allowing him to rest in peace with some dignity. I still miss him very much. He was a good friend to me and I'll never forget all the things he did to help me.

After this terrible ordeal I decided to cheer myself up by reorganising the garden. Too busy with work commitments to do it myself, I employed a garden designer friend of mine to put together a plan for a low maintenance and simple style. Although I love flowers, I haven't the time to look after anything too fussy, and anyway, I always forget to feed them. She came up with several lovely ideas, but the one I chose was based on a series of different patios, with a central water feature, set into the middle of a square area. This was filled with large ornamental pebbles and stones, out of which grew several varieties of small, clump-forming bamboos. One of the first tasks was to remove all the grass because Giles either dug it up or urinated on it. He was given his very own sunbathing patio, constructed of white paving slabs with a sand pit for all his toys. I know what you're thinking; yes, he is spoilt and I'm a soppy old fool. Inside the fence are several evergreen shrubs, interspersed with small trees. Finally, around the edge of my brick patio, where I have the table and chairs, there's a boxed, raised border housing lots of different flowering shrubs; such as Camellia, Japonica and Hydrangea. It has lived up to the brief in every way, being very easy for me to manage. As for the front garden, I'm afraid it went the way of many others these days; becoming a paved car standing area, with a just a few pot plants under the window.

In 2006 John Yorke became Controller of Drama at BBC but every now and then he would pop back to see us all. I shall always be indebted and grateful to him for the longevity of the Slaters. We had a succession of executive producers after John's departure, but none more successful than Diederick Santer. Sensing that the viewers were missing some of their favourite characters, who had departed Walford, he set about reintroducing some of them; for example ex-husband and wife Bianca and Ricky and the wicked

Janine who was the black sheep of our Walford family. Some new faces appeared in the form of the two glamorous sisters Ronnie and Roxy Mitchell and a short time later we had the pleasure of meeting their sly and extremely cunning father, Archie. He brought the Masood family to Walford and later introduced the controversial topic of homosexuality.

As Charlie Slater, I don't have much to do with these characters other than the odd word or two if my character happens to be in the Queen Vic. Charlie tends to keep himself to himself and concentrates on looking after his extended family. One by one his daughters leave home. The first to leave was Lynne in 2004. As I mentioned earlier and has been well documented so there's no need for me to elaborate here, Elaine had her own personal problems. My heart went out to her. Then Kat left home in 2005 when she went off with Alfie, followed a short while later by Zoe. Little Mo decided she'd had enough of being downtrodden and abused, deciding to make a fresh start somewhere else, and left Walford finally in 2006, with her son Freddie. Poor old Charlie was left with only his niece Stacey to look after and missed all his daughters. I'm sure many viewers could identify with this, because parents do feel an empty space when their offspring flee the nest. Stacey was a wayward and troublesome teenager when she moved in with the Slaters, giving Charlie more trouble over the next few years than his daughters ever did. For a start, her storylines featured drug abuse, alcoholism, an affair with her father-in-law, mental illness and accusations of murder and so on. Well, that's enough isn't it? Played brilliantly by Lacey Turner, whom I have a special friendship with. I know we're generations apart but we seemed to hit it off right from the start. She's a very beautiful girl and is definitely popular with the lads. Occasionally, we go to our favourite restaurant, Wagamamas, in St. Albans for a spot of lunch.

When I'd been on *EastEnders* for about two years, I began to relax about money. For the first time in my acting career, I felt that I would be in for the long haul on a series, so I could afford to splash out on a few luxuries. At last I could begin to contemplate buying the holiday apartment I'd dreamt of since Tenerife days, somewhere warm. For many years I'd favoured Portugal, having spent so much time there with the charity golf tournaments, but I also fancied a new challenge. It just so happened that my old mate, Rod, had moved to Majorca and I'd spent many long weekends there. On one of these visits, I set about the task of looking seriously; with Rod's help and guidance of course, because he knew all the things to watch out for; the pitfalls, best estate agents as well as all the legal stuff.

Whenever I went to the island, I'd tour around, and it didn't take long for me to work out the areas where I didn't want to be. Top of the list was Magaluf, or as it's referred to popularly by the locals, Shagaluf. I'll let you work that one out for yourselves. Typical of the worst of the tourist 'hot spots' taken over by the British holidaymaker; mainly singles and lager louts, it's popular as a stag weekend venue. Say no more. It's very sad though, because Magaluf was once a very pretty coastal village. Fortunately, the Spanish government has realised since, all the earlier mistakes, such as those made at Torremolinos, and is much stricter and more vigilant at preserving the most valued areas. Height restrictions are in force on Majorca, so it's unlikely to become too built up or over-populated. The only downside being that property prices remain high.

Known as 'The Jewel in the Mediterranean,' it lives up to its reputation in every way. From the air, as you cross over the Spanish mainland heading south, the rugged, northern mountains loom up ahead and it seems to take forever to reach the island. Then, as the plane takes an easterly bank, in preparation for the descent and final approach, the true magic of the landscape becomes visible. A stunning coastline to the south, with dozens of little sandy coves all shimmering in the sunshine; beautiful olive, orange and lemon groves; with rich farmland in between. The airport is one of the most sophisticated in Europe and I can't really complain about anything on that score. Added to which is the fact that the journey from Luton takes a mere couple of hours, depending on the wind direction of course.

Most of the tourist areas, stretching right around the island, are busy throughout the season; from March to October. I wanted to find a place where the locals lived as well, and a short walk away from the beach, so that I could get away from it all. Another consideration was this. Wherever I go in England I'm recognised, and with the popularity of *EastEnders*, it's not surprising. Lots of people will stop and ask me for my autograph, or to have a photo taken with me, usually by someone else in the crowd. After a few minutes, several more people will gather round and soon it becomes impossible to get away, until they've all had one. I never mind this publicity, because I try to remember that it's the public who pay my wages, and I take the view that it comes with the territory. Most actors want to be famous and have the money and trappings that come with celebrity status, but for some, as soon as they're lucky enough to achieve this goal, they go all coy and want to be "left alone". To my way of thinking, that's a selfish attitude but I accept lots of people won't agree with me.

It took a few trips to Majorca before I found a fabulous three bedroom, double apartment in Paguera. Originally two - a one bedroom and a two bedroom - knocked through to provide a very spacious home. It has three separate balconies, one leading off each of two bedrooms, and a large entertaining space which extends from the dining room. One of the great joys of being abroad, in such lovely warm sunshine, is being able to slop around in shorts and t-shirts, without a care in the world. No socks and shoes, just a pair of leather flip-flops. Bliss! It may have taken me 30-odd years to get here, but it's certainly been worth the wait. David and Jonathan love it too, and it wasn't long before Jonathan moved to the island permanently. As a graphic designer, he's never short of work. David is a keen diver, and comes out for holidays regularly, so I'm very glad with my decision to buy a place here.

Originally, when I embarked on buying my apartment, I had a vague idea it might be useful for my retirement one day, in case I changed my mind about living outside England. I'm too much of an Anglophile to do it though and anyway, luckily for me, I don't envisage I'll ever retire. I hope to drop off, on stage or on the set of a television programme, when the time comes for my number to be called.

The Walford Gazette is an in-house newspaper, for cast crew and production. When I'd been at *EastEnders* about three years someone asked me if I'd like to write a film review column and I agreed readily. Before long this had developed into almost a page, with snippets about Giles, my favourite recipes, poems or jokes, as well as general thoughts and ideas. The paper also has Sudoku, quizzes, crosswords, adverts, birthday announcements, film and book reviews and articles. Most of us contributed to its success in some way, and we all read it regularly. After a while I stopped writing a full page, but sent in the odd poem or joke. Caption competitions were my favourite, usually of a photo, taken during filming a scene, when one of us had been caught off guard. Some of the winning entrants had a wicked sense of humour and I found them hilarious.

As an actor in a long running soap, it's impossible not to be affected by real life tragedies that strike other artists. We all knew that Wendy Richard had been battling with cancer for several years but we thought it had been conquered. She left *EastEnders* for personal reasons when she became disillusioned with Pauline's storyline, and not because of illness, as some people thought. In 2007 she won the British Soap Awards' Lifetime Achievement Award, and I was delighted to be invited to a special luncheon, held in her honour, at The Dorchester Hotel later that year. Stories began appearing in the tabloids that her cancer was back and sadly they were right. When Wendy died in 2009 I attended her funeral, along with hundreds of friends and family. Although we were all sad, it was a happy day in one sense, being a celebration of her life.

When Mike Reid died it affected me deeply because we'd had some fun times playing golf in Portugal and I considered him a personal friend. We went back a long way and shared the same roots although Mike was brought up in Hackney. He was a terrific comedian both on and off stage and his catch phrase word "wallop" was picked up by virtually the whole country (said correctly Mike's way as "Waaalop!") in the '70s, after hearing it regularly on the TV show *The Comedians*. A few years earlier, in 1990 Mike's own son had committed suicide. It's ironic how often the actors' off-screen dramas seem intertwined within the programme's storylines. It just goes to show the writers must be getting something right, that's all I can say. From time to time we hear some scathing comments about soaps not being worthwhile. To me that's rubbish because they address real life issues as they occur for the vast majority of ordinary folk. Talk to anyone about families and they will admit to some bizarre stories of their own. You only have to look at the private lives of the soap stars themselves to see that the storylines ring very true.

John Bardon has become a good friend since working together on the show, although we knew each other very well from the charity golfing days. He had married a lovely lady called Enda and moved to a converted barn in a village not far from me. I used to visit quite regularly, and I was amazed to discover that he is a marvellous artist; mainly water colours and pen and ink sketches. When I started on the show he showed me the ropes a bit, and one of the first pieces of advice he gave was to join the Equity Pension Scheme, which now gives me a small pension, since it has run its course. One morning I got a call from Enda. She was shouting down the phone, telling me John had collapsed. I told her to ring 999 quickly, which she did. They took him away in an ambulance and we discovered later that he'd suffered a severe stroke. That was three years ago now and I think it's marvellous how the producers worked this real life drama into the script. After Jim spent time in a nursing home recovering from a stroke, he moved back in with Dot in 2009; another instance where true life is reflected in the soap.

Although this year, 2010, marked my 10th in *EastEnders*,

I've never known anything to go by so quickly. It feels as if it was only three years ago that I started. They say time only flies when you're enjoying yourself and I count myself very lucky to have been able to do a job where I go to work with a smile on my face and return home still smiling; and get paid for it to boot. If I'm not in a storyline for a week I get withdrawal symptoms and can't wait to get back to work.

Every now and then the production team releases me for the odd outing – time off for good behaviour I like to call it. Sometime during 2005, David Walliams asked me if I would like to appear as a guest on series one of *Little Britain*. We had worked together in *EastEnders* when he played Alfie Moon's cousin Ray in the Christmas special. On the first rehearsal day, Matt Lucas came up to introduce himself to me. He said, "Hello! I'm Matt Lucas. I'm Jewish and I'm gay!" To which I replied, "That doesn't make you a bad person!" Matt was quick off the mark again with, "Oh, you'll do!" We got on really well after that. I played myself, in Fat Marjorie's Club, where I'd gone to lose weight. All Marjorie (played by Matt Lucas) really wanted to know was the low-down and gossip on *EastEnders*, as well as future storylines and secrets of the cast. At the end I storm out indignantly because I'm not being taken seriously. Those who saw it thought the sketch was funny and I must say it was great fun to work on.

On February 14 2008 Laila Morse and I did a Valentine's Day special of *Ready Steady Cook* with Ainsley Harriott. I was the red tomato and Laila, the green pepper. My professional chef was Phil Vickery (Fern Britton's husband), and we had a good laugh, especially when I pretended to cut my finger. Ainsley rushed over to me, showing great concern, until he saw it was a wind up. Phil and I were in charge of pudding, which was crushed chocolate eclairs, baked like toffee and served with a strawberry mousse, while Laila made the main course. The show is just as frantic as it looks when you watch it on TV but luckily I'm laid back so it didn't stress me out too much. To Laila's disappointment, the red tomatoes won on the day and the now famous white china plate stands on my kitchen dresser with the words; 'Winner of *Ready Steady Cook*' engraved in gold.

Since I started going to fund-raising events for several charities, I've met lots of very interesting people from different walks of life, many of whom do far more than me. To explain what I mean by my charity work, I'd like to set the record straight here. I turn up to major charity events as a guest, alongside many other artists, where I'm expected to mingle and socialise with party-goers, all of whom have spent huge amounts of money on tickets. These can cost anything from a few hundred pounds to thousands. Everyone wants to have a photo, usually with my arm round them, which adds to the excitement of their evening. For my part, I get to hug and kiss a lot of very lovely ladies I can tell you, and you won't hear any complaints from me. One of the celebrities (although I don't like that term for myself) will be asked to host the auction, raffle or hand out prizes and so forth. For the charity; we give them a higher profile for selling tickets because that's what people want out of the evening. I've been a supporter of Sparks for the last 10 years, a charity that researches children's diseases. I used to attend nearly all the golfing events but since joining *EastEnders* I've found it almost impossible to keep up, as mostly they're held during a weekday when I'm busy at the studios. My real congratulations go to the thousands of unsung heroes who give hours of their free time to organise these events.

Although I have a great time at all these fundraisers, I can't switch off completely and be myself. In my opinion, one of the best evenings out in London is to be found at The Brick Lane Music Hall on Docklands. Vincent Hayes who runs it is a very dear friend, whom I met first when he was landlord of The Lord Hood during the '80s. There, he would put on small, impromptu performances, on a tiny stage constructed of empty beer crates. He felt that it was a travesty not to have a proper music hall variety theatre in London, which was, after all, the home of music hall entertainment, and so he set about looking for suitable premises. In 1992 he found a disused building in Brick Lane; hence the name, which had been formerly a part of the Truman Brewery. Since then he has built up such a reputation that larger premises were needed. When Vincent acquired the current theatre in Silvertown, it was in a sorry state of repair. The former St Mark's church has been transformed, almost single-handedly, by Vincent, with the help of a few good friends, into the most lavish little 'palace'. Housed within a Grade II listed building the interior is extremely opulent and shows are booked for months in advance. For the entrance fee, I get a three course meal and entertainment, with some of the top variety acts around; people like Roy Hudd for example, and the ambience is terrific. Audiences are seated in a cabaret-style format, around the stage, so the acts can encourage them to join in. Sometimes Vincent will get me up on stage to draw the raffle prizes but the banter is all good fun so I don't mind at all. If I go to the afternoon matinee, I'm served a full afternoon tea, including scones and cream – no wonder my waistband is ever expanding. To tell the truth, it's hard to describe it and I can only recommend you see it for yourselves. I promise you won't be disappointed.

Friends are a very important part of my life and I'm fortunate to be blessed with a huge circle of good ones. Whenever I have a few days off, I do the rounds as I call it, travelling the length and breadth of the country. The trouble with getting to my age though is that so many of my closest friends are no longer here, and it takes a long time to adjust to their departure from this world. The viewers often assume that the cast of *EastEnders* are all good friends in real life because they see us as a 'family'. While some of the younger actors do socialise at weekends, going to discos and clubs, most of the older members have families or partners and tend to switch off at weekends. We have a large number of lines to learn whenever we're at home too, so I suppose working on *EastEnders* is just like going to a factory or an office, where you clock in and out. The only time we get to socialise is at award ceremonies and whenever there's a leaving party for a cast or crew member. There have been some romances and at least one, the relationship between Ricky Groves and Hannah Waterman, led to marriage. To be honest, I don't always see what's going on under my nose because I tend to keep my head down, do my work and go home, so I'm sorry to disappoint anyone who was hoping for more juicy in-house gossip in this book.

To say my private love life has been turbulent is true, but I don't seem to have had much more luck with my on-screen partners either. Having tried it on with Peggy Mitchell a few years earlier, followed by a mere hint of a relationship between Pauline Fowler and Charlie, my character has remained a steadfast bachelor. When Stacey attempts suicide he becomes depressed and so the ever interfering Mo colludes with Jean, putting an advert in a lonely hearts column on an internet dating site. After much arguing he agrees, albeit reluctantly, to go on a date. Soon he gets a reply and makes arrangements to meet up with a lovely lady from Clacton-on-Sea, called Brenda, who belongs to the Salvation Army. She comes to Walford to see him and I think their first outing is for lunch. They share some common interests such as gardening and after several more dates they fall for each other, only Charlie is absolutely useless at getting this message across to her. Needless to say, the relationship fizzles out, with Brenda making the decision to live abroad, in Madeira. He's doomed to spend the rest of his life alone. Since the Slater girls left, Charlie has appeared on the periphery of some major storylines and with the return of some of his family members, I hope to be more involved once again, until my departure at the end of this year. I thoroughly enjoyed filming the plotline of Charlie's arrest for drink driving a few weeks ago; it's exciting being at the centre of the action and what acting is all about.

In recent years my character has appeared more as the backbone of the Slater household, holding together what is left of his ever decreasing family. Mo relies on Charlie simply to be there for her, like the furniture, while Stacey still needs his guidance and support to keep her on track as she tries to handle her bipolar mental health disorder. He has had to help his sister-in-law Jean, at times because she suffers with the same condition. The storyline won the Mental Health Media Award in 2006 for capturing the essence of the illness so well. Both Lacey and Gillian Wright portrayed the symptoms superbly and I think it was one of the best ever storylines. I'd like to say here that Gillian is one of the finest actresses I've ever worked with and it's been both a pleasure and an honour to work so closely with her.

Last year, 2009, saw the introduction of a gay relationship between Christian (John Partridge) and Syed (Marc Elliott) which is full of pain and anguish because Syed refuses to give in to his true feelings. Because of his religious beliefs as a Muslim and in order to appease his mother who is the only member of the family to know the truth, he marries Amira. When I consider that years ago men in this position went through their whole lives leading a double existence, I feel very sad for them and I think it's good that this storyline was included. There are probably still men today, who are living this same lie, in order to protect their families.

Over the years, I've attended many award ceremonies, held at different venues, such as The Albert Hall, BBC Television Centre and the 02 Arena. They're always very exciting because we're all kept in suspense, wondering if our 'soap' has won. I'm happy to say that my Slater girls did their old 'dad' proud, winning many of the Best Actress categories. In the last five years alone, Lacey Turner has outshone everyone, and I've lost count of how many awards she's won. At the *Soap Awards* the competition is fierce, so everyone really pushes the boat out to look fantastic. The girls especially; and to me, they look every bit as stunning as the stars who attend the Oscars. Our arch rivals are *Emmerdale, Coronation Street* and *Hollyoaks*, and we always jibe each other throughout the evening – all good sportsman-like banter though, I have to say. A nervous tingle runs through me when the envelope is opened, as I wait to hear if we've won. Whoever wins, the whole cast goes on stage to receive the award while an elected member gives the "Thank you" speech. Even though they don't appear, all the behind-the-scenes crew are appreciated. From the cameramen, make-up artists, wardrobe, props and sparks to the runners – without whom none of us could be there. There's always a party afterwards, usually at a nearby venue, where we can relax and let our hair down. It's good to meet other artists from rival soaps; some we know already and others who become new acquaintances, with lots of showbiz gossip. With my fruit juice in hand, I mingle through the crowds saying "Hello," to old friends. These parties go on until very late but I normally leave at around midnight. Cocoa and my bed await, with the ever faithful Giles, who never fails to greet me with his wagging tail, as I open the front door.

Even though Archie Mitchell was the rogue we all loved to hate, and there were several times where nearly everyone in Walford would have liked to kill him, it's sad to see his character gone. In the end five suspects were interviewed by the police, and over a period of several weeks we were all left wondering who the true killer was. The cast and crew were as much in the dark as the viewers and we all had to wait for the live televised programme in February of this year, which marked *EastEnders'* 25-year celebrations to find out. It was a great piece of drama. Having filmed an ending, with each of the five suspects being the guilty party, it's hard to imagine that none of them knew either. I believe only two or three members of the production team knew. Lacey was informed on the day, just before the show went on air, that it was her. A week after the live show, Diederick left *EastEnders*, having announced he was leaving in November 2009 and we all missed him. In a long-running soap, I think it's important to bring in new blood every so many years, and I was looking forward to working with our new executive producer, Bryan Kirkwood. Unfortunately, this was not going to be the case for very long.

In April of this year, he called for me to meet him in his office. I thought this is it – I'm in for the chop. Bryan is known in the business as 'the axe man' because of his reputation with previous soaps. He got rid of several of the top stars when he took over at Hollyoaks so we were all feeling apprehensive about our roles.

He greeted me warmly, shaking hands and introducing himself. He reassured me straight away, that he wanted Charlie's role to become more centred around his cab, you know, conversations with fare-paying customers and so on, and to which he added, "Cab drivers have an opinion on everything!" He also said that there should be more family gatherings, and arguments, around the kitchen table and such like. I left the meeting feeling elated that my part would be secure for at least another year.

By now you will have realised that there's no such thing as 'safe' in this business! A couple of weeks later I received a call from Bryan's assistant to say he wanted to see me, but she didn't know what it was about. Because I was due to have knee replacement surgery a few weeks later, I assumed it was to wish me luck for the forthcoming operation. How wrong I was! When I arrived for our meeting, he told me he had bad news for me, so I knew instinctively, what was coming. Quite coldly, he revealed his revised plan - to kill off Charlie Slater.

I left with his words ringing in my ears. Yes, at the time I was gutted, upset and very disappointed, but in all soaps – all shows to be honest - actors never know when the axe might fall. This is part of the business and the gamble actors take when entering the world of film, television and theatre. Twenty-four hours later though, when the shock had subsided, I was ready to face the next chapter in my career. My agent got on the case immediately and offers began coming in.

That said, after agreeing I would be leaving *EastEnders* for good in September with a fantastic storyline which I won't spoil for you here, I was asked later to stay on a few more months, which I agreed to without hesitation. After all, I've had nothing but good times on the show and have only positive things to say about everyone I've worked with, from the rest of the cast and bosses to all the behind-scenes girls and boys who make this fantastic soap what it is.

So, as I write this, I'm still good old Charlie Slater but won't be for much longer. By the end of 2010 I will have filmed my final scenes, although I shall be on screen still into 2011 and of course, I'm eager to make my next move. Watch this space as they say!

CHAPTER ELEVEN

Grand Finale

During 2004, I was honoured to be invited to join the prestigious Grand Order of Water Rats. It has its roots, and history, in the entertainment business and dates back to the early 1880s. I knew about The Order because so many great people from the entertainment industry are members and I used to hear odd snippets about what goes on. I'd also been to lots of their charity functions as a paying guest. My *EastEnders* pal John Bardon proposed I become a member because he thought I'd make a good Rat. I made it known that I'd love to join and the first procedure was to go along to a few meetings, held fortnightly on a Sunday, at the GOWR's Lodge in Gray's Inn Road. I wasn't allowed to attend the Lodge meeting itself but had to mingle and get to know the others in the bar area. John Bardon proposed me and Melvyn Hayes (of *It Ain't 'Alf Hot Mum*) seconded me. The next stage was for my name to be read out at three Lodge meetings, followed by a postal ballot among the members, before an announcement made to say I had been accepted. I received a notification a while later telling me to attend an initiation ceremony on July 18 2004. It was a very proud moment for me. I felt as if I would be entering a new and exciting chapter in my life - and I was right.

Before I entered the Lodge, a blindfold was placed round my head, and since everyone had wound me up beforehand, telling me dreadful tales about what would happen at this juncture, I must say I felt a tad apprehensive. Obviously I can't reveal all the details but I can tell you that when it was all over, the reigning King Rat welcomed me into the fold by placing a special collar around my neck. It was all very moving. A fledgling member is known as a Baby Rat. The Baby Rat collar is cream and this is worn at every meeting until a new member joins, when it's upgraded to blue.

After a couple of years members can apply for various official posts and most aspire to take office as King Rat one day. My first post was that of Trap Guard, followed by Chief Trap Guard and later Prince Rat. Since its inception there have been only about 868 members altogether, so I feel privileged to be among them. Having come up through the ranks so to speak, today I feel part of the family and I'm very proud to tell you that 2010 is my year as King Rat. I took over from Graham Cole (PC Tony Stamp in *The Bill*) who was a superb leader. My companions include some very big names from the past such as Laurel and Hardy, Charlie Chaplin, Peter Lorre and Howard Hughes as well as new members, Tony Hatch and Tony Christie. When Laurel and Hardy became Rats they donated an ornate egg on a chain which is awarded to the person who tells the worst gag. I have the dubious distinction of having been awarded this egg the most times in the last two years and, since I'm not a comedian, I feel quite chuffed. In 1890, one of the founder members donated another medal on a gold chain which is awarded for the best gag – sadly, I've not won this one yet. We're not all oldies though and include some young blood too; our newest recruit being Richard Joy who is the drummer with Freefaller.

Nowadays, members include sportsmen, musicians, actors, variety acts, ventriloquists, and even royalty. Since taking over as King Rat I'm amazed at how much work is involved – organising events and meetings and so forth - but my fellow Rats have been an enormous help to me and everything works out well in the end. Now perhaps, I'll have more respect for those who follow in my shoes. In the six years as a Rat, I've made a vast new range of dear friends and my Lodge meetings are something I look forward to immensely. If only these could be recorded; with the jibes, gags, jokes, kindly insults and banter, alongside anecdotes and laughter, it would make a wonderful radio programme – after some careful editing of course! One of the best things to happen to me since becoming a Rat are these wonderful new friendships.

What we do is very interesting so I feel I must give you an insight into our work. The GOWR put on variety shows all over the country for charity, with many of the Rats performing. We raise enormous sums of money for all sorts of different charities. Venues include Hunstanton, Dartford, Long Eaton, Blackpool and Margate as well as fellow Rat Vincent Hayes' Brick Lane Music Hall. Every year, on the last Sunday in November, we hold our Grand Ball, at the Dorchester Hotel, which is attended by about 750 people. It's a fantastic night out with amazing food, entertainment and to say it's star-studded would not be exaggerating. Even though I'm in the business I still get star struck myself when I see who's there. At the end of the evening the offices for the following year are announced.

Some members are called Companion Rats, because although they might not be in show business, they still want to support the work of the GOWR. They play a much needed role in our organisation and their generosity knows no bounds. One such Companion is John Ratcliffe CBE. You'll see his name on the back of almost every truck - 'Ratcliff Hoist'. All the Variety Club coaches have been fitted out with hoists from John's company - just one among many other things he does for charity. He and his lovely wife Marsha Rae live quite near me in Hertford. Marsha is a former Vogue model and Miss California. She does a lot for charity through the Lady Ratlings, having been Queen Ratling in 2004. The Variety Club Gold Heart Appeal was her brainchild and to date it has brought in millions of pounds, having become one of the most successful appeals ever. Marsha has also written several children's books, is a talented cartoonist and has designed many of the front covers for the GOWR Ball. They are good friends of mine now and I'd like to share an experience with you from when I was invited to a pre-Christmas dinner not so long ago. Imagine stepping back in time to Dickens' era (he happens to be my favourite author). As I entered the gates, to what can only be described as acres of park land, I drove up to their Grade II listed mansion and knew, instinctively, I was in for a treat. Once inside, I took in my surroundings. The interior was in keeping with the style of the house - olde worlde yet not old fashioned. There were 16 guests seated around a beautiful, elegant table which had been laid for full silver service, with a stunning centre-piece floral arrangement. I felt we were on the set of a period film. We sat through five courses and I can tell you I ate and drank in the atmosphere in every sense. After dinner there was a knock at the front door. We were beckoned to enter one of the largest drawing rooms I've ever seen, while John went into the hall. About 15 carol singers from the village church had congregated in a circle, holding lanterns. One by one they filed into where we'd gathered for the final part of our evening, singing to us while we sipped mulled wine and nibbled into delicious petit fours. Everyone joined in to sing all the favourite and most popular carols. A fantastic evening and one I'll never forget.

Another Companion Rat who has become a good friend is Bob Potter OBE and his wife Barbara. He owns Lakeside Leisure in Frimley Green which is an enormous complex and includes three hotels, sports facilities such as golf, snooker, pool, squash, bowling and darts. Bob has worked hard to get where he is and I admire him very much. As a musician in the early days, he started to promote shows, building up a classy reputation for top entertainment by booking all the big stars of the day. By the early '70s he purchased a huge parcel of land, to include the lake, in Frimley, where he developed his company into the success it is today. The fact there are three hotels on this site with a fourth not far away, shows how popular the venue is.

Every year in January, the World Championship Darts finals are held here and I have attended for the last four years. The Rats are given a special table for lunch, where wine and beer flow non-stop until the match is over. Then, we adjourn to one of the three hotels within walking distance, inside the complex, to continue the evening with a monumental hot and cold buffet, the like of which I've never seen before. The prawns are so big they're almost the size of mice. Bob and fellow Rat Tom Anderson are having a big hand in refurbishing the Water Rats pub. Both are extremely generous gentlemen.

Tom is a fellow Chelsea fan and has a season ticket at Stamford Bridge for four seats, to include restaurant booking, and I'm extremely lucky, and grateful, that he often asks me to join him. In 2009 he invited me to Wembley to see Chelsea play Arsenal in the FA Cup semi-final. These two arch rivals certainly fill the stadium and the atmosphere is fantastic, with plenty of jibes between spectators, as well as the songs – mostly rude ones about each other, and the banter, making it a truly fun occasion. The match kicked off at an alarmingly fast pace and after 18 minutes Walcott scored for Arsenal. Then, after 33 minutes Malouda equalised for Chelsea. In the second half, Drogba put in the winning goal for Chelsea which made my year. These days, it's the only way to watch the game in my opinion.

Barbara and Tom celebrated their Golden Wedding anniversary not long ago at the Palace of Whitehall. The banqueting suite is a truly magnificent Grade 1 listed building that not many Londoners know about. It's open to the public and well worth a visit. The ceiling was commissioned to be painted by Rubens and is breathtakingly awesome. The only part that remains of the original Palace, it was used for all forms of entertainment and Court business and, I'm informed, that it was from this room that King Charles 1 was taken to the scaffold outside to be beheaded, in front of a huge crowd.

About three weeks after my first trip to Wembley with Tom, an invitation was posted on our notice board at the studios; from the Football Association, asking if five cast members and their guest, would like to go to the Cup Final at Wembley in May between Chelsea and Everton. I put my name down straight away, taking my son David, who is also a Blues fan, as my guest. Funnily enough, although they are twins, each son supports a different team, with Jonathan being a Southampton fan. On the due day, a car came to pick us up and we were treated to the best seats and a lavish four course lunch. Carlsberg and Eon were the official sponsors of the match. We got to our seats just in time for kick-off. Again, the game went at a furious pace, but this time we were in for a nasty shock because Everton broke away, with Saha scoring the first goal after just 25 seconds. Then Drogba equalised. Half time came around quickly and we went back to the dining area for tea and cakes. The second half was even more exciting, with each side desperately trying to find that winning goal. Thankfully, Lampard scored it and the trophy was ours. After the match, all the invited guests went back for more drinks, either to celebrate or commiserate. A well known caricaturist was there and he did a sketch of David and me, holding the coveted trophy, which now hangs proudly in our study. I can only keep my fingers crossed that we can retain the cup again this year.

While on the subject of important listed buildings, I must tell you about some other good friends of mine (who are not in showbusiness), David and Julie Banes. They live about half a mile from me in a magnificent Elizabethan house, built around 1541. Complete with ghost apparently - that of a 12 year-old boy who appears now and then – although I've never seen him myself. But whenever I'm in the drawing room, which is in the oldest part of the house, I do sense an atmosphere. Or perhaps it's just me being fanciful. I only discovered how near they were by accident, whilst in conversation during a charity event in Radlett a few years back, which is where we first met. Julie's grandfather had been the chairman of Lloyds of London at one time and in her youth she'd been a singer with a band. The former boardroom table (which can seat at least 20 people), is now in their dining room. Summer barbecues are a speciality, held in the most spectacularly impressive gardens. Earlier this year, I was asked if I would be Godfather to their grandson Blake. I was honoured to accept and the christening was held on February 28 this year at the beautiful St. Michael's church in St. Albans. I'm Godfather to several children, although most have grown up now, so it's nice to be involved with a small child again, and I feel privileged to be asked.

About five years ago I went to one of the Queen's Garden Parties at Buckingham Palace. As I drove through the gates I got an unmistakable feeling of entering somewhere special. Even though I'd been with Mum and Dad 65 years earlier, I couldn't really remember much and children don't see in the same way as adults. I wished with all my heart though, that they had been alive to see me here again. Once inside the great central expanse that I'd admired only from outside until now, I was ushered through an archway into another central courtyard and told where to park. Next, I was escorted through a pair of grand, ornate oak doors, down a long corridor, where I couldn't even stop or linger to admire the sumptuous décor. I remember the feeling of soft thick carpet under my feet as well as a sense of grandeur though, before being taken outside again into the gardens. This was June, so the borders were full of colour with an abundance of every conceivable shrub and plant, giving off lovely fresh smells of summer. I was lucky, because the sun was on its best behaviour for the occasion. To give you an idea, the whole area including the lawns, is about the size of Wembley Stadium. Dotted around the central area are several marquees where soft drinks, sandwiches and cakes are displayed on long tables. There are lots of tables and chairs for guests to sit and rest, but most people want to mingle among the crowds, hoping to see and be seen. I hadn't been told that I would be introduced to Her Majesty but we all try to catch a glimpse if possible.

Everyone is dressed resplendently. The men in lounge suits, while the ladies get dolled up in their best finery – I imagine many women buy a new outfit for the occasion. Most ladies wear a hat so it reminded me of being at Ascot. I met up with fellow Rat Michael Black and his wife Julie Rogers, a well known singer from the '60s, who'd had a number one hit with *The Wedding*. Michael is a highly regarded agent who, for many years, managed the Astor Club in London's West End. All the big stars of the day appeared there and it became known also for its more infamous clientele of London and American gangsters, who could be spotted among the audience. This year Michael is Prince Rat to my King and we've been invited again as members of the GOWR. I confess I'm tempted to try out the throne for size this time! Michael and Julie live in a lovely detached modern house not far from the studios. Beautifully furnished, like something out of one of those glossy magazines; tasteful, not flashy, and if I get a chance I pop round sometimes during my lunch break. They are a very warm, hospitable couple and often as not they'll offer me smoked salmon and cream cheese bagels because they know how much I love them.

After a couple of hours we became aware of noises and shuffling, as the ushers guided all of us into a tunnel formation, ready for the Queen to make her way down the aisle. She smiled and greeted everyone, making a point of looking at each individual, as she glided past us. I bowed when she got to me but by the time my head came up again, I'd missed her. As King Rat, I sincerely hope to be introduced this year but I haven't heard anything as yet.

I'm smiling to myself as I write this because I have to remember that once I was so shy I couldn't arrange to meet someone in a pub unless they were in there first. I'd hang around outside to make sure, before entering. Now, though, I'm completely at ease with who I am and can meet anyone, from any walk of life, and feel confident. If only I could have had that attitude years ago because real shyness is a handicap, believe me.

My life is extremely busy these days. I turned 77 this year and, difficult as it may be to believe, I hardly have an evening to myself. Not only is my work schedule at the studios pretty tight – although this will soon be coming to an end - but the charity events keep me on my toes. The old knees give me cause for concern and I've had to postpone further golf tournaments, but apart from that, I'm very fit and healthy. I love to be busy working and hope, that as Charlie Slater will not be a part of Albert Square for much longer, that there will be new characters for me to play.

I rarely venture into the West End for anything unless for special functions or GOWR meetings. What with congestion charges, parking problems and never ending traffic jams it hardly seems worth the effort. Let's face it, at my age I've been there, seen it, and worn the T-shirt, several times over. One place I keep meaning to go to though, and would venture into town for, is an evening at the reopened Quaglinos. I still think that a dinner venue with live entertainment is the best form, and I hope it makes a comeback so that the younger generation learn to appreciate it. Perhaps I'm just sounding old. I tend to stay local, and eat at some excellent restaurants; my favourite Italian being 'Al Fresco' in Whetstone, which has a great buzz and atmosphere. The minute I walk in I'm transported to Rome for a moment as I take in the smell of lovely fresh garlic and all the bustle around me as the waiter escorts me to my table. My favourite local Chinese takeaway is just five minutes away but if I fancy going a bit more upmarket for special occasions, I go to The Good Earth in Mill Hill. I'm not pretentious about food and although I love sampling food from across the globe, I still don't think you can beat good old fashioned English fare. I'm not a bad cook myself, and can make a tasty spaghetti bolognese, sirloin steak – which I think has more flavour than fillet, Sunday roasts and casseroles. If the boys are at home with me for Christmas then I usually do most of the cooking, although I confess to buying the turkey breast all stuffed, basted and ready for the oven – no fancy preparation from me!

If I'm taking a lady out for dinner then I do enjoy going somewhere special. Although I've frequented a few of the top London restaurants over the years, there are some wonderful ones locally, such as West Lodge in Cockfosters and Hanbury Manor in Ware. My all time favourite restaurant used to be Le Radier in Cookham Dene which was run by husband and wife team Lucien and Margaret. Lucien was an extraordinary chef, very tall, at about six feet five, and his petite wife Margaret, who stood no more than four feet 11, was room director. Chris and I used to go there a lot but when we split up I lost touch with them. I often wonder if I'll see their sign up somewhere one day – it's unmistakeable, as Le Radier is an unusual name and one which I've never come across since.

You might be wondering about any women I may have dated over the years while I've been a bachelor, but I'm too much of a gentleman to speak about such matters. Some things are private, but as far as is possible, I've told you my entire story – both the good and bad parts, as promised.

While reflecting on people I miss, I must say that I often hope Frankie Palmer will pop up from out of nowhere. It's sad to lose touch with a good mate. After getting married, blokes often lose touch with one another as life moves forward in a different direction. I wonder if he's still around to see my success, because of all the people I've ever known, he alone understood how badly I wanted to be an actor.

I've had a few regrets in my life, but none more so than the fact that my past relationship with Chris, when we split up, consumed me with so much animosity that all through the boys' formative years, both David and Jonathan were left with resentments towards both of us, in different ways. I am saddened that David has chosen to continue this bitterness towards Chris to the extent that their relationship has been fraught for many years. He is entitled to feel bitter about certain things, but Chris was a really good Mum and it has left me with a deep sadness that we can't be together, as a united family.

When Chris and I patched up our relationship, things seemed to run along smoothly for a while, and we spent a few Christmases in north London with Chris and her husband Clive, and used to visit regularly, but for the past four years David has ceased all communication with his Mum because there are some things he has trouble coming to terms with, and he has found it hard to forgive. The only thing that would make my life complete now, would be a reconciliation between them both. I know from Chris, that she is deeply sorry for the past and finds it difficult to cope with the rift. Sometimes, when Chris and I are in Majorca visiting Jonathan, we wish with all our hearts that David could be with us.

My one true wish would be that I see David and Chris reunited before too long.

So, where do I go from here? I doubt much more excitement will come my way but I seem to be as busy as is possible at my age. This year I shall be starting to tour the theatre circuit in *An Evening With...* which is a show that visits venues all round the country, and where different celebrities are interviewed on stage in front of a live audience. Last year I tried one to see if I'd get on all right in this scenario.

As it transpired, I thoroughly enjoyed myself and the audience made me feel very welcome. This was in a small but very nice seaside town in Norfolk; one of my favourite counties. Hunstanton has a lovely theatre right on the seafront and it reminded me of everything that's good about our British seaside resorts – clean, vibrant and welcoming. Many years ago, I had friends there and used to love walking along the beach at Holcombe Bay to unwind from the stresses of London life. Walsingham is another must while in that area, especially a visit to the magical Slipper Chapel.

Also I get asked to give after-dinner speeches from time to time and the fact I can get up and talk to a room full of strangers is down to my amazing good fortune at being in The Business and without which I would never have lived or fulfilled such a dream. However old I am, I still feel only 25 in my head. Some people might say I've had an interesting life. There's an old saying that if you're lucky in gambling, then usually you're unlucky in love, and I think I've had periods where both have applied. In the late autumn of my life there are still things I want to do: visit Hollywood, home to all my heroes and legends of the big screen. Who knows, perhaps one day soon? I haven't always been tolerant and I'm prone to snap, but, as I get older, I have more time to reflect and slow down (except where driving is concerned) and I tend to stop and think first before putting my foot in things. What I'm trying to say is – ease up and think first.

I hope you've enjoyed reading my story, with all its ups and downs, trials and tribulations, and I hope too, that some of you will have been encouraged by my journey. I set out to demonstrate how anyone can change their life around, whatever the circumstances of their birth, as long as they are prepared to be patient, admit mistakes and move on. We all have dreams and ambitions but you may have to adapt them a little and be satisfied if you achieve a 70% or 80% target. Yes, years ago, I would have loved to go to Hollywood and become a big movie star; that was my original dream but it didn't happen. Nonetheless, I'm very happy and proud of what I have achieved, and if I had to pass on one thing from my experiences it would be this – never stick at any job unless it's the one that fulfils you totally. If you stop to think how many hours of your life are spent at work, it seems ridiculous not to enjoy every minute. I feel privileged to have worked with so many wonderful people who have given me such happiness and pleasure. I know it's hard to believe but I don't think I've had a day as an actor where I clock-watched or wished I could go home early. It saddens me when I hear people say that about their jobs. I've made lots of mistakes, especially in my private life, but then who hasn't? I consider myself blessed. Throughout my journey I've met some amazingly kind and generous people who have helped me. I have my Brother Rats whom I enjoy great companionship and camaraderie with, and I have two wonderful sons who mean everything to me - and I can't ask for anything more.

An East End Life

Postscript

There are many people I have to thank for helping me to get my memoirs published. First and foremost, I owe my ex-wife Chris a huge debt of gratitude, for it was she who suggested I write my story. So far I have not explained that my ghost writer, Christine An Poster is, in fact, my ex-wife! This might be an unusual twist to the tale but she has helped me enormously, to put my life story, ideas and thoughts down on paper.

It was Chris who was determined I should tell, what she considered to be a remarkably successful and compelling life story – from my humble beginnings, to my rise to fame. It is amazing how close we've become in the last 10 years, as we've been able to put the worst parts of our past firmly behind us. Writing this book has taken us on a marvellous journey - of soul-searching, forgiveness and friendship, and I think we've both learnt a lot about ourselves, as well as each other.

Also, I have to thank Shoba Vazirani and Steve Clark of Splendid Books for all their help and encouragement, throughout the many processes involved in getting this book published, and for having so much faith in me. My greatest thanks go to my two sons David and Jonathan, who have given me so much happiness and pleasure over the years, and without whom I can't imagine how my life would have been.

THE RAGAMUFFINS

THE RAGAMUFFINS

ANNA KING

LITTLE, BROWN

First published in Great Britain in 2002
by Little, Brown

Copyright © Anna King 2002

The moral right of the author has been asserted.

*All characters in this publication are fictitious and any
resemblance to real persons, living or dead, is purely coincidental.*

A CIP catalogue record for this book
is available from the British Library.

ISBN 0 316 85826 9

Typeset by Palimpsest Book Production Limited,
Polmont, Stirlingshire

Printed and bound in Great Britain by
Clays Ltd, St Ives plc

Little, Brown
An imprint of
Time Warner Books UK
Brettenham House
Lancaster Place
London WC2E 7EN

www.TimeWarnerBooks.co.uk

For my parents, Peggy and Bill Masterson.
With love, respect, pride and finally gratitude
for always being there when I need them.

These sentiments are echoed by my siblings
(listed in order of age): Tony, Maggi, Billy,
Helen, Michael, Teresa and Peter.

Acknowledgements

To my husband, Dave, for his support during a difficult period in my life. Also to my doctor, Ian Hannah, for putting up with my weekly visits. Without them, I might not have finished this book.

And also a special thank you to my agent, David Grossman, and my editor, Barbara Boote, for their patience and understanding.

CHAPTER ONE

'He's 'ere again, Missus. D'yer want me ter send him packing, or yer gonna give the brat more of Mr Mitson's hard-earned livelihood?' Agnes Handly shot a malevolent glance at the young woman standing behind the shop counter, not bothering to hide the animosity levelled towards her employer.

Ellen Mitson, fully aware of Agnes' feelings towards her, and knowing the reason for it, simply shrugged. 'Mr Mitson is well aware of the boy's visits, Agnes, and, like myself, sees no harm in giving the poor child a few cakes and a loaf of bread now and then. As for your comments concerning the boy's scrounging, you know full well he always works for whatever food he receives.'

Checking the till once more to make sure there was enough change for the day's business, Ellen Mitson shut the drawer with a loud bang that caused the scowling Agnes to jump.

1

Ignoring the surly woman, Ellen crossed to the shop door. Her lips spread wide in greeting, she opened it and smiled at the shivering young boy waiting outside the shop. 'Good morning, Micky. Have you been waiting long?'

The boy grinned back at the young woman, who didn't seem to be much older than himself, and answered cheekily, 'Nah, I only just got 'ere. I was gonna come straight in, 'cos it's blooming freezing out 'ere, but I saw that old bat glaring at me, so I thought I'd better wait till you came ter the door.'

Behind her, Ellen heard Agnes take a sharp intake of breath and, adopting an air of conspiracy, she winked at the boy, saying loudly, 'You mustn't be afraid of Agnes, Micky. After all, she only works here, and has no authority to make any decisions.'

As soon as the words left her mouth, Ellen felt a wave of shame sweep over her. It wasn't in her nature to be nasty, but Good Lord, that woman would make a saint lose patience. Ushering the boy into the warmth of the bakery Ellen said briskly, 'Well now, young man, there isn't any work for you today, but if you'll just wait a minute, I'll get your usual provisions. I can't risk losing a good worker like you.'

Instantly the boy's face lost all trace of merriment. Staring into Ellen's brown eyes he said quietly, 'I don't want charity, Missus. If yer ain't got no work fer me, then I can't take anything from yer.'

Ellen's heart skipped a beat as she gazed into the proud eyes of the shabbily dressed boy. Even though it was the middle of January and bitterly cold, the child wore no coat or gloves. The grimy knitted umper covering the small chest was full of holes, beneath which could be seen a grey linen vest, and Ellen couldn't help wondering what sort of mother would send her child out in such bitter weather without so much as a scarf to warm the boy's dirty neck. Before she could speak, Agnes uttered a sarcastic laugh.

'Bleeding 'ell. A beggar wiv a conscience. That's a turn up fer the books. He probably—'

Ellen rounded on the middle-aged woman angrily.

'This is no concern of yours, Agnes. And speaking of work, isn't there something you can be getting on with? I'm sure Mr Mitson would be grateful for some help. And I know how much you like helping out where my husband is concerned.'

At Ellen's words, the older woman's head snapped back as if she'd been slapped. Lowering her head, she sidled past Ellen with her eyes downcast, yet Ellen could see plainly the look of bitterness etched on Agnes' homely face. Putting out her hand, Ellen caught hold of her arm, saying quietly, 'I'm sorry, Agnes, that was uncalled for, I . . .'

Brusquely Agnes pulled away from Ellen's grasp, muttering, 'Don't yer worry about me, Missus. It'll take more than the likes of you ter upset me feelings. Now if yer'll excuse me, I'll go and see if I'm wanted in the kitchen, 'cos I ain't bleeding well wanted 'ere, am I?'

When the grim-faced woman had disappeared behind the curtain separating the shop from the large bakery at the back, Ellen turned her attention once more to the boy.

3

'Now then, me laddo. I've enough on my hands with Agnes without you giving me a hard time.' She smiled, taking the sting out of her words. 'It's all very well to be independent, it's an admirable trait, but sometimes we have to swallow our pride for our own good. As I said, there's no work for you today, but it'll be a different story tomorrow when the coalman makes his delivery. I keep on at my husband to have a trap door fitted to the basement, like most businesses have, but he keeps forgetting. So until he gets round to doing something about it, it falls on me to carry it downstairs every month. It's a horrible, back-breaking job, and filthy into the bargain, so I'd be much obliged if you'd come along at six tomorrow and help me.'

The boy's face brightened. 'You leave it ter me, Missus. And don't yer worry about 'aving ter help me. I can do it by meself. I might be thin, but I'm strong. Honest, you wait an' see.'

Ellen's lips twitched in amusement at the boy's eagerness. She wasn't about to tell him that Mr Dobbs, the coalman, had been carrying the monthly consignment of coal to the basement for years – for a small remuneration, of course – and he wasn't going to be too pleased when he discovered his monthly bonus of five shillings would no longer be forthcoming. She was going to be popular tomorrow. It was bad enough having to put up with Agnes' sour face day after day, now it looked as if she was going to be in the coalman's bad books as well. Arching her eyebrows she stifled a giggle. Oh, to hell with them both! The child needed the work, and the money, more than Mr Dobbs.

4

'What yer smiling about, Missus?'

Jerked out of her reverie, Ellen replied merrily, 'Nothing, Micky. At least nothing that would be of interest to you. Now then, are you going to take your wages in kind, or would you prefer money today?'

The young boy hesitated for only the briefest of seconds. The smell of the newly baked bread was like torture to his undernourished body; moreover he hadn't only himself to think about. There was someone else with an empty belly who would be waiting anxiously for his return. Hitching up his torn, soiled trousers that came to a halt just below his knees, he answered cheerfully, 'Thanks, Missus. I'll 'ave some grub, please. I'm so hungry, me belly thinks me throat's been cut.'

'Well, we can't have that, can we?' Ellen was already behind the counter putting six currant buns and a large loaf of bread into a brown paper bag. 'Here you are, Micky, you get off home while it's still hot. I'm sure your mother must be very proud to have a hard-working boy like you, though you must try and get a more permanent job now you've left school . . .' Ellen stopped in mid-flow, her hand flying to her mouth as she realised she sounded as if she was poking her nose into the boy's affairs. 'Oh, I'm sorry, Micky, it's no business of mine what you do. After all, I've only known you a few weeks.' Giving a nervous laugh, she said, 'I seem to be putting my foot in it with everyone today, and it's not even six-thirty yet.'

As she spoke, the bell over the shop door tinkled heralding the first customer of the day. Taking his

5

chance to escape any more probing questions, Micky thanked Ellen once again, adding quickly that he would be round bright and early the next day, then quickly vanished into the cold, dark morning.

When the boy left the shop, Agnes returned saying sullenly, 'Mr Mitson wants ter see yer. I'll take over here.'

As Ellen passed through the heavy curtain to the room out back she heard Agnes make some remark about it 'being all right for some', but Ellen had heard such disparaging remarks from Agnes for so long she no longer took any notice.

A blast of heat hit her full in the face as she entered the bakehouse. Arthur Mitson was in the act of taking a batch of piping hot loaves from the oven when he became aware of his wife's presence. Tipping the six crusty loaves from the large, flat shovel on to a nearby workbench, he mopped his sweating brow with the back of his hand and smiled tenderly.

'You all right, love? I've just had Agnes giving me an earful about encouraging beggars. I take it she was referring to the young lad that's been hanging around for the last couple of weeks?'

Ellen stepped forward and placed a kiss on her husband's chubby cheek. 'Don't you worry about me. I can handle Agnes, and yes, she was referring to Micky. The poor little soul. And he's no beggar, Arthur, as you well know. When I told him there wasn't any work for him today he refused to take any form of payment from me, when it's painfully clear to see he's desperate for a decent meal. I had to invent a job for tomorrow, just so he could justify himself in taking a loaf of bread and a half dozen buns.'

Arthur appraised his wife wryly. 'And what, may I ask, is this important job you have lined up for the young lad?'

Casting her eyes over the top of her husband's thinning hair, Ellen said guiltily, 'I pretended I needed help with tomorrow's coal delivery.'

Arthur Mitson's eyebrows seemed to meet across his forehead in a worried frown. 'Oh, now, love, you shouldn't have done that. You know Mr Dobbs has always seen to the coal delivery. He's done it for the last ten years or more.' Shaking his head anxiously he added, 'You've put me in a bit of a spot now, love. I mean, how am I going to explain to the man that his job's been given away to some street urchin?'

Ellen's eyes clouded. 'Micky's no street urchin, Arthur, any more than he's a common beggar. He's just a decent young boy trying to make do the best way he knows how. As for Mr Dobbs, huh!' The mirthless laugh made Arthur flinch. 'I've hardly taken away his job; blooming hell, Arthur, he runs his own business. The only reason he carries the coal down to the basement is because of the five shilling tip you give him. He doesn't do it out of charity, and that young boy needs the money more than Mr Dobbs.' She stared hard at her husband. 'I'll tell you what, Arthur, come tomorrow, I'll tell Mr Dobbs he won't be getting his extra five bob any more, then we'll see what he says. If he still insists on carrying the coal to the basement for nothing, then I'll apologise. But if he makes a fuss, then I'm going to give the job to Micky. What do you think of that?'

7

The thinning head shook from side to side help-lessly as Arthur tried to remember the girl he had married. A girl who had been totally dependent on him. The young woman now facing him bore no resemblance to that memory. His plump face grave, Arthur said anxiously, 'All right, all right, love. Let's not fall out over it. After all, the boy might not even turn up tomorrow.'

Even as he said the words, Arthur knew it was only wishful thinking on his part. Of course the boy would show up. Where else would he get fresh food and five bob for an hour's work? It wasn't that Arthur resented the boy, quite the contrary. He had only met him once, but the lad had seemed a decent sort – not like some of them around these parts. No, it wasn't Micky that was the trouble. If it hadn't been him, it would be someone or something else for Agnes to complain about. Now it seemed that, come tomorrow, he would have Mr Dobbs to contend with as well. Sighing loudly, Arthur Mitson reflected that life would be a lot quieter if only Ellen would act like other busi-nessmen's wives and stay out of his place of work.

Ellen watched her husband's silent battle and felt a wave of compassion for the kindly man. She knew how Arthur loathed any form of confrontation, and was saddened that she had heaped further worries onto his shoulders. The poor man had enough on his plate dealing with Agnes on a daily basis without her adding to his troubles. If it had been anything else she would have backed down, but she had promised Micky a job tomorrow and she wasn't going to go back on her word.

8

'He'll turn up, Arthur,' she said softly.

'I know he will, love,' Arthur replied, the tone of his voice resigned to the inevitable. Then he had an idea. Clearing his dry throat he said carelessly, 'Tell you what. How about you having a lie-in tomorrow? I don't like you having to get up so early, especially when Agnes is here to do the work. There really is no reason for you to get up at the crack of dawn. And don't worry about the boy, I'll see to him, I promise.' He looked into his wife's face, his countenance earnest.

Ellen returned the look, then shook her head wistfully, knowing full well how her husband's mind worked. He was simply trying to get her out of the way tomorrow so that he could create another job for Micky, thereby keeping his promise to see to the boy, and thus appeasing Mr Dobbs into the bargain. Her eyes flickering, Ellen fought down a feeling of resentment. It wasn't Arthur's fault he had no gumption; some people were born that way, but that didn't mean to say she was going to encourage her husband's weakness. Keeping her voice low she said softly, 'You know I don't like lying in bed, Arthur.' Actually, that wasn't quite true. She loved her bed and would happily stay in it all morning if she could do so without feeling guilty. Though she did allow herself a full half hour after Arthur had risen. Then she would stretch out luxuriously, revelling in the opportunity of having the large four-poster bed to herself, even if it was only for a short time. 'Anyway, I like to earn my keep. Speaking of which, Agnes said you wanted to see me. Do you want me to keep an eye on the bread

9

while you see the delivery man? He's due soon, isn't he?'

The factory where Arthur bought his supplies delivered every Tuesday morning. And such was the high regard her husband engendered, partly due to the large order he placed every week, that the owner of the factory always brought Arthur's purchases personally. And once their business was concluded, the two men would indulge in a glass of port upstairs in the drawing room above the shop where their living quarters were situated. 'I know how much you enjoy Mr Stone's weekly visit, as does he.' She paused; then, with a mischievous grin, she said playfully, 'And of course, there's always the added bonus of the usual tipple to warm him up on the journey back to his factory.'

Arthur made a face at his wife, while at the same time sliding another batch of loaves into the hot oven, followed by a large tray of currant buns which he placed on the shelf below the bread. His task completed, Arthur Mitson looked at his young wife, and as always when he saw her, his heart began to race with love – and fear. With love because he worshipped the very ground she walked on, and for the joy she had brought into his life. With fear, because he was constantly afraid she might leave him one day. Even though she had never once, in the nine months they had been married, shown any sign of discontent, Arthur feared there would come a time when she would see him for the overweight, balding, middle-aged man he was. If he had married a woman of his own age, then his fears would have been unfounded.

10

But Ellen was only just eighteen, and even though she wasn't what one would term beautiful, she had a pretty face and a kindly nature.

'What's the matter, Arthur? You look as if you're miles away.' Ellen was gazing at him quizzically.

Blinking the sweat out of his eyes, Arthur answered quickly, 'Oh, you know me, love. Always in a world of my own.' Taking off the coarse linen apron he always wore when baking, he carried on, 'Look, you go back into the shop while I finish tidying up.' Nodding his head towards the custom-built oven he added, 'Those last two trays should see us through the day. If we do start to run low, I can always bake some more.'

Ellen nodded, glad to get away from the stifling heat of the small room. 'I'll let you know when Mr Stone arrives. In the meantime I suppose I'll have to put up with Agnes' delightful company for a while longer.' With a wry smile, Ellen winked playfully at her husband before closing the door behind her.

Alone once more, Arthur lowered his large frame onto a three-legged stool. His face, red from the heat of the oven, was pensive as his mind travelled down a well-worn path of distant memories.

He had struck up a friendship with Eric Simms while still at school and that friendship had remained firm for over thirty years. Arthur had been best man at Eric's marriage to Mary Sumner, a childhood friend of them both. A year after the wedding, Mary had given birth to their only child, a daughter they had named Ellen. Arthur could still remember the awe he had experienced the first time he had held the tiny

11

bundle of humanity, and the overwhelming feeling of love that had been generated inside his body and heart towards the child cradled safely in his arms. Over the years he had watched Ellen grow from a helpless infant into a lovely, warm-hearted young girl, not realising she had taken over his life. He had only existed from one Sunday to the next. A lonely man, with no other friends or family, his entire world became centred on that one day; the day he visited his friends and their captivating daughter.

Then there had come that dreadful night, fifteen months ago, when a fire had swept through the terraced house he had come to look on as his second home, killing his dear friends, and leaving their only child an orphan.

Ellen would have suffered the same fate had she not been staying the night at a friend's house. Naturally distraught, Ellen had turned to Arthur for comfort. She had been sixteen at the time of her parents' untimely death, a very naive and trusting sixteen. Arthur hadn't planned what had happened next – it just had.

At first his only aim had been to comfort the young girl in her hour of need. He was a decent, hardworking man and the only thought in his mind was that of caring and providing for Ellen until such time when she would be able to fend for herself, no matter how long it took. The idea of taking advantage of the young girl in such circumstances would never have entered his mind.

So he had brought her here to recover from her grief. She had no living relatives; it was only natural that

12

Ellen should turn to Arthur, a man she had always known and loved, for help in the darkest moments of her young life.

The first six months had been the worst as Ellen slowly came to terms with her loss. Then Arthur had begun to notice the looks directed at him by his women customers, the same women who, when Ellen had first arrived, had applauded Arthur for his generosity in taking the orphaned girl into his home. The disapproving looks had soon escalated to open hostility and accusations at the state of affairs existing between himself, a middle-aged man, and a young, unchaperoned girl.

Arthur had been horrified. The very nature of the cruel implications had made him physically ill. He had been content just to have Ellen nearby, but he'd had to admit the whole set-up looked decidedly unsavoury to the outside world – the unfounded notions no doubt helped along by Agnes' bitter tongue.

For a brief moment, Arthur's conscience hung heavily on him. There had been a time when Agnes had been more than just an assistant to him. But that had been a long time ago, before Ellen had entered the world and his life. If he'd had any sense at all, he would have fired Agnes years ago. But, being the timid man he was, he had simply taken the line of least resistance and let life slip by. Though he had to admit Agnes hadn't caused him any trouble back then. She had seemed happy enough to continue working for him with no strings attached – until the day he had brought the distraught Ellen into his home.

Overnight, Agnes had turned from a pleasant, easy-going woman, into a hard-faced, bitter harridan. Yet even now, confronted and hounded by the woman whose wages he had paid every week for the past twenty years, Arthur still couldn't pluck up the courage to dismiss his one-time lover who was now the bane of his life.

His shoulders hunched, Arthur gave a long, shuddering sigh of self-pity. He was truly sorry he had caused Agnes so much hurt, but, oh, how he wished the blasted woman could put the past behind her and be happy for him.

The sound of raised laughter coming from the shop wrenched Arthur from his maudlin thoughts and brought a smile to his lips. That was Ellen's laughter he could hear, he would know that sound anywhere. Yet even as he smiled, a sudden stab of fear shot through him like a knife. What if she *did* leave him one day? What would he do then? She was his whole life. Without her he would be nothing.

Gripping the edge of the table for support, Arthur tried to steady his rapid breathing while he reminded himself that it was Ellen who had first brought up the idea of marriage. Faced with the prospect of having to leave her new-found stability and, like Arthur, afraid of facing life without each other, Ellen had tentatively suggested that they should marry in order to silence the wagging tongues. It had seemed the best thing to do at the time. The irony was, that if Agnes had kept her spiteful tongue quiet, he and Ellen would most likely never have even contemplated marriage. And in due course, Ellen would

14

probably have moved out of his home and made a
life for herself – a life that might not have included
him.

Getting to his feet Arthur gave a wry shake of his
head as he realised, for the first time, that he had
Agnes to thank for his wedded state, and wondered
if Agnes was aware of that fact.

'Arthur, Mr Stone's here.'

Arthur jumped. He hadn't heard Ellen enter the
room. 'Oh, oh, all right, love. I'll be right out.' Glad
of the diversion, Arthur planted a wet kiss on Ellen's
cheek saying jovially, 'Thanks, love. I won't be long.'

When the portly figure had disappeared to meet his
visitor Ellen puffed out her cheeks, her hand waving
in front of her face in an effort to combat the heat of
the room. Looking for something to do, she made
herself a mug of tea, then realised the milkman hadn't
called yet. Knowing she had used the last of the milk
earlier she walked over to the back door and looked
out, her ears straining for the sound of the milkman's
horse and cart. After the searing heat of the kitchen,
the cold February wind was a welcome relief, but only
for a few seconds.

Soon shivering with cold, Ellen wrapped her arms
around her waist for warmth, her eyes peering down
the narrow, pitch-black alley, hoping to catch sight
of the swinging lantern that would herald the arrival
of the milkman.

'Morning, Mrs Mitson.'

The sound from the darkness caused Ellen to
stumble back into the doorway.

'Oh, Mr Parker, you made me jump.' Feeling a little

foolish Ellen forced a smile to her face to hide her confusion.

'Sorry about that, Mrs Mitson, I didn't mean to scare you.'

The light from the bakery washed over the man standing before her, making it easy for Ellen to recognise Ted Parker, one of her regular customers.

Smothering a nervous laugh, Ellen replied, 'That's all right. I just came out to see if there was any sign of the milkman.' She heard her words come out in a high-pitched tone and silently chastised herself for acting like a fool.

'Oh, he's just turned into Shore Street, he should be here soon. I'll wait with you if you're nervous.'

The note of mockery in the man's voice caused Ellen to draw herself up to her full height, her manner now defensive. Feeling the rush of blood to her face she replied tersely, 'That won't be necessary, Mr Parker. I'm sure I'm quite safe on my own doorstep. Anyway my husband is within calling distance if I should need any assistance.'

The man tipped his hat towards her. 'I'm sure Mr Mitson's presence is very reassuring. It would take a brave man to tackle him.'

This time there was no doubting the sarcasm in the man's tone, but before Ellen could make a suitable rejoinder, the clip clop of horses' hooves broke the silence of the early morning – and the uncomfortable atmosphere.

'Oh, here he is,' Ellen cried thankfully.

The man stepped back, a sardonic smile on his lips. 'Good morning to you, Mrs Mitson.'

16

'Good morning, Mr Parker,' Ellen said stiffly, painfully aware of her beating heart.

Some time later, as she sat with a mug of tea in her hands, Ellen went over the small incident in her mind, cringing as she recalled how stupid she must have sounded – not only stupid, but childlike. Aware of her still-shaking hands, Ellen gripped the mug tighter. She knew most women would have handled the situation with more aplomb, most of them even enjoying a bit of harmless flirting. But most women of her age had some experience of life and she'd had none.

Suddenly impatient with herself she slammed the mug down on the table with an angry thud. What was the matter with her? Letting a trivial incident upset her so much. She really was acting like a child now. But isn't that what she was? Oh, she might have a wedding ring on her finger, but that didn't make her a woman. She wasn't a woman in any sense of the word, not even in the four-poster bed she shared with Arthur.

Apart from an affectionate cuddle and a peck on the cheek, her husband had never tried to take things any further, thank God!

Appalled at her thoughts, Ellen got to her feet in confusion. She had to find something to do, something that would occupy her. Getting a bowl of water and a scrubbing brush, Ellen got down on her knees and began attacking the floor. But still her mind would give her no peace. For the first time since her wedding, Ellen was experiencing the pangs of discontent. And all because of Ted Parker!

Resting back on her heels, Ellen stared into the

17

empty room. She was only eighteen and married to
man old enough to be her father. She had never know
the thrill of being courted by a man of her own age
never had the chance to experience the world, or th
people in it. And now she never would.

Young, exciting men like Ted Parker were out of he
reach for ever. She must accept that fact and learn t
live with it.

Yet as she scrubbed at the scrupulously clean floo
with renewed vigour, the feeling of resentmen
continued to surge through her body.

If only people hadn't been so nasty about her livin
with Arthur she wouldn't have been in such a rus
to get married. But she mustn't forget what she owe
to Arthur. Without him she might have ended up i
the workhouse.

Her thoughts tumbling around her head she remem
bered the conversation she had unwittingly overhear
a week before the hastily arranged wedding.

She had been rudely awoken by the sound of a fierc
argument. Still half asleep she hadn't recognise
Agnes' voice and when she did, she had crept out c
bed, tip-toeing down the carpeted stairs, hardly abl
to breathe. She hadn't realised at the time why sh
had been so careful not to be heard, but at the bac
of her mind she had known there was somethin
going on between Arthur and Agnes. Sitting on th
bottom step in her nightgown, she had listened i
stunned silence as Agnes had begged Arthur to ca
off the wedding. It had been obvious Agnes was cryin
by the tremor in her voice as she reminded Arthur c
the love they had once shared, a love she sti

rboured for him. Arthur's reply had been too soft
hear. There had followed a strained silence, a silence
great that Ellen was afraid the sound of her rapidly
ating heart would give her presence away. Then
gnes, her voice low and bitter, had said harshly,
on't give me that load of old rubbish, Arthur. If all
r wanted was to give the girl a proper home without
eople gossiping, yer could 'ave offered to adopt her,
fter all, you're old enough to be her father, ain't yer?'

Shaken and disturbed, Ellen had crept back to bed.
e had never mentioned to Arthur that she had over-
ard the heated conversation of that night. But by
od! She wished she had.

Back then, she had been so naive, so unworldly, so
raid of losing her new home and the comforting
esence of Arthur. She had trusted him implicitly.
ow she had to question his true intentions. It was
wonder Agnes hated her so much. Given the
rcumstances, Ellen didn't blame her.

It was as Agnes had said that night. If all Arthur
id wanted was to provide a home for Ellen, then
hy hadn't he done what Agnes had suggested and
lopted her?

Getting slowly to her feet, Ellen sat down at the
ble, her expression thoughtful.

Since her marriage she had begun working in the
op, and the experience of coming into daily contact
ith the colourful people of the East End had quickly
ened her eyes to the ways of the world.

But by the time she had realised she could fend for
rself, Arthur had already made her his wife.

* * *

19

Ted Parker turned at the top of the alley into Mornir Lane, a wry smile on his face. He shouldn't hav tormented the poor cow like that, but he hadn't bee able to resist it. He had been at the end of the alle making his way towards the tram stop when the ligl from the back of the bakery had caught his attentic and, without thinking, he had walked towards tl light. As might any man, only some men might hav taken advantage of the situation. What was h husband thinking about anyway? Letting a your girl, and that's all she was, a girl, stand about in tl doorway of the pitch-black alley. Good God! Anyor could have walked by. It was ten years since the la Ripper murder in 1888, but they'd never caught hir had they? For all anyone knew, the maniac could st be walking the streets. The clanking of the tra brought his mind back to the present. At such a early hour Ted easily got a seat, and, after paying h fare, settled back on the wooden slat, his fa thoughtful. Old Mitson must have thought his bo had come in when Ellen had agreed to marry hir He was old enough to be her father, or grandfath come to that.

Ted gave himself a mental shake and turned h mind to other matters. But he couldn't get the imag of those big, brown, trusting eyes out of his min nor the image of the silky chestnut hair caught u in a bun at the back of the slender neck. A girl Ellen Mitson's age should have her hair falling nat rally, not bound up like some woman twice her ag Oh! To hell with it! What was he concerning himse about anyway? It was no business of his what sl

20

did. Yet, some hours later, as he bantered good-naturedly with customers at his stall in Roman Road market, he still couldn't get Ellen's sweet face out of his mind.

CHAPTER TWO

Micky Masters hurried along the cobbled pavement, clutching the hot parcel close to his chest for warmth, the heady aroma of the package wafting tantalisingly up his nostrils. Ignoring the rough pebbles that dug cruelly into the soles of his feet through his worn boots, the boy turned into a side road, his hurried steps taking him towards a derelict building that stood out amid a pile of rubble that had once been a row of terraced houses. Micky was nearing his destination when he saw the shadowy figure of a man lurking in front of the building he was heading for. With a loud cry Micky sprang forward.

'Oi, you! What yer hanging around 'ere for? Go on, piss off, yer dirty old man.' His grimy face etched with fear, Micky leapt towards the figure barely visible in the dark, winter morning. Stooping quickly he picked up a broken piece of brick and, without thinking, threw it with all his might at the figure.

Startled, the man began to back off, then, hitching
p the collar of his thick coat, he hurried away.

'An' don't come back, d'yer hear me?' Micky
houted after the retreating figure. His heart beating
ast, Micky waited until the man had disappeared
efore running into the ruin calling out fearfully,
Molly? You all right, Moll?' Silence greeted him,
ausing his stomach to lurch and increasing the rapid
eating of his heart. Then, out of the darkness, a soft,
emulous voice replied, 'I'm here, Micky. I'm up here.'

At the sound, Micky's heart slowed its frantic
eating. With a bound he raced towards a piece of
ope dangling from the rotting roof and, with the
exterity of youth, pulled himself up into what had
nce been a bedroom. Peering into the gloom he
issed, 'What yer doing sitting in the dark? Yer scared
e living daylights outta me.'

Relief turning to anger he felt around the dirty floor
or the candle and matches. Finding both he quickly
truck a match and ignited the tallow wick. The flare
f the candle instantly lit up the gloomy room, and
e tear-stained face of the little girl crouched in the
ir corner, her back tight against the wall.

'I'm sorry, Micky. I . . . I had ter put the candle out,
:os that man came again. He was calling for me . . .
n' I was frightened. So I thought if I put the candle
ut, he might think there was nobody here. Why does
e keep coming 'ere, Micky? He scares me . . . I don't
vant yer to leave again. Please, Micky, don't leave me
n me own again.'

Averting his gaze, Micky made a great play of
ulling the warm package from the inside of his

23

jumper muttering, 'I can't, Moll. Yer know I can't. 'ave ter look fer work, an' I can't do that with yo tagging along.' Breaking off a chunk of warm brea he handed it to the forlorn figure, adding in moc cheerfulness, 'C'mon, Moll, 'ave some breakfast. I gc some buns too. An' they're still hot. Go on, 'ave some

The little girl stretched out a grubby hand to tak the food, her hunger overcoming her earlier fear. He confidence returning now her big brother was bac with her, Molly asked through a mouthful of breac 'Yer not going out again, are yer, Micky?'

Micky lowered his head saying gruffly, 'Now, com on, Moll. We've been through this all before. Yer know I've got ter work. How we gonna get a place of ou own if I don't work?'

Molly's lips began to tremble. Spraying out a spittl of dry crumbs she said tearfully, 'But what about tha man, Micky? He always comes when yer not here. H must be watching all the time. What does he wan Micky? Why does he want me?'

Again Micky felt a wave of helplessness sweep ove him. How could he explain to his eight-year-old siste that certain men liked little girls instead of womer Especially when he didn't understand it himself. Wha he did know was that his little sister was in constar danger whenever he wasn't around to protect her. Ye what else was he supposed to do? As he'd tried t explain to Molly, he had to find work. If he didn' how would they survive? At the same time he had t look out for his sister. He was all she had now. It wa up to him to provide for her and to keep her safe. Bu how was he to do both? If there had been work fc

im at the bakery, he would have been gone for hours.
uppose that man had managed to get to Molly during
is absence? The very notion brought a wave of bile
p from his empty stomach into his throat. Forcing
he disgusting thoughts from his mind he broke off
wo more chunks of bread and, handing one to Molly,
aid, 'Look, he's gone now, ain't he? So get on with
er breakfast an' forget about him. I'm 'ere now, ain't
? And he ain't gonna come back while I'm 'ere, is
e?'

Molly immediately brightened. Her childish mind
ased, she forgot her earlier fears and concentrated on
he food her brother had provided.

Micky too was now thinking only of his stomach.
tuffing the warm bread into his mouth with relish
e thought how good it would be to have a hot mug
f sweet tea to wash it down with.

Instead he filled two tin cans from a bucket of tepid
vater he had fetched from the stand pipe at the top
f the street earlier that morning.

In the soft candlelight he gazed lovingly at Molly
s she drank noisily from the tin can. Her thirst
uenched, she gave a loud sigh of contentment.

'That was lovely, Micky, thanks.'

Micky shuffled awkwardly, saying gruffly, 'Don't be
aft, I'm yer brother, ain't I? There's no need ter thank
he fer feeding yer, that's what I'm 'ere for.'

Looking into the large, blue eyes staring at him so
rustingly, Micky felt a lump gather in his throat. Then
is gaze travelled to his sister's matted hair that, when
vashed, fell to her waist in golden curls. But it had
een a long time since Molly's hair, and body, had

seen any soap and water. He too was in dire need o
a good wash. The nearest either of them had ha
recently was a quick sluice over their hands and fac
from the water bucket.

Their breakfast finished, Micky looked at th
currant buns longingly then shook his head. He'd sav
them, and the rest of the bread for later. Not trustin
himself to resist the delicious treat, Micky carefull
put them back in the paper bag. Conscious that Moll
was staring at him anxiously, he gave her a playfu
nudge and grinned. 'All right, I'll stay. You go bac
ter sleep, then later on, I'll take yer down the marke
The bloke on the fish stall said he might 'ave som
work fer me. Yer might as well come along.' Pushin
his face close to hers he laughed, adding, 'Mayb
someone might even give you a job, if we're luck
then we could stay together all the time.'

The enormity of his words banished the smile fron
his face, yet the words had the opposite effect on hi
sister. Her pretty face lighting up, she breathed wist
fully, 'Wouldn't that be wonderful, Micky? D'yer thin
that might happen one day?'

Micky averted his eyes, not daring to meet hi
sister's gaze for fear she might see the desolate loo
on his face. Adopting a lighter mood, he said, 'Look
seeing as how I ain't gotta go back ter the baker
today, why don't we get some sleep? I don't kno
about you, sis, but I could do with another couple o
hours' kip.'

Her eyes stretching wide with happiness, Moll
squealed, 'Oh, yes, Micky. I'd love ter go back te
sleep.'

Less than ten minutes later the young girl was fast asleep. Lying close by her side on top of a soiled mattress they had found in the ruins along with three equally filthy blankets to cover them against the cruel winter months, Micky stared up through the broken roof waiting for daylight to break. His mind, as always when there was nothing else to occupy it, returned to the reason he and Molly now found themselves in such dire circumstances. Blinking to hold back tears that threatened to flow, Micky angrily brushed the back of his hand across his eyes. Bleeding hell! He was going soft. It was lucky Molly hadn't seen him like this. In her eyes, her brother, at the grand age of fourteen, was almost a man. Composing himself, he rested his arm against the back of his head and let his mind wander.

This time last year he and Molly had been at home; home being a modest two-bedroom house in Hoxton. Their parents, like the majority of people living in the East End, had always had to struggle to make ends meet. Their father, a big, gruff man they had both idolised, had worked down the docks. His wage had varied from week to week, but Annie Masters had always boasted she could make a penny stretch further than any other woman in the street. They had been poor, but never hungry or cold, their mother had seen to that. It was only now that Micky realised how much their parents had gone without in order that he and Molly didn't suffer. Now they were both dead, their deaths occurring with such alacrity that Micky still couldn't believe he'd never see either of his parents again. Shifting restlessly he carefully turned so as not

to disturb Molly who, now her mind was at peace and
her belly full, was deep in slumber.

The last time they had seen their father he was going
off to work. He had never returned home. One of the
managers from the docks, accompanied by a police
man, had called at the house, their grave expression
giving no need for words. There had been an accident
involving a crane down at the docks and their father
had been killed.

Annie Masters had never been the same after her
husband's early demise. In order to earn a living, she
had found a cleaning job. But her health had never
been good at the best of times, and she too had died.
For the two children who were still grieving for their
father, the death of their mother so soon after losing
their father had sent them into shock.

Yet further tragedy was about to strike.

Micky, who had just finished school, had imagined
himself capable of looking after his sister once he had
found a job, but the authorities had thought other
wise. Despite anguished protests, the two children had
been taken to the workhouse by two grim-faced offi
cials. Molly had been content enough to have some
kind of stability, but Micky, independent by nature,
had kicked his heels in protest against their new envi
ronment, his agile mind looking for the first oppor
tunity to escape the oppressive building. The children
had been in the workhouse for three months before
the chance of getting out was presented to them. Due
to a severe winter, a good deal of the staff had taken
to their beds with influenza, their misery resulting in
a severe shortage of staff. Micky, who had been biding

his time, had quickly seen the diminished staffing arrangements as a stroke of luck, and had lost no time in taking advantage of the situation. With the remaining staff struggling to keep order, it had been relatively easy to simply walk out of the workhouse with their meagre possessions tied up in a small bundle. They had walked for what seemed an age, with Micky expecting to feel the hand of the law on his shoulders at any second. And when he had realised they were free at last, Micky had been ecstatic. But he hadn't taken into account his little sister. Molly, excited at first, had soon become fretful as the early January evening began to draw in.

Micky too had become increasingly anxious as the darkness closed in around them, his earlier euphoria deserting him as stark reality set in. Alone, cold and hungry, without any money, the two children had quickly found themselves at the mercy of the elements. With Molly crying with fear, cold and hunger, Micky, who was close to tears himself, had become desperate. Then their luck had changed. Just as Micky, worn down by Molly's pitiful cries, had almost decided to go back to the workhouse, they had stumbled on the derelict house. With no light to guide them the two children had felt their way though the pitch-black house, stumbling time and time again as their feet tripped over unseen objects scattered throughout the crumbling building. Guided by touch alone, Micky had found a mattress and a pile of blankets, the filthy condition of their find not becoming apparent until the following day when the morning light had flooded their new dwelling. Even then, they had been so glad to have somewhere to stay, the appalling condition of the house had seemed a palace.

Molly, worn out by the eventful day, had quickly fallen asleep on the heavily soiled mattress. And Micky, bone-tired himself, but knowing that if he allowed himself the luxury of sleep, he and Molly, who hadn't eaten since the bowl of lumpy porridge they had consumed that morning in the workhouse, would wake up ravenous. As tired as he was, Micky knew it would be better if he went out now, while it was still early evening. While Molly slept, Micky crept out of the building, his weary footsteps trudging towards the market in Well Street where, hopefully, he could earn enough money to buy some sorely needed food.

He had managed to earn a couple of shillings by running errands and helping to clear away the stalls for several market traders. He had also been given a bag of ripe apples and pears for his hard work. Knowing the effect such food could have on an empty stomach, Micky had decided to buy a loaf of bread to supplement the impromptu supper. Once again, his luck held, guiding his footsteps towards the bakery at the top of Morning Lane.

There he had met the baker's wife, a lovely young woman who, sensing his need, had refused payment for the bread, insisting she was going to throw it out anyway due to the lateness of the day. Micky had known the young woman was just being kind. Yesterday's bread was always sought after by women eager to buy a loaf or some cakes at half price.

Beside him, Molly stirred restlessly, throwing off her

covering. Gently, so as not to disturb her, Micky pulled the blankets up around her neck, thinking as he did so how horrified his mother would have been to see her beloved children living in such filthy surroundings.

If only that was all he had to worry about! They could survive the way they were living for quite a while. At least, he could; he wasn't so sure about his sister. It would be better once summer came. And he didn't know how long the house they were occupying would remain standing. Why this house alone had escaped being demolished Micky didn't know. But what he was sure of was that, sooner or later, when the council decided what it planned to do with the vacant plot of land, they would waste no time in removing the last remaining house. In the meantime, he had to work and work hard if he wanted to get them into some kind of home where they would be safe. His plans were somewhat hazy, his mind closed to the pitfalls ahead, but one thing he couldn't shut from his mind was the man. His lips tightened, his arms automatically going around the small innocent form lying beside him as he thought about the stranger.

He had turned up ten days ago. At first Micky had feared he was an official come to take him and Molly back to the workhouse, but the man had been quick to reassure Micky that that was not his intention. The man, who had introduced himself as Kenneth Wells, had gone out of his way to be friendly to the two orphans, and for the first time since running away, the children had begun to feel safe. He had begun by

31

bringing food and making the children feel as if they had found an ally – and Micky hadn't been too proud to admit that they needed an adult in their lives. Every day the man would turn up, always bringing some treat with him, usually food, his manner genial and sympathetic to their plight. A week later, when the children had become comfortable in his presence, the man had sent Micky off on an errand. The youth, not having any reason to distrust their new-found friend, had gone off willingly. On his return, he hadn't noticed that his normally bubbly sister was very quiet, almost subdued. The next day, when Micky, a florin clutched tightly in his hand, prepared to go off on another errand, Molly had grabbed his hand, her eyes imploring him not to go. To his everlasting shame, when Molly had needed him most, he had let her down. But something had nagged at him until, cursing himself for a fool, he'd raced back to the building. The sight that had met his eyes would remain with him until his dying day. Closing his eyes tightly, he tried not to remember the vision of the man holding Molly on his lap. His dear, sweet Molly, her tiny frame rigid with fear as the man slobbered over her face, while his hands . . . Oh, God! Those hands. Hands that had been stretched out in friendship and been gratefully accepted, had turned into vile, despicable instruments fondling and groping the young, innocent child Micky had left in his care.

The image had been burned into his brain for ever. At the time, his mind had seemed to close down. The next thing he remembered, he was on the man's back, screaming, kicking and punching with all the strength e possessed. Taken by surprise by the unexpected, erocious assault, the man had fled. For the next two days Molly hadn't left her brother's side, nor had he wanted her to. But they'd had to come back to reality. n order to survive, Micky had to work, and he couldn't work with Molly alongside him. So he had come up with a plan.

Together they had carried the mattress and blankets o the top of the house. Then they had removed the ickety staircase, the rotten wood coming away easily n their hands. Micky had then attached a rope to the only solid beam left in the upper part of the house, nabling him and Molly to climb up to their new living quarters, and then pulling the rope up after them, thus epelling any unwanted visitors. It wasn't an ideal olution, but it was the best he could do for now. udging by the man's presence outside the house this morning, it was obvious that Kenneth Wells, if that was his real name, wasn't going to be put off so easily. The only consolation was that Molly, innocent and rusting, simply thought the man only wanted to kiss nd cuddle her, like her dad used to do before she vent to bed. But even very young children knew what hey did and didn't like. Molly had loved her father learly and she knew that his loving embraces bore no esemblance to the way that horrible man had slobered all over her. She had been badly frightened by he man's unwanted attentions, but fortunately was till oblivious of his true intentions.

Forcing his mind to other matters, Micky thought head to tomorrow. The baker's wife hadn't said how nuch he would be paid for the morning's work, but

33

whatever she offered would be fair. He only wished he hadn't had to lie to her. Then again, he hadn't actually lied. She had assumed, quite normally, that Micky had a home and family, and Micky had simply chosen not to enlighten her on that small matter. He wondered briefly how old she was. She only looked about sixteen, but she must be older than that. Though he had nearly put his foot in it on meeting the baker himself. Seeing them together Micky had naturally assumed the baker was the girl's dad. Luckily for him Ellen Mitson had immediately introduced the portly man as her husband.

He had been very pleasant and friendly too. Letting out a soft sigh, Micky tried to get some sleep. If only there was a proper job to be had at the bakery. No matter how menial the work, Micky would jump at the chance of having a regular wage to look forward to. That was his dream. To have somewhere for him and Molly to live without fear. To have their own front door, to sleep once again between clean sheets, to be able to have a proper bath and clean clothes to put on. There were plenty of boarding houses in the East End where he could find a room with no questions asked. All he needed was that elusive job. Flopping onto his side, his face tilted up at the hole in the roof, Micky waited for daybreak. He would give Molly another hour then take her with him around the local factories and shops. There must be somewhere that was looking for a strong, willing boy.

An idea struck him, bringing a smile to his lips. Maybe the baker's wife knew of somewhere. After all she said he should look for a job. It was worth asking.

34

xcited at the notion, Micky closed his eyes, waiting
or Molly to wake up. But when, some time later,
Molly awoke, she found her big brother fast asleep.
miling happily, the little girl snuggled against the
warm body of the boy who, in her eyes, was her
rovider and protector. Nothing bad could ever
appen to her while Micky was around.

CHAPTER THREE

'Five bob!' Micky looked down at the two, shiny hal
crowns nestling in his blackened palm, his fac
stretched incredulously. Shaking his head h
muttered, 'This can't be right, Missus. Not just fer a
hour's work. Yer must 'ave made a mistake.'

Ellen, her own face a picture of happy satisfactior
smiled. 'There's no mistake, Micky. That's the amoun
my husband paid the coalman – until I offered the jo
to you.'

Two bright blue eyes stared out of the blackene
face in bewilderment. 'But yer said you always ha
ter shift the coal by yerself.' His voice, still quiverin
with excitement at the money in his hand, now hel
an accusation. 'Did yer just pretend yer had ter shi
the coal yerself, just so yer could give me the money
'Cos, like I told yer before, Missus, I ain't taking n
charity, not even from you.'

Finding herself on the offensive, Ellen shifte

guiltily. 'Now, Micky. It isn't quite like that. It's true
did lie, and I'm sorry for that, but that money in
your hand is money you worked hard for. You're enti-
led to it. I've always resented the money my husband
nsisted on paying the coalman, a man who owns his
own business, when there are many people who, to
my mind, need the work and the money more than
he does.'

Micky held Ellen's gaze, his need for the money
wrestling with his conscience. Slowly his fingers
closed over the coins. He would be mad to throw it
back, especially when he and Molly needed it so much.
But he hated being treated as a charity case. It was
only for Molly's sake that he was prepared to swallow
his pride and take the money. But instead of feeling
a sense of worth for a job well done, Micky felt cheated
somehow. Not only because of the money, which was
almost a full week's wage for some men, but because
of the young woman who had given it to him. He had
thought they could become friends. He had wanted
to please her and had thought he was helping her by
taking on the job. Now it seemed she only felt sorry
for him. To her, he, Micky, was just another street
urchin, and he was surprised and somewhat bewildered by the unfamiliar emotions swirling inside his
chest.

'Micky?' Ellen was staring at him anxiously. They
were both of the same height, and, with his entire face
blackened with coaldust, the only way the young boy
could be recognised was by his eyes. And for the first
time, Ellen was struck by their bright, almost cobalt
blue. For a few seconds they stared at each other, the

boy and the young woman. No words were spoken. Ellen appeared to be mesmerised by the boy's unflinching stare. Then a jolt rippled through her body bringing her sharply back to her senses.

Good Lord! What was happening to her? First she had made a fool of herself in front of Ted Parker, now she was being intimidated by a mere youth.

'I'll be off then, Missus. Thanks ... yer know ...' Micky nodded at his closed palm. 'It was kind of yer.'

Ellen gulped. 'I wasn't being kind, Micky. The job had to be done, and I thought you deserved the work. Call by tomorrow, and I'll see if there's anything else needs doing.' Regaining her composure, Ellen gave a small laugh. 'I hope you told your mother the nature of the job you had lined up for today. Goodness, you look as if you've spent a morning up a chimney. Go on now, get yourself home. I expect your mother will have a hot bath waiting for you.'

Micky nodded, his eyes now averted. He wished he could tell Mrs Mitson the truth. But even if she seemed very young, she was still an adult, and might turn him and Molly over to the authorities, thinking she was doing it for their best interests.

'Yeah, you're right, Missus. I'd better be off.' Micky hesitated, his thoughts jumbled. Then he asked hopefully, 'I was wondering if yer knew of anyone that wanted a young lad for regular work?' Giving a nervous laugh, he added, 'Like yer said yesterday, now I've left school I should be looking for a permanent job.'

Ellen thought hard. There was nothing she would like better than to take the boy on permanently, but here simply wasn't the work. It was only a small bakery. In fact they were overstaffed since she had begun working in the shop. Arthur and Agnes could run the business perfectly well between them, as they had done for many years before she had arrived. As Agnes was always pointing out to her.

Then a thought struck her. Walking slowly with Micky to the door she said quietly, 'I can't think of anyone off hand, Micky, but I'll certainly ask around.' Conscious of Agnes' curious stare, Ellen continued. Look, let me have a word with my husband, and we'll see what we can do, though I can't promise anything.'

Micky nodded. 'Can't ask fer more than that, Missus. Ta. See yer in the morning.'

'Yes, all right, Micky. Take care. 'Bye.' Ellen stood at the door until the slim figure had disappeared into the morning gloom.

'If yer don't mind shutting the door, I'd be ever so grateful. Only it's bleeding freezing fer us old 'uns. The cold gets right inter me bones. That's if it ain't no trouble, like.'

The sarcasm in Agnes' voice was lost on Ellen, whose thoughts were elsewhere. Closing the door, she said absent-mindedly, 'I'm just going to make some tea. Look after things please, Agnes.'

Agnes glared after the retreating figure. 'I think I can manage, Missus. After all, I've only been doing the job fer twenty years. And I wouldn't say no ter a cuppa, if there's one going.'

Her mind still elsewhere, Ellen replied amiably, 'Yes, of course, Agnes. I'll bring one out to you.'

Taken by surprise, Agnes mumbled, 'Oh, right
Yeah, thanks.'

Arthur, as usual at this early hour, was busy baking
Glancing up, he looked at his wife and gave her a cur
nod, before returning his attention to the job in hand
Ellen sighed impatiently, then shrugged. So he wa:
still sulking, was he? Well, let him. Putting the kettle
on, Ellen thought back to earlier that morning wher
Mr Dobbs had arrived, his sooty face wreathed ir
smiles. That was until Ellen informed him his serv·
ices in unloading and carrying the monthly supply o
coal to the basement would no longer be required
Arthur had been present at the time, but instead o
backing her up, he had launched into a spate of apolo
gies. Reliving the scene Ellen felt a fresh burst of anger
Watching and listening to the pitiful spectacle, Eller
had cringed. And when Mr Dobbs, his countenanc·
no longer amiable, had begun a blistering attack or
Ellen for what he termed an act of treachery, Arthur
instead of making a stand and taking his wife's side
as most men would have done, had quickly washec
his hands of the whole affair, placing the situatior
squarely on Ellen's shoulders. Ellen could still feel th·
shame at seeing her husband, the man who wa:
supposed to put his wife first, humiliating himself
She had thought that hearing Mr Dobbs berate he
would have infused some gumption into Arthur. Bu
he had let her down and for that she would neve
forgive him, nor respect him ever again. Ignoring th·
bulky form, Ellen set about making the morning tea

'Well! Don't you have anything to say?' Arthur'
voice cut into the silence of the stuffy room.

Turning to face him, Ellen looked at the plump, red
ace, filled with self-righteous indignation and immediately went on the defensive. 'Excuse me, Arthur?'
he answered, her voice deceptively soft. 'I'm not sure
what you mean. Unless of course you're referring to
that embarrassing spectacle you made of yourself this
morning.'

Still smarting after being, as he thought, put into an
impossible position, Arthur flinched as the truth
struck home. His lower lip quivering, he tried to
restore his humiliated ego, even though, deep down,
he knew full well he had disgraced himself. Not only
in the eyes of Mr Dobbs, whose scathing look had said
more than mere words could ever convey, but also in
the eyes of the one person he so desperately wanted
to impress. But instead of admitting his shame, Arthur,
like most ineffectual men, tried instead to shift the
blame on to the nearest person, and that person was
Ellen.

Drawing himself up to his full height he said angrily,
'You made me look a right fool in front of Mr Dobbs.
And all for some little guttersnipe. Huh! It says a lot
for me, doesn't it? How do you think I felt with you
taking over the conversation, pushing me out of the
way as if I counted for nothing . . .'

Ellen rounded on her husband, her fierce anger
more than a match for Arthur's feeble blusterings.
'How do I think you felt?' she shouted. 'How do you
think I felt having to witness my husband, the one
man I thought I could depend on for support, practically grovelling to the coalman, apologising over and
over until I felt I would be sick with shame. Even if

you didn't agree with me, you should have stood b
me; that's what husbands do. I wouldn't have minde
you having a go at me in private, but to take Mr Dobb:
side against your own wife, well that says it all, doesn
it, Arthur?'

Her voice had risen and Arthur, already humiliate
once today, didn't want everyone in the shop hearin
his wife laying into him as well. Adopting a differer
tack, he put his hands up in a feeble attempt to stifl
Ellen's tongue. 'All right, all right, love. There's n
need to broadcast our private lives to everyone.'

Coming nearer he laid a tentative hand on Ellen'
arm, his face now sheepish, but Ellen, who onc
would have relented, now shook off the offendin
hand with disdain. 'There you go again, Arthu
Thinking of yourself as usual. All you're worrie
about is saving face, but I think it's a bit late for tha
don't you?'

The colour in Arthur's face deepened, and it ha
nothing to do with the heat of the kitchen. His stomac
churning, he tried once again to pacify Ellen. 'Pleas
love, let's leave it, eh? I mean . . .' He uttered a smal
nervous laugh. 'There's no point in going on about i
is there? I mean, it's done now, so let's forget abou
it, all right, love?'

Ellen's gaze remained stony. In their short marrie
life, there had been plenty of times she had kept quie
or given in, just to keep the peace and to keep Arthu
happy. But that had been when she was still in aw
of the man who had saved her from the workhous
and was willing to be a pliable and good wife. Bu
things had changed. *She* had changed. With a sudde

art of awareness, Ellen knew that her life would
ever be the same again.

Arthur, too, was experiencing the same emotions,
id felt a surge of blinding panic. What he had always
ared now seemed to be in danger of happening. His
verish mind turning this way and that, he tried to
ink of the best way of defusing the situation. Should
e be compliant and ask Ellen's forgiveness? Or
iould he do what he should have done that morning
id make a stand? To be the strong man Ellen wanted
m to be. The silence in the stifling room was
coming unbearable, then Arthur made his decision.
nfortunately it was the wrong one. Adopting a
anly stance, he said firmly, 'Now then, Ellen. I think
ve been very patient with you over this sorry affair.
et you humiliate me in front of a very close friend,
st to keep you happy, but no more. In future the
inning of the business will be mine and mine alone.
ou may continue to serve in the shop, if you wish,
it you will disassociate yourself from making any
cisions and you will also sever all ties with the boy.
iere'll be no more encouraging the boy to come here
r hand outs in return for some small job that could
sily be done by either you or Agnes.' Well into his
ride, Arthur began to pace the room, his hands
asped behind his back.

He should have looked instead at his young wife
see her reaction to his words. But he was too far
to his new persona to notice the danger signs in
len's face. 'I know it will be difficult for you, so I
ink it would be wiser if you stayed upstairs
morrow and let me deal with the lad. Don't worry,

43

I'll let the boy down gently. Now then, why don't w
kiss and make up.' Stretching his arms wide he smilec
'Come here, you silly little thing. Come and give n
a cuddle, and we'll forget all about it.'

Her entire body seething, Ellen, not trusting herse
with what she might do or say if she stayed here
moment longer, shot Arthur a withering look, an
said, 'You know what you can do with your cuddl
Arthur. Oh, I'm getting out of here. I can't bear to t
in the same room with you.' Grabbing her coat fro
behind the back door Ellen shrugged her arms int
the heavy sleeves, for once not noticing the stiflir
heat of the kitchen.

Behind her Arthur hovered anxiously. 'Hang o1
love. Where d'you think you're going at this time d
the morning?' Frantic now, he began gabbling. 'No'
look, love, there's no need for this. You're blowing tl
whole business out of proportion.' Unthinking, h
grabbed hold of Ellen's arm. With an angry twist st
broke free and without bothering to look back, st
strode out of the back door into the dark alley.

Never in her life had Ellen walked the streets i
the dark, either in the morning or at night. Yet
would have taken a brave man to accost her in tl
mood she was in. Gradually, her anger turned int
a new emotion, a feeling of elation, but more tha
that, for the first time she felt a rush of self-respec
No longer would she be dependent on Arthur; st
didn't need him any more. She knew now she wa
well capable of looking after herself. But the feelir
of euphoria was shortlived and quickly replaced b
a wave of shame. Her footsteps slowed as a wave c

emorse swept over her. Poor Arthur. It wasn't his
ault. After all he had done for her and this was the
hanks he got. Her steps dragged as reality returned.
he had to go back. There was nowhere else for her
o go. She had no one to turn to. Even if she had,
he would never be so cruel as to just walk out
vithout a word. She owed Arthur more than that,
nuch more.

'We must stop meeting like this.' A deep voice cut
hrough her thoughts.

Her head coming up sharply, Ellen felt her body
elax when she saw who the man was. With a genuine
mile, she said merrily, 'Good day, Mr Parker. And
ow are you this fine morning?'

Ted Parker tipped his hat back further on his head
o see better, thinking at first he had mistaken Ellen
or someone else. But the light from the end of the
lley reassured him that this bright, seemingly care-
ee woman was indeed Ellen Mitson. Yet the change
n her compared to yesterday's encounter was so
narked that Ted wondered if she was unwell.

'You all right, Mrs Mitson? You seem different
oday. Has something happened?'

Ellen was standing so close to the man their breaths
ningled in a fog of white mist. The semi-darkness
overed them like a cloak and Ellen felt again the pull
f attraction. In spite of the fact they were in an open
pace, that the dawn was just breaking and the sound
f people's voices as they set about the start of a new
ay floated all around them, never had Ellen experi-
nced such a feeling of intimacy. Gathering her wits,
he spoke crisply. 'I'm fine, Mr Parker, but thank you

for asking'. Ellen had to tip her head to see Ted'
concerned gaze.

'Well, in that case, I'd best get off, else I'll miss m
tram.' Again tipping his hat, Ted Parker made to wal
on, puzzled by the sudden change in Ellen Mitson
Moments later his eyebrows rose in amazement whe
he felt himself being halted in his tracks by a sma
but strong hand on his arm.

'You own your own stall, don't you, Mr Parker?'

Thoroughly confused now, Ted looked down int
Ellen's enquiring eyes. 'Yeah, that's right. But what . .

Linking her arm through his, Ellen smiled broadl
'I was just wondering if you could do me a favou
Mr Parker. Oh, and please call me Ellen . . . Ted.'

Feeling more confident than she had ever felt in he
life, Ellen hugged the muscled arm tighter as sh
walked with Ted towards the tram stop, chatting awa
as if she had known the handsome man all her life.

Her newly found confidence would have bee
shaken if Ellen had known she and Ted Parker wer
being sharply observed by a pair of malicious eyes.

CHAPTER FOUR

gnes, her weathered face alight with mischief,
anded over a penny change to the last customer from
e early morning rush. 'There yer go, Edna,' she said.
orry yer had ter wait, but Miss Fancy Pants decided
r take herself off somewhere.' Tapping the side of
er nose Agnes winked, leaned over the counter then,
wering her voice, she added, 'Now I'm not one ter
ssip, Edna, am I?'

Edna Brown, a regular visitor to the bakery, shook
er head in agreement, while privately wondering
ho Agnes thought she was kidding. Everyone knew
gnes Handly was the worst scandalmonger in the
strict. But not wanting to miss out on a bit of juicy
ssip she said vigorously, 'Nah, Agnes, yer ain't like
at. An' yer know I can keep a secret. Come on,
oman, spit it out.'

Looking over her shoulder towards the kitchen to
ake sure Arthur wasn't in earshot, Agnes preened

herself and said gleefully, 'Seen her with me own tw
eyes I did. I'd just popped out ter see if the milkma
was in sight, 'cos I was gasping fer a cuppa, an' wha
d'yer think I saw?' She paused, relishing the momen
a moment she'd been waiting for ever since that litt
madam had turned her world upside down. 'Her lady
ship, walking down the street, as bold as brass, wit
that Ted Parker. Arm in arm they was, talking an
laughing for all the world to see, like they was
respectable couple walking out, and poor Mr Mitsoi
not knowing anything about what his wife's gettin
up to.'

Edna Brown looked at Agnes with distaste. Sh
didn't like her, not many people did. Yet Agnes ha
once been popular, always good for a laugh and a ch.
– until young Ellen had arrived on the scene. Nov
Agnes was a bitter, middle-aged woman, whose onl
enjoyment in life was in trying to put young Elle
down at every possible opportunity. But Agnes hadn
finished yet.

'I don't know what ter do fer the best, Edna. I mea
ter say. Should I tell Mr Mitson what's going on, c
keep quiet? What would you do in my place?'

Engrossed in their conversation, neither woma
heard the tinkle of the bell heralding another custome
in the shop until an icy voice, dripping with scor
snapped angrily, 'I know what I'd do, Agnes Handl
I'd keep me bleeding gob shut, before someone doe
it fer yer, yer spiteful old cow.'

Both women jumped as the familiar voice filled th
bakery.

Whirling round, Agnes opened and shut her mout

48

ke a fish out of water. 'Oh . . . sorry, Nora, I didn't
e you there,' she spluttered, her face reddening in
e force of Nora Parker's anger.

The newcomer looked at the woman behind the
unter, her sharp eyes taking in every detail of
gnes' body from top to toe. As usual, Agnes was
essed in the drab brown skirt and black shiny
ouse she always wore in the shop. Her hair, scraped
ck from the plain face was a dull brown, liberally
reaked with grey strands. For a split second, Nora
arker felt a spark of sympathy for Agnes. Everyone
new of her feelings for Arthur Mitson, but even
enty years ago, Agnes Handly had been a plain
oman, and the passing years hadn't been kind to
er. What chance had she against the youth and
auty of Ellen Mitson? Then Nora remembered the
ndictive words she'd overheard, and any sympathy
e might have had for Agnes disappeared in a
newed rush of anger.

Hugging her thick black shawl tight to her chest she
apped, 'That's bleeding obvious, otherwise yer
ouldn't have been shouting yer mouth off about my
ed. And I'll tell yer something else, Agnes Handly.'
he short, stout woman bristled furiously. 'My Ted
uld 'ave any girl he wants. He don't 'ave ter go
iffing round a married woman, like some men. So
u mind what yer say in future, understand?'

Caught out, Agnes had no choice but to try and
uff her way out of the awkward situation. 'Now,
ng on a minute, Nora. All right, so I shouldn't 'ave
en talking about your Ted, but I know what I saw
id—'

'I don't give a monkey's what yer think yer saw. my Ted was with young Ellen, then it was all perfect innocent. Not that you'd think that way. Yer've 'ad in fer that young girl from the start, an' we all kno the reason why . . . don't we?'

Caught between the two sparring women, Edr Brown stood back to enjoy the spectacle of Agne getting a taste of her own medicine, but her enjoy ment was shortlived.

Desperate for some kind of diversion, Agne turned on the hapless bystander. 'Is there anythin else yer want, Edna?' Edna Brown squirmed uncom fortably before shuffling grudgingly out of the warr bakery.

Left alone, the two women eyed each other, neithe willing to give ground. 'Well, d'yer want somethin or is this just a social visit?' Agnes, back in contre once more, glared at the equally angry woman on th other side of the counter.

Still fuming at hearing her beloved son's nam muddied, Nora Parker wrestled with her conscienc There was nothing she'd like better than to tell Agne Handly where to stick her bread, but Arthur Mitson bakery was the best one in Hackney. Besides, it wasn as if her custom was lining Agnes' pockets, and sh had no quarrel with Arthur. Squaring her shoulder she said waspishly, 'No, it ain't a social visit. If I wa wanting a bit of company, I wouldn't come ter yo for it. I'll 'ave a large cob, and half a dozen buns . . please.'

Her face sullen, Agnes wrapped the bread and bur and was placing them on the counter when Arthu

me through from the kitchen into the shop, a
orried frown on his face.

'Have you seen Ellen, Agnes? Oh, hello, Nora, I
dn't see you for a minute. How are you?'

Shooting a warning glance in Agnes' direction, Nora
arker answered pleasantly, 'I'm fine, thanks, Arthur.
nd yourself?'

Forgetting his troubles for the moment Arthur
niled. 'Oh, same as always, Nora. Hot and flustered.'
ot one for idle chatter, Arthur trailed off self-
nsciously.

Her heart going out to the kindly man and knowing
gnes would stick her poison in at the first available
pportunity Nora said casually, 'I saw your Ellen a
tle while ago, Arthur. Me an' my Ted met her outside
out . . . Ooh, ten, fifteen minutes ago. She said she
ncied a bit of fresh air, so my Ted offered ter stay
ith her. He's like that, my Ted. Didn't want ter leave
llen on her own, not round these parts, even if it did
ake him late fer work. Not that it matters what time
e gets ter Hoxton, seeing as he's his own boss, like
erself, Arthur.' She smiled at Arthur with genuine
ndness. Seeing the look of relief that crossed the
lump face, Nora shot a gloating look at the seething
gnes thinking, 'That's scuppered your plans, yer
iteful old cow.'

The bell over the shop jingled again and all eyes
rned to the door as Ellen entered the bakery. Sensing
e strained atmosphere, Ellen looked from one face
the other, her conscience stabbing at her like a knife.
ora quickly came to her rescue.

'Hello, love. I was just telling Arthur 'ere how me

and Ted met yer outside and stopped fer a bit of natter. I hope he walked yer back before he went t work.'

Ellen shot her a grateful look. 'Yes he did, Nor thanks.' Guilty at her earlier treatment of Arthur, Elle strolled over to her husband's side and took hold his hand. 'Actually I was trying to talk Ted into givir young Micky a job. I'm afraid I made a bit of nuisance of myself.' Looking back at Nora, Ellen sai sheepishly, 'Will you tell Ted I'm sorry for waylayir him in the street, please, Mrs Parker. He's much to nice to tell me off for putting him on the spot.'

Nora patted Ellen's arm affectionately. 'Don't b daft, love. He may be kind, but he ain't no fool whe it comes ter his business, but I'll tell him what y said.' Putting her purchases into a straw basket sh smiled widely at Ellen. 'I'll have ter get a move o or I'll be late fer me cleaning job. Not that I 'ave t work . . .' She directed a triumphant look at the no dejected Agnes. 'My Ted's always telling me ter sta at 'ome and put me feet up, 'cos he earns enoug without me working. But like I said ter him, What el: would I do with meself all day? Nah! I like ter kee busy. Still, it's nice ter know there's someone ter loc after yer when you're getting on in life; not like som poor cows with no family or friends ter fall back o Anyway, I'll be off now. 'Bye love, 'bye Arthur.'

The deliberate snub to Agnes was not lost on Elle but Arthur, his mind put at rest, didn't notic Squeezing Ellen's hand he asked tentatively, 'All righ love?'

Ellen smiled at him. 'Yes, Arthur, I'm fine now.

just needed to get out for a while. I feel much better now.' Turning to Agnes she said, 'If you want a break, Agnes, I'll take over now.'

Her teeth gritted tightly, Agnes answered scathingly, 'I've only been working an hour. I think I can last a bit longer before I need a break.'

Ellen and Arthur exchanged amused glances, their differences forgotten. Relieved beyond measure that his fears had been unfounded, Arthur placed an affectionate arm around Ellen's shoulder. 'In that case, Agnes, I think me and Ellen will take our break now while you hold the fort. It may be just on eight, but we've been up since five-thirty.'

Humiliated beyond measure Agnes lowered her eyes and began to busy herself rearranging the already carefully stacked bread.

As soon as Ellen and Arthur had left Agnes stopped in her task. Praying there would be no more customers for a few minutes so she could have some time to herself she let her body sag. Then, like a woman twenty years her senior, she wearily sank down on the three-legged stool behind the counter, her mind in turmoil. When she had seen Ellen and Ted Parker together she had been sure she'd finally got one over on the young scut who had ruined her dreams of one day marrying the man who had been the centre of her life since she was nineteen – over twenty-three years ago. Twenty-three wasted years.

She had just turned nineteen when she'd come to the recently opened bakery in search of a job. At that time, Tom Mitson, Arthur's father, had been in sole charge of the baking while Arthur served in the shop.

Wanting to train his only son in the same line of work, Tom Mitson had taken Agnes on so that Arthur would be free to learn his father's trade. Tom had been a widower for five years and Agnes had become almost like a daughter to her employer. He had been a lovely man, kind and compassionate, always treating Agnes like family instead of an employee. She had been devastated when he had died of a heart attack at the age of fifty.

Arthur too had been beside himself with grief and, for a time, Agnes had thought the distraught young man would go to pieces. If Agnes hadn't been there for him, to offer a shoulder to cry on, to listen to his outpouring of grief any time of the night or day coupled with genuine affection and support, Arthur would have shut himself away and let the business, the business his father had spent so many years building, go to the wall. At the time, all Agnes had wanted was to see Arthur through his grief. Then, about a month after his father's death, Arthur had asked Agnes to stay the night and she had been only too happy to agree. The affair had been brief. While Agnes had fallen head over heels in love, it had soon become increasingly obvious that Arthur was regretting the affair. He would find excuses to avoid being alone with her and, being the timid man he was, he hadn't been able to pluck up the courage to address the problem. Loving him as she did, Agnes had ended it, simply to ease his peace of mind. She had imagined that, given time and space, Arthur would come to love her as much as she loved him. But that had never happened. Over the years Agnes had been forced to accept that Arthur would only ever see her as a friend and she had been content with the arrangement. Like most people, just being in close contact with a loved one had kept her happy.

Then he had brought the young, frightened girl into their lives, and Agnes had known immediately the reason why Arthur had never married. She had known where he spent most of his weekends, for he would regale her with all the news of his friends, and their beautiful daughter. Agnes had listened dutifully, glad he was spending his spare time with old friends. But how could she have imagined that one day the child Arthur was besotted with would end up as his wife. Shaking her head in misery, Agnes lowered her head into her hands as she remembered that she had encouraged Arthur to keep in contact with his friends, believing that by doing so there would be less chance of him meeting another woman.

When his friends had died, it was Agnes who had helped him, once again, to deal with his grief. And although she had been genuinely sorry that the couple had died in such horrible circumstances, nonetheless she had been grateful to be needed again. She had even welcomed his decision to bring the orphaned Ellen into his home. But the moment she had clapped eyes on the pretty young girl and seen the open adoration shining from Arthur's eyes whenever he looked at her, Agnes had known all the years she had devoted to the man she loved had been in vain. But what caused Agnes the most pain was the certain knowledge that she had forced the hasty marriage. If she hadn't started to spread rumours, Ellen would have grown up eventually and moved on and out of Arthur's life. But no, she had been so eaten up with jealousy she hadn't been able to stop her tongue from cultivating vicious gossip. Banging her hands on her knees in despair she whispered to the empty shop, 'Why couldn't you have kept your big gob shut? If you'd welcomed Ellen with open arms it would have been easy enough to bring up the suggestion of adoption to Arthur and he would have done anything to keep Ellen by his side.' And, in due course, she, Agnes, might have been able to persuade Arthur to make his family complete by marrying her. All this could have been possible, if she had made a friend of Ellen. Because, to be fair, the young girl had a kindly nature and would have been grateful to have an older woman to talk to, especially at a time when she was still getting over the loss of her mother. But Agnes, hurt beyond words and feeling betrayed, had turned into a nasty, spiteful woman. She knew too that Arthur wanted her out of the shop, but was too timid to sack her and that the new Mrs Mitson might not have any such qualms.

The change in Ellen since her marriage was incredible. During the past few months she had become more confident, more at ease with the customers, and had toughened up considerably. Judging by the fierce argument she had overheard about the coalman and the subsequent sighting of Ellen arm in arm with Ted Parker, Agnes was sure that Ellen was beginning to regret tying herself to an older man. The only hope Agnes had now was that the marriage would fail. Yet even if it did, unless she changed her ways she would never have Arthur.

Like Ellen, Agnes had also changed, but she had changed for the worse. She didn't even like herself and if she didn't, how could she expect anyone else to?

Was it too late to change? More importantly, could she change?

The bell sounded and immediately Agnes rose to her feet, a smile pasted on to her lips, ready to greet two of her regular customers.

Above the shop Ellen too was wrestling with her emotions. The short time she had spent in Ted Parker's company had been a revelation to her. She had felt like a different person. Ted had made her laugh like she'd never laughed before and the memory of her close proximity to the charismatic man was enough to send shivers of delight tingling up her back. Then the image changed to the look of utter relief on Arthur's face as Nora, bless her, had quickly defused what might have been a tricky situation. Well, she'd had her moment of reckless enjoyment, but it must never happen again. Not that anything untoward had happened between her and Ted, but she knew that in different circumstances things could have turned out very differently. She was painfully aware of the attraction she felt for Ted and, although she was still naive, she wasn't that inexperienced to realise Ted Parker felt the same way.

Later that night, as she lay awake beside the sleeping Arthur, she tried to recapture the pleasant memory of being in Ted's company, knowing that was all she would ever be able to have, a pleasant memory.

Yet instead of conjuring up the handsome features, the image that floated into Ellen's mind was that of a pair of striking blue eyes staring out of a blackened face.

CHAPTER FIVE

'Coo, Micky, are we rich? Can we get a place of our own now?' Molly, her blue eyes as wide as saucers, stared in fascinated awe at the silver coins lying in her brother's open palm. The open hero worship mirrored in Molly's eyes was a much needed balm to Micky's bruised ego. Now he was back at the place he called home, he forgot the feeling of hurt pride he had experienced on learning the deception Ellen had engineered in order to give him a job – and a very well paid job at that. He had been so proud, thinking he was helping the pretty young woman, until he'd realised she had only given him the work out of pity. All the way home he had felt a curious feeling of despondency, unable to understand why he felt so low when he had five shillings in his pocket. The money was a small fortune to someone in his position, so why, he had kept asking himself, wasn't he jumping for joy? Now he was with Molly, basking in her adoration, Micky found his self-respect returning.

Feeling quite pleased with himself he strutted up and down the cramped room. After all, he had every reason to be proud of himself. It wasn't even eight o'clock yet and already he had earned five bob. As soon as they had breakfasted on the currant buns Ellen had slipped under his arm on his way out of the shop he intended to try the markets to see if he couldn't earn another couple of bob. Of course, to earn even a shilling, he would have to work without a break for the remainder of the day. The job he'd had this morning was a one off: he wouldn't be that lucky again. And he said as much to his little sister who was still staring at him in awe, her cheeks bulging with the remains of one of the freshly cooked buns.

'Come on, Moll, eat up. The sooner we get down the markets, the sooner I can earn some more money.'

The hope in Molly's eyes dimmed. 'Does that mean we're not rich, Micky? Have we got to stay here for ever?'

Seeing the disappointment in his little sister's eyes and hearing the resignation in her voice, Micky felt his elation deflating like a balloon suddenly deprived of air. Reaching out he caught hold of the small hands. 'No, we're not rich, Moll. But I promise you we ain't gonna stay 'ere for ever.' But Molly remained unconvinced. Gently lifting her chin so he could look her straight in the eyes he said softly, 'We'll 'ave ter stay 'ere fer a while longer, Moll. I don't like it any more than you do, but I'm doing the best I can.'

Her chin wobbling, Molly asked tearfully, 'Couldn' we get a room somewhere, Micky, just fer a few nights?'

I hate it 'ere when yer not with me. I'm always fright-ened that man will get me, but I wouldn't be fright-ened if we was in a proper room with a lock on the door. Can't we, Micky, please? Just fer a little while.'

Swinging his head from side to side Micky muttered, 'I'm sorry, Moll, honest I am. I know five bob seems like a lot of money, but it won't last long if we go spending it on lodging houses, then we'll be right back here. And maybe even this place might be gone soon. If the council knocked the other 'ouses down, then they must be planning ter build some-thing else here. That's why I want ter save up as much money as I can so we can get a proper place ter live fer good, not just fer a few days.' Pulling a face, Micky gave his sister a playful shove. 'Come on, girl, eat up. Unless yer want ter stay here on yer own while I'm down the market.'

The threat, although made in a joking way, galvanised Molly into action. 'All right, Micky, I'm hurrying,' she said anxiously, swallowing the last remnants of food in a loud gulp. 'You'll 'ave ter have a wash first though, Micky. You look filthy.'

Taken aback, Micky looked down at himself. He'd forgotten he was covered in coal dust. Then he had an idea. They may not have enough money for proper lodgings, but they could afford a trip to the local baths. Micky quickly added up the money he had put by. With the five bob he'd earned this morning, plus the one and threepence he had hidden behind a loose brick in the bedroom, he had enough not only for a much needed bath for himself and Molly, but also, if they looked carefully around the stalls, they might even be able to afford a change of clothing. In their hasty departure from the workhouse, Micky hadn't given a thought to the practicalities of life.

'Yer right, Moll. I ain't gonna get any work looking like this. Mind you, yer ain't exactly smelling of roses either. How about we treat ourselves ter a real bath, and a new set of clothes . . . Well! Not new clothes, but we should be able ter pick up something on the rag stall. What d'yer say, Moll?'

Molly's eyes lit up. 'Oh, that'd be lovely, Micky. Will we 'ave ter have a cold bath? Or can we afford a hot bath with real soap and a soft towel?'

Micky cast a reproachful look at his sister. Hot baths with nice soap and soft towels were a luxury they couldn't afford, not at fourpence each – especially when they could have a cold bath with carbolic soap and a rough piece of cloth to dry themselves with for tuppence. Those opting for the second-class cubicles had to be in and out within ten minutes. Which, given the conditions, was all the time anyone wanted.

'Hang on, Moll. I just told yer we 'ave ter be careful with the money we've got. A hot bath with soap and proper towels will cost eightpence for the pair of us, that's unless we share a bath, an' I don't think that's allowed . . . Oh, what the hell,' he grinned, wanting nothing more at this minute than to put the smile back on Molly's face. 'All right, we'll 'ave the best. After all, there's no telling when we'll be able ter afford it again. Besides, we deserve a treat. Just don't go getting used ter the good life, girl. Don't forget what Mum used ter say. Look after the pennies, and the pounds will look after themselves.'

At the mention of their mother, Molly's eyes filled with tears, her lower lip beginning to quiver as she whispered, 'I miss me mum, Micky, and me dad. I wish they was still alive and we was all back in our old house.'

Looking into Molly's tearful face Micky felt his own eyes begin to prickle. Sometimes, in those few seconds after waking, he would often forget the past, and expect to hear his mother shouting up the stairs for him to get up. Then harsh reality would set in. He would look at the sleeping Molly beside him, both of them lying on the filthy mattress, covered by blankets that were practically crawling. But it was the smell that sickened him the most. And not just the smell from the bedding, but from Molly and himself. A sudden resolution rose in his chest. If he had to work every minute of the day and night to get Molly out of this hell hole, then he would. In the meantime, he was going to give his little sister a day to remember.

At five o'clock that evening, Micky and Molly, tired but happier than they had been in a long time, returned to their dilapidated home. Two hours later Molly was fast asleep, leaving Micky to think back over their day.

First they had visited the second-hand clothes stall where Micky, after much good-natured haggling, had bought a thick jumper, a heavy black jacket and a pair of boots that still had plenty of life left in them. But his most cherished purchase was his first pair of long trousers. For Molly, he had splashed out on a red woollen dress and a grey coat. As she hadn't been pounding the streets every day as he had the past months, Molly's boots were still in reasonable condition. When it had come to the question of undergarments, however, the embarrassed Micky had left those essential purchases to his sister. Which would have been fine if Molly, never having shopped before, hadn't picked up a pair of grey long johns, calling out at the top of her young voice, 'Micky, will these fit yer? Come an' 'ave a look.' As amused glances came their way, Micky, mortified as only the young can be at being shown up in public, had quickly grabbed the offending garment, stuffing it into a tatty canvas bag someone had dropped in the street.

Their next stop had been the public baths in Mare Street. The attendant had looked at the two filthy children with open distaste. But Micky had stood his ground and when, some twenty minutes later, they had emerged clean in body and clothing, they had looked at each other and grinned widely. Their soiled clothing had been left in a cubicle, as a kind of present to the snooty attendant who had treated them so shabbily. Feeling very grown up in his long trousers, Micky had tried to maintain some kind of dignity. But Molly, her waist-length blonde hair freshly washed and dripping wet, had grabbed his hand crying joyously, 'Come on, Micky, race yer ter the market.' And Micky, forgetting his new status, had broke into a run, dragging the laughing Molly alongside him.

The exciting day had continued with Micky getting six hours' work in Well Street market. Even Molly had earned fourpence by fetching mugs of tea from the local café for the stall holders. By the time the traders had begun packing up for the day both children were exhausted. Yet it was an exhaustion tinged with happiness, for it was the first day since their escape from the workhouse that they had spent the entire day together.

To round off the day, Micky had bought fish and chips for their supper, and they ate the hot food straight out of the greasy paper.

The only damper was having to return to the hovel they'd occupied for the past months. In that time they had grown accustomed to the filthy conditions, grateful only that they had a roof of sorts over their heads. Now they were clean, it was doubly difficult for them to lie on the stained, damp mattress. But, as Micky had told Molly, it was either that or sleep standing up until they could afford decent accommodation. When Molly had fallen asleep, Micky counted the money he had left by the light of their last remaining candle, which reminded him he would have to buy some more tomorrow. Which also meant forking out more money. Sighing softly he removed the loose brick. Keeping sixpence back, he placed the rest of the money in his secret hideaway, a satisfied smile on his lips. Even with the visit to the baths and the new clothes plus the fish and chip supper, he still had almost six shillings left, thanks to the generosity of the market traders. Grimacing with distaste, Micky forced himself to lie down beside Molly. If he knew for sure how long they could remain here, he would do his best to make the place habitable. Second-hand furniture and bedding could be bought reasonably cheaply if you weren't that fussy. And anything would be better than their current living conditions.

The long day started to creep up on him, his eyes becoming heavier despite his efforts to stay awake. He wanted to make plans for tomorrow, but his tired body had other ideas.

His last conscious thought was of Ellen Mitson as he wondered if she had remembered his plea to ask around in search of a permanent job for him. He doubted she would have found anything for him yet. After all, he had only asked her this morning. Still, there was no harm in going to the bakery to enquire. Also he was anxious for the baker's wife to see him in his new finery. His face flushed in the darkness and with an angry shrug of his shoulders, he muttered, 'Soppy sod.' Blowing out the candle he turned on his side and let sleep overtake him.

CHAPTER SIX

It was a bright, sunlit day and Ellen was preparing to go shopping. The reason for her expedition was double-edged. She normally did her weekly shopping down Well Street market, but today, as she had for the past month, she was going to Hoxton instead. Passing through the bakery she stopped to speak to Agnes. 'I won't be too long, Agnes. Is there anything I can get you while I'm out?'

Agnes, in the process of serving a customer, looked up and, in a pleasant tone, said, 'No thanks, Ellen. I got my shopping yesterday.'

Buttoning up her light blue, three-quarter-length coat, Ellen said, 'Are you sure you can cope, Agnes? After all, Saturday is our busiest day.'

Agnes passed over a large crusty loaf to the bemused customer, whose face was etched in surprise at the friendly chatter between the two women who were normally at each other's throats. After all, half the fun of coming to this bakery was listening to Ellen and Agnes trade insults. Yet even though, on the surface at least, the women appeared to have patched up their differences, there was an undeniable air of tension, as if they were merely playacting.

'Don't yer worry about me,' said Agnes. 'I can cope fine on me own. You 'ave a nice day, an' don't worry about rushing back. After all, the trams'll be packed. You'd be better off going ter Well Street, but if yer've taken to going ter Hoxton, you'll 'ave ter fight yer way onto the tram. Couldn't be bothered meself. Still, I expect yer want ter see how young Micky's getting on now Ted Parker's given him a job.'

Feeling her cheeks growing hot, Ellen pulled on a pair of cotton gloves, adjusted her straw hat and said lightly, 'Well, yes, I am interested in how Micky's getting on, but Hoxton's a much bigger market than Well Street, and besides, it's nice to have a change of scenery now and then.'

Agnes nodded sagely. 'Course it is, love. You get off now, and enjoy yer day . . . Oh, by the way, your hair looks much better hanging loose; takes years off yer.'

Ellen nodded, a fresh rush of blood staining her cheeks, then held the door open for the customer, her sharp eyes noting the curiosity mirrored in her face. But she wasn't going to waste time gossiping, especially as whatever she said would be elaborated on. With a pleasant 'Good day, Mrs Stone' Ellen walked towards the tram stop, her nose sniffing the warm, spring air. It was amazing how the arrival of spring, with its warm weather and longer days, could lift one's spirits.

Stepping out quickly, Ellen was lucky to catch a tram straight away. As it was now ten-thirty, the morning rush was over and Ellen found herself with a choice of seats. Skipping up the circular stairs, she flopped down on a wooden, slatted bench, her gaze centred on the street below and the people going about their daily business on this fine day.

Once she had paid her fare, she was left alone with her thoughts and as she recalled the events of the past month, a tender smile came to her lips.

Not only had Ted Parker given Micky a trial run, starting with one day a week, Micky had impressed Ted so much that he now employed the young boy four days a week. And the change in Micky was nothing short of a miracle.

That first day he had come into the shop, wearing his long trousers and thick jacket, his face a mixture of self-consciousness and pride, Ellen's heart had gone out to the boy who was trying so hard to make an impression. Even Agnes had made a kind comment about Micky's appearance, causing the young boy to look at her suspiciously, as had Ellen, especially as it was only the previous day that Agnes had tried her best to make trouble between her and Arthur. If it hadn't been for Nora Parker's intervention, Ellen's moment of recklessness in waylaying Ted, which had been perfectly innocent, could easily have turned into a very nasty situation.

The following day Ellen had braced herself for further remarks, and had been taken aback when Agnes had arrived at her normal time and, for the first time since Ellen had known the woman, had greeted Ellen with a smile and a pleasant 'Good morning'. Then Micky had arrived, and he too had been greeted in the same vein. Ellen and Micky had exchanged bemused glances, and Ellen was trying to think up some small job for Micky to do when Ted had entered the shop and offered Micky a day's work on his stall down Hoxton Market. Ellen could still remember the look on Micky's face as he glanced from Ellen to Ted, not wanting to let Ellen down, but desperate for the chance of a real job. Ellen could also remember the joy that had spread over Micky's handsome features when she had told him there wasn't any work for him that day and to go along with Ted. He would break a few hearts, would Micky, when he got older. In fact he was already charming the women and girls that frequented Hoxton Market.

For the past month Ellen had visited Hoxton every Saturday and for the life of her she didn't know who she most liked seeing, Micky or Ted.

Taking a deep, satisfying breath of air, Ellen relaxed against the wooden seat. Everything seemed to be going well in her life and for that reason alone she felt a slight shiver of apprehension. Her misgivings centred solely on Agnes' sudden change of character. Not suspicious by nature, Ellen had been trying her utmost to establish a fresh acquaintance with the new, amiable side of Agnes, but it was hard going.

Then she shrugged impatiently. What was she worrying about? Maybe she was wrong and Agnes really had turned over a new leaf. According to Arthur, Agnes had once been a friendly, pleasant woman. He hadn't added that Agnes had only changed since their marriage; he hadn't needed to, that much had been evident. But maybe Agnes had accepted the situation and was now finally trying to make amends for her surly behaviour since Ellen had arrived at the bakery.

Her stop approaching, Ellen got to her feet, then, gripping the iron rail, she carefully descended the twisting stairs to the safety of the platform.

Joining the bustling crowd, Ellen made her way to Ted's stall, her stomach churning as it always did when she was about to see the man who had helped turn her life around. For if she hadn't bumped into him on that fraught morning, she would probably have returned home, still angry and frustrated, her minor triumph over the coal delivery soon paling into insignificance. Instead, something in Ted's character had brought out qualities in her she hadn't known she possessed. She had begun the slow process of growing into adulthood, her inner strength already coming to the fore. But since making a friend of Ted, she had found herself growing stronger each day. In an ironic twist of fate Ellen was following in her husband's footsteps. For where Arthur's life had revolved around his weekly visits to her parents' house, so was Ellen's life revolving around her weekly visit to Hoxton Market – and Ted. Approaching the fruit and vegetable stall, Ellen's face broke into a wide smile as she heard Micky shouting out to the passing crowd as if he'd been working the market all his life.

Standing back a pace so Micky wouldn't know she was watching him, Ellen looked on fondly, thinking as she did so how much Micky had changed from that first meeting when he had appeared outside the bakery, a bedraggled, filthy urchin who, even in dire need, had refused to take charity. Most people, Agnes for instance, would have quickly shown the young boy the door, or even called the police and turned him in for begging, a practice the police frowned on. But Ellen had seen past Micky's outward appearance to the dignity and character that lurked beneath his ragged apparel. And she had been proved right. She soon spotted Ted who had been hidden from her view by the large crowd. Unconsciously she adjusted her straw hat and flicked a long, thick strand of chestnut brown hair over her shoulder before walking towards the stall.

Ted was talking and laughing with two women, while at the same time filling brown bags with items of fruit and vegetables. One of the women was flirting openly with Ted, who was obviously enjoying every moment of the attractive woman's attention. The sight caused Ellen's stomach to constrict as if she'd been physically punched. All her earlier elation vanishing, Ellen, her heart thumping, her throat tight, turned to go. Then Micky spotted her.

'Oi, Ellen, hello. Ain't yer gonna buy anything today?'

Caught out, Ellen was forced to approach the stall, a tremulous smile on her lips. 'Hello, Micky. I was going to have a look around first, but don't worry, I'll be back later to get my usual order.'

Micky grinned. 'I'll get it ready fer yer, Ellen. Then yer can pick it up when you've finished looking round. Or I could drop it off on me way 'ome tonight; save yer carrying it all the way back home on the tram, won't it?'

'Thanks, Micky, that's kind of you. I might take you up on that offer,' Ellen said, her eyes flickering towards Ted, who was still enjoying the flirtatious banter with the two women.

Following her gaze, Micky's smile faltered. Pushing back his flat cap, he called out over-loudly, "Ere, Ted, Ellen's here.'

Immediately Ted turned away from the hovering women, the grin on his lips widening. Teasingly he said to the woman who was practically draping herself over his body, 'See yer next week, darling. Don't do anything I wouldn't do.'

The blonde woman smiled brazenly. 'Don't leave much fer me ter do then, does it, Ted?'

Her face burning, Ellen fiddled nervously with the clasp of her leather bag. Then she looked at the woman and her spirits lifted once again. For the woman was looking daggers at her and Ellen, knowing her presence had caused a pique of jealousy, felt a surge of confidence.

'Hello, love.' Ted's deep, throaty voice brought the smile back to Ellen's face. Especially as he had dismissed the two women in favour of her company. 'Managed to get away from the sweat shop then?' He leant nearer, his body almost touching hers, sending a delicious shiver of delight down her spine. Then his hand reached out and touched the long, shining chestnut hair, adding softly, 'I prefer your hair like this. That other style didn't suit you at all, made yer look like an old married woman.'

Ellen's smile wavered. 'Well, I am, aren't I? Well . . .' she laughed self-consciously. 'Not exactly old, but I am married.'

Ted leant his head back as if to get a better view, then, his voice sombre, he said, 'Yeah, I know. I'm reminded of it every time I walk past the bakery.'

Her eyes met his and, for a brief few seconds, their gazes locked. Then someone pushed past them and the spell was broken.

Embarrassed by the chemistry that flowed between them and anxious to get the conversation back on a safer level, Ellen looked over at Micky and asked, 'How's Micky getting on?'

Following her gaze, and knowing what she was feeling, Ted replied, 'He's a natural. I admit I only gave him a chance as a favour to you, but it's turned out the other way round. I've lost count of the boys I've had working for me over the years, hoping I'd find someone reliable and honest, so I could set up another stall at one of the other markets. And with Petticoat Lane on Sunday morning, I could make a lot of money. But none of 'em was any good; well, not so much that, but there wasn't any I could have trusted to run me stall without me keeping an eye on 'em. Now I think I might just 'ave found the right bloke – 'Ere, just listen to him.'

Ellen turned her attention to Micky, smiling fondly as she heard him shouting out to the crowd with all the confidence of a grown man. 'Come on, ladies, yer won't find anything better than this stall if yer looking fer fresh fruit and veg.'

An elderly woman was busily inspecting a pile of

74

oranges. 'These fresh, are they, mate? I don't wanna get 'ome and find 'em as dry as me old man's throat on a Saturday night.'

'Fresh?' Micky picked up an orange and threw it in the air. Catching the large piece of fruit he said loudly, 'Picked 'em meself from an orchard in Kent at five o'clock this morning.'

The woman grinned, showing more gums than teeth. 'Yer cheeky devil. Go on then, I'll 'ave three, not that I believe a word of what yer say, but yer deserve a sale fer yer cheek.'

Deftly depositing three large oranges in the woman's shopping basket, Micky added, 'What about some nice juicy apples ter go with 'em?'

Fishing around in her purse the woman looked at Micky with a twinkle in her eye. 'I suppose yer picked those fresh this morning an' all?'

Micky winked, his cherubic face a picture of inno-cence. ''Course I did. I wouldn't lie ter a nice lady like yerself, now would I?'

Chuckling loudly the woman nodded. 'All right, lad, I'll 'ave a couple.' Again Micky had the apples in her basket before she could change her mind. But he wasn't finished yet. Knowing he was being watched by his new boss and Ellen, Micky, anxious to make a good impression, took the woman's money saying quickly, 'How about a bit of veg, love? Can't 'ave a good roast Sunday dinner without veg, can yer?'

Thoroughly enjoying the banter, the woman turned to another customer waiting to be served and cackled, 'Cheeky little beggar, ain't he? An' handsome into the bargain. Gawd, if I was thirty years younger I'd put a smile on yer face that'd last fer a week. Go on, I'll 'ave a cauli and half a pound of Brussels and that's me lot, mate. Yer'll 'ave me skint at this rate.'

Ellen and Ted exchanged amused glances, glances that were tinged with pride. As they were shoved once again, Ted, his eyes twinkling mischievously said, 'Look, we can't stand 'ere, we'll be trampled. How about 'aving a bit of lunch with me? I was gonna go for me dinner about now anyway.'

Ellen hesitated. There was nothing she would like more than to spend time in this man's company, but she was treading on dangerous ground. Then her head came up defiantly. Why shouldn't she enjoy herself? After all, nothing could come of her association with Ted. It wasn't as if she was planning to have an affair with the man. Even as the thought crossed her mind, an image floated before her eyes and such was the nature of her thoughts she blushed as if she had spoken her deepest secrets out loud. 'Thank you, Ted. I'd like that very much. Will Micky be all right on his own?'

Ted gave a hearty laugh. 'Get on with you. Ain't I just been telling yer how pleased I am with him? 'Course he'll be all right.' Taking hold of her arm he bent down and whispered in her ear, 'I suppose you know the lad's got a crush on you, poor little bleeder. Still, he'll get over it in time. At his age I was always falling in love with a different girl every week. Mind you, it's a different kettle of fish if it happens when you're older.'

Deliberately ignoring the last comment, Ellen's eyes darted to where Micky had a queue of women waiting to be served. Startled, she said, 'Don't be silly. He's just a boy and I'm a married woman.'

Ted snorted, 'You don't have to keep reminding me you're married. As for Micky, he's nearly fifteen, and you're not much older . . . Look, let's go and get something to eat, 'cos if one more person pushes me I'll land 'em one.' His disarming smile was evidence he would do no such thing. Then without warning he put his arm around her shoulder pulling her tight to his side, the sudden action sending a jolt through her entire body. For a second, a picture of Arthur swam before her eyes, but she instantly dismissed him from her mind. She wasn't doing anything wrong, she kept reminding herself, as she allowed Ted to lead her through the busy market towards a pub on the corner.

She was still telling herself the same thing when she emerged from the pub, slightly tipsy from the large gin and tonic she had swallowed without thinking. Not used to alcohol, the beverage had gone straight to her head.

Ted, amused at first, had become concerned at the thought of Ellen travelling home on her own in the state she was in, especially as it was his fault. Sitting her down on a bench outside the pub, he went back to the stall and told Micky he was taking Ellen home and would be back as soon as possible.

On the journey home, Ellen leant against Ted's side, revelling in the close, intimate contact of the man she was falling in love with . . .

Arriving at the bakery, Ted, his face troubled, now said, 'You'd better go in the back way and have a lie down before anyone sees you.'

Ellen giggled. 'Don't care if they do. I've had a wonderful day, well worth a telling off for. Thanks, Ted.' Fumbling in her bag for her key Ellen stumbled. Ted's arms came out circling her waist. The giggle that was forming instantly died as she stared up into the intense eyes, for once holding no trace of mockery.

Then his lips came down on hers. It was merely a touch, but the effect on Ellen was overwhelming. Instantly sober she pulled away, saying in a trembling voice, 'I'd better get in. Arthur will be worrying. Goodbye, Ted.'

Ted released her reluctantly. Well aware of Ellen's emotions he touched her lips with the tip of his finger saying tenderly, "Bye, darlin'. See you next week.'

Her legs weak, Ellen let herself into the bakery. Quietly she made her way up the stairs to the bedroom, repeating over and over in her mind Ted's last words. He had called her darling. She knew the term was used frequently by East End men to any woman. It meant nothing – or did it? Hearing Arthur calling out to her as he came up the stairs, Ellen quickly lay down on the bed. She heard Arthur saying her name, but pretended to be asleep. For what seemed an age Arthur hovered beside the bed while Ellen fervently prayed for him to go. There was no way she could face him, not just now. When he finally closed the door, Ellen peered cautiously over her shoulder, sighing with relief at finding herself alone. Making herself more comfortable on the four-poster bed, she closed her eyes, intending to go over in her mind the events of the day and where she was going to go from here. Her emotions in turmoil, she vowed never again to visit the market. And if Ted came into the shop, she would treat him like any other customer. Yes she would, she told herself vehemently. But no matter how hard she tried to convince herself, she knew that come Saturday she would be back in Hoxton, to spend what little precious time she could with Ted.

CHAPTER SEVEN

After Micky had delivered Ellen's fruit and vegetables as promised, he hurried home, worrying as he always did if Molly was all right. He hated leaving her alone. It had been bad enough when he was doing a few hours' work here and there, but since Ted had taken him on four full days a week she was on her own from early morning until he got home. In all the months he had been praying for such an opportunity, Micky hadn't thought of what would happen to Molly once he was gainfully employed. As he broke into a run, he pondered on life's ironies. Here he was, getting what he and Molly had dreamed of since they had run away from the workhouse, yet neither of them had thought of the practical side of Micky working permanently.

Then there was the fear he might come back one evening and find the place they called home demolished and Molly taken into care. If that happened he

would have no chance of getting her back. And, as if
that wasn't bad enough, there was also the constant
worry of the pervert Kenneth Wells hanging around.

'Molly, Moll, I'm home, mate.'

Instantly Molly's pretty face peered over the
balcony. 'Ooh, I'm glad you're 'ome, Micky, it's really
lonely being on me own.'

Scrambling up the rope, Micky gave his sister a hug.
'I know, Moll, but it can't be helped. Anyway, it's not
so bad now the days are lighter for longer. And I've
got a treat fer yer. I got us some pie and mash for tea.
Ted gave me an extra tanner, 'cos he 'ad ter leave me
looking after the stall on me own this afternoon. It
was only fer a couple of hours, but he didn't 'ave ter
pay me extra. I'd've done it fer nothing. He's a good
bloke is Ted. Anyway, like I said, seeing as I got a bit
extra, I thought we deserved a bit of a treat – you
especially.' Reaching out a hand he stroked her cheek
lovingly. 'You're a good girl, Moll, and brave. I know
it must be horrible fer yer being on yer own all day.
It wouldn't be so bad if yer could go out an' play, but
yer can't, not with that . . .' He stopped abruptly. Molly
didn't need reminding of Kenneth Wells. The poor
little cow was terrified of even putting her nose out
of the door in case he was lying in wait. Then there
was the possibility of a truant officer spotting her.
Laying out the hot food, Micky sighed. Gawd, but life
was difficult.

They were halfway through their meal when Micky
had an idea. 'Listen, Moll. It's the Easter holiday next
week. How about yer come with me down the market?
I mean, no one will notice why you're out of school,

'cos like I just said, all the schools will be closed down. What d'yer think?'

With a loud shout of pure joy, Molly flung her arms around her brother's neck. 'Oh, Micky, d'yer mean it? Will I be able to help yer out on the stall?'

Micky held her for a few seconds before gently disengaging her arms from the stranglehold she had on his neck. 'Hang on, mate. You can come with me, but yer won't be able to work with me.' Seeing the joy fading from the heart-shaped face, Micky said softly, 'Look, Moll, just think about it for a minute. No one knows about you. If I'd told Ellen and Ted I had a sister, it'd be all right, but if I suddenly turn up with you in tow, they might become suspicious and start asking awkward questions.'

Molly, her face solemn, said timidly, 'They might not, Micky. You could always just say you'd never mentioned me 'cos yer didn't think about it.'

Shaking his head Micky answered, 'Nah, that wouldn't work. It's been bad enough lying to Ellen and Ted that I've got a mum. I've got really friendly with both of them and they'd know something was wrong if I suddenly produced a sister. They're not stupid, Moll. Maybe neither of them would wonder why I'd never mentioned yer, but I don't think they would. Besides, now things are looking up, why take the chance?'

'Well, what am I gonna do all day down the market?' Putting the last morsel of pie into her small mouth she said excitedly, 'What if yer said I was a mate of yours, an' yer was looking after me during the school holidays while me mum was at work?'

His mouth full, Micky stared at his sister in amazement. She might be only eight, but she had the sense of a girl twice her age. Ellen and Ted wouldn't question Molly's presence if he followed her suggestion. Why hadn't he thought of it himself? Her idea was perfect.

Grinning widely he said, 'You sure yer only eight, Moll? Yer ain't a woman midget, are yer?'

Molly looked back at him in surprise. 'Don't be silly, Micky. You've always said if someone wanted something badly enough there was always a way round it. And if yer can't tell anyone I'm yer sister, then it's obvious yer could say I was just a mate you was looking after during the school holidays.'

Micky could only look at Molly in awe, mingled with pride and relief. Give her a few years and his sister would be able to look after herself – she might even end up looking after him too. Chuckling quietly Micky gave Molly an affectionate hug.

With the problem of the Easter holiday out of the way, the two youngsters talked until the evening turned into darkness. As always, her stomach full, her mind at rest, Molly was asleep by nine o'clock, leaving Micky to his dreams.

He now had nearly two pounds saved, enough to get them a room in a boarding house. Yet even though he was sure Ted would keep him on, after so long of worrying about money, Micky was afraid to touch his savings in case something happened and he lost his job. Then he looked down at the sleeping Molly. So young, so vulnerable, so brave, never complaining, other than of her fear of being left alone. In that instant

Micky made up his mind. On Monday he would take Molly with him to work. And once the school holiday was over he would look for a room, preferably with a landlady who didn't ask awkward questions. A frown crossed his forehead. That was something else he had to sort out. At some point he would have to get Molly into a school: he didn't want her growing up without any education. But that particular problem wasn't pressingly urgent. Even if he waited until he was sixteen, legally a man, he could still get Molly four or five years of schooling.

His head reeling with all the difficulties he had to deal with, Micky pushed everything to the back of his mind for the time being.

The minute he did that, his thoughts turned to Ellen. And as always, his stomach began to churn and he could feel his cheeks burning.

Even if he was older, he still wouldn't have a chance with her, not with her being married. And even if she wasn't, he knew he hadn't a hope in hell with Ted in the picture. He had seen the way they looked at each other and, each time he witnessed the growing affection blossoming between them, he experienced pangs of jealousy. Angry with himself he punched his pillow. He was fond of both Ellen and Ted and at the same time he was jealous and for that alone he felt guilty. Ted had been good to him as had Ellen. It wasn't fair for him to resent the man who had given him a job when no one else would. Not only that, Ted had bought Micky another change of clothes from the second-hand stall. And now Micky had a regular wage coming in, he was able to buy Molly two cotton dresses from a similar stall at the other end of the market. Both of them slightly faded, but to Molly, who had always been so particular about her appearance, the dresses could have been brand new, so delighted was she with them. They could even afford a bath every week, so what was he moaning about?

To take his mind off things that were so painful to him, Micky instead turned his thoughts to finding accommodation. No matter what lodgings he found Molly would still have to stay out of sight when he wasn't around, but at least he wouldn't have to worry about her, not once she was safely installed behind a proper door that locked. But for the next couple of weeks she would be with him every second of the day; more importantly she would be able to roam the market without fear and be able to smell and savour the spring air, instead of the fetid odour that pervaded the derelict house.

As Micky thought about his future, Ellen was doing much the same thing. Seated in her dining room with Arthur fast asleep in the armchair opposite her, Ellen put down the book she had been trying to read and leant her head back against the winged armchair.

The alcohol she had consumed earlier had long since worn off, leaving her with a throbbing headache and a guilty conscience to match. What had she been playing at leading on Ted like she had? She was now feeling deeply ashamed of her behaviour. Looking across at the sleeping man Ellen felt a surge of affection for her husband. She owed him so much, he deserved better. If only they could get away for a holiday. Oh, that would be marvellous.

For not only would it do Arthur, who to her knowledge hadn't had a holiday in the past twenty years, a power of good, it would also take her away from the temptation of Ted Parker. Excited by the notion, Ellen visualised her and Arthur, just the two of them, enjoying some time together, with nothing or no one to disturb them. Then common sense set in, ruining her plans. Arthur would never agree to close down the bakery for a weekend, never mind a couple of weeks. It wasn't that he couldn't afford to take a holiday, he was comfortably well off, but being the type of man he was, he'd be afraid of losing the loyal custom he'd accumulated over the years.

Arthur stirred, yawned loudly and smiled tiredly. 'Sorry, love. I don't seem able to stay awake once the day's business is over; must be a sign of old age creeping up on me.'

Quickly taking advantage of his words, Ellen left her chair and came and sat by his feet, resting her chin on his lap. Staring up into the plump face she said earnestly, 'Arthur, why don't we have a holiday? God knows you deserve one. What do you think, Arthur? Why, a couple of weeks by the seaside would do you a world of good.' Looking up at him anxiously Ellen felt her spirits drop at the look of agitation that crossed his face.

Running a shaking hand over his chin he replied, 'You know I can't just take two weeks' holiday, Ellen. I mean who'd look after the business? No, I'm sorry, love. It's out of the question.' Seeing the look of resignation on Ellen's features Arthur added kindly, 'Please, love, don't look like that. I'd love to go off for two weeks with just the two of us, but you must see it's impossible.'

Angry and frustrated, Ellen went back to her chair, her face sullen with disappointment.

'Look, Ellen, what if we had a weekend away? I could prepare the bread on Friday and leave it to rise overnight, like I always do and, if Agnes agrees, she can come in early Saturday morning and put them in the oven. As for the cakes, Agnes can make those by herself. In fact I could ask her to stay overnight, it would make it easier for her. I'd have to offer her extra money of course, but I'm sure she'd love the chance of running the place by herself. Then we can get away after the shop closes on the Friday we plan to go away and stay until Sunday night. I know it's not what you wanted, but at least that's better than nothing . . . Ellen . . . Ellen, love, say something.'

Staring at the wall, Ellen said dully, 'Forget it, Arthur. It wouldn't be worth the effort. By the time we got anywhere, we'd be lucky to have a couple of hours before it was time for bed. We'd have Saturday, but you'd want to get an early start on Sunday morning, so as you'd be back in time to prepare the bread for Monday. No, forget I said anything. If we can't get away for a proper holiday, then I'd rather stay at home.'

Judging by the set look on Ellen's face, Arthur knew he had found himself in a no-win situation, so he did what he always did and took the line of least resistance. Yawning excessively, he stood up and stretched.

'I think I'll have an early night, love. That's if you don't mind?' He peered at the downcast head, a sure sign his wife was not in the mood for talking.

'I'm sure I'll manage without your company until bedtime.' She glanced up at the mantel clock, adding scathingly, 'Though that'll be some time yet, seeing as it's only just on eight o'clock. Still, I'm sure I can find something to occupy me. I can read my book, or if I get really desperate, I could always ask Agnes up for a cup of tea and a chat. She is still downstairs, isn't she? She always stays late on Saturday to give the shop a good clean, all ready for Monday morning.' Throwing her head back she uttered a mirthless laugh. 'Good God! I must be desperate for company.'

Sheepishly Arthur said, 'I thought you two were getting on better lately.'

'Huh! You mean she's making an effort. She doesn't like me any more now than she did when I first arrived. But, yes, if she's willing to make the effort, then I suppose I should do the same and give her the benefit of the doubt . . . Oh, go to bed, Arthur. You're making me nervous hovering there like a lost soul.'

Tentatively Arthur moved forward to kiss Ellen good night, but Ellen was in no mood for his embrace, which she made evident by turning her head sharply, leaving Arthur's pursed lips landing inches from her ear. Dispirited, Arthur gave up trying to make amends and left the room, grateful for some time to himself.

The door had barely closed after him when there came a tap on the dining-room door. Without looking up Ellen called out, 'Come in, Agnes.'

Agnes entered the room. 'I just come up ter say I'm

leaving. Everything's done downstairs.' As she spoke, Agnes' eyes roamed the room. It was a modest size and comfortably furnished. The walls were papered with red and gold flock wallpaper, which complemented the dark red carpet. A highly polished cabinet took up most of the far wall. In the middle of the room stood a table big enough to seat six people, its mahogany surface covered by a green baize, tasselled tablecloth. There were various knick-knacks on the shelves, and on either side of the elaborate fireplace were two dark green, velvet armchairs. The mantelpiece itself held an assortment of figurines, that had once belonged to Arthur's mother. The centrepiece was a beautiful, gold-edged clock that had been in the Mitson family for over a century. Agnes had been in this room countless times over the years, yet each time seemed as if it was the first. It was a room she had once imagined would be hers and Arthur's.

Ellen watched Agnes' face closely, trying to imagine what was going through her mind. 'Thanks, Agnes. It's good of you to stay behind on Saturday.'

Agnes shrugged. 'It's what I've always done. Anyway, I'm off now.' Her eyes darted to the closed bedroom door. Ellen could plainly see the disappointment mirrored in Agnes' eyes as she realised she wouldn't be seeing Arthur now until Monday.

In a moment's compassion Ellen said quietly, 'Why don't you sit down for a minute, Agnes? I was going to make a cup of tea. Maybe you'd like to join me?'

Taken by surprise by the unexpected request, Agnes hesitated, but only for a few seconds. There was nothing or no one to hurry home to. She had been living on her own since her mother's death fifteen years ago. Which was why she stayed in the bakery for as long as she could, especially on Saturdays, in order to put off returning to the dreary terraced house to spend yet another lonely evening on her own. Lifting her shoulders she said, 'Yeah, all right. Ta, Ellen.'

'Well, come and sit down then, Agnes. Make yourself at home while I put the kettle on.' When Ellen had left, Agnes walked across the room, her steps slow and awkward, half expecting that Ellen was making fun of her and would return and retract the invitation. Seating herself in the chair Arthur had recently vacated, she perched uncomfortably on the edge. There was much Agnes disliked about Ellen, but she had to admit the young woman wasn't of a spiteful nature. If she had been, then she, Agnes, would have been given her marching orders long since. With this thought in mind she removed her black shawl and wriggled her bottom further back in the velvet chair.

'Here we are.' Ellen came bustling into the room carrying a silver tray. 'I've brought some cakes too. I hope you're hungry. I know I am.' Setting the tray down on the occasional table between the armchairs she said brightly, 'Help yourself, Agnes. Don't stand on ceremony.'

Ellen poured out the tea, then held the china cup to Agnes. Amiably she said, 'Actually, Agnes, I wanted to ask you a favour.'

Agnes, having just taken a sip of the hot beverage, spluttered and began coughing. 'A favour! From me?' Her initial thoughts returning, Agnes laid down her cup and asked suspiciously, 'You 'aving a laugh at me, Ellen? 'Cos if yer are, then it's a rotten trick ter play. Pretending ter be all friendly an' . . .'

'Just a moment, Agnes,' Ellen interrupted quickly. 'You know me better than that. I know we're not the best of friends, but I would never make fun of anyone out of spite.'

Relaxing slightly, Agnes picked her cup up and took a long swig before saying warily, 'Yeah, sorry, Ellen. It just came as a bit of a surprise, that's all. You asking fer my help, I mean.'

Anxious to put the older woman's mind at rest, Ellen, cutting two large slices of sponge cake, said tentatively, 'The thing is, Agnes, I've been trying to get Arthur to take a holiday, but it's like talking to a brick wall. As far as I know he's not had a holiday since his father died and that's over twenty years ago.' Handing over a generous slice of cake Ellen gave a short laugh. 'Hark at me telling you something you already know. After all, you've known Arthur much longer than me. By what Arthur's told me, his father was very fond of you, looking on you as part of the family. That's why I'm asking you for help. You're the only one I can think of to help me. Surely there's some way to persuade Arthur to take a holiday, without worrying about losing the custom he's built up over the years.' Staring at Agnes over the top of her cup Ellen asked, 'Can you help, Agnes? I mean, isn't there someone who could see to the baking while you ran the shop? And of course you'd be compensated for the extra work. You might even think about taking some time off yourself later on in the year, because you've never had a holiday either. And with all the hard work you've put in over the years you deserve a break. But of course, that's up to you. So, what do you think?'

Agnes' mind was racing furiously. This was the last thing she had imagined Ellen would ask of her. Taking a bite out of the sponge cake she said, 'How long was yer thinking of being away?'

Now it was Ellen's turn to feel uncomfortable. Her voice hesitant she said, 'I was thinking of two weeks ... but I'd be happy with just a week,' she added swiftly as she saw the surprised look on Agnes' face.

'Two weeks! Bleeding 'ell. You ain't asking fer much, are yer? People like Arthur and me don't go on holiday fer a fortnight. A long weekend in Southend is as much as we can look forward to.'

Ellen's face fell in disappointment. 'That's just what Arthur said,' she replied dismally. 'Thanks anyway, Agnes, it was worth a try.'

'Hold yer 'orses, Ellen. I said a weekend was all most people have, I didn't say it was impossible. Give me a minute ter think, will yer?'

While Agnes consumed her cake, Ellen waited in trepidation. Then, putting her cup and plate down, Agnes nodded. 'I might be able ter help. I ain't promising, mind.' She peered at Ellen.

'Oh, no, I understand,' Ellen answered eagerly. 'I don't expect you to come up with an answer tonight, but if you could think of anything I'd be ever so grateful.'

Silence settled on the room again with Ellen holding her breath expectantly, then Agnes, coming to a decision, said briskly, 'I could ask Bill Cummins. He's been retired for two years now, but he might be grateful fer two weeks' work. Arthur knows Bill well. He's a good baker, is Bill. And if yer trust me ter look after the shop fer a couple of weeks, and Bill agrees . . . Well, I don't see as how Arthur could object, especially if yer work on him. He'd do anything ter keep yer happy, would Arthur.' A note of bitterness had crept into Agnes' voice. Rising to her feet she said, 'I'll go round ter Bill's 'ouse tomorrow, and see what he says. Don't get yer 'opes up though, but I'll do me best.' Getting to her feet she glanced at the book lying on the arm of Ellen's chair and asked, 'Good book, is it?' She picked it up, her eyebrows rising. '*Less Miserables*. That sounds like a barrel of laughs. What's it about anyway?'

Without stopping to think Ellen said, 'Actually it's pronounced, *Les Miserables*, and it's a bit complicated to explain.'

Immediately Agnes went on the defensive. 'In other words, I ain't clever enough ter understand.'

'Oh, no, that isn't what I meant at all,' Ellen said quickly, seeing the fragile truce disappearing. 'I'm having trouble with it myself. Victor Hugo's books are hard going. Basically it's about a young man who steals a loaf of bread to feed his starving family and ends up spending eighteen years in prison before escaping while on parole and a policeman who won't give up looking for him. That's the gist of it.'

Agnes' eyebrows rose as she handed the heavy tome back to Ellen. 'Eighteen years fer stealing a loaf of bread, that's a bit steep, ain't it?'

Ellen smiled. 'Well, he had extra time added on for trying to escape, but the story was written nearly thirty years ago and set in France. I imagine their laws are much harsher than ours. At least, I would hope so.'

Finding the conversation increasingly difficult, Ellen began to fidget nervously. Here she was, discussing a literary classic, when it was painfully obvious that Agnes' idea of a good read was a penny romance novel. An uncomfortable air pervaded the room as each woman tried hard to say something that would be of interest to them both, but it was no good. They simply had nothing in common.

Agnes was the first to speak. Standing up she said over-loudly, 'Well! I'll be off then. Like I said, I'll pop round ter see Bill tomorrow, an' I'll let yer know what he says on Monday, all right?'

Relieved Agnes was going, Ellen smiled gratefully. 'Thanks, Agnes. I really appreciate your help.'

Showing Agnes to the door Ellen hesitated slightly before putting out her hand in a gesture of friendship.

For a few awkward seconds her hand hovered uncertainly in the empty space between them. Then Agnes, her face betraying her embarrassment, reached out and clasped Ellen's hand.

'Yeah, well, I'll do what I can.' Agnes, her face averted in confusion, relinquished the soft palm.

''Bye, Agnes and, once again, thanks.'

Ellen had hardly closed the door when Arthur appeared from the bedroom. 'What on earth did you ask her up here for?' he demanded.

Swinging round, Ellen replied tartly, 'I thought you wanted an early night. As for Agnes, it's you that's always moaning about me trying to get on better with her. And since she's been a lot friendlier lately, I thought it only fair to meet her halfway.'

Wearing an ankle-length, striped nightshirt Arthur looked a comical figure, but his face wasn't wreathed in his usual amiable smile. 'Yes, well, I've been thinking about that. I've known Agnes a lot longer than you, Ellen, and I don't trust her. If she's being friendly, then she's up to something, you mark my words.' Running a hand over his thinning hair, Arthur looked deeply disturbed. He admitted to himself that in the beginning he had prayed for Agnes and Ellen to get on, but he had now changed his mind. In fact, he wanted rid of the woman whose very presence always caused him to feel guilty and uncomfortable. He wanted to forget the past, and he couldn't do that while he was daily reminded of his brief, reckless fling all those years ago. His face reddening, Arthur mumbled, 'Look, Ellen, she's got to go. I know she's been on her best behaviour lately, but to be truthful, I always feel uncomfortable in her presence. It's time she went. She'd be better off. And I was thinking that maybe, once she's gone, I could offer young Micky some extra work when he's not working for Ted on the stall.'

Ellen's face was like stone. 'And who's going to tell Agnes her services are no longer required, Arthur? Because don't think I'm going to do your dirty work for you. If you want Agnes out of the shop, then you can tell her yourself. But I think it's a pretty dirty trick to play on a woman who's given the best part of her life to you.'

Ellen sat down, her face set. 'I'm going to read for a while, Arthur. And I'd rather be on my own. Goodnight.'

Agnes was at the shop door when she remembered she'd left her shawl upstairs. She was outside the door of the dining room when she heard Arthur's voice. And what he said made the blood drain from her face. She couldn't believe it. Not only did he want her out, but he was intending to give her job to that little guttersnipe Micky Masters. Her feet like lead, Agnes, her shawl forgotten, slowly descended the stairs. Once out in the street she didn't notice the chilly nip in the air. She didn't notice anything. All she could hear was Arthur's voice, and with each word she died a little inside. She was outside her house when she suddenly couldn't face another night on her own. Turning round she made her way to the nearest pub. Maybe a couple of gins would wipe away the hurtful words she had overheard.

But they would still be there in the morning. They would be with her for the rest of her life.

CHAPTER EIGHT

It was just after ten-thirty when Agnes staggered out of the Red Lion, her legs stumbling as she drunkenly tried to negotiate the cobbled road.

Passing the fish and chip shop she was suddenly reminded she'd had nothing to eat since the slice of sponge cake Ellen had given her and that wasn't enough for a woman of Agnes' healthy appetite. Finding the heady aroma irresistible, she weaved into the shop and ordered plaice and chips.

Too hungry to wait until she reached home, Agnes tore at the greasy paper and began cramming the delicious, greasy food into her mouth.

As she turned into the next street she saw a youth running in front of her. Normally she wouldn't have paid any attention. But even at this distance, she was sure she knew the young boy from somewhere. Her bleary eyes followed the running figure and when the boy passed under the street lamp on the other side of the road Agnes realised why the figure looked so familiar.

It was that brat, Micky Masters. Agnes followed Micky, not knowing why she was bothering, but powerless to stop herself. Finishing off the tasty meal, she threw the wrapping into the gutter, her eyes never leaving the figure in front of her. Then she stopped abruptly and ducked behind a wall as Micky furtively looked up and down the narrow street. Her forehead screwed in bewilderment as he stopped in front of a derelict house, before running inside.

A crafty smile crossed Agnes' lips. So that was it, was it? No wonder the boy was always cagey whenever the subject of his parents and home came up. The little bleeder was a runaway, though obviously not from the police or else he wouldn't have come regularly to the shop, or taken Ted Parker's offer of a job. Nah! He must be a workhouse brat on the run. Her thin lips spread into a grim smile of satisfaction. So, Mr bleeding Mitson was gonna give her job to Micky Masters, was he? Well, she'd soon put a stop to that idea. Then the smile dropped from her face.

What if he was just some orphan squatting wherever he could find a place to stay before moving on? Also she knew how fond Ellen was of the lad, not to mention Ted Parker. He was another one who had taken the young boy under his wing. Not quite so confident now, Agnes knew she had to have time to think before she did or said anything.

Then she let out a scream as a man stepped out in

front of her. Her first thought was of Jack the Ripper. He'd come back to his old haunting grounds!

'Dear me, I'm sorry I startled you, dear lady. I mean you no harm I do assure you.'

Agnes eyed the well-dressed man suspiciously. There was only one reason a man like this one was hanging round these parts, and that wasn't just to do a bit of sight-seeing.

Backing away she said harshly, 'Look, mate. If yer looking fer a tart, you've picked on the wrong woman. You'd best get yourself down ter Bethnal Green Road. There's plenty of 'em 'anging about down there.'

Kenneth Wells barely restrained himself from laughing in the old hag's face. As if any man would be interested in an old soak like her. The only reason he had accosted her was the fact she seemed to be interested in young Micky's business.

Stepping back a pace to remove any threat he might pose, he waited to judge the woman's reaction. The gesture worked. His sharp eyes noting the slight relaxation of the scraggy body, he raised his top hat, saying smoothly, 'Please, Madam, I'm a happily married man, and . . .'

Agnes laughed sneeringly. 'That ain't never stopped a bloke before, mate.'

Kenneth shook his head reproachfully. 'I do assure you, Madam, my intentions are quite honourable. The reason I'm down these parts is because I'm trying to keep an eye on my nephew and niece.'

Seeing the puzzled look cross Agnes' face he continued. 'You see, I noticed you too seemed interested in my nephew Micky, and I wondered if we might be of assistance to each other.' He stopped, then seeing he had her attention, hurried on. 'My brother and sister-in-law died just before Christmas, God rest their souls.' He bowed his head in a reverent manner. 'Naturally I asked their children to come and live with my wife and me. Young Molly was only too willing, poor little soul. Lovely child, she is. But Micky, now he's a different kettle of fish altogether. He refused point blank my offer of accommodation, saying he was capable of looking after himself and his sister. Well . . .' He spread his arm towards the derelict house. 'I ask you, dear lady. Does that look to you like a respectable place for a young girl to be left on her own while my no-good nephew walks the streets looking for work?'

''Ang on a minute, mate,' Agnes interrupted him. 'I know Micky well enough, but he ain't never mentioned no sister before.'

Again Kenneth pointed towards the ruined building with his gold-capped walking stick. 'Of course he hasn't. He knows that if the authorities were informed of Molly's present mode of living, she would be taken away immediately. But, if I may ask, Madam, what is your interest in my nephew?'

Agnes hesitated. There was something about the well-spoken gentleman she didn't like.

Kenneth was quick to note her sudden distrust. Doffing his hat he said smoothly, 'As it seems we have something in common, may I buy you a drink? We can talk in comfort instead of standing out here on the street.'

Again Agnes hesitated, then nodded. It wouldn't

do any harm to listen to what the bloke had to say. And she'd get a few free drinks into the bargain.

Side by side they walked back towards the main road.

CHAPTER NINE

''Ere, what's up with Agnes? I ain't seen her looking
so pleased with 'erself since before Arthur went an'
got himself married. If I didn't know better, I'd think
she'd got 'erself a bloke. I told yer my Bert saw her
with some toff just before the Mitsons went away, but
I didn't think nothing of it at the time. I mean ter
say . . . !' Mabel Smith raised her eyebrows in disbelief. 'The poor cow would be 'ard pressed ter find an
ordinary bloke, let alone one with a bit of class. What
d'yer think, Nora?'

Nora Parker cast a disparaging glance first at the
woman by her side, then to the object of their discussion. Both women had known Agnes for over twenty
years and, as her neighbour Mabel had just commented, neither of them had seen the middle-aged
woman looking so happy, nor as smart since the
early days when Agnes had imagined that one day
Arthur would eventually get around to proposing

to her. Yet since the Mitsons had gone on holiday, leaving Agnes in charge of the business, a remarkable change had come over the once dowdy woman, a change that hadn't gone unnoticed by her regular customers.

Agnes, well aware of the speculation surrounding her and thoroughly enjoying her sudden elevated status, smiled sweetly at the elderly woman at the front of the queue as she put a large crusty loaf into a wicker basket. 'That'll be tuppence, please, Mrs Cox.'

'Thanks, Agnes . . . Er, um, so how yer been lately, ducks? Got any news ter share with yer mates, love? Only we couldn't 'elp but notice how 'appy yer've been lately, an' we was wondering like, if yer had anything ter tell us? 'Cos I was only saying ter me daughter the other day, "Rene," I said, "if anyone deserves a bit of 'appiness, it's Agnes; especially after the way Arthur treated her."' The grey head bobbed up and down as if to add weight to her words. 'Now, I ain't just being nosy, love, you've gotta lot of friends round these parts . . . Nah, it's true, ducks, honest.' The bird-like features of Mrs Cox crumpled at the look of scorn that suddenly flashed across Agnes' plain face. Shuffling her small frame awkwardly she murmured, 'Well, I can't stand 'ere gossiping all day. I'll see yer, ducks.' Nodding to the two other women waiting to be served, both of whom had been listening intently to the conversation, the red-faced woman hurried out of the warm bakery.

Agnes, her expression betraying none of the pleasurable churning in her stomach at finding herself the centre of attention, asked airily, 'Made up yer minds yet, ladies? Only yer've been 'ere long enough ter buy up 'alf the shop. Unless yer've just come in ter 'ave a nose round.'

Instantly the two remaining customers sprang to life, their faces turning hard at the insulting tone in Agnes' voice.

As Nora Parker made to come back at Agnes with a suitable retort, Mabel quickly gave the irate woman a discreet nudge in the ribs. Then, her features folding into a warm smile she said sweetly, 'Don't be daft, Agnes. We was just wondering who your gentleman friend was, that's all.'

Taken by surprise, Agnes' cheeks began to burn in confused embarrassment. Noting her uncomfortable reaction, Mabel hurried on gleefully. 'Ah, that surprised yer, didn't it? My Bert saw yer with him in the Nag's Head just before Arthur and Ellen went away. Proper toff my Bert said he was. Now yer can't blame us fer wondering who he is. I mean ter say, it's only natural we should be curious.' Agnes lowered her head in startled bewilderment, and Mabel smiled triumphantly at Nora before resuming her probing. 'Come on, woman, don't keep us in suspense. Who is he? Where d'yer meet 'im?'

Regaining some of her composure Agnes raised her head and stared hard at the two women. Women who had been coming into this shop for years and never before had they shown any genuine interest in her, apart from the time Arthur had brought Ellen here to live. Oh, they'd been out in force then, the nosy, hypocritical old cows. Making snide remarks and looking at her with feigned sympathy. How she had come to hate them all. These women with their boring, dependable husbands and snotty-nosed children, children who were now grown and rarely visited their parents, unless they were after something, apart from Nora, whose son Ted still lived at home and supported his widowed mother. The rest of them were still living in tiny houses, for ever in debt and having to watch every penny. And they had the cheek to feel, not only superior to her, but sorry for her as well! At least she owned her own house and she had a few bob in the bank, which was more than the majority of her customers could lay claim to.

Now she had a man in her life. And not just any man, but a man of means, a real gentleman.

The only fly in the ointment was Kenneth's wife.

Kenneth had been very open about his marital status right from the start and, as their friendship had blossomed, brought about by their mutual interest in young Micky Masters, Kenneth had confided in her that his wife's health, which had never been robust, was now so bad the doctors had told Kenneth to prepare himself for the worst. It was that evening that he had taken hold of her hand and, his eyes locked onto hers, had asked her gently if she would wait until he was free. A tingle of excitement ran up her spine as she recalled the intimate moment.

'Well, come on, woman, out with it.' The loud voice jerked Agnes back to the present and the naked curiosity that filled the faces of the two women. They were both smiling at her as if they were close friends, but their eyes slyly mocked her. Agnes recognised the look at once; after all, it was a look she had witnessed hundreds of times over the years. But now things had changed. Now she was the one holding the upper hand and she revelled in the new experience. It had been a very long time since she had felt any self-worth or respect for herself. Now she had both and she wasn't such a fool as to imagine that these women had suddenly become her bosom friends. Still, she was only human, and the desire to show off quickly overcame her reticence. But she must be careful how much she divulged. Kenneth had been most insistent about their relationship remaining a private matter between the two of them. But once Kenneth's wife was dead, there would be no more need for secrecy.

Assuming a superior air, Agnes straightened her back and, with her head held high, said, 'As a matter of fact I do have a gentleman friend, but I can't say any more at the moment.' She hesitated, then, unable to maintain her lofty attitude and desperate to talk about Kenneth, her mouth opened and the words she had fought to keep quiet came tumbling out in a rush of excitement. 'Oh, all right then, I'll tell yer. But yer've gotta promise ter keep it to yerselves.'

Both women edged closer to the counter, their faces agog with excitement.

Looking first over their shoulders to make sure no one else was about to enter the shop Agnes took a deep breath. 'Like I said, I can't say too much at the minute, but let's just say I might not be working 'ere fer much longer. My gentleman friend is very comfortably off, an' once we're married he'll expect me ter

tay at 'ome, especially with the little one ter . . .' Agnes
broke off, her face registering her horror at the near
lip she had made in referring to Kenneth's niece.

But the inference hadn't gone unnoticed. Immedi-
tely Mabel exclaimed, 'Bleeding 'ell, Agnes. Yer ain't
pregnant, are yer? Gawd love us, yer can't be, not at
'our age.'

Before the startled Agnes could reply Nora Parker
napped loudly, ''Course she ain't too old, Mabel.
'here's plenty of women that's been caught out 'cos
hey thought they was too old ter get pregnant.'
'ocking her head to one side she added slyly, 'An'
'er only in yer early forties, ain't yer, Agnes?'

Agnes' face had turned scarlet, both in embarrass-
nent and deep despair. It had been her life's wish to
lave a child of her own, but as the years had passed
'y she had reluctantly resigned herself to the fact that
he would never have the joy of hearing a child call
ler mother. There was also the fear that one day soon
Illen would announce she was pregnant and that
vould be her undoing. The thought of watching
Illen's stomach swell, and Arthur strutting around as
he expectant father was enough to make Agnes'
nsides knot in silent agony. She wouldn't be able to
'ear it, she knew she wouldn't. Yet now she was to
ave a second chance. Once Micky was out of the way
eaving Kenneth the chance to rescue the little girl
rom the squalor in which she lived, then she, Agnes
Iandly, would become a mother to the orphaned child
once Kenneth was free to make her his wife. And
naybe, just maybe, she might still have a child of her
wn one day. Though deep down she knew that her

chances of becoming a mother at her time of life were very slim.

Gathering her startled wits she said bitterly, 'No, ain't pregnant. Chance would be a fine thing, wouldn' it?'

The raw, naked pain on Agnes' plain face momen-tarily silenced both women, causing them pangs o guilt as they remembered how they had treated Agnes in the past. Nora Parker cleared her throat as i preparing to speak, but no words came. In those few moments it was as if a veneer had been stripped from Agnes' face, leaving in its place an anguish so painfu to behold that both women dropped their gaze, a genuine feeling of sympathy engulfing them.

Nora was the first one to speak. For once at a disad vantage she said softly, 'Sorry, Agnes, we didn't mean any harm, did we, Mabel?' She looked to her friend for support.

'Oh, no, Agnes, 'course we didn't.' Her eyes flick ering to Nora, Mabel continued uncomfortably. ' mean ter say, we wouldn't be deliberately spiteful honest.' Floundering now she glanced back at Nora breathing a sigh of relief as her friend took over the strained conversation.

Anxious to change the topic of conversation Nora asked pleasantly, 'Well now, 'ow long is Arthur and Ellen away for?'

Her composure back in place once more, Agnes made a great play of rearranging the display of cakes on the counter before replying, 'They went fer two weeks, so they'll be back at the weekend.'

Their purchases bought and paid for, the women

prepared to leave, anxious to get outside so they could discuss Agnes and her gentleman friend in more detail. It was as they reached the door that Nora remarked casually, 'I still can't believe Arthur let Ellen talk 'im into 'aving a holiday. I wouldn't be surprised if they came back early, especially as Arthur's never been away from the place fer over twenty years. He's probably worrying 'imself sick his business will go ter rack and ruin while 'e's away. Mind you, I gotta say, Bill's baking ain't a patch on Arthur's, though don't tell Bill I said so. Anyway, see yer tomorrow, Agnes. 'Bye.'

No sooner had the women departed when the bell over the shop announced another customer, and it was one o'clock before Agnes had the chance for some time to herself.

With Bill minding the shop, Agnes took her dinner break in the kitchen. And as she ate a crusty cheese roll, she thought back over the past three weeks, her eyes and mouth softening at the memories. For the first time in twenty years she had a purpose for getting up in the morning, apart from going to work. Finishing her snack she wandered over to the mirror hanging over the sink and took stock of her reflection. And once more she marvelled at the difference a bit of hair dye and new clothes could make to a person's appearance. She looked ten years younger, but, she reflected sadly, no amount of hair dye and new clothes could make her more attractive. She was still as plain as she'd always been. Then she brightened. Kenneth obviously thought her attractive. In fact he had been lavish in his compliments on her new appearance. Idly smoothing down the ruffles on her new white blouse she then inspected her hair. She had toyed with the idea of letting it hang loose, but had quickly dismissed the notion. The last thing she wanted was to look like mutton dressed as lamb. She had, however, left a few wisps of hair framing her face, giving her features a softer look. The rest of her hair was neatly plaited and pinned to the back of her head. Turning her head this way then that, she was suddenly overwhelmed by a wave of frustration as she recalled all the wasted years. If only she hadn't been so stupid as to hope that Arthur would one day rekindle the romance of their early days. And where had her hopes and loyalty got her? Cast aside, her heart broken, her self-esteem shattered. If only she'd had the sense to move on when the affair with Arthur had ended she could have been married, maybe even had a family by now. If only! The two most tragic words in the world. But, by some miracle, she had been given a second chance of happiness and she wasn't going to waste it this time. Checking the mirror to make sure she had no crumbs on her mouth she suddenly recalled Nora Parker's comment about Arthur coming back early and the memory of those casually spoken words brought Agnes' head up sharply.

Arthur would never have consented to such an arrangement if she and Ellen, for once allied against the weak-willed man, hadn't constantly kept on at him, day after day, until the poor, harassed baker had finally agreed, just to get a bit of peace.

Pouring herself another mug of tea, Agnes' mind whirled anxiously, her thoughts going round and round her head like a pet mouse on a spinning wheel.

If she was to have any chance of a new life with Kenneth she would have to move quickly. Only last night Kenneth had pleaded with her again to put their plans into motion, but for some inexplicable reason she had continued to stall for more time. But now she realised there was no more time to prevaricate. Once Arthur and Ellen returned and, knowing Arthur, who must by now be champing at the bit to return home, they could well turn up any time now, she would have no opportunity to get Micky out of the way. She knew too, that, once the deed was done, she would have to leave her small terraced house. For once word got round, as it would surely do, she, Agnes, would no longer be welcomed in the East End. Her head drooped as the enormous consequences of what she was about to do hit her like a physical blow to her stomach. Then she stiffened her resolve. The plan was well worked out. Once Micky was out of the way, she would move into a small hotel, paid for by Kenneth, and there she would stay until they could finally be together. In the meantime he would put her house on the market with a reputable estate agency. Once the house was sold, the money earned would go into her bank account. She would feel easier in her mind once she knew there was a comfortable nest egg to fall back on if things with Kenneth didn't go well.

Not that she expected that to happen, she rebuked herself sharply, but she of all people knew that life didn't always work out as one expected.

Taking a deep breath, she swallowed the last of her

tea and came to a decision. She would do it this evening. Yet even as she tried to convince herself she was doing it with the best of intentions, she couldn't stop the nagging guilt gnawing away inside.

CHAPTER TEN

Micky hastened his steps, a huge grin on his face. Everything was going well for him. He had been able to have Molly with him over the Easter holidays as he had promised her. No one had questioned her presence, accepting at face value his explanation that he was looking after the small girl as a favour to one of his neighbours. The change in Molly had been nothing short of a miracle. That time, as brief as it had been, had given Molly new hope for the future. Micky's grin widened, his whole body alight with happiness. Just this morning Ted had told him that next week he was going to trust Micky with the running of the stall in Hoxton, while he, Ted, looked for a regular pitch down Roman Road. It would only be for one morning, but if he did well Micky knew that Ted would eventually give him more responsibility. His step jaunty, Micky skipped along the pavement. He wouldn't let Ted down, not ever. Although it would be some time before Ted would let Micky run the stall by himself full time. He had even gone so far as to say that come Micky's sixteenth birthday, they would make permanent arrangements pertaining to the running of the stalls. Whistling under his breath Micky did a quick sum in his head. He would be fifteen in May, so it would only be a matter of just over a year before he would be given the chance to be a proper stall holder. For the present though he had to content himself with the knowledge that he had a regular wage coming in each week. The only thing that worried Micky was the fact that he was deceiving both Ted and Ellen, the two most important people in his young life, apart from Molly. He'd lost count of the times he had nearly blurted out the truth to Ted as they worked side by side down the market, but mercifully he had managed to keep his tongue in check. Even though he was sure Ted wouldn't turn him over to the authorities, Micky wasn't sure of the law regarding minors. Maybe Ted would get into trouble if he knew of Micky's living conditions and didn't report it. No! Micky shook his head. He couldn't risk it. Yet sometimes the need to unburden himself was so strong he had to leave the stall on some pretext for fear he might reveal the truth. Anyway, with his future looking set he would soon be able to look after Molly legally. His mind skirting around the many pitfalls he would have to overcome Micky turned his attention to tomorrow, his half day off. He hadn't told Molly yet, but now he had a few pounds put by he was going to get the *Hackney Gazette* and look for lodgings. He would have to be careful.

f course. The first sign of a nosy landlady and he
vould be off like a shot. There were plenty of places
round the East End where the owners of the
oarding houses asked no questions. And all he and
Molly needed was one room – with a stout lock, that
vas the most important thing of all. If everything
vent well, he and his sister should be safely housed
y the weekend, His grin broadened still further as
e imagined Moll's face when he told her he'd found
omewhere for them both to live without fear.

As he approached the bakery he thought of Ellen
nd, as always when he thought of the pretty young
voman, his heart gave a leap of happiness. He was
ld enough to know that Ellen was out of his reach,
ut that didn't stop him from loving her.

Passing the bakery he was startled to hear Agnes
alling his name. Stopping, he turned to face her, his
yes wary. He hadn't set foot in the bakery since Ellen
ad gone on holiday, preferring instead to buy his
read from the bakers down Hoxton, rather than have
face that old bag. Now here she was framed in the
oorway, her face radiating pleasure at seeing him.
Micky paused. Life, since his parents had died, had
ardened him and made him suspicious. But even if
e hadn't changed, he would have been wary of the
ospitable welcome when he knew Agnes didn't like
im, had never liked him. He blinked, then looked
gain. She was still smiling at him as if he were a dear
riend. Assuming a defensive stance he said guard-
dly, 'Yeah, what d'yer want?'

Agnes, her heart thumping at what she was about
do, managed a watery smile. 'Well, that's a nice

welcome, I must say. And here's me saving the usual
bread and cakes Ellen always puts by fer yer.'

Thrown off balance by the kind words and friendly
face of the woman who had always treated him like
something you'd scrape off your shoe, Micky re
mained where he was.

Agnes immediately noted Micky's suspicion and
swallowed hard. This wasn't going to be as simple as
she had first thought. Micky might be a mere boy, but
he had the intelligence of someone twice his age. A
feeling of desperation gripped her. The plan Kenneth
had outlined must be accomplished. With a supreme
effort Agnes gave a wry smile. 'Look, mate. I know
we ain't exactly been the best of friends, but I'm trying
Can't yer give me another chance . . . eh?'

Still Micky hesitated. But his nature, kind by heart
was willing to give Agnes the benefit of the doubt
His eyes met Agnes' as if trying to gauge her true feel
ings and saw true remorse mirrored in her eyes. What
he didn't suspect was the real reason behind the
remorseful look. His body relaxed slightly, but his feet
dragged awkwardly as he followed Agnes into the
shop.

'Thanks, Agnes. Ta. I've been buying me bread and
cakes down the market, but they ain't as nice as the
are 'ere.'

Her back to him, Agnes grabbed the parcel she'd
put under the counter earlier on, then, her heart
hammering so hard she was sure the boy must hear
it and realise the truth behind her actions, quickly
handed it over. 'There yer go, mate . . . Nah! Put yer
money away, love,' she exclaimed as Micky reached

into his pocket. 'It'd only go stale. Besides, Ellen never charges yer, does she?'

His face flustered Micky muttered, 'That was when I was doing odd jobs, I don't expect ter keep getting me grub fer nothing.'

Bustling quickly now in case someone came into the shop and witnessed the transaction, Agnes hurriedly ushered Micky out into the street. 'Sorry ter rush yer, love, but I want ter shut up fer the night.'

Still feeling awkward and ill at ease, Micky was only too pleased to leave. Then he paused. Looking back at Agnes he smiled and said shyly, 'Yer look nice, Agnes. An' thanks fer the grub. See yer.'

Agnes watched him go, her hand clutching her throat. Those few simple kind words had thrown her completely. As the minutes ticked by her troubled mind was screaming that what she was planning was wrong. She still didn't like the lad, but he'd never done anything to her, and just now, he had been so nice to her. And the words he had spoken had been genuine.

Then Kenneth's face floated before her eyes, and before she could change her mind she let out a loud shout. 'Stop 'im. Stop thief. The little bleeder's nicked me supper.'

Micky was halfway down the street when Agnes' strident voice reached him, and in that awful, heart-stopping moment he knew, knew that his earlier suspicions had been right. In the split second it took to realise he had been set up he thought of going back and facing Agnes and her lies, then he thought of Molly and his feet took flight, his hand discarding the parcel of food as if it had suddenly turned into a burning flame. And as he ran Agnes' voice followed him, high and screeching. Doors were flung open and people poured into the street to see what the commotion was all about. Then Micky was ducking and diving past them all, dodging their grasping hands.

Quiet now, Agnes watched until Micky disappeared from sight, a small crowd chasing after the young, terrified boy. To her surprise tears sprang to her eyes, making her blink. Then she stiffened as a loud voice boomed, 'What's up, Agnes? What's all the excitement about?'

Police Constable John Smith, the local bobby, loomed in front of Agnes as if he had been conjured out of thin air.

Gulping nervously Agnes stuttered, 'It's that Micky Masters. He's gorn an' nicked stuff from the shop. I just turned me back fer a minute, an' . . . an' the next minute he'd grabbed an armful of stuff from the counter and legged it.'

PC Smith's eyes narrowed. 'Now, Agnes, I know the lad slightly. He doesn't strike me as a thief. And anyway, why should he steal? He's got a good job with Ted now, he doesn't have any reason to thieve.'

Stepping nearer the trembling woman the policeman asked gruffly, 'Look here, Agnes, you sure it was young Micky? 'Cos I just can't see it myself.'

Agnes looked at the scepticism in the policeman's eyes and braced herself. It was done now, there was no going back.

Assuming an injured air she drew herself up to her fullest height and replied frostily, ''Course I'm sure. I ain't daft. Like I said, the boy came into the shop asking when Ellen was coming back, and while me back was turned he grabbed the parcel I'd laid out on the counter ter take home fer me supper and was gone before I could stop 'im.'

PC Smith pushed his helmet further back on his head, his eyes still sceptical. 'All right, Agnes. I'll see to it, but I gotta say I can't see Micky stealing, he's not the type.'

Her aggression coming to the fore, Agnes, feeling more in control of herself, bridled, 'You calling me a liar, John Smith? 'Cos if yer are then say it ter me face, instead of making sly comments.'

The veteran constable stared back at the small woman, his shrewd eyes noting the furtive look in Agnes' eyes before she dropped her gaze. 'All right, I'll take your word for it – for now. But I'll tell you something, Agnes Handly, there's something fishy about the whole business, so I hope you're right, for your sake.'

With a curt nod the police officer strode off in the direction Micky had taken, his hobnailed boots ringing out loudly on the cobbled streets as he moved quickly after the small crowd, all of them relishing the unexpected bit of excitement.

Micky, his face streaming with sweat and fear, ran on, but he had no chance of outrunning the baying mob chasing him. Not heeding where he was going, Micky turned a corner, then stopped; he had run into a dead end. Frantically looking around for a way out Micky began to cry. And that unexpected act of weakness was the final straw for the proud young boy.

Knowing he was trapped Micky angrily wiped the tears from his cheeks and turned to the excited crowd.

'I ain't done nothing. I didn't steal anything, honest. That old cow . . .'

A thick-set man moved forward grabbing Micky by the scruff of his neck. 'Yeah! That's what they all say, yer thieving little bastard. Let's see what the coppers 'ave ter say, shall we?'

Micky struggled wildly in the vice-like grip, then a loud voice of authority rang out. 'That's enough, Ron. I'll deal with this, let the boy go.'

All eyes turned to the uniformed man, their ghoulish enjoyment slipping from their faces as they realised the matter was now out of their hands.

The man called Ron, self-appointed leader of the crowd, reluctantly loosened his grip on Micky, the excitement disappearing from his fleshy features. 'All right, keep yer hair on. I was gonna take 'im down the station. Yer've saved me a trip.'

'Yeah, I'm sure you were, Ron. You certainly know the way, don't you?'

The deliberate reference to his shady past brought a flash of anger to the man's face, then he gave Micky a vicious push towards the stern-faced officer.

''Ere, take the thieving little bleeder. I'll tell yer something else an' all. It's the last time I try an' do the law any favours.'

'Well, I'm sure the force will be able to struggle on without your help, Ron. Now, on your way, the lot of you.'

One by one the crowd dispersed, their low mutterings fading as they returned to their homes.

Left alone with the police officer Micky looked up at the familiar burly man, his eyes pleading. 'I didn't steal anything, Officer, honest I didn't. She . . . I mean Agnes, she gave me the parcel. I offered ter pay fer it, but she said I could 'ave it fer nothing.' The tears began to spurt again, but Micky, in his agitated state, didn't realise he was crying. 'Please don't take me in, Officer. I ain't done nothing wrong. Ellen . . . I mean Mrs Mitson'll tell yer I ain't no thief . . .'

The officer looked at the tear-stained face with pity. There was something very wrong here. Although he didn't know the boy well, John Smith knew his patch, and the people on it. He had seen the young boy frequently, and knew of his friendship with the baker's wife. There wasn't much that went on around these streets that the veteran police officer didn't know about. He also knew Agnes Handly, and of the two he was rather inclined to believe the boy, though why Agnes should try and get the boy arrested was beyond him. But a crime had been reported and he had to take the boy in for questioning.

His voice low and sympathetic he said kindly, 'I'm sorry, son, I've got to take you down the station. But look, as soon as I've booked you in, I'll go round and have a word with Ted Parker and get him to come down, unless you'd rather I fetched your parents.'

Micky's heart leapt in fright. 'Oh no, don't . . . I mean, I ain't got a dad, an' me mum ain't been well . . .' Surprised at how easily the lies were tumbling from his lips Micky added, 'I don't want ter worry 'er, Officer. So could yer get Ted, please?'

Taking hold of the boy's arm PC Smith led him out

121

of the alley and into the main thoroughfare, his soothing voice erasing some of Micky's fear. 'Don't you go worrying, son. Ted'll sort this mess out, he's a good bloke, is Ted Parker.'

Wiping his face across the sleeve of his jacket Micky nodded dumbly, his spirits rising at the kindness in the policeman's voice. Quieter now he walked alongside the officer, his only thought being of Molly. As they entered the station in Mare Street Micky squeezed his eyes tightly shut and prayed silently – 'Please God, let Ted come quickly and make this nightmare go away so I can get home to Molly . . .'

Micky sat on a damp, smelly bunk bed, his eyes never leaving the closed cell door. He was finding it hard to breathe in the small, confined space. There wasn't even the luxury of a cell to himself, for lying on a similar bed only inches from his was a filthy, drunken tramp, whose snores were guaranteed to keep Micky awake all night. Not that he was planning on sleeping. Instead he closed his eyes, his mind saying over and over, 'Ted will be here soon.' He would. Ted wouldn't let him down. But the cell door remained shut tight, and the fear that had entered his heart the moment he had been thrown into the cell was fast turning into sheer terror. His only comfort was his unwavering faith in Ted Parker. He looked over at the tramp then dropped his face into his hands.

'Please, Ted. Hurry up. Come and get me, Ted, please. I'm so frightened. I've never been so scared in all me life. Please, Ted, come and get me . . . please.'

* * *

PC John Smith resumed his beat, his mind still on Micky Masters and the boy's refusal to give his address for fear of upsetting his ailing mother. Of course the woman would have to be informed of her son's arrest: he was bound by law to inform the next of kin of any prisoner. First though he would find Ted Parker. If anyone could help the young lad out of his present predicament, then Ted was the man to do it. He was only a few minutes away from Ted Parker's house when the local pub doors opened and a pile of men spilled out onto the street and proceeded to brawl. Sighing loudly, PC Smith waded into the fight. Luckily for him, two of his colleagues were soon on the scene and between them they managed to break up the fight, arresting four men in the process. With his hands full, the kindly police officer forgot all about young Micky. He only remembered when he returned to the station some hours later to sign off his shift. Guilt stricken, he raced to find Ted, praying that the man would be at home. His prayers were answered. Not a man to waste words, the officer, a friend of Ted's for over ten years, quickly explained the situation.

Within twenty minutes Ted was at the station, and with John Smith backing him up, the duty sergeant agreed to let Micky out on bail, providing that Ted, in the absence of a parent present, took full responsibility for the boy, and the charge levelled against him until the case came to court.

When Micky emerged from the cell, cowed and shivering, his handsome face blotched and swollen with tears, it took all of Ted's willpower not to sweep the stricken boy up into his arms. Then Micky looked up at him and, like a small child, ran towards the man he had come to love and threw himself against the strong, safe body. It was then that Ted, with a low groan of pity, picked Micky up and held him tight against his chest. And as he carried him from the police station, his voice softly whispering against Micky's ear, a feeling of rage against Agnes Handly and her foul accusations threatened to overwhelm him. Forcing himself to keep his emotions in check Ted took the still shivering boy to his home, vowing that, come tomorrow he would find Agnes and, if need be, shake the truth out of the lying, spiteful bitch.

The trauma of the past few hours had taken its toll on Micky, but not enough for him to have forgotten about his sister.

Wrapped in a warm blanket, with Nora Parker bustling around him and plying him with food and drink, it was difficult to get a word in as the irate woman continued to vent her anger against Agnes who had been the instigator in the whole sorry business.

Finally, conscious of the time and unable to keep quiet any longer, Micky caught hold of Nora's hand and, looking up at her beseechingly, he stuttered, 'Me sister. I've gotta get home ter me sister. She'll be so afraid . . . She's on— only eight. An'. . . an' there's a man after 'er. A bad man. He . . . he wants ter . . . ter . . .' His trembling voice trailed off, not able to speak of the vile intentions Kenneth Wells harboured against his little sister.

Ted and Nora exchanged glances, then Ted, drawing up a chair next to Micky, said quietly, 'You ain't got any mother, have yer, Micky?'

Fresh tears spilled from Micky's eyes as he shook his bowed head, ashamed to look Ted in the eye.

Glancing first at the startled Nora, Ted drew a deep breath and said kindly, 'I think yer've got some explaining ter do, mate.'

And Micky, too tired and scared to lie any longer, started to talk, his voice rising with agitation as he imagined Molly, alone, terrified out of her wits, wondering what had happened to him. But what really turned Micky's blood cold was the thought of Kenneth Wells getting his hands on the vulnerable child.

Before Micky had finished talking, Ted already had his coat on, his face grim. 'Come on, then. You'd better show me where you've been living. And after we've got Molly safely back here, there's gonna be some serious talking to be done.'

Micky lowered his gaze, thinking that Ted was angry with him for lying for so long. Then his chin was being pulled upwards, and Ted was smiling.

'Take that miserable look off yer face. You should 'ave told me what was going on from the start, but I suppose in your shoes I'd've done the same. Anyway, we know the truth now, and yer don't have ter worry any more. We'll sort it out . . . won't we, Mum?' He turned to look at the hovering Nora.

Her eyes misty, the normally stalwart woman flapped her hands at them crying, 'Of course we will, yer daft sod. Now go an' fetch that poor little mite. She must be scared ter death by now.'

Outside the house Micky tentatively caught hold of Ted's hand, a gesture he wouldn't have dreamed of a

125

few hours earlier. But he needed comfort, needed to feel safe, and Ted made him feel safe. His throat tightening, Ted gave a loud cough before saying briskly, 'Well, come on then, let's go and get this sister of yours.'

As it was dark and nobody could see, Micky kept a tight hold of Ted's hand, as if he was afraid the man beside him would suddenly disappear. Twenty minutes later they were standing inside the derelict building and while Micky called out for his sister Ted looked around the filthy ruin in horror. The thought of two children living in these conditions for so long brought a lump of sadness coupled with anger to Ted's throat. His eyes sweeping the darkness he vowed silently that if it lay with him, Micky and his sister would never again have to live in such appalling conditions.

Micky climbed up the rope whispering, 'Moll, Moll, it's me, Micky. I'm sorry I'm so late, but I got into a bit of bother.' Silence greeted him. Screwing up his eyes he moved nearer the bed he shared with Molly, his stomach beginning to churn with fear. Blindly feeling his way towards the bed, he moved his hands over the smelly blankets expecting to come into contact with the small lump that was Molly, but the bed was empty. His eyes stretched wide in horror and disbelief as he opened his mouth and began to scream.

He'd come too late – Molly was no longer here. Someone had taken her, and he didn't have to think hard as to who had abducted his little sister. Unable to face the horror of what had happened to Molly,

Micky gave a low anguished groan. Red spots danced before his eyes – and then he was falling.

Falling into a warm, welcoming black hole where there was no feeling, no fear, just peace – lovely, wonderful peace.

CHAPTER ELEVEN

About an hour before Micky was rescued from the prison cell by Ted, Sadie North, a local prostitute was walking alongside a punter she had just picked up, chatting away nineteen to the dozen to keep the nervous man from changing his mind and making a bolt for it. She'd had a lot of men like the one shuffling awkwardly by her side, their shifty eyes darting from left to right for fear of being seen with the flamboyant prostitute. Middle-aged men who weren't getting any loving from their worn-out wives, women who were ground down by the daily existence of living, terrified of falling for another child to feed when there was barely enough to survive on as it was. The man who had picked her up on the corner of Mare Street had just staggered out from the Nag's Head, his courage bolstered by three pints of ale, and a small whisky; money that should have been used to feed his wife and children. Now the drink was wearing off and with it the beer-fuelled bravado.

Not for the first time Sadie wished she had somewhere local she could take her customers, instead of having to walk the streets in search of a dark alley. Her profession was sordid enough without having to perform her business down a darkened sidewalk. But her two-room flat that she was so proud of was her haven and her home, somewhere she could change out of her working clothes, and into respectable clothing and forget about her unsavoury occupation for a brief period of time. If she was lucky, a customer would offer to pay for an hour's pleasure in any one of the dozens of boarding houses and run-down hotels that asked no questions, but usually, like tonight, it was up to her to find somewhere to ply her trade. Still, she comforted herself with the thought that this man was to be her last punter for tonight.

Tucking the man's arm tighter to her side Sadie looked for somewhere suitable to conclude her business. Stopping outside the only building still standing among a pile of rubble that had once been a row of terraced houses, Sadie quickly pulled the man inside the pitch-black building. Safely off the streets and out of sight of any passers-by, the pot-bellied man regained his courage. Not bothering with the niceties of foreplay, the man grabbed Sadie's large breasts, his slobbering lips sucking at her neck and face. Anxious to get the familiar routine over with as quickly as possible, Sadie averted her face and lifted her skirts as the man began to unbutton his trousers, his breathing becoming ragged and harsh. Pressed up against the crumbling wall, Sadie gazed over the man's head, her eyes blank, her mind shutting out the act in which she was participating. Automatically murmuring encouragement to the sweating man, she urged him on, moaning and panting as if she was enjoying the experience as much as he, while her mind was wondering if she had enough food in the flat for her supper. Sadie waited impatiently for the man to finish. From experience she knew it wouldn't be long and, moments later, she was proved right as the man gave a loud shuddering sigh, his head falling onto Sadie's shoulder. Glad the unpleasant act was over, Sadie was about to ask for her money when a frightened scream from above their heads caused both parties to jump in fright.

Crouched on her bed, Molly, already scared and anxious at Micky's lateness, had heard the man and woman come into the building. She was used to tramps coming into the house, especially when it was cold and raining, but they never stayed for long, and Molly always remained as quiet as a mouse, as Micky had instructed her. But when the man had started to make loud, strange noises, and the woman had begun to moan and call out in a muffled voice, Molly, her heart beating fast, had crawled carefully over to the edge of the room. Not allowed to light her candle until Micky was home, Molly squinted into the gloom below, trying to make out the two shadowy figures in the darkness, her only source of light being a thin stream of moonlight shining through one of the many holes in the roof. But it wasn't bright enough to light the lower part of the house. Hearing the man's harsh breathing become louder coupled with the woman's low screams, Molly had curled herself up into a tight ball praying for her brother to come home. The sounds became increasingly louder, and Molly, thinking the man was hurting the woman and unable to keep quiet any longer, scrambled closer to the edge and screamed wildly, 'Stop it! Stop it! Let her go, you 'orrible man. You're a bad man. Stop hurting the lady.'

Recovering her wits, Sadie squinted her eyes up towards the sound of the childish voice. The man, quickly taking advantage of Sadie's distraction, rearranged his clothing and took to his heels. Hearing the sound of running footsteps, Sadie spun round, her face hardening as she realised she had been conned out of her money, bloody well-earned money at that, considering what she had to do for it. At any other time she would have given chase, but knowing there was a frightened child somewhere in the rotting building Sadie had no option but to let the man go. But it wasn't in her nature to let the crafty bleeder off completely.

'You stinking bastard. Don't think yer've got away with fleecing me. I'll catch up with you, you take me word. An' when I do, I hope your poor wife'll be with you. You won't be so bleeding cocky then.'

Panting with rage, Sadie glared down the dimly lit street, then her attention was brought back to the presence of the unknown child by the sound of muffled sobbing. Careful not to frighten the poor little mite more than she had been already, Sadie called out softly, 'It's all right, love. The bad man's gone, you can come out now.'

When no answer came, just the continual quiet sobbing, Sadie moved cautiously nearer the sound, her eyes raised. She saw the rope dangling from the old beams and thought of climbing it, then common sense quickly dismissed the idea. That particular route might be all right for a small child, but no way would it take her weight.

Standing directly beneath the rope she again called out, 'I know you're scared, love, but I ain't gonna hurt you,' but the sobbing only intensified.

Sadie was in a quandary. It was obvious the child needed help, but if she wasn't going to trust her enough to show herself, then there wasn't much Sadie could do. On the other hand, she couldn't just leave the child in this dump on her own. She wouldn't be able to sleep nights if she walked away and abandoned the child to the mercy of any passing pervert, and God knows there were plenty of them about. Trying a different tack she said calmly, 'All right, love. I don't blame you for not coming down. I mean to say, yer don't know me, but I don't want to just go off an' leave you, not after you helped me. After all, one good turn deserves another, don't it? You scared off that nasty man, didn't you? I don't know what I would've done if you hadn't of been here. But if you want me to go, then I will. Thanks for helping me, love, I'm really grateful.' Sadie paused, her ears pricked for any sound from above. 'I'm leaving now, love. 'Bye.' So saying she walked loudly on the spot to make it sound as if she was going.

Up above, Molly sat huddled on her bed, her young mind struggling to know what to do for the best. She was tired, cold and hungry, but most of all she was desperately frightened.

Even though she had no clock, Molly knew that her brother should have been back hours ago. She knew too that for Micky to be so late something terrible must have happened to him. And she couldn't even go and try to find him in case that horrible man was waiting for her to step outside the safety of her home.

In her young life she had only known two men. One was her father, whom she had adored and who had made her feel safe and loved. The other man was Kenneth Wells. He had been nice at first, until . . . Her immature mind quickly shut down on what the man had been trying to do when Micky had come running back that day. Micky had saved her. From what exactly, Molly wasn't quite sure, but she knew enough to know it was bad and nasty, and that just thinking of it made her feel sort of mucky inside.

From her limited experience of life she had imagined that there was only one bad man she had to avoid, but now she knew better. Her world, until now, had been very black and white for Molly. She stayed in the derelict building while Micky was at work, so that the bad man couldn't get her. Now she realised there were plenty more men of his type, and that newfound knowledge struck a chill into her heart. What if Micky didn't come home? What if something terrible had happened to him? What would she do then? She couldn't stay up here for ever. She desperately needed help, and down below there was a woman who might be able to provide that help. But if she showed herself Micky might be angry with her for disobeying his orders. But Micky wasn't here, was he? And if she had any chance of finding him she would need the help of a grown-up. If it had been a man downstairs, Molly wouldn't have dreamed of asking for help. But women didn't do nasty things to children; it was only men who did those nasty, dirty things. And the lady sounded nice. Still Molly hesitated, then she heard the woman's footsteps leaving, and in that moment Molly made up her mind. Scrambling to the edge of the floor, she leant over the edge, crying out in a trembling voice, 'Wait, lady. Don't go. I'll be down in a minute.'

Sadie watched as the small figure deftly slid down the rope with expert ease making it obvious the young girl had done it many times before.

Then the woman and girl were facing each other in the faint light of the moon shining through the rotting roof. Moving slowly, so as not to frighten the girl, Sadie gently took the small, cold hand and moved over to the empty doorway where, in the light shining brightly from the lamp post on the opposite side of the street, the two females took stock of each other. Molly's huge eyes stared in amazement at the lady dressed in a bright red dress with matching feathers stuck on top of equally bright auburn hair. Her mouth agape, Molly, momentarily stuck for words, continued to gaze at the gaudy creature, a sight she had never seen before.

Guessing what was going through the girl's mind, Sadie laughed merrily. 'Gawd 'elp us, love. Close your mouth before a moth flies in. I take it you've never seen anyone dressed like me before, 'ave you?'

134

Instantly contrite at having been caught out in her thoughts, and aware she was displaying bad manners, Molly stuttered, 'I'm sorry for staring, lady. Me mum always said it was rude to stare.'

Her face softening, Sadie asked kindly, 'And where is your mum, love?'

At the mention of her much missed mother, Molly's eyes, already moist, began to well up with fresh tears. 'She died . . . and me dad, an' all. An' . . . an' I don't 'alf miss 'em.'

Her face tender, Sadie crouched down and said softly, 'I'm sorry about that, love, I really am. But who looks after you now? You can't be caring for yourself.'

Sniffing loudly, Molly answered, 'Me brother Micky looks after me. He's nearly grown-up now, he'll be fifteen in a few weeks' time. But . . . but he hasn't come 'ome yet, an' . . . an' he's usually back by now.' She gave another loud sniff. 'And I'm scared something's happened to 'im, 'cos he'd never leave me on purpose. He's me brother, an' he loves me.'

When the strange woman's arms went around her shoulders Molly flinched then, needing physical comfort, the comfort her mother used to provide, she relaxed against the soft, sweet-smelling woman. Feeling the small frame nestled so trustingly against hers Sadie swallowed hard. It had been a long time since she had felt contact with another human body. Her punters didn't count. Contact with them was limited to the minimum amount of time possible. But that kind of contact was devoid of any warmth or affection; it was simply business. Now, with the child's head nestled in the voluptuous folds of her breasts,

135

Sadie felt a surge of tenderness and fierce protective-
ness.

Hugging the small girl tighter Sadie thought
quickly. She couldn't leave the child here to fend for
herself; on the other hand there was the brother to
think of. There could be any number of reasons why
he was so late. And when, or if, he turned up and
found his sister gone he would be frantic. She would
have to leave a message of some kind. But how? She
wasn't in the habit of carrying writing material on her
person. Maybe the child could help. Tilting Molly's
chin upwards she said, 'Now look, love, I can't leave
you 'ere, so I'll have to take you home with me . . .
Hang on, mate, don't be frightened . . .' she added
quickly as she felt the girl begin to struggle in her
grasp. 'What I was thinking was, we could maybe
leave your brother a message, to let him know where
you are. I can't just take you away without leaving
some sort of note for him, can I? I mean to say, what'll
he think when he comes home and finds you gone?
Why, the poor little sod'll be out of his mind with
worry. The problem is, I ain't got no paper or pen.
How about you, love? You got anything we could
write a note to your brother on?'

Molly chewed her lip thoughtfully, her confused
mind torn between the desire to go with the lady, or
to stay here in the dark and cold waiting for Micky
to turn up. What if he'd had an accident? No one knew
about her, no one would come and tell her if Micky
was hurt or . . . Her mind shied away from the
unimaginable possibility to explain Micky's absence.

Watching the girl struggle with her conscience Sadie

said wryly, 'Unless you'd rather I fetched the law, 'cos I can't leave you 'ere on your own.'

Instantly Molly's eyes filled with fear. Her body trembling she cried, 'Oh, no, please! Don't tell the coppers. They'd take me away an' put me back in the workhouse. An' . . . an' it's 'orrible there.' Grabbing hold of Sadie's hands Molly hung on to them like a drowning man clinging to a life raft. 'We could write a note on me slate. Micky got it for me and some chalk so I could learn to spell and add up, 'cos I can't go to school any more. Wait a minute, I'll go and get them.' Scrambling up the rope she paused halfway and stared hard at the gaudily dressed woman, a woman Molly was now desperate to hold on to. 'You won't go, will you, lady? You will wait for me, won't you?'

Sadie nodded. ''Course I won't leave yer, you silly cow. Go on, get your slate and chalk.'

Molly was up and back down the rope in record time. ''Ere you are, lady. You'll 'ave to write the message, I ain't that good at writing yet. But I'm learning. After all,' she whispered sadly, 'I ain't got nothing else to do all day.'

Taking the slate, Sadie again moved out of the building into the street where the light was better, and after a moment's thought asked the hovering Molly, 'What's your brother's name again, love, I've forgotten. Come to think of it, I don't know your name either. In fact, we ain't been properly introduced.' Holding out her hand she said in mock formality, 'I'm Sadie North. How do you do?'

A shy smile lit up Molly's face as she solemnly took

the proffered hand saying, 'My name's Molly, and me brother's name is Micky, Micky Masters.'

'Hello, Molly, pleased to meet you. Now then, we'd best get a move on.' Raising her gaze to the darkening sky she added, 'It looks like it's going to chuck it down any minute.'

Finishing off the brief note that merely gave her name and address and that Molly was safe with her, Sadie put the stub of chalk in her beaded bag. Going back into the damp-smelling building, Sadie, with Molly close behind, looked around for somewhere to leave the slate so that Micky would be able to see it the minute he returned. The trouble was that with no proper lighting, except that from the street lamp on the other side of the road, and the weak stream of moonlight, it was difficult to think of where to place the slate where it would be easily seen.

Voicing her dilemma, Molly said earnestly, 'I know, lady, I'll put it on our bed. That's the first place Micky'll look for me.' Once again Molly scrambled up the rope, placing the slate at the foot of the double mattress.

She was about to descend the rope when Sadie called up, 'You'd better bring your coat, if you've got one. It's turning bleed— I mean it's turning bitter, an' it's starting to rain.'

'Oh, yes, I've got a coat, Micky bought me one at Easter. I'll get it. Hang on, lady, I won't be a minute.'

The desperate fear in Molly's voice caused a tightness in Sadie's throat, while at the same time she wondered what she was letting herself in for. For all she knew, this Micky character might be a thieving ruffian. Then she uttered a short laugh. What was she thinking? After all the years on the streets she was more than able to look after herself – she'd had enough practice. And if she could handle grown men, she didn't think she'd have much difficulty in managing a young lad of fourteen.

Terrified the lady might leave if she dallied too long, Molly grabbed her coat, bouncing on the mattress as she shrugged her arms into the thick sleeves. 'I'm coming, lady, I'm coming,' she called out anxiously, still afraid that the lady might change her mind and leave her here alone. As she bounded off the bed she noticed the slate fall to the floor. Hurriedly she laid it back upright at the foot of the bed, placing it directly under the moonlight so that it would be easy for Micky to see when he got back.

Once down in the lower part of the building Molly gazed up at the painted lady, her heart beating rapidly, still not sure she was doing the right thing.

Then Sadie stretched out her hand and Molly hesitated no more. Pausing only to look one more time down the street hoping to see the familiar figure of her brother racing towards her, Molly's face fell in disappointment. Clasping Sadie's hand tightly, Molly didn't utter another word as she went trustingly with her new-found friend.

Back in the building the rain Sadie had forecast began to pour down heavily. Most of the water missed the mattress which Micky had wisely pushed up against the furthest wall for just such occurrences. But the foot of the mattress was unprotected. As the rain poured through the hole in the roof, the rivulets quickly washed the carefully worded slate clean, completely obliterating the hastily chalked message.

CHAPTER TWELVE

Micky was inconsolable. Seated hunched by the fireplace in a worn, comfortable armchair back at Ted's house he stared miserably into the fire, watching the flames jump and lick at the heaped coal and wood laid in the grate, but inside he felt cold, so desperately cold.

It was now gone eleven and Nora, after much prompting and gentle bullying from her son, had finally, albeit reluctantly, gone to her bed leaving the young lad in the safe hands of Ted, but not before she had put a liberal dose of laudanum in Micky's cocoa. Just in case the lad got it into his head to try and sneak out to trawl the streets in another desperate attempt to find his sister. Then she and Ted would have two children to worry about, and Lord knows, one was enough!

Drawing up the matching armchair Ted pulled the chair closer to the silent youth until his knees were touching Micky's thin ones. 'Look, mate. There's nothing we can do tonight. I know you're half outta your head with worry – bleeding hell, I would be in your shoes – but yer've gotta look on the bright side. Maybe she just wandered off, you know, looking for yer, and . . .' Ted's words trailed off miserably. He was only making things worse by trying to give the lad false hope. Despite his attempts to comfort Micky, deep down Ted was imagining the worst. After all, the girl was only eight and, knowing their circumstances, would be unlikely to walk into the nearest police station to ask for help. Even so, Ted had gone back to Mare Street police station to ask if any lost young girl had been brought in by some kind passer-by. Then he'd had to answer some difficult questions as to why he was inquiring about a lost child, especially as he'd only just bailed out a young lad suspected of theft a couple of hours previously. Ted had hoped to find John Smith still on duty, but unfortunately that kindly man had gone back on his beat, and Ted couldn't waste time looking for him. His main concern had been to get back home to Micky whom he had left with his worried mother.

Receiving no response, Ted touched the slim leg lightly, then gave a tired smile. The laudanum had finally taken effect. Easy in his mind now he knew Micky would sleep for a good few hours, Ted took the opportunity to do the same.

But sleep didn't come easily to Ted. Not when his mind was filled with images of a young, vulnerable child in the hands of a pervert. Yet even with the horrendous images, the long day, coupled with worry, finally caught up with him. Exhausted beyond measure Ted's last thought was his planned visit to the bakery in the morning to find out just what that old witch Agnes had been up to, accusing and getting Micky arrested for stealing. And by God, he'd find out, even if he had to shake the truth out of the malicious old cow.

Agnes was in the scullery making herself yet another mug of strong tea in an effort to stay awake when the loud knocking resounded through the small terraced house.

Hurrying through the parlour to the front door, her smile of welcome was wiped from her face when, instead of a happy Kenneth holding a small child in his arms, there stood a man she hardly recognised, so contorted was his face with savage rage. Kicking the door shut behind him, Kenneth grabbed Agnes' arm in a vicious grip as he snarled, 'Where is she, you deceitful bitch? Where's my Molly?'

As the pain shot up her arm, Agnes tried not to cry out for fear of alerting the neighbours, if the loud banging at her door at this hour of the night hadn't already done so. Groaning pitifully she gasped, 'Please, Kenneth. You're 'urting me arm. I don't know what you're talking about. I did what you told me to, you know I did. If the kid ain't where she's supposed ter be, I don't know where she is. Why on earth would I?'

The pressure on her arm eased as Kenneth flung her to one side, striding past her into the parlour without so much as a backward glance at the quietly crying woman.

Timidly following him, Agnes looked at the tall, well-dressed figure with growing unease. It was the same figure who, only earlier that evening had held her in his arms, his face wreathed in smiles as he'd told her over and over how grateful he was to her for giving him the opportunity to rescue his niece.

Swallowing hard she moved nearer and when she tried to speak her voice came out in a croak. 'Are yer sure you went to the right place, Kenneth? I mean, maybe, you know, in the dark, like, you . . .'

Kenneth's fist came down hard on the mantelpiece making Agnes jump in alarm. Then she began to retreat as the murderous-looking man bore down on her.

'You stupid bitch. Of course I went to the right place. It's the only house still standing in that road.'

As he approached, Agnes stepped back further, her heart racing with fear. There was something wrong here, something terribly wrong. She could understand Kenneth being upset at not being able to find his niece, but nothing, at least, nothing normal, warranted this terrifying display of emotion.

'You were the only one other than me who knew where those brats were living. So I'll ask you again, and this time I want the truth, or so help me God I'll wring your scrawny neck.'

As he came nearer Agnes tried to run, then screamed in pain as she felt her hair being pulled viciously by the very roots from her head.

Instantly a loud thud on the adjoining wall broke the highly charged atmosphere in the small room.

'You all right in there, Aggie?' a strong voice called

from behind the parlour wall. And at the sound Kenneth came to his senses. That was all he needed, a nosy neighbour. With a supreme effort he released his hold on Agnes, then, with a great theatrical gesture he stumbled to the couch and slumped down, dropping his head in his hands – afraid to look at the hovering Agnes for fear he might not be able to contain his rage. Then he heard Agnes call back, 'Yeah, I'm all right, Doris. Just knocked me leg against the table. Thanks anyway.'

Breathing a sigh of relief Kenneth kept his face averted and whispered, 'Oh God, Agnes. I'm so sorry. I don't know what came over me. To go for you of all people, the only person whom I can trust implicitly. Will you forgive me, Agnes? I'll understand if you want me out of the house this instant. It's no more than I deserve after such despicable behaviour.' His hands still covering his face Kenneth held his breath as he waited for some response from Agnes, while cursing himself for his inability to contain his frustration. And it wasn't the first time. Good God, no! If he wasn't careful it would be the undoing of him one day.

Still deeply shocked and unnerved by Kenneth's actions Agnes felt behind her for a chair to steady herself, gratefully sinking down on the padded seat before her legs gave way beneath her. She couldn't believe what had happened. Kenneth, her kind, gentle Kenneth, a man who wouldn't hurt a fly, to have suddenly turned into a madman. If anyone had told her he was capable of such savagery she would have laughed in their face. Yet she had seen it for herself.

Then she heard a loud groan of anguish from the man sitting opposite and all her reservations vanished as Kenneth, looking at her with bloodshot eyes, eyes he had carefully rubbed until they had hurt to get the desired effect, gazed at her in mute contrition. And Agnes, firmly pushing any lingering doubt to the far recesses of her mind, went to the man she loved. With a cry of joyous relief she fell into Kenneth's outstretched arms sobbing, 'Don't worry, love. I understand. Finding yer niece gone like that would make anyone act crazy, especially when yer was so near to rescuing her from that filthy hovel. Now, don't you worry, darling. We'll find the girl, I promise. She can't 'ave got far. She probably got scared when Micky didn't come home and went out looking for 'im. I bet yer anything she's gone back to that place they call 'ome. After all, where else could she go? You probably just missed her. If yer'd waited a while longer, you might have caught her coming back.' Feeling herself being gently but firmly pushed from Kenneth's embrace, Agnes fidgeted with the laced-edged neck of her white frilly blouse, her thumping heart beginning to calm its erratic beat. 'Look, you sit and rest while I make us a nice cuppa, then we'll decide what to do, all right?' She looked at the averted face hopefully.

Conscious he had to make an effort, Kenneth looked up and smiled wanly. 'Thanks, Agnes. I don't deserve you, especially after the way I behaved earlier. I'm so ashamed. I don't know what got into me.'

Agnes' body relaxed. 'Now don't say another word about it, Kenneth. It's all done and forgotten. You ust sit there while I fetch the tea. I won't be long.'

Left alone Kenneth allowed his true feelings to surface once more, his devious mind going over the past few weeks. Weeks he'd had to try and pretend he found the ugly old hag attractive. God! How stupid could some women be? Still, if the woman in question was as desperate for a man as Agnes was, she'd believe anything. His upper lip curled in contempt as he recalled how proud Agnes had been of the plan she had thought up to get Micky temporarily out of the way. She'd gone on about a book she'd just finished reading, a book that had given her the idea for getting Micky locked up for stealing some bread. A snort of derision came from his mouth. As if a woman of her limited intelligence could possibly understand the work of Victor Hugo. The stupid woman hadn't even been able to pronounce the title properly, pronouncing it as 'Less Miserables'. Up until that moment Kenneth hadn't had much occasion for humour, but he'd had to stop himself from laughing in her simpering face as she proudly tried to get her tongue around the French title. Obviously someone of higher intelligence had read the famous book and told Agnes snippets of the plot. But out of all the complexties of the story, all Agnes had remembered was the part about Jean Valjean stealing a loaf of bread. Stupid, ignorant cow! And he'd had to look impressed at her supposed knowledge.

Still, it had been worth it. Or so he had thought at the time. When he had met Agnes earlier that evening and she had told him that Micky Masters was safely locked up in Hackney police station, Kenneth had wanted to shout his elation to the very heavens. He'd had no intention of ever seeing Agnes Handly again. He'd had everything planned so meticulously. First he would go to the ruin and wait until Molly finally showed herself. He had expected a long wait as he knew the young girl was under strict instructions from that brat of a brother to keep indoors until he was home. But a child as young as Molly would eventually become frightened and venture out to find her brother, and then he would have her. How he had hurried through the streets, his mind filled with the delights to come once he had the girl safely installed in a secret place he had stumbled across quite by accident, and he was confident that she, like her predecessors, would entertain him for many months, or even years. It all depended on how young they were when he got them. But eventually children grow up then, sadly, Molly would have to be got rid of, the same as all the others he'd taken over the years. But all that was in the future. Then, after all his scheming, all his fantasies, and, worst of all, the loving attention he'd had to shower on Agnes to keep her sweet, to then find the child gone had been a crushing blow.

He had searched the ruined building frantically when it had become apparent that the house was empty. His first reaction had been one of stunned amazement. Then the anger had begun to burn into a raging hate against the world. A world that didn't understand men like him. Needing to vent his anger on someone he had turned instinctively on Agnes. She was the only other person he could think of who could have taken the child. But now it was evident Agnes knew nothing of the girl's disappearance. More importantly he had almost given himself away. Any other woman with an ounce of pride would have shown him the door immediately, but not Agnes, who still obviously thought the sun shone out of his backside. Even so, he would have to be more careful until he had Molly. Even a woman as lonely and desperate as Agnes would become aware something was wrong sooner or later.

And he still needed Agnes – for the time being. Hearing footsteps Kenneth composed himself and smiled as Agnes reappeared bearing a tray carrying china cups and a plate of sandwiches.

'Shall I be mother?' Agnes simpered coyly.

Shuddering inwardly, Kenneth nodded. 'Please, my dear. Then I must be off. I won't be able to rest until I know my niece is safe.'

Agnes bent her head as she poured out the tea trying to hide her disappointment. She had hoped Kenneth might stay awhile, but it wouldn't be proper to suggest such a thing. Besides, she mustn't forget Kenneth had a wife to go home to.

'Is there anything I can do to help, Kenneth?' she asked wistfully. 'You know yer've only gotta ask.'

Kenneth shook his head. Downing his tea and ignoring the carefully cut sandwiches, he rose to his feet. 'I'm grateful, Agnes, but like I said, I must get off. I'll do what you suggested and go back, just in case Molly has returned.'

Rising with him Agnes walked alongside the immaculately dressed man to the door. 'Of course, Kenneth, I understand, and you've got yer wife to think of an' all, poor soul. I hope she doesn't 'ave too much of a shock if you don't manage to find your niece and bring her home with you tonight.'

For a moment Kenneth looked at her in puzzlement. 'Who . . . ?' he asked vaguely.

Agnes swallowed hard, her previous suspicions returning. 'Yer wife, Kenneth,' she replied, a tremor creeping into her voice. 'I expect she'll be worrying an' all, and that can't be good for a woman in her poor state of 'ealth.'

Immediately Kenneth's brow cleared. 'Good Lord!' he exclaimed, his lips parting to reveal white, even teeth in a wan smile. 'I nearly forgot about poor Margaret. I must get off. Goodnight, my love.'

Following him to the door, Agnes' forehead creased in confusion. Kenneth had just referred to his wife as Margaret, but she could have sworn he had told her his wife's name was Marjorie. Oh, stop it, she chided herself. She must have made a mistake. After all, the two names were similar.

On the doorstep Agnes held her face up for a kiss, and Kenneth obliged by giving the lovelorn woman a peck on the cheek.

Doffing his bowler hat, Kenneth was about to take his leave when a strong, sneering voice boomed in the night air. 'Well, well! If it isn't Kenny Stokes. I haven't seen your ugly mug around these parts for a couple of years. When did they let you out? If it was up to me I'd've thrown away the key, you filthy pervert. You still up to your old tricks, Kenny? 'Cos if you are, then you'd better be careful, as I'm going to be keeping an eye on you now I know you're out. And so will the rest of the nick once they know you're back on this patch.'

Under the street lamp, Kenneth's face drained leaving his handsome face bloodless. But more frightening to Agnes was the look of sheer terror that filled every inch of Kenneth's face.

Stumbling backwards, Kenneth cast a wary, frightened look at the glaring police officer before turning and, almost at a run, made off into the night.

'Well, nice company you're keeping these days, Agnes.' PC John Smith bore down on the startled woman. 'First you stitch up young Micky, now I find you with a piece of scum like Kenny Stokes.'

Her stomach churning, her heart racing, Agnes faced the stony-faced officer bravely. 'I don't know what you're referring to, John Smith. Copper or not, you've no right to be nasty to friends of mine, just 'cos you don't happen to like him. As a matter of fact, Kenneth and me are . . .' She gulped nervously. 'Well, if you must know, we're sort of courting. Only we've gotta keep it quiet, 'cos his poor wife's dying. And his name ain't Stokes, it's Wells, so there,' she added somewhat childishly.

To her horror, the uniformed man stared at her in amazement then threw his head back and laughed loudly. 'Bleeding hell, woman. Talk about there's no fool like an old fool. I don't know what that pervert's been telling you, Agnes, but I can tell you you're a bit too old for Kenny Stokes' tastes. About forty years too old, I'd say.'

Agnes opened her mouth to reply but no words came. All her earlier misgivings, all the suspicious thoughts she had harboured and squashed as soon as she saw Kenneth now came back at her with a vengeance. Yet still she refused to believe what the policeman was telling her, though deep down, in that special place where no one can hide the truth, not even from themselves, she knew with a sickening start that she was hearing the truth. And if that was true . . . Her knees buckled as the full horror of what she had done hit her like a physical blow. If John Smith hadn't moved quickly she would have fallen. When she came round she was in her armchair, John Smith's concerned face bending over her.

'Here, Agnes, old girl. Get this down you.' The smell of brandy wafted under her nose as she gratefully grabbed at the glass. Draining it in one go, she laid her head back, her eyes filling with tears. Dear God! What had she done? Closing her eyes her mind ran down the years to a time in her life that she had tried to obliterate. But, like all memories, sooner or later they surfaced, usually when least wanted or expected.

She was nine years old again, and she was lying on a comfortable sofa with her Uncle Cyril, a horsehair blanket thrown over them. Agnes' mother was in the room, smiling down at them, teasing Agnes for being such a miseryguts when she had such a special uncle who thought the world of her. And all the time under the blanket, in full view of her mother, her Uncle Cyril was touching her down below. Touching and hurting her, and she was powerless to stop him. For if she told, then her mum and dad would go to prison, and so would she for being such a bad little girl.

Her eyes flew open as John Smith said firmly, 'Come

on, old girl, tell me what you know.' The grim-faced officer was seated opposite her, just like Kenneth had done only a short time ago.

'Can I 'ave another drink, John? Gawd help me, I need it.'

Getting to his feet the constable answered kindly, 'It's your brandy, Agnes, but I want to know what's been going on with this Stokes bastard.'

Agnes nodded tiredly. Taking the replenished glass she took a long swallow, then, all the fight knocked out of her, she began to talk.

Micky stirred, a low whimper escaping his lips as he tried to wake himself from the nightmare, but his tired mind was too weak to obey his unconscious demand. Molly was calling for him, but he couldn't get to her. He tried – Oh God, how he tried – but it was no use. The closer he got to her, the further away she went, still calling his name, her pretty face awash with terror.

Then another face appeared in his dream. But this face was soothing, the eyes and lips assuring him everything would be all right. He just had to hang in there, he had to wait until she could get back, and then the nightmare would be over.

His body thrashed this way and that, but still he slept on. He could hear her voice so clearly, and after a while his body relaxed slightly. Then he called out into the darkness, 'Ellen, Ellen, come home. Please! Please, Ellen, come back.' Yet still he remained deep in slumber.

Opposite the young boy, Ted awoke with a start. 'Micky! Micky! You awake, mate?'

There was no answer from the slender form

153

huddled up in the armchair. Satisfied Micky was still asleep, Ted made himself comfortable while wondering if he had indeed heard Micky call out for Ellen, or if he himself had dreamed it. Either way, she was needed back here, as much for his sake as Micky's.

But would she come back if asked? There was only one way to find out. And Ted fully intended to do just that.

CHAPTER THIRTEEN

The Grand Hotel was in a prime position overlooking the sea front in the popular holiday resort of Southend. Visitors staying at the Grand were only five minutes away from the multitude of entertainment facilities which included theatres, amusement arcades and plenty of other activities to occupy the ever-increasing stream of holiday makers who had chosen Southend for their annual vacation. The Council boasted that their fair town had something for everyone, whatever their age. But, despite all the attractions of Britain's much loved resort, Ellen was bored out of her mind.

On this spring morning, Ellen was sitting out on the balcony adjacent to their first-floor room staring at the wonderful view of the sea front and sighed heavily. She had imagined that having some time to themselves would bring her and Arthur closer. Instead it had only served to emphasise how little they had in common. They had been fine back home – at least Ellen had thought so. Now she realised that it was only the fact that, during their short marriage, she and Arthur had spent very little time alone together. During the day they were both busy in the shop, and at night, tired out by the long day, and knowing they had to be up early, they normally only spent an hour or so in each other's company before retiring to bed. And then, she was usually reading while Arthur dozed off after his evening meal. Both of them had become accustomed to their daily routine, not realising they were, without knowing it, forming a kind of barrier between them, unconsciously masking the insurmountable differences in their personalities.

The holiday had started off well. The change of scenery and the chance to relax had been wonderful. Their days had been filled with exploring the seaside resort and all the sights it had to offer, but when they were alone in the hotel suite, or dining out at one of the local restaurants, it had soon become painfully clear to both Ellen and Arthur that their conversation was becoming more and more stilted and awkward. In some respects they were like a couple thrown together by chance and were now realising they had nothing in common. In all honesty Ellen had to admit that the sad state of affairs wasn't solely Arthur's fault; she was as much to blame for the tension that existed between them. The main trouble was that all of Arthur's conversation revolved around the bakery and the day to day running of his beloved business. Whereas Ellen, now she had broadened her horizons, due mainly to her friendship with Ted Parker and Micky, plus the various stall holders she had become friendly with over the past months, had plenty to talk about and humorous stories to tell. But whenever she tried to share her thoughts, Arthur would quickly change the subject and revert to his pet love – the bakery, the tradesmen, and of course, his loyal customers. It was as if he was trying to pretend that Ellen didn't have a life of her own now. And if he told her once more about the rise of prices in flour, yeast and everything else they needed to run the bakery she felt she wouldn't be responsible for her actions. Even that wouldn't have been so bad if the stories varied, but they were always the same. Yet Arthur continually regaled Ellen with his narrations as if imagining his wife was hearing them for the first time. And Ellen, heartily sick of hearing the familiar anecdotes again and again, had to restrain herself from screaming at him in frustration. The only thing that had saved her sanity was making the acquaintance of a middle-aged couple, May and George Bradley.

They had met at dinner in the hotel dining room and, after the initial embarrassment of being mistaken for father and daughter, the atmosphere had quickly changed. Much to Ellen's surprise, Arthur, who normally shied clear of meeting strangers, had taken to the pleasant couple with uncharacteristic warmth and enthusiasm. At first Ellen had been stunned to find her husband suggesting they make up a foursome, until she realised that Arthur too was aware that things weren't going well between them. And this knowledge only made Ellen feel more guilty. In a fit of desperation she had suggested they cut their holiday short and return home. She had been sure Arthur would jump at the idea, but there she had been wrong. For someone who had had to be dragged metaphorically kicking and screaming into taking a holiday, Arthur now seemed to be thoroughly enjoying himself. Or maybe he just wanted to keep Ellen away from London – and Ted Parker – for as long as possible. She was beginning to wonder if she had underestimated her husband.

She had imagined he was blissfully unaware of her growing attraction to the engaging stall holder, but now she wasn't so sure. He hadn't actually come out and said anything – that wasn't Arthur's way, for he hated any form of confrontation – but certain little things he had said, in a perfectly innocent manner, had caused a flutter of anxiety in Ellen's already guilty mind. If Arthur had indeed suspected anything, there was one thing of which Ellen was absolutely certain – those ideas had been planted in his mind by somebody. Arthur was intrinsically too honest and trusting to think of such a thing left to his own devices, and it didn't take a genius to figure out who that person was. She could just see Agnes making veiled remarks with her spiteful tongue. From the moment she and Arthur had married, Agnes had been looking for just such an opportunity to split her former lover and his young bride apart.

As this thought came to mind, Ellen's body gave an involuntary jump. Her heart began to beat faster as she imagined what it would be like to be free of

Arthur, and immediately she was once more assailed by guilt. But after the last disastrous ten days she knew she couldn't go on the way things stood. If she was bored and dissatisfied with her life now, how, in God's name, would she feel ten, or twenty, years from now? She shuddered at the thought. Arthur could live until his eighties or even nineties, by which time she would be in her fifties, an old woman, childless and bitter at the waste of her life. And as that thought crossed her mind, another one entered it. This must be how Agnes felt.

Ellen couldn't help but feel a pang of pity for her adversary. But she, Ellen, was still young enough to start again – if it wasn't for Arthur. Her eyes flew open in horror. What was she thinking? It was almost as if she were wishing Arthur dead so she could be free. No! No! She mustn't entertain such awful thoughts. She didn't wish Arthur any harm, it was just that . . . well! She couldn't help but wish he would just . . . just disappear. To go off somewhere, somewhere he would be happy, and in doing so set her free. A wry smile touched her lips. Maybe he would rediscover the feelings he had once held for Agnes and run off with her? The frivolous notion quickly vanished. 'I should be so lucky,' she muttered sadly. Getting to her feet she began to pace the small balcony, her thoughts in turmoil. She could always ask Arthur for a divorce, but even as the idea entered her mind it was gone. If she were to take such action, Arthur would be devastated. Not only that, he would also be deeply humiliated at being jilted by his child bride. It was what everyone who knew them was waiting for, and she couldn't do that to Arthur. Whatever his faults, he was a decent man and didn't deserve to be made an object of ridicule.

No! She would just have to put up with her life and make the most of a bad job. What was that old saying? She'd made her bed and now she must lie in it.

But she had been so young. Young and terrified of what was to become of her. She had jumped at the idea of marriage without giving a single thought as to what she was letting herself in for. If she'd had more experience of life she wouldn't have married a man twice her age just for a sense of security. But in that respect, Arthur hadn't been entirely blameless. As Agnes had so bitterly reproached him, he could have adopted her, or applied for legal guardianship. Ellen's eyes hardened. She at least had the excuse of innocence for her part in the hasty marriage; Arthur, on the other hand, had no such excuse. He had known exactly what he was doing.

Leaning her arms on the intricate iron railing of the balcony she squeezed her eyes shut. It was no use going over and over the same ground. The rights and wrongs of the past were done and couldn't be undone. That didn't mean to say the future couldn't be changed. Because the way things were now, it wasn't fair to either of them. Not for her, nor Arthur. He deserved better than a wife who didn't love him, not in the way a real wife should. And she deserved the chance for a proper marriage, with a husband she loved and children. She had always wanted to be a mother, but that would never happen while she was still tied to Arthur. Then there was Ted. With his laughing eyes and daredevil ways. Ted, a man who could turn her legs to water just by looking at her in that intimate way she both loved and feared. She knew he was just waiting for her to say the word, and he wouldn't think twice about taking her away from Arthur. Men like Ted took what they wanted without fear for the consequences. And that sort of man, if she was brutally honest with herself, was exactly what she craved. Only she wasn't brave enough to take that ultimate step. And that knowledge made her want to cry out in anguish and disgust at her own weakness.

She was rudely awoken from her daydream by the sound of her voice being called. Leaning over the balcony she groaned at the sight that met her eyes.

Standing outside the hotel looking up at her, his face beaming, was Arthur. Beside him, also smiling brightly, were the Bradleys, the middle-aged couple who had appeared like a godsend to Ellen. In their company Ellen could have a rest from the growing ordeal of making conversation with her husband. It had also meant she no longer had to entertain Arthur, much as one would with a young child, for, from the moment they had arrived in Southend, Arthur had clung to her side like a boy fearful of losing sight of his mother. If the Bradleys hadn't arrived when they had, Ellen didn't know how much longer her frayed nerves would have held out. With gentle persuasion she had encouraged Arthur to spend as much time as possible with their new-found friends, leaving her some much needed time to herself. He had objected at first, been almost frightened at the idea of branching out on his own without the presence of his wife to steer him in the right direction, and of course, to step into the conversation if it became stilted. Now it seemed he no longer needed her by his side every waking minute of the day, and for that reason alone, even if, after the holiday, she never saw either of them again, she would be for ever grateful to May and George Bradley.

'Ellen, Ellen, love. We're going down to the front to watch a game of bowls, maybe even have a game if we can. Do you want to join us?'

Ellen smiled back weakly. Watching a group of middle-aged men playing bowls wasn't her idea of entertainment; given the choice she'd rather watch paint dry. But if she could get Arthur and the Bradleys out of the way she could take a long stroll along the promenade, looking in the shops, relishing the time to herself. She might even go for a paddle, and hope Arthur didn't see her. He'd have a fit if he were to see her with her dress up around her knees showing her legs to all and sundry.

'Would you mind very much if I didn't, Arthur? I was looking forward to spending the day window shopping.'

Arthur waved his hand airily, his face a picture of husbandly indulgence. 'Of course I don't mind, love. If you're sure you'll be all right on your own.'

Biting down a moment's irritation Ellen smiled down at the trio. 'I'll be fine, Arthur. You get off, and I'll see you later for afternoon tea.'

With further waving and assurances they would

meet up later the trio finally walked off, disappearing into the swarm of people that filled the promenade. A sigh of relief escaped Ellen's lips. Getting to her feet she breathed in a deep lungful of sea air and walked back into the adjoining room, her eyes glancing at the mantel clock. It was now just after ten, which meant she had a whole five hours to herself. Grinning broadly she picked up her bonnet and bag and, like a child looking forward to a day off school, she made her way down to the foyer.

She was so engrossed in planning the precious time ahead of her she didn't hear her name being called at first until the receptionist called again.

'Mrs Mitson, there's a telegram for you. I was just about to send the bell boy to your room to deliver it.'

Taken by surprise Ellen took the brown envelope being held out to her, her mind whirling as she tried to think of who could possibly have sent a telegram. Nobody liked receiving the official-looking envelopes, for they usually contained bad news, and Ellen was no exception. Seating herself into a plush armchair in the foyer she carefully opened the envelope, and what she read brought her quickly to her feet.

'Is everything all right, Madam?' The male receptionist had appeared by her side, his face showing concern.

Gathering her thoughts, Ellen answered quickly, 'Yes! I mean, no, not really.' Folding the telegram she looked into the curious eyes of the smartly dressed man. 'There's been some trouble at home. I'm afraid we're going to have to cut our holiday short. Would

163

you kindly prepare our bill while I fetch my husband.'

'Of course, Madam. I trust it's nothing too serious,' he said, his tone hopeful as if waiting for further information. But here he was disappointed, for Ellen, with an absent nod, swept out of the hotel in search of her husband.

'I still don't understand why we have to give up our holiday just because Ted Parker sends a telegram asking us to come back because young Micky's in trouble. I mean to say, it's not as if he's a relation, is it? What about his parents? Surely it's them who should be taking responsibility for their child. Unless they're incapable of looking after their own son. Still! They wouldn't be the first to neglect their offspring. Probably a couple of drunks, sponging off respectable, hard-working men like me.'

His fleshy face quivering petulantly Arthur failed to notice the anger building on Ellen's face.

'Besides, what could be so important that it couldn't have waited a few more days? I was really enjoying myself, and it was you who made such a fuss about taking a holiday in the first place. When I think of the inconvenience, not to mention having to let the Bradleys down, well . . .'

Ellen turned sharply to the red-faced, indignant man by her side and answered in no small voice, 'First of all, there was no mention in the telegram of you being needed, or wanted for that matter. You could have stayed behind with the Bradleys, I told you that, but of course you wouldn't hear of it, would you? Oh, not because you were concerned for

164

me travelling back to London on my own, but because you were worried what it might look like if you had.'

Almost bouncing on the padded seat Ellen's voice rose a notch higher, much to Arthur's embarrassment.

'I wish to God you had stayed behind. You've done nothing but moan and whine about the inconvenience to yourself, with not a word of concern about Micky. Ted Parker wouldn't have gone to all the trouble of contacting us if it hadn't been important. But then, other people's troubles have never been high on your list of priorities, have they, Arthur? Unless of course you aren't put out in any way, then you're all smiles and affability. Well, I'm not like you. I care for my friends, and Micky is a friend. Maybe not a friend of yours, but he certainly is one of mine. And if he needs me, then I'm going to be there for him.'

Her steadily rising voice was attracting the attention of the other passengers aboard the train heading back to London, and immediately Arthur changed tack. Smiling inanely at two women seated on the other side of the aisle he bent his head to Ellen's and hissed nervously, 'Keep your voice down, woman. We don't want all and sundry knowing our business. We'll have plenty of time to discuss this unfortunate incident when we get home.'

Angrily Ellen shifted away from her agitated husband, a feeling of distaste rising inside her body that this two-faced, petulant man was her spouse. 'There you go again, thinking of yourself as usual. I should have come back on my own. After all, as you've

165

so forcefully pointed out, Micky's problems are of no concern to you. And as I've already said, you could have stayed on at the hotel, I did tell you to. In fact I almost begged you to stay behind. But, oh no! That would have meant showing your true colours to your new friends, and that would never do, would it?' A slow shudder rippled through her body. 'God! Every time I think of the way you expressed genuine concern for Micky, it makes me feel sick. You were so convincing, I nearly believed you myself. But it was all an act, just so you could portray yourself in a good light for the Bradleys' benefit . . . Oh, get away from me . . .' Ellen pulled her hand away from Arthur's clammy grasp. 'I'm going to the dining car, and don't even think of following me, or I swear I'll really show you up.'

She glared down at the florid, quivering face and again felt a wave of shame – shame that this man was her husband. Arthur made no further move to stop her. Taking out the newspaper he had bought at the station he made a great study of burying his attention in the day's news.

Steadying herself against the rocking motion of the train Ellen entered the dining car and was immediately shown to an empty table. Suddenly realising she'd had nothing to eat since breakfast she ordered a pot of tea and a large cream cake. As she tucked into the delicious treat she reflected wryly that Arthur's stomach must be rumbling by now. If he hadn't been so preoccupied with having his holiday spoiled he would have made a beeline for the dining-car the moment they had boarded the train. For if there was one other love he had apart from the bakery, it was his stomach. But she had no fear he would follow her, not after the harsh words she had levelled at him.

Gazing out of the window as the train swept past the picturesque countryside Ellen wondered what could have happened that would make Ted take such drastic action as to send for her. Her hand flew to her mouth as an awful thought struck her. What if something terrible had happened to Micky? Oh, God! No, not that. An image of that sweet, handsome face floated before her eyes and her stomach lurched in alarm. Despite what Arthur said about the young boy not being any relation, Ellen felt differently. To her Micky was like the younger brother she'd never had. Ever since he had appeared at the door of the bakery, cold, hungry and ragged, yet maintaining an air of dignity in spite of his obvious plight, Ellen had felt an overwhelming responsibility for the young lad. And since Ted had taken him under his wing the change in Micky had been remarkable. He was a different person to the one she had first encountered, and Ellen couldn't help but feel a certain amount of pleasure and satisfaction that she had been instrumental in helping Micky forge a better life for himself.

But Arthur was right about one thing. Why would Ted take the drastic measure of sending for her unless matters back home were indeed serious? If so, then where were Micky's parents in his hour of need? Closing her eyes Ellen let the gentle rolling of the train lull her into a light sleep. Telling herself she could do nothing until they knew more about the situation, she let her body relax. She had a feeling she was going to need all her strength in the days to come.

CHAPTER FOURTEEN

Ellen, Ted and Arthur were sitting in the living room above the shop, the light refreshments Ellen had prepared and laid out on the dining table forgotten. The Mitsons listened in stunned silence as Ted recounted what had transpired during their short absence. When finally Ted stopped talking, Ellen stared at the dark-haired man she had missed more than she cared to admit, her thoughts whirling. So, poor Micky was an orphan on the run from the workhouse. Not only that, but he had an eight-year-old sister who was utterly dependent on him. Why, oh why hadn't he confided in her? But then, as Ted had pointed out, Micky had been too afraid of being sent back to the workhouse. Also the loyal young man hadn't wanted to take the chance of making trouble for his new-found friends. But all that paled into insignificance beside the horror of Molly Masters abducted by a known pervert, aided and abetted by Agnes Handly.

And that was what Ellen was finding so hard to believe.

Ellen knew her employee was capable of many things, but never in a million years would Ellen believe that even Agnes would stoop so low as to deliver an innocent child into the hands of a child abuser. There must be a mistake, there must be.

Arthur too was finding it hard to believe, but, unlike Ellen, Arthur's mind was working along very different lines. For years he had been trying to find a way to rid himself of the woman who caused him daily embarrassment and shame at the way he had treated her. Up until now he'd been unsuccessful in his quest, but now! His chest swelled, his heart began to beat erratically as he saw himself dismissing Agnes in a great show of moral outrage, preferably in the presence of an audience. No one would blame him. There was an unwritten code amongst the criminals of the East End. Stealing, extortion, violence and even murder were looked upon as a way of life because life was hard and people did what they could in order to survive. But there was one brand of low-life that even the most hardened of criminals wouldn't tolerate, and that was child molesters. The second most reviled person or persons were those who helped the sick, depraved men attain their innocent prey.

Arthur's mind was working furiously. This was the perfect opportunity for killing two birds with one stone. On the one hand he would be rid of the woman who had been a thorn in his side for years, and in doing so would raise his status in the community. No longer would he be looked upon as just good old Arthur. Dependable, dull Arthur. Tolerated and treated with the same kind of affection one would show to a faithful, aging dog. His chest swelled further as he envisaged the future. The new respect he would see mirrored in people's eyes, the deference he would command in the community. Of course he would have to make the dismissal of Agnes public, and the more witnesses to Agnes' humiliation the better. He frowned as a sudden thought struck him. After what had happened it was doubtful Agnes would dare show her face in public for quite some time. Then he relaxed. If she wouldn't come to him, then he would go to her, bringing with him as many observers as he could attract along the way.

The inner feeling of euphoria almost caused Arthur to rub his hands in glee. Fortunately he stopped himself in time. But in his vivid imagination there was no thought for the Masters children, even for the child Molly. It wasn't that Arthur was an unfeeling or unkind man, and if he were to witness a child being hurt he would step in to help if he could. But people like Arthur, who hadn't the gift of empathy, were incapable of feeling other people's pain, especially that of strangers. So wrapped up in his own private world was Arthur that everyone and everything was as of no consequence. His face and portly body rigid with self-importance, Arthur rose slowly to his feet. Sticking his chin out from the white starched collar of his shirt, he stuck his thumbs into the lapels of his jacket, rocked back on his heels and boomed pompously, 'Well, this is a fine state of affairs I must say. Though if the young man in question had been honest with us in the first place, none of this appalling business would have happened. But it has, and now we must try and minimise the damage.'

Ellen, brought out of her reverie with a start, could only stare open mouthed at the puffed-up features of her husband. Flickering her gaze at Ted she winced at the look of disgust that crossed his rugged face. Yet she couldn't blame him, for she too was experiencing the same sense of loathing.

Remaining seated she looked up at her husband and said icily, 'Minimise the damage! Is that all you can think of, Arthur? Why don't you just come straight out with it? What you really mean is how this is going to reflect on you, and the business. But don't worry, once word spreads they'll be queuing down the road from here to Mare Street, just on the off chance they might be able to pick up some juicy gossip. People are like that, not all of them, but most. They love to see other people's misery, it must be a distraction from their own dreary lives. Ghouls, that's all most people are, ghouls, and you're no better than any of them.'

Gripping the sides of her chair Ellen gritted her teeth as she almost spat the words at him. 'Ever since we arrived home and heard what Ted had to tell us, your only thought has been for yourself, and how my involvement with Micky might affect you . . .'

Aware of Ted's contemptuous glare Arthur's head snapped back on his neck. His colouring heightened further as he attempted to regain some home ground. 'Now look here, Ellen. I won't have you talking to me in that tone. Don't forget you are my wife, and as such will conduct yourself in a like manner.'

Ellen's face twitched in amusement at the unfamiliar tone. Their short acquaintance with the Bradleys had obviously rubbed off on Arthur. But where the Bradleys' way of talking was natural, Arthur merely sounded ridiculous. She could almost visualise him twirling the ends of a waxed moustache, if he'd possessed one. But the moment of humour was short-lived. For as she stared into the puffy face suffused with self-righteousness she realised that whatever feelings she had once held for Arthur were now gone. With his callous disregard for the plight of eight-year-old Molly, and the anguish Micky must be going through, he had killed the last vestige of affection and loyalty she had held for him as surely as if he'd severed them with a sharp blade. Worst of all, although she had never been in love with him, she had always respected and liked him as a person, and had held a great fondness for him. Now she found she didn't even like him any more, and she knew sadly that she would never feel the same about her husband ever again.

A sudden movement opposite her brought her attention back to Ted. The tall brooding man was on his feet. His eyes cold with contempt he turned his back deliberately on Arthur and, looking at Ellen, said shortly, 'Micky's at my house, if you want to see him. He's in a terrible state, poor sod. But who wouldn't be, in his shoes? You'd have to have a heart of stone not to feel for him right now.' Out of the corner of his eye Ted saw Arthur's lips twitch nervously and thought angrily, Yeah, that was directed at you, yer selfish, fat bastard. 'I haven't slept for more than an hour since Molly went missing.' He gave a short grunt of derision. 'Not that I can take any credit for that. Anyone with a bit of compassion would feel the same. Me mum's in a right old state, an' she don't even know the girl. But that don't make no difference. A child's a child whether you know them or not. And anyone with an ounce of decency would feel the same.' This time Ted made no attempt to disguise his contempt as he turned and stared coldly into Arthur's ruddy face. And such was the fury in Ted's eyes that Arthur stepped back a pace, his jowls quivering in fear and apprehension, knowing he was no match in either verbal or physical strength to Ted.

Inwardly squirming, Arthur made one last desperate effort to regain control of the situation. Directing his gaze at Ellen he said, 'Well, at least you won't have to concern yourself with Micky Masters any more. Now the truth's out, he'll be sent straight back to the workhouse, and if he's any sense he'll stay there until he's lawfully released . . .'

His words were cut off abruptly as Ted sprang across the room, his hands grabbing at Arthur's jacket in a vicious hold.

'Micky's going back to no workhouse, yer unfeeling bastard. He's staying with me an' me mum, and little Molly too when she's found. And I will find her. If I have to knock on every door and walk every mile of the East End, I'll do it.' Even as he said the words Ted knew he was grasping at straws where Molly was concerned. She could be anywhere. She might never

174

be found. She wouldn't be the first child to go missing and never be seen again. But if he couldn't help Molly, he could provide a proper home for Micky. It wouldn't be easy. He'd have the authorities to deal with first. But if the worst came to the worst he'd up sticks and move away from the East End, because there was no way on God's earth he would let Micky go back to the workhouse; it would be like signing the boy's death warrant.

'Ted! Ted, for God's sake, let him go. This isn't solving anything. Please, Ted, stop it.'

Startled, Ted looked down at Ellen, then he felt her hands pulling at him and realised his own were wrapped around Arthur's flabby neck. Recoiling in shock, Ted's hands released their grip as quickly as if he'd been holding red-hot coals.

Severely shaken and gasping for breath Arthur staggered backwards, falling in a heap into the armchair he had so recently vacated.

The atmosphere was charged with tension. Then Ted, his face grim, turned to a pale-faced Ellen and said tersely, 'You coming with me or staying here? It's up to you.'

Faced with the option of going with Ted or staying here with Arthur, Ellen didn't hesitate. 'Of course I'll come,' she replied, picking up her cotton gloves and straw hat. Not looking back she said quietly, 'I don't know what time I'll be back, Arthur. Don't wait up for me.'

With Ted by his wife's side, Arthur could only watch helplessly as Ellen swept from the room.

* * *

Passing through the empty bakery Ellen forced herself to put from her mind the unpleasant scene she had just witnessed and focus her thoughts on Micky. Then, her eyes bewildered, she asked Ted, 'I know there's no love lost between me and Agnes, but I can't believe she would do such a despicable thing. She must have been duped into doing what she did.' Fiddling with the clasp of her bag she lowered her gaze adding, 'I want to see her, Ted. I have to know exactly what happened while we were away . . . I know, I know . . .' she held up a hand as Ted made to protest. 'I've heard all the facts, but I want to hear Agnes' side of it.'

Ted's face darkened. 'You go and see her if you want, but I ain't going anywhere near the old bitch. I wouldn't trust meself within a mile of her.'

It was only five minutes' walk to the row of terraced houses where Agnes lived, and during the short journey neither Ted nor Ellen spoke. It was as if they had made an unspoken agreement not to mention what had happened back at the bakery; that particular topic would have to be put on hold for the time being. But it wasn't going to go away. Sooner or later there was going to be a confrontation between herself, Ted and Arthur, and it wasn't something she was looking forward to. But for now Micky and his missing sister were her top priorities.

As they approached the road Agnes lived in, the first thing they saw was the burly figure of John Smith standing guard outside the green door. The second thing that caught their attention was the fact that the front window had been smashed in.

'Afternoon, Mrs Mitson. Glad to see you back, love. Young Micky'll feel a lot better when he sees you, poor little sod. It was good of you to cut your holiday short.'

Ellen smiled wanly. 'To tell the truth, Officer, I was glad of the excuse. I know it was my idea to get away, but I was bored stiff after a couple of days.' Aware she was stalling for time, Ellen stepped forward, her hand gesturing towards the closed door. 'Could I see Agnes, Officer? Like I've said to Ted, I'd like to hear her side of the story before I make any judgment.'

Constable John Smith's face softened. She was a nice young woman was Ellen Mitson. She of all people would be justified in taking satisfaction from Agnes' present predicament. It was common knowledge how Agnes had tried her hardest to make life difficult for the new Mrs Mitson. Yet now, when Agnes needed friends, only Ellen was prepared to give her the benefit of the doubt. He himself had no liking for the acid-tongued woman, but after hearing her pitiful story, and seeing the genuine distress she was in, he had volunteered to stand guard outside Agnes' home, knowing the outcry that would ensue when word got around about what had transpired. He had no doubt Agnes had been tricked by a master craftsman, and was as much a victim as the child that had gone missing. Kenneth Stokes, or Wells, as he was now calling himself, had had plenty of practice in duping vulnerable women in his perverted search for fresh young bodies. PC John Smith, like his fellow officers, could only stand by and watch in frustration as men like Stokes got off time and time again. Men like him were clever. They targeted poor families, worming their way into poverty-stricken homes, playing the benevolent gentleman, offering to take one of the children and find them a live-in job. Of course, the hungry, desperate mothers jumped at the chance of having at least one of their children taken care of. Of course there was no job and when Stokes and his kind were finished with their victims they would bring them back, cowed and too terrified to tell their parents what had happened to them.

Men like Stokes were the scum of the earth, not fit to breathe God's air. To make sure of their victims' silence, these so-called gentlemen would always leave a small amount of money to keep the parents quiet. But every now and then, an outraged parent on learning the truth had refused to be intimidated and had gone to the police, but rarely had the case ever come to court. For when it came to the day, with help from local bully boys, paid to instil fear into those brave enough to stand up to them, the parents in question would reluctantly withdraw their complaint. And no amount of police assurances were enough to convince them they would be kept safe until the trial was over. And who could blame them? John Smith thought sorrowfully. For every police officer stationed in the East End, there were ten villains who would cut their own granny's throat for the price of a pint of beer. In the twenty years Kenneth Stokes had been prowling the East End, he had been jailed only twice, both times sentenced to a poxy three years. But then, men like Stokes had money, and money bought the best solicitors.

'Of course you can see her, love. She needs all the help she can get right now.' Nodding towards the broken glass he added, 'As you can see, word's out already. If I hadn't turned up, things could have got a lot worse. Anyway, you go on in, love, while I have a word with Ted here.' He looked at Ted, saw the naked hatred in the dark eyes and shook his head, wondering if there was any point in trying to put Agnes' version of events to the normally cheerful stall holder. Well! He had nothing better to do, did he? It was worth a try.

Ellen passed through the green door and stepped warily into the small hallway. Swallowing nervously she called out, 'Agnes. Agnes, it's me, Ellen. May I come in, Agnes? I'd like to talk to you, if that's all right.'

Only silence greeted her words, but Ellen remained where she was. Obviously Agnes had heard her. Equally obviously, she was suspicious of Ellen's arrival. Knowing this, Ellen took another few tentative steps nearer the front room, talking all the while.

'I know you can hear me, Agnes. Agnes! Look, I don't blame you for being suspicious, but I promise you I haven't come to cause you any more trouble. I only want to help. I've always believed in making my own decisions, so until I hear it from your own lips, I'm not going to take any notice of the talk that's all around the streets.'

Still there was no answer. Then into the eerie silence came the sound of quiet sobbing, a sound that wrenched at Ellen's soft heart.

Her mouth dry, Ellen entered the front room, and there, curled up in a shabby armchair, was Agnes, her thin body wracked with heart-breaking sobs.

At the sight of her old adversary's distress, Ellen let out a low moan of pity. 'Oh, Agnes.' Dropping her bag on the dining table, Ellen knelt down by the armchair and laid a hand on the shuddering form. 'Look, shall I make some tea? I know it's an old cliché in circumstances like these, but it'll give me something to do while you try to compose yourself.'

Still there was no response from Agnes. It was only when Ellen put her hand on the thin arm that the body in the armchair suddenly came to life. With a frightening change in demeanour Agnes sat bolt upright, slapping Ellen's hand away viciously. 'I've already been taken for a mug, but I ain't a complete idiot.'

Her plain face ravaged by hours of crying, Agnes glared at the pretty young face staring back at her. And saw only pity and compassion mirrored in the clear blue eyes. Yet still she remained wary, and with good cause. With their past history why should Ellen Mitson worry about what happened to her?

Swallowing loudly, Agnes swivelled around in the chair, her gaze focused on the floor. 'I know why yer've come. Couldn't resist the opportunity ter gloat, could yer? Well, now's yer chance. So go ahead an' get it over with, then yer can piss off back ter where yer came from.'

Drawing herself up from her crouching position Ellen said quietly, 'I'll put the kettle on, it'll give me something to do while you think about what you've just said. And while you're thinking, ask yourself if you really believe I'm the sort of person you've just described. If you decide I am, then I'll go and not trouble you again. But you and me know each other well, Agnes, and that's why I'm here. I don't believe for one moment you would deliberately conspire to hand an innocent child over to a pervert. All I ask is that you give me the same courtesy of the benefit of the doubt as to why I'm here. I'll be back in five minutes for your answer.'

Out in the scullery Ellen made herself busy, and when she returned carrying a tea tray Agnes was sitting upright, her red-rimmed eyes holding a tentative spark of hope.

Her voice quivering she asked, 'You really mean it? You really wanna 'elp me, hear my side of the story?'

Pouring out the tea Ellen smiled. 'That's why I'm here, Agnes.'

At Ellen's words Agnes' body slumped with relief. Now she had two allies – and that was two more than she had dared hope for. Maybe with John Smith and Ellen backing her up, there might still be a future for her in the East End.

As Agnes talked, Ellen listened and as the whole sordid tale unravelled she realised that her own problems seemed insignificant in comparison. Pushing all other thoughts from her mind, Ellen gave her undivided attention to Agnes.

CHAPTER FIFTEEN

'Put 'er outta yer mind, son. Yer only setting yerself up for a load of grief if yer carry on 'oping she'll leave 'er 'usband for you. It just ain't done, mate . . . Well, not very often. And even then, yer've gotta 'ave a bleeding good reason fer wanting to get shot of an 'usband or wife. Yer can't just get a divorce 'cos yer fed up with yer spouse. Gawd 'elp us, if it was that easy, there wouldn't be very many married couples still together.' Nora Parker shot a quick look at her son, her heart missing a painful beat at the look of misery etched on his face.

Moving away from her only child Nora began setting out plates and cutlery for the fish and chip supper Ted had picked up on his way home, her thoughts racing in despair. Her Ted was a good-looking man, with a quick wit and overpowering personality and charm that had had the girls running after him since he was in short trousers. He could have had the pick of any woman, but who does he go and fall for? A bleeding married woman, that's who. Bustling around the small scullery Nora looked through to the sitting room where Ellen was sitting on the sofa, the pitiful figure of Micky Masters snuggled close to her side. So wrapped up in her thoughts was she, that Nora jumped when Ted's answer came.

'I'm a grown man, an' I'll make me own mistakes, just like I've always done, and not be frightened to face the consequences. Now, let's get this grub eaten before it gets cold. There'll be plenty of time to say your piece, 'cos you ain't gonna let it drop, no matter what I say. But not now, eh, Mum? Right now looking after Micky and finding his sister is more important than my love life, or lack of it!'

He grinned at Nora, and that lop-sided smile made even her, his own mother, want to reach out and grab hold of him. And in that respect she was lucky. As his mother, she could hold him any time she chose. With a wry smile she said affectionately, 'Give over. You'll never go short of female company, an' yer know it.'

Ted gazed down at her fondly, then winked. 'What can I say, Mum? I can't help being irresistible to women, now can I?'

But behind the jocular manner, Nora knew that there was only one woman he was interested in. And her looking barely older than the child she was comforting. A sharp slap on her backside propelled Nora forward, the impact almost upsetting the tray carrying their supper. Entering the living room she glanced up at her son and said waspishly, 'You'll smack my ars— backside once too often, me lad.

You're not too old ter get a good clout if I put me mind to it; just you remember that, mate.'

Handing out portions of the tempting food Ted chuckled. 'You don't have to mind your words in front of Ellen, Mum. I don't think she'll go into a swoon if she hears the word arse, would you, love?'

Ted's eyes were fixed on Ellen, and Nora, her heart sinking, saw the adoration shining from Ellen's eyes as she answered cheerfully, 'I very much doubt it. Working in the East End has toughened me up considerably. Mind you, I probably would have a couple of years ago before . . .' Her voice trailed off, her manner suddenly solemn as she remembered Arthur waiting at home on his own. But she felt so at ease here in Ted's home. She already knew Nora from the shop, and although their home wasn't a patch on her own rooms above the bakery, she felt more comfortable here than she'd ever felt anywhere else since her parents' death. Aware she was in danger of putting a damper on the evening, and realising that Micky needed to be in a positive atmosphere she said brightly, 'Goodness, I'm starving. I haven't had anything to eat since one cream cake on the train coming back, and that smell is heavenly.' Shifting her position to ease Micky from her side she said softly, 'Come on, Micky. Sit up properly and have your supper.'

His arms clinging to Ellen, Micky said tremulously, 'I ain't 'ungry.'

Gently but firmly Ellen extracted herself from Micky's fierce hold. 'Now look here, Micky. I know . . .' She looked at Ted and Nora. 'We all know how

184

worried you are, but like I've already told you, that man hasn't got Molly. Agnes said . . .'

Micky twisted angrily away from her. 'I don't believe that old cow. I wouldn't believe anything she said. It was her fault I was nicked, just to get me outta the way so that pervert could get his 'ands on my Molly. He's been after 'er for months, but I looked after 'er. I protected 'er. But now . . . now . . . he's got 'er. An' . . . an' . . .' He broke off, his voice failing him as he dissolved into heart-rending sobs.

The three adults looked at each other helplessly, but it was Ellen who quickly took charge of the situation, making Nora realise that despite her youthful appearance, Ellen had a good head on her shoulders, which was more than could be said of some of the women Ted had brought home, none of whom had lasted long. But Ellen was speaking, bringing Nora's attention back to the two young people cuddling on her sofa.

In a strong, firm voice, Ellen took hold of Micky's shuddering shoulders and said, 'Now look, Micky, that man hasn't got your sister.' As Micky tried to pull away from Ellen's grasp, he found his face cradled in two soft hands, then his chin was lifted upwards and he was staring into Ellen's blue eyes.

'I don't blame you for not trusting Agnes, especially after the way she set you up for shoplifting. But think, Micky, think! If that man had got hold of Molly, then why would he have come back to see Agnes? And why would he have attacked her? Because he thought she had told on him. Either that, or she had changed her mind and got to Molly first. If that evil man had Molly, he'd have been long gone by now. He certainly wouldn't still be hanging around the East End.'

Micky's eyes flickered as he tried to take in Ellen's words. Part of him wanted to believe that Molly was safe somewhere, but his tortured mind was afraid to get his hopes up. Yet what Ellen was saying made sense. The only reason Kenneth Wells had sucked up to that old cow Agnes was to get his dirty hands on his beautiful, innocent sister. But if he didn't have Molly, then where was she? Oh Gawd, his head hurt, his stomach was churning, and he had a sensation in his chest he hadn't experienced since the death of his parents. He couldn't think straight. All he wanted to do was curl up in Ellen's comforting arms, and wake up to find his sweet Molly's face smiling at him.

'Micky! Micky, have you been listening to what I've been saying?'

Like an old man, Micky shrugged his shoulders and nodded wearily. 'Yeah, I heard you, and . . . and I want to believe what you're saying 'cos it makes sense. But if . . . if that's true, then where is she?' He looked at Ellen, then Ted and finally Nora, as if praying one of them would say something to reassure him, but they all averted their gaze, unable to endure the pain and terror in the frightened eyes.

Another awkward silence descended on the room. This time it was Nora who stepped into the breach. Clucking her tongue impatiently, she barked, 'Well, we're not gonna be able to think on an empty stomach. Now then, get that food inside you all before it goes stone cold. And while we're eating, we can 'ave a think an' maybe one of us'll come up with a brainstorm.'

Not bothering with the plates she had set out on

the table, Nora plonked the still warm, greasy parcels into everyone's laps. No one in the room would have thought they could eat at such an emotional time as this, but their empty stomachs soon proved them wrong. With the food consumed, followed by two mugs of strong, sweet tea, the occupants of the small, cosy room, their bellies full, their strength returning, began to talk.

Taking a long, loud slurp of her tea, Nora said, 'Now then, let's get our thinking caps on. From what Micky's told us, young Molly wouldn't 'ave left their 'ouse, unless she was really desperate. Now the way I see it, the poor little cow probably got frightened when Micky didn't come 'ome and wandered off trying to find him. She probably only intended to go outside so she could have a proper look up and down the street so she would see Micky as soon as he turned the corner into their road. We've all done it when we're waiting for someone. It's like if we keep looking outta the window, or out in the street, it'll make that person turn up quicker. Maybe she only intended to walk up to the top of the road, then lost her bearings. She's only eight, an' she ain't used to going out at night, an' what with it being dark ... Well, like I said, she probably got lost and she's hiding out somewhere waiting for Micky to come and find her.'

Nora smiled at the anguished face of the young boy, her smile fading at the look of utter hopelessness on Micky's deathly pale face.

Sitting on the edge of the sofa, his legs apart, his arms hanging limply between his knees he said flatly, 'What! For two nights? So where's she been sleeping?

And what's she been doing for food and drink? Who you trying to kid, Mrs Parker? I ain't stupid, you know.' His voice cracked and, sinking to a whisper he said, 'Someone's got her, and if it ain't that Wells bloke, it might be some other pervert. 'Cos he ain't the only man who likes little girls, is he?' Raising his head he looked directly at Ted and asked simply, 'Why are some men like that, Ted? I don't understand. Are they born like it, or do they change as they get older? Before this happened I couldn't wait to grow up. Now I ain't in such a hurry, 'cos right now I feel ashamed to be a man.'

Startled, Ted could only look to his mother for help, but on this occasion Nora wisely thought that this particular topic was best left to a man. Gathering up the greasy papers she said to Ellen, 'Give us a hand clearing up, will you, love? I think I've still got some fruit cake left for afters. That's if Ted ain't finished it off, greedy sod. He must 'ave hollow legs, 'cos the amount he eats he should be like the half side of an 'ouse.'

Ellen, as eager to leave the room as Nora, gratefully followed the stout woman into the scullery. 'What would you like me to do, Mrs Parker?'

Rinsing the mugs under the cold tap Nora looked over her shoulder saying, 'You can drop the Mrs Parker for a start. Me name's Nora to me friends, and I'd like us to be friends.' As the words left her mouth Nora was amazed she had uttered them. Only a short while ago she had been trying to think of ways to stop Ted from seeing the young woman who was smiling at her so openly. Yet, painful as it was to admit her son wasn't going to give up easily in his pursuit, and that ultimately there would be a high price to pay, Nora couldn't help but warm to Ellen. If only she wasn't married, she, Nora, couldn't have wished for a better daughter-in-law. But there it was, she reflected sadly, life was rarely easy, or fair. Which brought her mind back to the wretched boy desperately looking to Ted for answers that no ordinary person could possibly answer. From the other room she could hear Ted's low, soft voice and her heart went out to him, and the young boy whose world had been turned upside down in the cruellest way imaginable.

Nodding towards the open door she said flatly, 'It don't look good, does it, love?'

Ellen too looked towards the sitting room and said simply, 'No, it doesn't.'

They were seated at the kitchen table, neither of them anxious to return to the other room.

'Micky's right, you know.' Nora's voice was heavy, both with fatigue and worry. 'His sister ain't wandering round the streets looking for him. John Smith's got all the coppers on the beat looking out for 'er. And when it's a child gone missing, all coppers from miles around go that extra mile to find them. It ain't unknown for a lot of 'em to carry on looking even when they're off duty. Every derelict 'ouse'll be searched. Every man seen walking along with a young girl'll be stopped and questioned. An' it ain't only the coppers'll who'll be looking for her. Most of the East End knows what's 'appened by now an' they'll be keeping a look out an' all. So, if she was out there,

189

and she ain't been found by now ... Well! Like I said,
it don't look good ... 'Ere, you all right, love? Yer look
clapped out.'

Ellen smiled tiredly, the long day finally catching
up with her. 'I am tired, but I think it's more mental
than physical tiredness. I still can't quite take it in. I
mean Micky having a sister and living in a filthy ruin
both terrified of being caught and sent back to the
workhouse. The poor, poor little souls. What they
must have been through, and now this, it's just ..
just too cruel ... Oh, I'm sorry ...' Ellen dabbed
quickly at the tears springing to her eyes. 'You've
enough on your plate without me falling to pieces as
well.'

Immediately all motherly concern, Nora made to
comfort the distressed girl, but Ellen, sensing her
intention, quickly composed herself. There would be
plenty of time for tears later when she was on her
own – and she still had Arthur to face! Thinking of
the confrontation to come she gave her eyes a good
wipe with her handkerchief and said shakily, 'No
you're right, God help them, it doesn't look good. But
if the worst has happened, I only hope the poor little
mite didn't suffer, and that she's found soon. At least
then Micky can mourn her. Because the more time
goes by the more he's going to suffer. But whatever
the outcome, he'll always blame himself, and it's much
harder to forgive oneself than to forgive others.'

Nora gave a derisive snort. 'Yeah, it is normally.
But I doubt young Micky'll ever forgive Agnes
Handly for her part in this whole sorry mess – my
Ted too for that matter. Gawd! When he found ou

what she'd done! I've never seen him so angry, and I've seen him in many a foul temper, I can tell yer. It's lucky she's a woman, 'cos if it'd been a man, my Ted would 'ave beaten the shit outta him.' Darting a furtive look towards the front room, Nora lowered her voice and, leaning across the table added, 'I've tried ter reason with him, especially since I heard 'er side of it, but he ain't 'aving any of it. For what it's worth, I believe her. Like you, there ain't no love lost between me and Agnes, but I remember back when we were younger, yer wouldn't 'ave recognised 'er then. She was always good fer a laugh was Agnes. Oh, I know it's hard ter believe now, but she was a nice young girl. Felt a bit sorry fer 'er, to be honest. Stuck in that 'ouse, with her mum. Right old cow, she was, Audrey Handly. No wonder old Billy slung his hook when he did. Give 'im his due, he waited till Agnes left school. But the first week she brought 'ome a wage packet, he was off. No one ever saw him again . . .' Her words trailed off as she realised she was babbling. And the reason for her sudden discomfort was sitting only inches away from her. For the past hour, Nora's thoughts had been focused on Micky's troubles, but now, the worry of her Ted and Ellen Mitson came flooding back to torment her frayed nerves.

Seeing the elder woman's distress, and sensing the reason for it Ellen impulsively reached out and took hold of the plump hands lying on the table. 'It's all right, Nora. I know it must be awkward for you, having me here, I mean. But don't worry, I'll be going shortly . . . And, Nora . . .' She caught Nora's gaze and

191

held it firmly. 'I don't intend making trouble. I'm a married woman, not happily married . . .' She tried to smile at her attempt at humour and failed. Dropping her gaze she whispered, 'I'd better be going. Arthur will be wondering where I've got to. You know how fussy he is.' Now she was the one babbling. 'I'll just say goodbye to Micky. I only wish I could take him home with me, but I can't. I doubt he'd come with me even if it were possible. No! Micky's far better off here with you and Ted. You can give him hope and stability and that's what he most needs right now, especially Ted. Micky looks up to him and feels safe knowing Ted's around.'

'I know. He 'as that effect on people, does my Ted.' Nora's voice was filled with motherly pride as she followed Ellen back into the sitting room.

'Yer ain't going, are you, Ellen?' Micky, his bright blue eyes staring piteously out of a white, strained pinched face. He would have run to her side if Ted's strong hand hadn't stilled his flight.

Gripping the thin shoulder Ted said, 'Now then, Micky. We've already been over this, ain't we? You know she can't stay here. You don't wanna get her into trouble, now, do yer?' Gently folding his fist into a ball Ted playfully brushed Micky's cheek. 'You stay here, mate, while I walk Ellen home. Me Mum will look after you until I get back, so don't you go giving her any trouble while I'm gone, d'yer hear?'

Ellen was shrugging her arms into the light blue summer coat she'd had on since leaving Southend, her head coming up sharply as she heard Ted's jocular words. Buttoning up the linen coat she glanced quickly towards Nora and saw plainly the anxiety etched on the plump face.

Turning all of her attention to the task in hand, Ellen, her heart thudding at the prospect of being alone with Ted, fastened the last button saying brightly, 'Oh, that's all right, Ted. It's still light outside, and besides, it's only a few minutes' walk from here.' Putting out her arms to the slight frame huddled up in the wide, comfortable armchair she said softly, 'Do I get a hug, Micky?'

The words were scarcely out of her mouth before Micky rushed into the warmth of the slim arms. Caught off balance momentarily Ellen stumbled, her hands grasping at Micky's wiry body in an attempt to remain on her feet. Then Ted was holding them both, and to the fearful Nora watching the sombre trio, they seemed to belong together. Even she, here in her own house, felt out of place. It was as if she was being shut out, put aside, and she knew then how Arthur must be feeling.

Jerking herself out of her reverie she said over-loudly, 'Be careful, lad. You nearly had the lot of you over.' Bustling around the room she added in an off-hand manner, 'Don't yer worry about Ellen, love. I'll walk her 'ome. Like she says, it's only a few minutes away, an' I need ter pick up a few things while I'm out.'

'And where yer gonna get anything this time of night?' Ted asked sardonically, knowing full well the reason why his mother was anxious not to let him and Ellen spend any time alone together. 'It's nearly half nine now, it'll be dark soon. So don't give me any old flannel about having ter get some shopping, all right? I'm walking Ellen home and that's an end ter it.' Giving the forlorn Micky's shoulder a firm squeeze of reassurance, Ted stood back as Ellen bent to kiss the pale cheek.

'I'll be back first thing in the morning, Micky, all right?'

Micky nodded listlessly, the pathetic action jerking at Ellen's already frayed emotions. Avoiding Nora's glance, she said, "Bye, Nora . . . And thanks.'

Nora, now standing by Micky's side, merely nodded as the young couple left the house.

At the same time in the top floor in a tenement building in Shoreditch, Sadie North, her face devoid of make-up and wearing a pale blue woollen dress, was tucking her newly found charge into the brass-headed double bed Sadie had slept in alone since she'd bought it over fifteen years ago. Her policy of not bringing her punters home had never wavered. This two-room flat was her haven, her escape from the sordid world she lived in. When she had first moved in, the flat had been in a disgusting state; it had also been cheap. Over the years she had gradually reno-vated the two rooms, discovering she had a talent for spotting good, second-hand furniture. The final touch to her new home had been the purchase of two off cuts of carpet, which she had proudly fitted herself. No one else in the building had ever been invited into Sadie's domain, the other occupants of the tenement block preferring to keep themselves to themselves, which suited Sadie just fine.

But now she had been landed with an unexpected guest and was at a loss as to what to do about the child she had taken under her wing.

'I don't suppose yer've remembered the name of that bakery, or the names of your brother's friends, 'ave yer, love?' she asked hopefully. At the time, taking the child home with her had been the only option open to her, but she had hoped that Molly's brother, after reading the note left for him, would turn up to collect his sister. Now, after two days, Sadie had to face the possibility that something had happened to the boy. And the only way to find out was to track down Micky Masters' friends. Taking a deep breath she tried again. Tucking the eiderdown round Molly's neck she asked quietly, 'Your brother must 'ave told yer where he was working, love. If I know where to look, I can go and find him. You do want ter see him again, don't yer?'

But the girl remained mute, only her eyes showing her apprehension and fear, and it wasn't hard to understand why the child was so frightened.

That first night, the young girl hadn't stopped talking about her brother and every word and action had been filled with pride. Yet even then Sadie had detected a note of fear. And she had been right. For the next day Molly could barely remember her own name. The poor little cow was scared her brother wasn't coming back for her, not because he didn't want her, but because he couldn't. If that was the case then Molly must be hoping that Sadie would look after her. Her heart sinking, Sadie looked down into the large blue eyes staring out of a heart-shaped face. What on earth was she going to do if the brother couldn't be found? Smoothing down the bedcovers, she gently stroked the soft cheek saying, 'All right, love, don't worry. You 'ave a good night's sleep and perhaps you'll remember something in the morning. 'Night, love.'

''Night, Sadie,' Molly replied sleepily. 'God bless.'

Leaving the bedroom door slightly ajar, Sadie made herself a light supper, her mind whirling round in circles, wondering what to do for the best.

She'd already lost two nights' work, and while the rest had been very nice she wasn't going to earn any money sitting on her backside. Yet if she was to be honest with herself, these past forty-eight hours had been the happiest time of her life. For those short two days she had been able to pretend she was a normal, respectable woman and she realised she was in danger of taking that fantasy one step further and begin to think of herself as a mother. It was a dream she had harboured for over twenty years, but Sadie was nothing if not practical. She was a whore, a thirty-eight-year-old whore who had no desire for a permanent man in her life. Also, unlike many in her profession, she had never fallen pregnant, thus saving her from risking her life at the hands of the many back street abortionists that worked the East End.

Her inability to conceive may well have been due to being forced to go on the game at the tender age of twelve, urged on by her own mother, a blowsy, gin-soaked tart who had thought nothing of setting her only daughter on the sordid and often dangerous road of prostitution.

Brought up in a cramped, dirty bedsit where Bertha North had entertained her clients, Sadie had grown up watching different men come and go at all hours of the day and night. She had heard the groans and squeaking of the double bed from her straw-filled pallet tucked away into the furthest corner of the room. Sadie had never thought to question her mother when she had brought home her daughter's first client, for Sadie had never known any other way of life. Yet from that first, brutal encounter something inside Sadie had died. The only way she could survive in her new world was to build a protective barrier around her mind to block out the loathsome men that used her for their own pleasure without a thought for her as a person. And with each new punter her heart had hardened, until she was incapable of feeling any emotion.

Even when her mother had died from a venereal disease at the relatively young age of thirty-six, Sadie hadn't shed a single tear. She had paid for the cheapest funeral she could find, and, before the coffin lid had been nailed down, Sadie had looked down dispassionately at the bloated, ravaged face that could easily have been taken for a woman in her late fifties. Sadie had sworn then she would never end her days as a tuppenny whore.

With her mother gone, Sadie was left alone with no real friends or family to turn to. She had never known who her father was; then again, neither had her mother. From that day Sadie had started to make plans for her future. With steely determination she had promised herself that she would retire the day she

turned forty, for she knew only too well that once a
prostitute reached that landmark, it was a slippery
slope into middle age then a sharp skid towards the
grave. Sadie had seen too many old tarts, like her dead
mother, desperately touting for trade, their looks gone,
their bodies diseased, all alone in the world with only
a gin bottle for company. With military precision she
had estimated it would take that long to build up her
growing nest egg, allowing herself a comfortable
lifestyle until she was ready to embark on a new life

Oh, she'd had it all mapped out. Her ultimate goal
was to one day be able to set up a little business of
her own. The precise nature of that business had yet
to be decided, which was why she forced herself out
onto the streets every night, desperate to earn as much
money as she could before she reached forty, only two
years away. Once her flat had been made into a home
every spare shilling she earned had been put into the
bank for safe keeping and to earn interest. There was
something else she'd promised herself, and that was
to take herself out to the most expensive restaurant
she could find and order the dearest meal on the menu
In short she planned to spoil herself rotten. Those
plans and dreams had kept her going, kept her sane
in her lowest, darkest hours, and God only knew there
had been plenty of those. But her greatest pleasure
would be the day she bundled up all the cheap, tarty
clothes that had been her trademark for so many years
and donate them to the Salvation Army. What that
holy organisation would do with the obvious cast-off
clothing of a prostitute was anyone's guess, for Sadie
would be long gone before the bulky parcel was

opened. Oh, yes, Sadie North had had her future well planned.

Then she had met Molly. And when, on the walk home that night, she had felt the small hand clasp hers so trustingly, it was as if a chisel had pierced a hole in the armour she had built around herself for so long. And the longer she spent with the sweet-natured girl, the wider the chink in her amour was spreading. Staring towards the open bedroom door Sadie felt her eyes misting over, and the shock of experiencing the first real emotion she could remember brought her sitting bolt upright. She had imagined she was no longer capable of such feelings, but a person would have to be made of stone not to be affected by the loving child. And though Sadie had tried her hardest to remain impervious to the little girl's innocent charm she now had to admit that, despite her best efforts, Molly had already wormed herself into Sadie's heart. And the longer Molly stayed, the harder it would be to give her up. And Sadie had had enough pain and let downs in her life; she wasn't going to allow herself to be hurt any more. First thing in the morning she was going to go to all the markets in the East End, and start asking questions. Market traders were a close-knit community; it shouldn't be too hard to track down Molly's brother – if he was still alive.

Hardening her defences once more, Sadie headed for the bedroom, undressed and, careful not to disturb the sleeping child, climbed into the double bed.

Then the small form turned over, snuggling against Sadie's voluptuous body and Sadie was lost. The feel of the warm body cuddling against her brought tears

199

to Sadie's eyes, and this time she let them fall. There was something else Sadie had never experienced, and that was any form of genuine warmth and love.

She didn't know what tomorrow would bring. But for now she was going to cherish this precious moment, hold onto it for as long as possible, sadly acknowledging that tonight might be the last chance she would ever have to hold a child's warm body, innocent and trusting, next to hers.

CHAPTER SIXTEEN

'Please, Johnny, yer can't go off and leave me on me own. You know what will 'appen when yer've gone. I've already had me window smashed in. If you go it'll be me face next.'

Constable John Smith shook his head tiredly. 'I'm sorry Agnes, but I can't stop here for ever. I've already stayed too long as it is.'

Buttoning up his tunic the kindly policeman looked with genuine pity at the pathetic figure reeking of brandy, but what more could he do? Fixing his helmet firmly in place, he thought quietly before saying warily, 'Look, how about asking young Ellen if you can stay with her and Arthur . . . just until you get yourself sorted.'

Agnes' jaw dropped in amazement, then, her eyes hardening she spat out, 'Yer 'aving a laugh ain't yer?' A bitter sound erupted from her lips. 'Yer really think Arthur Mitson would offer to take me in when he's been trying to get rid of me for years? Nah! He'd laugh in me face and enjoy doing it.'

Taking his leave, PC Smith replied sympathetically, 'Maybe Arthur would, but Ellen wouldn't. She's a nice young woman, and she did offer to help if she could.'

Seeing the hope slowly enter her eyes, the uniformed man quickly pressed home his suggestion. 'Look, what if I come to the bakery with you? Arthur might be a bit more amiable with me alongside you. In fact, how about me having a word with him first, eh? And with Ellen siding with me, I can't see Arthur refusing, not with both of us pleading your case. You know what he's like, strength of character has never been Arthur's strongest point, has it? Poor old sod.'

Agnes' lips curled in disgust. 'Bleeding gutless, that's what Arthur's trouble is, always 'as been.' Rolling her eyes she added spitefully, 'Gawd help us. I must 'ave been blind all those years. If . . .'

Tired and impatient to get home to his long-suffering wife, John Smith interrupted Agnes' deliberate ploy to keep him talking. For a few brief moments he had considered inviting Agnes to stay at his modest house for the night. Horrified the thought had even crossed his mind John Smith rubbed his chin in agitation. His Sarah, wife of thirty years this coming August, was one of the sweetest-natured women he had ever known, but she was no mug. Giving up his spare time to help Agnes was one thing, bringing the said woman home with him was another matter entirely. Adopting a more professional manner he said crisply, 'Get your coat, and put a few bits in a bag for the night. If Arthur does dig his heels in,

I'll find you somewhere else to stay, I promise.'

Knowing John's word was always good, Agnes was soon dressed for the outdoors, a shopping bag containing her nightwear clutched tightly in her hand.

Thinking it more prudent to leave by the back door, the constable was caught off-guard as a chunk of brick sailed by his ear, hitting Agnes on the back of her covered head, causing her to cry out in pain. John swiftly put his bulk in front of the crying, terrified woman, his sharp eyes peering into the failing light, and focused on two shadowy figures lurking in the alley opposite.

'Get yourself off home before I run you in for disturbing the peace,' his authoritative voice boomed out into the silence of the night.

Then came the sound of running footsteps, and a sneering voice called out defiantly, 'Yer can't 'ave the bobbies looking after yer for ever, yer wicked old bitch. We'll get yer. You're gonna get what's coming to yer.'

Cursing beneath his breath, the constable could only watch helplessly as the would-be assailants ran off, their taunting threats still ringing in his ears. Taking a deep gulp of air he turned to the trembling woman hiding behind him and said brusquely, 'Come on, old girl. Let's get you to Arthur and Ellen's place before anyone else decides to take the law into their own hands.'

Cowering behind the safety of the broad, reassuring figure, Agnes tentatively reached out and caught hold of the policeman's arm, holding her breath, as if fearful of rejection, and when, after a few seconds, a heavy, warm hand covered hers, she let out a shuddering sigh of relief. A silence settled on the incongruous couple as they walked the short journey to their destination.

In the sitting room above the bakery, Arthur, his fleshy face sweating with anxiety, could still see the contempt in Ted Parker's eyes, still feel the tremor that had rippled through his body as he had gazed into those hard, cold eyes. A shudder racked him as the memory returned to haunt him. It wouldn't have been so bad if Ellen had spoken up for him: he was her husband after all. But no. Instead of performing her wifely duties she had sided with Ted Parker. Fresh beads of sweat broke out on his brow as he looked down at the dwindling remains of whisky in the cut crystal glass. Downing the last of the drink he rose unsteadily to his feet and staggered over to the sideboard, pouring another glass from the depleted decanter. Returning to his armchair he slumped down into the comfortable cushions, spilling some of the alcohol onto the carpet, but Arthur was too drunk to notice.

The one thing he had feared most had come to pass. He was going to lose Ellen.

If he was honest with himself the change in Ellen had been going on for some time. And he could almost pinpoint the time Ellen had begun to change. It had been when that brat Micky had first come knocking on the door. Because of him, Ellen had forged a friendship with Ted Parker in order to get the boy a job. From that moment on, Ellen had begun to grow further and further away from him. So when she had suggested going on holiday, Arthur, at first, worried about his business, had hesitated, mainly out of habit.

But it hadn't taken him long to realise that a holiday might be his only chance to put their ailing marriage back on familiar ground. And for a short time the impromptu holiday by the sea seemed to have worked. Then the telegram had arrived, and Ellen had insisted she must return home that very day, her abrupt decision making it perfectly clear where her loyalties lay. And, as if he hadn't been humiliated enough in front of their new-found friends, the Bradleys, he'd had to endure a confrontation with Ted Parker in his own home.

Tears of self-pity pricked his eyes. Why was this happening to him?

Suddenly he was jerked back to the present by a hammering on the back door. Shuffling over to the slightly open window, he peered down, squinting to make out the figures standing below.

'Ellen, is that you?' he slurred, hopefully.

'Open up, Arthur, it's me, John Smith. I've got Agnes with me. Come on, man, I haven't got all night.'

The amount of alcohol Arthur had consumed had left him confused and disorientated. Not a big drinker by nature, Arthur was totally unprepared for the transformation he felt within himself. Filled with dutch courage he sauntered down the stairs, his expression set, determined that this time he would take control of the situation. Halfway down he tripped, grabbed the handrail to stop his fall, then, pulling himself up to his full height, he threw open the door and said, in what he hoped was a manly tone, 'Well, what d'you want?'

Hearing the aggressive note in Arthur's usually

placid voice, PC Smith hid a smile at Arthur's obvious attempt to be assertive. The constable gave a cough to cover his mirth before answering, 'Come on Arthur, let us in before the neighbours come out to see what's going on.'

Reluctantly Arthur gestured them in, trying to keep up the charade of masculinity. Unfortunately the weak-willed man couldn't quite pull it off. Faced with an officer of the law, albeit a man he had known for years, Arthur soon crumpled under the stern gaze. He heard himself agreeing to let Agnes stay until Ellen got home, noting with self-disgust the look of sympathy that crossed John Smith's face, a look that only served to remind Arthur how he appeared to the outside world. A bleeding mug! That's how people saw him, and usually they would be right. But not this time. Oh, no! There was no way Agnes Handly was going to get the better of him. If she thought she was going to spend the night under his roof, then she was going to be sorely disappointed. No sooner had the back door slammed behind the uniformed man, than the fixed smile dropped from Arthur's face, leaving in its stead the fury that was bubbling inside him. With eyes almost bulging out of his head, Arthur turned on Agnes, who had flopped gratefully into one of the armchairs placed either side of the fireplace. Grinding his teeth in anger he growled, 'Don't get yourself too comfortable, you ugly old cow.'

And Agnes, who for the first time that day had just begun to relax, heard the raw hatred in Arthur's voice and immediately the fear came surging back.

Arthur saw the look and his chest swelled with

renewed confidence. 'You can look surprised. You didn't think I was really going to welcome you back into this house with open arms, did you? 'Cos if you did, then you're even more stupid than I thought you were.'

Agnes remained where she was, her eyes hardening as she realised that the blustering façade Arthur had presented to the constable was merely the result of too much whisky. She should have known better. Like everything Arthur tried to do, getting drunk only made him appear more pathetic than he normally did. His newly found courage would disappear as soon as the drink wore off. Until then she wasn't moving. Grimly churning inside, Agnes remained quiet as the maddened man raged on.

'Bleeding hell, I always knew you were desperate for a man. You proved that when you carried on hanging around my neck when I made it perfectly obvious I wasn't interested in you any more. But I kept you on here out of the goodness of my heart, when what I should have done was to send you packing. But I didn't think even somebody like you would be that desperate that you'd hand over a little girl to a pervert just to keep him interested in you.'

As Arthur's cruel words continued to beat inside her head, Agnes, her knuckles white, gripped the side of the armchair as she slowly raised herself to her feet, her lips settling into a tight grim line. Taking one step towards him she kept her voice low, but there was no disguising the menace in her tone.

'Yer bloody hypocrite. 'Ow you can stand there and preach when you're no better yerself. For two years

I've 'ad to put up with the thought of you in bed with a mere child. 'Cos that's all she was when yer married 'er. All that putting on a front as the respectable businessman to make excuses for marrying a poor little orphan out of the goodness of your 'eart just to cover up your true colours. You think that everyone round these parts was thinking what a kind man you was, when all the time they've been sniggering behind your back. And yer've got the nerve ter call me names. All right, what I did was a terrible thing ter do. But as God is my witness, I didn't know what that man was like. If I had, I'd've turned him over to the nearest copper. 'Cos yer wrong, Arthur. I'd never see a child hurt, never, and if you think I would, then yer never really knew me – just like I never really knew you. Or maybe I did, and wouldn't believe it. People are like that, yer know. They can be very blind to a person's faults, especially when they're in love. And I did love you, Arthur. Now I see yer was just a dirty old man, and yer still are.'

Advancing on the startled man Agnes continued her barrage of abuse, her fears forgotten. Arthur backed away, his face reddening as Agnes went on relentlessly, her voice dripping with scorn. Shocked into silence, Arthur could only stand mute, shocked at the venom in her voice.

'When I think of her living here before yer married her. Carrying on all the time. Did yer think no one knew?' Arthur blanched as the true meaning of her words began to pierce through his fuddled mind. Oblivious of his distress Agnes hissed, 'How old was she when yer first fancied her? Seven? Eight? Or do you like 'em younger? All those years you was playing the dutiful friend, when all the time you was only going round there just to get yer 'ands on the kid.'

Stung into action at the outrageous thought Arthur leapt forward, his hand grasping Agnes' arm in a vicious grip. Ignoring her cry of pain Arthur hissed, 'I've never slept with Ellen now or in the past, not in the way you mean, you filthy-minded bitch.'

Spittle sprayed from Arthur's lips over Agnes' face, but she didn't flinch, for despite Arthur's murderous countenance Agnes knew she was in no danger. Arthur was, and always would be, a coward at heart, ready to back down if faced with a stronger character, and Agnes wasn't a woman to be easily intimidated – especially by the likes of Arthur Mitson. So wrapped up in their own private war were they, neither heard the door open, or were aware Ellen and Ted had entered the room until Ellen's anguished voice cut through the heavy atmosphere like a knife.

'Arthur . . . please . . .'

Releasing his hold on Agnes Arthur whirled round to find the couple staring at him in surprise. But whereas Ellen's face portrayed hurt, the expression on Ted Parker's face could only be described as triumphant.

And in that moment, Arthur realised his world, as he knew it, was finished. But worse still was the knowledge that he had condemned himself out of his own mouth. Knowing anything he said now would be futile Arthur turned and, stopping only to grab the depleted whisky decanter, he walked with as much dignity as he could muster into the safety of his bedroom, closing the door quietly behind him.

Ignoring the dumbfounded Agnes, Ted took hold of Ellen's arms, his face alight with excitement. 'Why didn't you ever tell me? Don't yer know what this means? You ain't properly married. You can walk out now, and there's nothing Arthur can do. I ain't no expert on divorces, but I do know yer can get a marriage annulled if it ain't been . . . well, you know . . .'

But Ellen, her face burning with embarrassment at having her most personal and intimate secrets aired in public, had no intention of giving the avidly watching Agnes any further information about her private life. Pushing Ted's arms away she said firmly, 'I can't talk about it now, Ted. No matter how badly Arthur's behaved, he doesn't deserve this public humiliation. I want you to go, Ted.'

His face screwing up in bewildered lines Ted said, 'What are yer talking about, love? Don't you understand, you're free. We can be together now. Look . . .'

Ellen turned on him. 'I asked you to leave, Ted. This is Arthur's home, and whatever you say, I am still his wife until the law says otherwise.'

Looking into Ellen's determined face Ted's mouth tightened. 'All right. If that's what you want, I'm going. But don't leave it too long, Ellen. I love yer, but I ain't gonna wait around for ever. You get things sorted with Arthur, and soon.'

When Ted slammed out of the room Ellen turned wearily to Agnes. 'It's all right, Agnes, I know why you're here. We met Constable Smith on the way home. You can stay for the night, but I'm afraid you'll have to sleep downstairs. I'm sorry I can't offer you a bed, you'll have to make do with the armchair in the kitchen. I know it's a bit battered but it's quite comfortable, and after all, it is only for one night. Now I'm going to bed. I've had just about enough for one day. Goodnight, Agnes.'

When Ellen entered the bedroom Arthur was standing by the window, his hands clasped behind his back, his body ridged. But although his body was still, his mind was churning. All he could hear was Ted Parker's voice filled with glee, mocking him for his inability to be a proper husband to his young wife, and try as he might, Arthur couldn't get those words out of his mind. But if Ted Parker was gloating over the true state of affairs between himself and Ellen, that old bitch Agnes must be over the moon at the news. No doubt when the fuss concerning the Masters children was forgotten, his one-time lover would waste no time in regaling the whole sorry business to all and sundry – that's if Ted Parker didn't beat her to it.

His head drooped in despair. It wasn't fair. All his life he'd tried to be kind and easygoing, and where had it got him? Ridiculed and despised by all who knew him, that's where! Even Ellen was turning against him. Oh, she might have sent Ted Parker packing tonight, but for how long? Slowly turning he looked to where Ellen was getting ready for bed. She normally undressed in the adjoining bathroom, immersing herself in the flannel nightdress that covered her from neck to ankle before getting into bed. And the fact that she felt comfortable disrobing in front of him only inflamed his already maddened, whisky-fuelled mind. Did she think he was made of stone? Or maybe she imagined he was incapable of acting like a normal red-blooded man, a man like Ted Parker!

Unaware of her husband's thoughts Ellen said tiredly, 'Would you mind sleeping in the spare room tonight, Arthur? I think we both need some time alone.'

And those words, spoken without rancour, were for Arthur the final straw, and something inside him snapped.

Not recognising his own voice Arthur answered, 'Yes, I would mind as it happens. You've made a right mug of me today, and I've had enough. D'you hear me, I've had enough.'

Ellen's eyes widened in surprise as Arthur advanced towards the bed, and for the first time a flicker of alarm tugged at her chest. Clutching her nightdress close to her breasts she tried to keep her voice light.

'Don't be silly, Arthur. Look, we're both tired, let's not start an argument now. We can talk properly in the morning . . . Arthur. Arthur, what are you doing?'

His face grim, Arthur growled, 'I'm getting undressed for bed. My bed, with my wife.' Stripped to his undergarments Arthur gave a low, mirthless laugh. 'Yeah, my wife. And I think it's about time you started to act like a wife.'

Thoroughly frightened now, Ellen began to rise from the bed. 'Stop it, Arthur. Look, you're drunk, you don't know what you're doing. Please, Arthur, you're beginning to frighten me . . .'

A heavy hand pushed her back onto the bed, then Arthur was on top of her, his heavy bulk crushing her into the mattress.

Tears stung her eyes as Ellen tried futilely to push Arthur away, but it was no use. Feeling as if she were in a nightmare, Ellen could only lie helpless as sweaty hands roamed over her body. But she couldn't stifle the cry of pain as a red-hot pain seemed to tear her insides apart.

Arthur heard the cry, but he was too far gone to stop. Then it was over, and with it came stark reality.

With a soft moan of despair Arthur rolled off the trembling body. 'Oh, God! Ellen, I'm so sorry. I don't know what came over me. Please . . . please, Ellen, say something.'

But Ellen, traumatised by the violent assault, could only lie still, her face turned into her pillow, while Arthur sat on the edge of the bed, his large frame heaving with sobs of remorse.

And when, some time later, he staggered from the room, Ellen remained still. It was as if she had lost the use of her limbs. Only her mind remained active. And her thoughts were more painful than her bruised body.

All her secret dreams of one day being with Ted, living with him, bearing his children and growing old together were gone for ever.

For with that one brutal act, Arthur had bound her to him for life.

CHAPTER SEVENTEEN

'Now, Mrs Knight is gonna keep an eye on yer while I go to work. All right? Be a good girl. I'll be 'ome as soon as I can.' Sadie rested her hands on Molly's shoulders as she tried to reassure her that she wasn't about to run off and leave her behind.

Molly, her blue eyes filling with tears, answered tremulously, 'I promise, Sadie. I'll be good. You will be coming 'ome, won't ya?'

A gruff voice from behind laughed, ''Course she'll be coming 'ome, yer daft little thing. Now, how about getting out from under me feet.' Waddling over to the open door, the heavily pregnant woman called out loudly, 'Billy, Charlie. Get yerselves in here.'

Two laughing, scruffy boys raced into the room, almost knocking Molly over. 'What d'yer want, Mum?' they cried in unison.

'Take Molly out ter play with yer for a while. I'll call yer when yer tea's ready.'

Before Molly could protest, the boys grabbed a hand each and dragged her out of the door. The last sight Sadie had of Molly was a sad, pleading look from big, blue eyes filled with unshed tears.

'Don't worry, Sadie, she'll be all right with them two.'

Struggling to appear unconcerned, Sadie replied, 'Yeah, I know, Lil, they're good lads. You know, I've only had 'er a couple of weeks, but it seems like she's always been 'ere. Anyway, I know I've said it before, but thanks for looking after 'er for me. Gawd knows what I'd've done without your help this past fortnight, 'cos I couldn't 'ave left 'er on 'er own, not the state she's been in. Right then, I don't know what time I'll be 'ome, but I won't leave it too late. After all, I've got someone else to think about now; bloody nuisance!'

The offhand remark didn't fool Lily Knight for a moment. 'Don't be daft. The boys'll be looking after 'er more than I will, and besides, I need the money yer pay me after that old git ran out on me as soon as he found out there was another one on the way.' Lily Knight wiped her face with a grimy cloth, then, her face suddenly guarded, she said hesitantly, 'Look, mate, I know it's none of me business, but yer ain't getting too fond of the kid, are yer? Only yer know 'er brother could turn up outta the blue an' take 'er away, an' I don't wanna see yer get 'urt.' Lily Knight's voice trailed off as a flash of anger crossed Sadie's face. Undaunted she took a deep breath and added,

'Now don't yer go giving me daggers, Sadie North. We've known each other too long fer playing silly buggers, and I know yer ain't been exactly breaking yer neck ter find that brother of young Molly's, 'ave yer?'

Swallowing hard Sadie lowered her gaze. 'Nah, yer right, Lil, I ain't. I did fer the first few days, yer know I did. But without knowing where ter look, it was a waste of time. All I know from what Molly told me that first night was that 'er brother did odd jobs in a bakery, then got a job down the market a couple of days a week. D'yer know how many bakeries there are round these parts? Bleeding dozens of 'em. It's the same with the markets. Yer know 'ow those market traders operate. They go from one market to the next, working different days at each one. Then there's the fly pitchers, an' if young Micky's taken up with one of those shifty bleeders, I'll never find 'im. Besides, maybe he ain't the loving brother Molly thinks he is. After all, a lad that age don't wanna be lumbered with a little sister hanging round his neck. For all I know, he might 'ave pissed off for good, and if that's the case, then he could be anywhere.'

Yet even as she spoke, the words sounded hollow to her ears. No one could engender the kind of love Molly had for her elusive brother unless that love was reciprocated.

Avoiding her friend's kindly stare, Sadie, her voice softer, said, 'I had me whole life mapped out, then I had ter go and find Molly hiding in that filthy hovel. She was so scared, Lil. But even then, when she 'eard me with that punter and thought he was hurting me,

216

she tried ter help me. And I've gotta say, I don't think I could 'ave been that brave in her circumstances. She's a good kid, Lil, and she's me last chance of ever 'aving a kid of me own. And I'll tell yer something else. Tonight's me last night on the game. I've got enough put by ter get a place for the pair of us, somewhere decent. She ain't gonna grow up like we did. She's gonna 'ave everything we missed out on. As fer her brother . . .'

She shrugged. 'Well, I'll just 'ave ter take me chances, won't I? Anyway, I'd best be off. The sooner tonight's over the better, 'cos ter tell yer the truth, Lil, I ain't got the stomach for it any more. Every night before I get into bed with Molly, I scrub meself from top ter bottom. She's so clean and innocent, and when I think of how I've spent the evening . . . Well! Like I said, I think I'm sort of contaminating her. That's why I'm giving it up, and I'll tell yer something else, I ain't gonna miss it. All these years I've managed ter turn off me feelings while some slimy bastard's mauling me, I can't do that any more. In fact I'm in two minds whether ter go out tonight, but seeing as I've got me glad rags on I might as well earn as much as I can, 'cos like I said, after tonight I'm gonna become a respectable woman. Can yer imagine that, Lil? Me, Sadie North, hard as nails, going soft over some kid I didn't even know existed two weeks ago.' She smiled at her closest friend, her only friend, but the smile held a distinctive air of defiance, as if daring Lily Knight to contradict her.

But that worldly woman knew better than to cross swords with Sadie, besides which she was genuinely fond of the brassy, straight-talking woman she'd been friends with for over ten years. She'd been a good mate to Lily Knight, slipping her a few shillings now and then simply because Lily's husband was a lazy good-for-nothing waster who'd never done an honest day's work in the last five years. It had been the best day of Lily's life when he'd walked out for good, but she didn't know what she'd have done without the odd shilling Sadie always left on her kitchen table whenever she visited. Now it looked like she was about to lose her dear friend, and she was going to miss her, and not just because when Sadie went, so would the much needed few bob she had come to rely on.

Nodding, Lily replied as lightly as she could manage. 'I don't blame yer, Sadie. Don't forget I was on the game meself once, though not as long as you. Anyway, yer get off, an' don't worry about young Molly. Me boys'll take good care of 'er.'

'Yeah, I know they will. Thanks, Lil, see yer later, or maybe sooner.' Sadie winked. 'Yer never know, I might change me mind an' come straight back 'ome.' As Sadie walked across the forecourt of the block of flats, she could hear the loud happy sound of children playing. Resisting the impulse of making sure that Molly was all right, Sadie turned and made her way to the High Street.

'Come on, Molly, you can do it.' Billy Knight, his impish face throwing out the challenge, said, 'Me and Charlie 'ave done it lots of times. We don't let scaredy girls in our gang. 'Course if you don't wanna play with us, you can always go running back to our mum.'

Molly, her stomach churning as she looked at the planks covering a large hole on a building site, swallowed nervously.

'I'm not scared,' she answered defiantly.

Then, tentatively testing her weight on one of the broad planks, she inched her way across to where Charlie Knight was waiting, a huge smile on his grimy face. Halfway across, the planks started to bow and creak, causing Molly to wobble. A loud cry of derision came from both boys and instinctively Molly put her fears to one side. With a look of determination, she made it safely across. With a loud shout both boys slapped Molly hard on the back to show their approval. 'Well done, Moll, you're the first gel to have got across without crying.' Their acceptance of her caused a warm feeling to course through Molly's slim frame. 'Come on, Molly, we'll show you our camp.'

Molly followed the boys happily, finally assured of the knowledge that she was among friends. For a few seconds she stopped and lifted her face to the sun, savouring the feel of the warmth on her skin. It was so good to be out in the fresh air, to be able to run and laugh with children of her own age, even if they were boys. A wistful look flitted over her face as she thought of Micky. Then Billy Knight shouted at her to hurry up, and with the resilience of a child, she ran after the two boys, thoughts of her missing brother pushed firmly to the back of her mind.

Sadie was sitting at an empty table in the Red Bull public house in Mare Street nursing a gin and tonic and fervently wishing she hadn't bothered coming out tonight. Apart from one old regular, she hadn't had one offer in the past two hours. She was about to leave when who should walk in but the punter who had run off that night she had first encountered Molly. Never one to let go of a grievance, Sadie immediately made a bee line for the unsuspecting man.

'Hello, mate. Remember me?' She stood directly in his path and had the satisfaction of seeing the look of fear leap into his eyes. 'Yeah, that's right, yer miserable old bastard. Now then, we've got some unfinished business, ain't we? Like the matter of the five bob yer owe me. I don't do freebies, at least not fer fat old bastards like you. So come on, hand over me money, 'cos I ain't leaving 'ere till I get paid what's owed me.'

The man, accompanied by two friends, floundered for a moment, then, emboldened by the presence of his companions who were watching the scene with great interest, drew himself up and said contemptuously, 'I ain't paying you a penny, yer old tart, though hang on a minute, on second thoughts, I will pay yer – here!' With much laughing from the onlookers in the pub the man took a coin from his pocket and held it out to the furious Sadie. 'There yer are, one penny. That's all you're worth, yer clapped-out old bag.'

Feeling very pleased with himself, the man dropped the coin at Sadie's feet and with much back slapping from his friends he sauntered to the bar. But he hadn't counted on a woman like Sadie North. He hadn't gone more than a few steps when he was spun round and, before he could utter another word, a heavy fist caught him square on the chin, sending him spinning across the room before he landed on the sawdust floor in an undignified heap.

Standing over him Sadie laughed, 'No one gets one over on me, yer little toe rag. You can keep yer penny. By the looks of yer, you need it more than I do. Oh, and by the way, give my sympathies ter yer wife. I've seen bigger fingers than your cock. In fact I didn't even know you'd done it till yer'd finished, and that didn't take long either. See ya!'

As she turned to go, the man, furious at being made to look a fool in front of the entire pub, stumbled to his feet and shouted after her, 'I ain't surprised yer can't notice when you're being screwed, 'cos an old slag like you would only notice if yer was shagged by an elephant. Maybe your new recruit will make yer more money. I saw yer take that little girl outta that old house. You teaching her all yer old tricks, 'cos if yer are, put me down for a visit. At least then I wouldn't begrudge paying . . .' The words were hardly out of his mouth when Sadie came rushing back at him, but this time the landlord, not wanting a full-scale riot in his pub, came out from behind the bar and grabbed Sadie roughly.

'Leave it, I don't want any trouble in 'ere, Sadie. Now go 'ome, there's a good girl. He ain't worth it. Go on, get yerself off outta 'ere, otherwise I'll have ter throw yer out, and I don't wanna do that.'

Her face still twisted with fury, Sadie shrugged off the restraining arms, and with one last murderous glare at the portly man standing within the safety of

221

his group of friends, she slammed out of the pub.

At the back of the snug, a shabbily dressed man who had listened avidly to the heated exchange quietly followed Sadie from the pub.

Storming down the road, the irate woman, still fuming from the vicious verbal assault, didn't notice she was being followed. Heading straight for home she was back at the block of flats within fifteen minutes.

Careful not to be seen, Kenneth Wells, né Stokes, watched Sadie disappear into the building.

So that's where young Molly had gone. At least he assumed the girl spoken about was his Molly. It was too much of a coincidence to be anyone else. Of course he might be wrong, but he didn't think so. There was only one way to find out for sure. Come tomorrow he would return and watch and wait. Making sure of the name of the road, he walked off whistling, a satisfied smile on his lips.

'I wish you didn't have to go out ter work, Sadie. I get scared something might happen to yer, like my brother.' Molly, her blue eyes reflecting her fear, stared at Sadie. 'I mean, I like living with you, Sadie, but I miss me brother. What if he's trying ter find me? He'll be so worried, 'specially with that nasty man . . .' Aware she had said too much, Molly clamped down on her tongue, but Sadie wasn't to be deterred so easily. Apart from their initial encounter, this was the first time Molly had revealed anything about her past life.

'What man, love?' she asked gently, careful not to frighten the child into silence once more.

222

Molly's childish emotions were running high. More than anything she wanted to tell Sadie about the man she still had nightmares about, but she was afraid to say too much in case Sadie decided to take her to the police. And if that happened, she would end up back at the workhouse, and she'd never go back there, she'd rather die first. But when Sadie lay down on the bed and took her into those warm, comforting arms, Molly found herself talking, and once she'd started, it was as if a dam had broken inside her. Between tears she told Sadie everything, starting from her parents' death to running away from the workhouse, and ending up in the ruins of the house in Morning Lane where Sadie had found her. But most of all she talked about her brother Micky and how much she missed him. She also revealed the whereabouts of the bakery, and of the kind woman who had given Micky work, and found him a job working on a stall with a man called Ted Parker.

And as Sadie listened, all her dreams of starting a new life with the golden-haired child crashed around her ears. She had imagined Molly had accepted that her brother wasn't coming back for her, but now she saw she had been deluding herself. Yet worse than that, she had put her own interests before those of Molly. Now she knew where to look she had no option but to make enquiries about Micky Masters. For if the boy was still alive, it would be the utmost cruelty to keep brother and sister apart. Even so she hoped the boy had abandoned his sister, and was immediately ashamed she could even think such a terrible thing. With a sinking sensation in the pit of her stomach she held the weeping child in her arms until she finally fell into an exhausted sleep.

Tenderly tucking the small form under the blankets, Sadie looked down on the beautiful little girl and, amazed, she felt tears prick the back of her eyes. She hadn't cried since she was twelve, after her first initiation into the seedy world of prostitution, and she hadn't shed a tear since. She had imagined any form of emotion had died on that awful night when her mother had handed her over to her first customer. Even after all these years she could still see his face, sweating and excited at the prospect of having a virgin. For even though she had only been twelve at the time, it was relatively unusual for a girl of her age to still be a virgin, especially in her new profession. She could even remember how much he paid. Five pounds, a fortune back then. But child prostitution was a lucrative business, even now. She could still see the large, white five-pound note, handed to her delighted mother when the man had finished with her. After a while the price went down. Child or not, she had become soiled goods.

With a heavy heart she left the sleeping Molly and settled herself in the sitting room she was so proud of. Looking around the room she saw the polished furniture, the deep piled carpet and the flock wallpaper she had put up herself, but for once the sight gave her no pleasure. She finally had to admit to herself she had been living in a fool's paradise. When she left these rooms she would take all her possessions with her to her new house, but given the choice she would give up all she had worked so hard for in exchange for Molly. It was the early hours of the morning before she climbed into bed. And, like Molly, she fell asleep with tears streaking her face.

CHAPTER EIGHTEEN

Arthur Mitson's modest bakery had never been so busy. In the past two weeks, a steady stream of customers had poured through its doors, but despite the constant ringing of the till, it was glaringly obvious that the owners of the thriving business appeared far from happy.

Along with the regulars had come the gossip-mongers, their curiosity fuelled by the story in the *Hackney Gazette* about the little girl that had gone missing, presumed abducted by a pervert well known to the police. Yet although every one of the idle curious were genuinely concerned about the fate of the missing child, the true reason behind their constant visits to the bakery was in the hope of meeting Agnes Handly, the woman who, according to the papers, had been in cahoots with the man it was said had snatched the eight-year-old girl.

Even though the newspaper articles had stated that

the former assistant at the Mitson bakery had gone to ground, it didn't stop the thrill seekers from visiting the place where the evil Agnes Handly had once worked – and she must be evil to have done what she had. But their efforts to elicit information from the young woman serving behind the counter had come up against a blank wall. Yet they continued to come. Unable to learn the truth they'd had to be content with the rumours that were circulating the streets surrounding the bakery, and a very juicy piece of gossip it was. As with most rumours, no one was quite sure where the original story had started. Some said it was old Ma Wilson who had started the ball rolling.

Apparently, the elderly widow had been woken by a frantic knocking on her door late one night. At first, fearful of being murdered in her bed, the terrified woman had stayed huddled beneath her quilted eiderdown praying whoever it was would get tired and go away, but the banging had continued relentlessly. It was only when she heard her name being called that she had ventured trembling from her bed and cautiously peered out of her window to see Agnes Handly's worried face staring back at her. Relieved to see the familiar face, the elderly woman had let the agitated Agnes into her house, asking what had led Agnes to her door at this hour of night. And the answer she had received was nothing short of sensational.

Playing down her role in the abduction of the Masters child – something Ma Wilson knew nothing about, for she rarely ventured out of doors, nor did she read the newspapers due to her failing eyesight

– Agnes had described her terror at the mounting mob of outraged people baying for her blood, and how John Smith had taken her to Arthur Mitson's home for her own safety – only for her to be terrorised by the very man the policeman had handed her over to for help.

'. . . I'm telling yer, that's what I heard.' A plump woman was holding court outside the bakery, her face alight with excitement. 'An' that's not all.' The woman stopped for breath, making her moment of importance last as long as possible. Then, seeing she had the undivided attention of the group of women surrounding her she carried on, 'It turns out old Arthur's never done the business with young Ellen, yer know, in bed . . . !'

A woman in the small crowd gave a derisive laugh. 'Is that all? Bleeding 'ell, Flo, I'd've been more surprised if he 'ad. I mean ter say, he's a nice enough bloke, but he ain't exactly the sort of man ter make a young girl go weak at the knees, or any other woman for that matter, now is he? Nah! I've always thought him and Ellen had what they call a marriage of convenience . . .'

'Cor blimey! Hark at you, Gladys Brown. Marriage of convenience, my arse. You've been reading those fancy magazines again, ain't yer?' Another woman broke into the conversation. 'Anyway, I don't believe a word of it. I mean ter say, Arthur might be a boring old fart, but he's still a man, ain't he? Yer can't tell me he's been sharing a bed with a pretty girl like Ellen for how long is it? Two years, an' kept 'is pecker tucked in 'is underclothes. Unless, of course, he can't get it up any more. An' let's face it, he can't 'ave had much practice, poor old sod.'

The woman called Flo, seeing her audience slipping away from her, raised her voice, desperate not to have her moment of glory taken from her. ''Ang on, I ain't got ter the best bit yet. Unless yer ain't interested in what else I 'eard.'

The group of women fell silent, their curiosity getting the better of them. Satisfied she had their attention once more, Florrie Baxter hurried on.

'Like I was saying, Arthur an' Agnes were 'aving a row when he told 'er he'd never touched Ellen in that way, when who should walk in but young Ellen and Ted Parker. Well! Agnes told Ma Wilson all hell broke loose. First Arthur stormed out of the room, then Ted pulled Ellen into his arms like they was a couple of sweethearts, and told her that her marriage wasn't legal . . . Well, not that exactly, but he was all excited, saying she could divorce Arthur on account of the marriage not being consummated; I think that's the word he used. Anyway Ellen told him ter go and according ter Agnes' version, Ted Parker told Ellen he loved her, but not ter keep him 'anging on too long, 'cos he wasn't gonna wait fer 'er for ever.'

Stopping for breath the delighted Florrie saw she had a captive audience and carried on quickly before someone else took it into their heads to steal her thunder.

'So off he goes in a right old temper, but Agnes didn't 'ave a chance ter talk ter Ellen 'cos she went straight ter bed. I gotta say, she's a nice girl, is Ellen, 'cos even though she must 'ave been in a right state

229

herself, she still thought of Agnes. Told her she could
sleep downstairs fer the night. And let's face it, she
could've chucked her out, 'specially the way Agnes
has treated Ellen since she married Arthur. Anyway
Agnes didn't fancy sleeping in a chair downstairs, 'cos
it'd turned chilly that night. So she stayed where she
was, thinking she'd be able to slip away quietly in the
morning, and Arthur and Ellen wouldn't be any the
wiser. She was just drifting off ter sleep when she
heard raised voices, an' yer know how nosy Agnes
Handly is.'

She nodded to the spellbound group, not realising
the hypocrisy of her words. As her eyes roamed over
her audience she noticed a woman she'd never seen
before. Unlike the others, this particular woman
although listening intently, didn't appear to be as
engrossed as the others. Mentally shrugging, Florrie
Baxter finally got to the crux of her tale.

'When she 'eard Arthur shouting, she didn't take
much notice at first, 'cos he'd been drinking, an' yer
know what men are like when they've had a few. But
then she 'eard Ellen trying ter calm him down, then
according ter Agnes, Ellen started crying. Well, Agnes
got worried, so she went over ter listen at the bedroom
door, an' you'll never guess what she 'eard . . .' She
paused for effect, delighting in the rapt faces of the
women crowding round her. 'Only Arthur saying that
it was time Ellen began ter act like a proper wife, and
poor Ellen crying and begging Arthur to stop and that
he was frightening her. The last thing Agnes 'eard was
Ellen cry out, like she was in pain, then it all went
quiet. Agnes was just wondering what ter do when

she 'eard Arthur coming towards the door. According ter her, she was frightened Arthur might rape her too' – a coarse laugh erupted from her thin lips – 'Bleeding wishful thinking if yer ask me. So she grabbed 'er things an' ran as if she 'ad a rocket up her arse. That's how she ended up at Ma Wilson's. She knew the old girl wouldn't 'ave 'eard about that business with the little girl and that pervert she'd got herself tangled up with. When Ma Wilson woke up next morning, Agnes had gone without so much as a thank you or by yer leave. No one knows where she is now. If she's any sense she'll stay right away from the East End. People 'ave long memories round these parts. The only chance Agnes Handly 'as of coming back 'ome is if that poor little girl's found safe and sound, please God! Though if Agnes' story about Arthur forcing 'imself on Ellen is true, I hope fer 'is sake Ted don't find out, 'cos if he does, there'll be murder done.'

With no more news to impart the woman fell silent, her brief moment at the centre of attention over.

Slowly the women began to disperse, all except for the stranger who had been listening to the lurid story in silence.

Sadie remained where she was, then, anxious not to attract unwelcome attention, she began to pace up and down, giving the impression she was waiting for someone. Then, curiosity getting the better of her she stopped and looked into the shop window, only to give a nervous start as she saw the young woman, whom she surmised was the object of the conversation she had overheard, staring straight back at her. Flustered, Sadie quickly moved away. Her mind spinning she wondered what she should do for the best. Under the circumstances she didn't think it a good idea to approach the baker's wife at the moment. If what she had heard was true then the poor cow had enough on her plate to deal with. Knowing she was prevaricating, and hating herself for wasting valuable time she made a decision. Glancing to her right she saw the woman who had been holding court and made her way towards her.

Florrie Baxter was only too eager to have a sympathetic ear, and, after having to listen to the same story again, Sadie finally managed to get a word in, getting to the real purpose for striking up a conversation with the garrulous woman. Fifteen minutes later she was on a tram heading for Roman Road market where she had been reliably informed Ted Parker ran his stall. For reasons of her own she hadn't asked about Micky Masters, telling herself it was best if she didn't let anyone know she was looking for the boy. But no matter which excuse she tried to assuage her guilt, deep down she knew she was still hoping the boy would be long gone, and then she would be able to keep Molly with her without raising anyone's suspicions as to why she was trying to locate the boy. It would also stop any awkward questions being asked.

But whatever the outcome, she must put her own feelings aside and do what was best for Molly.

When she alighted from the tram, she slowly made her way down the long lines of stalls, her feet dragging, a sick sensation in her stomach. It would have been quicker to ask the first stall holder where to locate Ted Parker, but she was in no hurry to find him. The longer it took her to find him, and ask about Micky Masters, the longer she could hold onto her dream of keeping Molly, of having a daughter to share her lonely life with.

'I bet they're having a field day out there, nosy cows. Still, I'm not complaining, we've never been so busy.'

Arthur, coming to relieve Ellen so she could have her lunch, attempted a jocular tone, but the icy look on his wife's face chilled him to the bone. The morning rush was over so it was safe for them to talk, until the next customer arrived.

His fleshy face reddening he said pleadingly, 'Please, Ellen, love. I've apologised over and over again. I was mad with rage at seeing you with Ted Parker, and hearing what he said about you being able to leave me and go with him. I was almost out of my head with worry that I was going to lose you, but I swear to God, I never meant to hurt you. You must know I'm speaking the truth. God Almighty, we've been married and sharing a bed for over two years, and I've never laid a finger on you. Now be fair, there's not many men would have done that. I'd cut off me right arm if I could turn back the clock, but I can't. What's done is done. But I swear to you, it'll never happen again. Ellen . . . Ellen! Please, love, say something. It's killing me having you look right through me as if I wasn't there. What more can I do for you to forgive me? Just say the word and I'll do whatever you ask.'

Taking off her apron, Ellen came out from behind the counter. Without looking at him she said in a cold, flat voice, 'It's not your right arm I'd like to cut off, Arthur. And no matter what excuse you use to try to justify what you did, the truth is you raped me. I know a husband can't be charged with raping his wife, the law doesn't recognise a woman's rights in that matter once she's married, more's the pity. You say you're sorry and it'll never happen again, and that much is true.' She turned to face him, and Arthur flinched at the dead look in those once sparkling eyes. 'Because I'll tell you now, Arthur, if you ever attempt such an act again, I swear I'll pack up and move out without a backward glance, and you'll never see me again.'

Arthur stared after the retreating figure, his entire body filled with an emotion he couldn't put a name to. The Ellen he had married was gone for ever. It was as if she had died. He felt what he could only term as a kind of bereavement. As the bell over the door tinkled, a wild thought entered his mind. Please God, let that one, never-to-be-repeated act result in a pregnancy. Only then would he be able to put his tortured mind at ease. For two long, agonising weeks he had been expecting Ellen to pack her bags and leave – and it wouldn't have taken a genius to work out where she would go.

But if she were to have a baby, then surely she would stay with him, if only for the sake of the child.

Putting his best smile on he asked the waiting customer, 'Yes, love, and what can I get you today?'

It was one o'clock and Sadie was sitting in the pie and mash shop drinking her third mug of tea. She was aware of the curious glances in her direction, not surprising since she'd been sitting in the same booth for the past two hours. Ignoring the other occupants of the café she sipped her tea, her eyes staring unseeingly out of the window. She'd had no trouble in locating Ted Parker. The first stall holder she had spoken to had pointed him out to her. Her heart beating like a drum, she had slowly approached the stall, her eyes darting back and forth in search of a glimpse of the young boy she had set out to find, but the tall, dark-haired man appeared to be working the stall alone. At any other time, Sadie would have appreciated the rugged good looks of Ted Parker, but not today. Today, the only thing on her mind was trying to find a way to keep the child she had grown to love.

But instead of enquiring of the boy's whereabouts she heard herself asking for a pound of apples and half a dozen oranges; Molly needed the good nourishing food she had long been denied. Oblivious of Ted's good-natured banter, Sadie paid for her purchases and, needing more time to get her thoughts in order, decided to treat herself to her favourite meal of pie and mash. She had just finished her third mug of tea when a man slid into the booth, sitting himself down comfortably on the bench opposite her. Raising her eyes she saw the dark-haired market trader staring at her with marked curiosity.

Without preamble he said, 'I hear yer've been asking about me. D'yer mind telling me why?'

Knowing men as she did, Sadie knew that, despite the man's good-natured tone, he wasn't the type to be fobbed off easily. With the ease of a man comfortable in himself he beckoned over the waitress and ordered a meal, a mug of strong tea, and another one for Sadie. By the way the waitress hovered coyly over him it was obvious that not only was he well known in the café, but that he was also very much a ladies' man. Ten, fifteen years ago, she would likely have felt the same attraction, but with the life she'd led, men no longer had the power to excite her.

'Well. You gonna tell me why you've been looking fer me, or do I have ter tie you down and beat the truth outta you?' Ted grinned amiably. 'Oh, thanks, darlin',' he said as the piping hot dinner was laid before him. The waitress darted a quizzical look at Sadie, then squealed with pleasure as Ted slapped her smartly on the backside. Giving her a broad wink he said laughingly, 'Bring us over another tea in five minutes, there's a good girl.'

Her cheeks turning a bright pink the waitress hurried to her next customer.

Tucking into his meal Ted said lightly, 'I'm still waiting, love. You must 'ave a good reason fer wanting to meet me, and seeing as I'm a curious bloke, I'd like ter know why, and you ain't leaving till you tell me.'

Behind the friendly tone, Sadie knew the man was deadly serious. Not knowing where to start, she swallowed nervously, then, deciding the best course of action was just to blurt out the truth, she said quietly, 'I've been looking fer a boy called Micky Masters and I was told he works fer you. I've got his sister Molly staying with me.' Even though she had been expecting some sort of reaction she wasn't prepared for the electrifying effect her words had on the market trader.

His dinner forgotten, Ted leant forward, his flippant manner replaced by one of desperate urgency. 'Listen, love, I don't know who you are, or if you're telling the truth. There's a lot of people who'll be grateful ter you for ever, including me. But if you're pissing me about, then you've got a bleeding sick sense of humour.'

Immediately on the defensive Sadie shot back angrily, 'Don't you talk ter me like that. What d'yer take me for? I found Molly hiding in a filthy ruin, and I took her home with me. All she talked about that night was her wonderful brother Micky, an' I thought I'd look after her fer the night then set about finding 'er brother the next day. Only it didn't work out like that, 'cos the following morning I couldn't get a word out of her. And believe me I tried. I mean, I didn't mind having 'er stay the night, but I certainly didn't bargain on 'aving 'er still with me a fortnight later. Apart from knowing 'er brother's name, and that he did some odd jobs for a nice lady in a bakery before getting a job with a man called Ted Parker who ran a fruit and veg stall. But she didn't say where the bakery or market was for that matter. And like I said, the morning after I couldn't get anything else outta 'er. I didn't 'ave anything else ter go on. It ain't easy trying ter find someone when yer ain't got a clue where ter look. I reckon the only reason she clammed up was because she was frightened something bad had happened ter her brother. In her little mind she was probably scared of being sent back ter the workhouse an' hoped that if she kept quiet and behaved herself I'd take 'er in and look after her.'

Impatiently pushing away his plate Ted said scathingly, 'Don't give me that. Bleeding hell, the story was splashed all over the front page of the *Hackney Gazette* for the first three days after Molly went missing. She's not headline news any more but the paper's still asking fer anyone who's got any information ter come forward. They've even offered a reward . . .' Ted's eyes suddenly narrowed. 'Is that what this is all about? 'Cos if it is then you're outta luck. You ain't the first one that's tried to collect the reward . . .'

He wasn't given the chance to finish his sentence, for Sadie, emotionally drained, her anger reaching boiling point, spat out bitterly, 'You bastard! I ain't interested in the money. I didn't even know there was a reward . . . Oh, yeah, yer can look at me like that, yer smug git, but it's the truth. And the reason I didn't know about it is because I don't buy the newspapers; there wouldn't be much point seeing as I can't read.' Her breathing rapid, Sadie carried on. 'If yer must know, I was hoping I wouldn't be able ter find Molly's brother. I know I said I was annoyed at first at being lumbered with her, but the truth is, I've grown ter love her. I thought, given time, she'd forget her brother, 'cos apart from that first night she hardly ever mentioned him. And like I said, I was 'oping, in time, she'd grow ter love and be happy with me. But last night, as I was tucking 'er into bed, she suddenly started crying for her brother. And once she'd started it all came tumbling out. The name of the bakery where he used ter do odd jobs, and she told me your name, but she couldn't remember the market where you worked; though once I knew your name it wasn't hard ter find you.' Her voice dropped to a whisper as she tiredly pushed back a strand of hair from her face.

'So there it is. First thing this morning I left Molly with a friend and came looking. I went ter the bakery first, then I lost me nerve and asked someone if she knew of a Ted Parker.' She bravely gave a watery smile. 'Seems you're well known, because the woman I asked knew exactly who you was and where I could find you . . .' She raised her shoulders, 'So 'ere I am, and before the day's out Molly'll be with her brother and everyone will be 'appy . . . except me.' Her voice began to tremble as the strain of keeping up a normal appearance finally got the better of her. Her eyes suspiciously bright, a sob caught in her throat as she said, 'It'll break me 'eart to let 'er go, but I've gotta think of Molly, and 'er brother . . . Oh, shit! Let's get outta 'ere, please, before I make a complete mug of meself.'

Throwing down some coins on the marble table Ted took Sadie's arm and led her from the café. Once out in the fresh air Sadie began to regain control of her emotions.

'So then, where is this Micky? I thought he was working fer you.'

'He is. Sometimes he puts in a full day's work, then there's times like today when he can't settle, and off he goes to search the streets for his sister. He often doesn't come 'ome till gone midnight, almost dead on his feet. He used ter be such a happy kid, but he ain't smiled since Molly went missing.' Ted paused before asking, 'Did Molly say anything about a man called Kenneth Wells?'

Sadie shook her head. 'No, I don't remember her mentioning anyone of that name. Though she did say something about a nasty man she was afraid of. Is that the man?'

Ted nodded grimly. 'Yeah, that's the perverted bastard. It's also why Micky's been almost outta his 'ead with fear that Wells had got hold of her. Look, give me ten minutes ter find someone ter take care of me stall, and then I'll take yer 'ome with me ter wait fer Micky. It'll give me the chance ter fill yer in with the rest of the story.' He hadn't walked more than a few steps when he turned and asked, 'I know it's none of me business, but what was yer doing in that derelict house at that time of the evening?'

For the first time in her life Sadie was suddenly ashamed of her profession. Then, lifting her chin proudly she replied, 'You're right, it ain't none of your business. But if yer must know I was entertaining a client. To put it more bluntly, I'm a brass; there, satisfied now, are yer?'

Ted walked back towards her, a smile on his face. Then to her surprise he lifted her off her feet and planted a kiss on her cheek.

'From where I'm standing, darling, you're eighteen carat pure gold.'

Then he was striding off, whistling happily, leaving Sadie feeling she had suddenly become someone special, and that feeling caused her chest to swell with emotion and pride. Her step lighter she began to browse among the stalls until Ted returned for her.

CHAPTER NINETEEN

At almost the same time Sadie was entering the pie and mash shop, three other people were also consumed with thoughts of Molly, each one for very different reasons.

Micky Masters had been pounding the streets since six o'clock that morning. After a sleepless night, his mind forming indescribable images of his sweet Molly in the hands of that dirty old man, he had finally given up hope of getting any rest and, careful not to wake Ted or Nora, crept out of the house, praying fervently that this might be the day he found his sister. The condition he might find her in was pushed firmly to the furthest recesses of his mind.

Walking the same streets he had trodden the last fortnight he stopped every person he encounted to ask if they had seen a girl answering his sister's description; the answer was always the same. Most of the people he stopped looked at the ashen-faced boy who seemed to have aged years in the short time his younger sister had gone missing, and smiled at him pityingly, wishing with all their hearts they could do something to help, but powerless to do more than pat the young man on the shoulder and try to reassure him his sister would be found soon while knowing that those chances were slim to the point of impossibility. After all this time there was no doubt in anyone's mind that Molly Masters was dead – and those brave enough to look straight into the boy's eyes saw that he knew it too, but would never rest until the body was found and given a decent burial. Yet for every person who stopped to offer some kind of sympathy or hope, there were at least three others who hurriedly crossed the road, or disappeared into the nearest shop to avoid the desperate young boy. As one woman remarked to her friend, the world could be a cruel place at the best of times, but a boy of Micky Masters' age should never have to experience the kind of pain he was suffering. She added grimly that when that Wells bloke was caught he should be handed over to the fathers and mothers of the East End. They'd make sure he never harmed a child again – not with his balls cut off he wouldn't.

Micky trudged on, his steps slowing as the sleepless night and five hours of walking began to catch up on him. His eyes felt hard and gritty, and every bone and muscle in his body ached, yet still he carried on. But if his body was bone weary his mind continued to taunt him.

It was all his fault. If he hadn't gone into the bakery with Agnes that night, he wouldn't have ended up in prison and Molly wouldn't have been left unprotected. He should have been suspicious of Agnes' sudden show of friendship, but she had seemed so genuine. Even so, based on past experience with that old bitch, he shouldn't have been so trusting. But the fact remained he had, and he would never forgive himself. Molly had trusted him unconditionally, and he had let her down. As he walked on, his head felt suddenly light and his vision became blurred. The next thing he knew his legs buckled at the knees, and if it hadn't been for a kind passer-by catching hold of his thin body, he would have fallen onto the hard cobbles.

'Come on, mate, let's get yer 'ome an' some grub inside yer, 'cos I bet yer ain't eaten today, 'ave yer? An' yer ain't gonna do yer sister any good if yer land up in the 'ospital.'

Micky peered up at the man holding him upright, trying to recall his name, but he was so exhausted he could barely remember his own. Without uttering a word he offered no resistance as the concerned man half-walked, half-carried the youngster to the Parkers' home.

Agnes was also feeling the strain. If anything had happened to the young girl she would never be able to live with herself again. She was honest enough to recognise her own faults and admit she had turned into a bitter, lonely woman. She was also aware that she didn't have one single person in the world she could call a friend, and that knowledge cut her deeply. Her life could have been so different if she had never gone to work for Arthur Mitson, and in doing so fall

243

in love with a man who had used her for comfort after the death of his father, then dumped her without a second thought. She could have been happily married to a man who loved her, and children – oh, how she had longed for children. For years she had kept hoping that one day either Arthur would renew their relationship, or, failing that, she'd hoped that she would meet someone else. And with each passing year her hopes faded until she was forced to admit she would never hear a child call her Mum. Mum! Such a simple word, yet so precious. Was it any wonder, starved of love as she had been, she had been so easily duped into believing the lies Kenneth had told her? How he must have laughed at her eagerness to please him, and she, stupid fool as she was, had fallen hook, line and sinker for his plausible patter. And in doing so had put an innocent child at risk of an ordeal she had suffered herself as a child at the hands of her uncle.

The only consolation she had was the fact that the smooth-talking bastard didn't have the girl. If he had got his filthy hands on Molly, he would never have come to her that night in a rage at being deprived of his prey. But despite the intervention of PC John Smith, she knew that men like Wells – she couldn't think of him by his real name of Stokes – didn't give up easily. Somebody had Micky's sister, and she had to find her before Wells did. But that was easier said than done. Sitting on a bench in Victoria Park she reflected on recent events.

Like Micky, she had also been walking the streets for weeks. But unlike Micky Masters, Agnes was searching for the man who had effectively destroyed

244

the lives of so many people, including herself. She was at present living in a one-room flat in Shoreditch, too frightened to return to her home, for fear of further reprisals. Even if the child was found safe and sound, there was always the chance she could return and find her home burned to the ground in retaliation for what many people deemed her part in being in league with a pervert.

Finishing the sandwiches she had brought with her, she rose reluctantly to her aching feet. It was just gone eleven. She would visit a few pubs before returning to her dingy room for a couple of hours' sleep, before venturing back out onto the streets once more. Making sure the black crochet shawl she had worn covering her head and most of her face since that night she had landed at Ma Wilson's door in case someone recognised her, she summoned up her waning strength and ventured forth once more. Stopping at a back street pub she ordered a large gin to keep her strength up. She was about to leave when the pub doors opened and a smartly dressed man sauntered in. Her jaw dropping in disbelief, her head swivelled round to follow his progress, unable to believe her eyes. The hair colouring was different, the once smooth face was now sporting a moustache and a goatee beard, while the upper part of his face was almost obscured by a pair of tortoise-shell eye glasses. But despite his best efforts to alter his appearance, Agnes recognised him straight away, and it took all of her willpower to stay where she was and not run across the pub and attack him with all the strength she possessed. A surge of rage swept through her. Her basic instinct was to scream his true identity to the entire pub before smashing her empty glass right into that smug, evil face. After that she would leave him to the mercy of the pub customers, and if there was any justice they'd tear him limb from limb. Her lips white with fury she gripped the empty glass. She had to think and think hard. Every fibre in her being wanted to avenge what he had done to her. For not only had he ruined her life, he had used her in the most despicable way known to man. No! She must keep her head. Even though he hadn't managed to get the child that night he had attacked her, there was always the possibility he had somehow tracked her down since. If that was the case then the only way to find the child was to follow Kenneth wherever he went.

Until then she would have to put all thoughts of revenge on hold. Her day would come, of that she had no doubt. Careful to keep her shawl half covering her face she ordered another gin and waited.

Taking a last look in the full-length mirror in the boarding house, where he had been staying since that nosy bastard John Smith had appeared on the scene the well-dressed man gave a satisfied smirk at the image that stared back at him. For weeks he'd had to dress like a working-class man, a scruffy, unwashed male of the lowest order in his books, in order to avoid being recognised. Now that period of time was nearly over. It had been hard to contain his frustration once he had ascertained that the slut Sadie North was the cause of all his misfortunes. His first instinct had been to confront the blowsy prostitute, but after witnessing the violent altercation in the public house he had quickly changed his mind. Instead he had followed the furious woman to a block of flats not too far from the pub. It was an area he was familiar with, so he didn't have to worry about finding it again. All night he had lain awake, thinking hard as to how he would get his Molly back – if indeed the child referred to was his Molly!

A sudden noise from the landing snapped him out of his reverie.

Briskly now, he took one last look in the mirror. Then, shutting the door behind him, he left the seedy building, his steps taking him back to the building he had visited last night, and was rewarded by the sight of Molly leaving the tenement building in the company of two young boys whose ages he judged to be between ten and twelve respectively. Five minutes later a plain, smartly dressed woman wearing a black skirt and a white silk blouse appeared at the door of one of the first-floor flats, looking the image of respectability. The sight of her threw him, for she bore no resemblance to the painted whore he had followed the previous evening – until she opened her mouth. From his position he heard her say clearly in a strong, common voice, 'Righto, Lil, wish me luck, mate. I ain't looking forward ter it, but now I know where ter look, I gotta try an' find Molly's brother. I think I'll try the bakery first, an' if I don't get no luck there, I'll ask after this bloke Ted Parker. 'Cos if young Micky was working fer 'im two weeks ago, he likely still is. Mind you, don't say anything to Moll about where I've gone. I don't wanna get 'er 'opes up, poor little love. Anyway, see yer, Lil.'

A slovenly, heavily pregnant woman came out into the street, her arm going round her friend's shoulders in a gesture of comfort.

'Don't worry, Sadie, love. Look on the bright side. If yer find the brother, yer might end up with two kids ter look after, just like a ready-made family. An' the best bit is, yer won't 'ave a bleeding 'usband getting under yer feet.'

From his vantage point, Wells saw a dispirited look pass over the prostitute's face.

'Thanks, Lil, but I don't think there's much chance of that, do you?'

Giving her friend another awkward pat on the back the pregnant woman re-entered her flat. Unaware she was being watched, Sadie's shoulders slumped for a brief moment, then, with a look of determination etched on her freshly washed face, she began to walk towards him. Quickly darting out of sight, he waited until she had disappeared before approaching the flat she had just left, unaware that he too was being closely scrutinised.

Agnes hadn't taken her sharp eyes off the hateful figure since she had followed him out of the pub. She too had overheard the exchange between the two women, and it didn't take a genius to figure out what was going on. Somehow, Kenneth had found out who had Molly, and where. Now she knew too. But what to do with the knowledge? Clutching her shawl tighter around her head she saw Kenneth knock at the ground-floor flat, and within a few minutes he had disappeared inside. Her eyes darting frantically up and down the street she looked in vain for a copper. Most days you couldn't walk more than a few feet without practically falling over one of them. Of course, when you really wanted one, there were none to be seen.

Unlike Wells, she hadn't seen Molly run off to play with the two boys. As far as she knew, the girl was inside the flat. Knowing how plausible Kenneth could be, Agnes had no doubt he would at this moment be spinning the same tale he had spun to her. She only hoped the woman who had been left in charge of Micky's sister wouldn't be as gullible as she had been. And if he couldn't persuade the woman to hand over the child to him, her supposed uncle, Agnes had no doubt he would take her by force. What was she to do? She was no match for a grown man if it came to a struggle. But if she left to find a copper, he could be long gone by the time she found one. Of course she could always scream for help. There must be plenty of people at home at this time of day. She nodded, her mind made up. That's what she'd do. If he came out of that flat with the little girl, she'd scream at the top of her lungs. Her plan of action settled, she leant back out of sight against the brick wall and waited.

Inside the flat, a none too clean mug of tea held in his hand, Kenneth Wells, disguising his distaste at his surroundings, turned on the charm he had perfected over the years and smiled at the straight-faced woman.

'So, Lil . . . If I may call you Lil?'

Lily nodded wordlessly, a clear look of distrust on her face. Kenneth saw the look and cursed silently.

The only reason he hadn't gone to Sadie North was because he had deemed her too worldly-wise to be easily taken in. Also it was obvious she had become fond of his Molly. Why else would she have taken her in and cared for her these past two weeks? Now it was becoming alarmingly clear that this woman, Lily Knight, wasn't going to be a pushover either. Keeping a tight rein on his temper, he put down the mug onto an equally grimy, sticky table, and curved his lips into what he assumed was a disarming smile.

'I don't blame you for being suspicious. Indeed, it does you credit that you should take your duties in looking after my niece so diligently, but you must try and see it from my point of view. I've been going out of my mind with worry, thinking the worst. It was bad enough when I knew Molly was being looked after by that young tearaway Micky – he's a bad lot, that one. I was never very close to my brother, I will admit, that's why I was unaware of my brother and sister-in-law's deaths. The authorities traced me eventually, but by the time I arrived at the workhouse, that scallywag Micky had already made his escape, taking Molly with him. It would have been far better if he had left her behind, but he was always a selfish boy. Anyway, what's done is done. Micky can look after himself, but I would be failing in my duties as Molly's legal guardian if I left her with a known prostitute . . .' Too late he realised he had said the wrong thing.

Her face cold Lily waddled over to the door and flung it wide. 'Yer must think I was born yesterday. People like you, with yer smart clothes an' fancy talk think us cockneys are all thick – well, we ain't. We might not be able ter talk posh, but we can smell a rat when we see one, an' you, mister, stink like a rotting corpse. D'yer really think I'd fall for that load of old cobblers? If yer was really Molly's uncle, yer'd 'ave brought the law with yer, or somebody from the authorities. Nah! I know who you are. You're the nasty man Molly told Sadie about. Scum, that's what men like you are, scum. An' yer've got the nerve ter look down on decent people just 'cos we're poor. Now! Get outta my 'ouse. And 'ere's something ter think on. I know what yer look like now, an' the minute Sadie gets back, we'll be straight down the cop shop. Now, piss off, yer disgusting bleeder. Go on, get outta my 'ouse.'

Still believing people like Lily Knight could be bought off if offered the right price Kenneth pulled out his wallet and threw down two white five-pound notes. Lily merely glanced at the two pieces of crisp paper. She had never seen so much money in her entire life, and probably never would again, but she'd rather cut off her arm than sink to the level of selling a child, any child. Her voice dripping with scorn she spat out, 'Go on, get yer stinking carcass outta my 'ouse, an' yer can take yer blood money with yer, yer smarmy bastard.'

The velvety veneer slipped from his face like paint stripped from a wall with a blow torch. His upper lip curling in anger he snarled, 'Don't go getting on your high horse with me, you fat slag. Do you imagine I don't know what you're after? Here! There's another five pounds. That's what you're really after, aren't you? More money. You're all the same, people like you. You'd sell your own mother if the price was high enough. So don't go pretending moral indignation on me, because it won't wash. Go on, take it,' he pointed scornfully to the small pile of money. 'You can split it with your friend when she gets back. Because let's face it, that's more than a pair of old slappers like you will ever earn in your line of work . . .'

The look on Wells' face turned to fear as, with a cry of pure rage, the woman grabbed a carving knife from the table and, holding it in front of her bulging stomach, she rushed at him, raising the wicked-looking blade so that it was only inches from his face. Instinctively he grabbed hold of her wrist, but not before the knife slashed across the back of his right hand. He had imagined it would be an easy task to disarm her, but he hadn't bargained for the tenacity of the East End women, especially when those women were mothers. And like all mothers, Lily fought her assailant with every bit of strength she possessed to protect the innocent child he had come for. But for all her fury, she was still a woman, and a heavily pregnant one at that. Yet still she would not relinquish the knife, her only form of defence. Gasping and sweating, Kenneth lifted his arm high, bringing it down viciously across Lily's perspiring face. Lily had often been hit by her husband, especially when he'd come home drunk, so she was accustomed to being used as a punch bag. In normal circumstances she would have weathered the blow, but, with her bulging stomach weighing her down, she was caught off balance and fell to the floor with a sickening thud.

His breathing still rapid, Kenneth tried to calm himself down and concoct another plan, for after today he would never get another chance to get his hands on Molly. Edging cautiously towards the still form, Kenneth, bracing himself for another attack, carefully turned the woman over, then reeled back in shock. For there, almost hidden by her huge belly, the carving knife she had tried to use on him was now embedded between her ponderous breasts. The sweat was pouring off him now. Then he heard the sound of laughing children approaching and with a swiftness of thought that surprised even himself, he practically threw himself across the room and behind the open door.

Billy Knight was the first to enter the room, as always a grievance on his lips about something his brother had done to upset him, only to come to an abrupt stop at the sight of his mother lying motionless on the floor, covered in blood, the wooden handle of the kitchen knife protruding from her chest. It was a sight that rendered him speechless with shock. Then he was being shoved out of the way by his older brother Charlie.

'Mum . . . Mum, Billy's nicked me conkers . . . Mum . . . Mum . . . !' The two boys were framed in the doorway, their eyes wide with horror and disbelief.

Blissfully unaware of the horrific scene, her view hidden by the two boys, Molly playfully pushed Charlie, laughing, 'Get outta the way, Charlie. I need ter go to the lav.' Using her elbows she tried to push the solid form out of her path, but he remained as if turned to stone. ''Ere, what's up? What's 'appened, Charlie? Where's yer mum?'

Suddenly stung into life, both boys rushed towards their silent mother crying piteously, 'Get up, Mum . . Please, Mum, get up . . .'

It was only then that Molly saw Lily and like the boys she was momentarily struck dumb with shock Then she opened her mouth wide and let out a blood-curdling scream of pure terror. The sound seemed to galvanise the boys into action. Charlie, older than his brother by a mere ten months, took charge.

'You, Billy, run for 'elp, quick.' When his brother stayed huddled over his mother, Charlie grabbed him roughly by the back of the neck shouting, 'Hurry, Billy Yer gotta get a doctor. Go on, run, Billy, run . . .' His voice broke, and shoving his brother out into the stree he turned to Molly who was still screaming. 'Shut up . . . shut up.' The harsh words were a brave attempt to adopt an adult demeanour. 'Look, get some sheets . . . or towels . . . Anything. We've gotta try an' stop the bleeding . . . We've gotta do something . . .' But for all his bravado, he was still only a child, a child terri-fied of losing his mum. His voice breaking on a sob his eyes bright with tears, he looked for help to Molly But Molly, although now silent, remained rooted to the spot. By now people were pouring out into the street to see what all the noise was about.

Still in his hiding place, Kenneth cursed his bad luck. Within seconds the place would be crawling with people, and if that fat cow was dead, then he'd hang But he wasn't just going to stay hidden behind the door, for once that crowd entered the flat he'd be discovered in seconds. Slamming the door shut he sprang forward at the unsuspecting Charlie, and with a clenched fist hit him hard around the head, the blow sending the boy falling across his mother's bleeding body. Then he turned to the petrified Molly. Picking her up with his good arm, he covered her mouth with the hand Lily had stuck the knife into, adding to Molly's terror as she tasted his blood on her lips.

The sound of voices was growing louder and nearer. Like a trapped rat he looked wildly around the tiny room to a narrow hallway. With his prize firmly held in a vice-like grip, he bounded out of the room, his eyes lighting up at the sight of the open window leading out to the back yard. He had just climbed through the narrow window when a small group of people burst into the room behind him. Dropping onto the uneven slabs beneath the window, Kenneth ran as if the devil himself was on his tail, the limp body of Molly, who had fainted, slung over his shoulders. Keeping to the back streets he managed to avoid being seen. Only when he was sure he was safe did he stop to staunch the wound in his hand with a linen handkerchief which he always wore in his breast pocket, before moving Molly's position from over his shoulder and into his arms, looking for all the world like a doting father carrying his sleeping child home.

Hailing a hackney cab, he clambered in, giving the cabbie an address in Essex. A satisfied smile of relief on his lips, he sat back on the leather seat, his eyes devouring the still form of the young girl. It had been the devil of a job to get her, but get her he had – and she was going to pay for all the trouble she had caused him.

* * *

When Molly screamed Agnes had jumped with fright, not having heard them come back. Then all hell seemed to break loose as a boy raced sobbing from the flat calling for help. Inching forward Agnes approached the open doorway, but before she could look inside the door slammed in her face. Running to the side window she witnessed Kenneth's assault on the boy, and him grabbing who she could only assume was the elusive Molly. Pushing open the door she too stopped in her tracks at the sight that met her eyes. Then she heard running footsteps and, following the sound, saw Kenneth make his escape with the girl through a window at the back of the flat. Although not as agile as she once was she managed to scramble out of the window and, careful to keep at a safe distance she followed the retreating figure, while at the same time keeping a look out for the law, or even a couple of strong men who would be able to stop Wells making off with the unconscious girl. But luck wasn't with her today. Nor for the bloodied woman left for dead, or maybe already dead, and the boy, also lying unconscious over his mother's body as if trying to protect her from further harm. The only way she could help the little girl was to find out where Kenneth was taking her. And as soon as she knew, she'd go straight to the law.

Then they were out of the back alleys and into the high street. And there was that pervert, looking to all intents and purposes like a loving father holding his child close to his chest. She saw him hail the cab and looked desperately around her for some kind of assistance. At this time of day, the high street was fairly busy, but before she could enlist any help, the cab was driving away, leaving Agnes crying in frustration. She couldn't believe he had got away with the child so easily, not in broad daylight. But as her mother used to say, 'the devil looks after his own', and if ever there was a personification of evil, it was Kenneth Wells and all men of his ilk.

Then she had the first piece of luck she'd had for weeks. For as the cab drove past her she heard Kenneth's voice through the open window, giving the cabbie the address he wanted taking to.

Repeating the address over and over in her mind, fearful of forgetting it, Agnes saw two policemen strolling down the high street.

She was only a few feet away from the uniformed men when she stopped suddenly, an idea forming in her mind.

She knew where to find Kenneth now. What if she went to the address she had now committed to memory, and rescued the child by herself? After all, she would have the advantage of surprise on her side, for Kenneth had no idea that anyone knew where to find him. And what if she was able to get the child away and back to safety? For not only would she be saving the girl from a known pervert's clutches, but she too would be able to return to her own home without fear. She had passed the two officers, her mind jumping forward, the unplanned thoughts gathering momentum by the second. Returning to the cheap boarding house, she quickly took some money from a box hidden under a loose floorboard, and hurried back out onto the streets. Within minutes she was settled in the back of a cab, an experience new to her, but for once she wasn't concerned how much money the journey was going to cost her. By the time she had asked directions and waited around for trams it might take hours to get to the destination she was heading for, and time was of the essence.

Aware she was trembling, Agnes slowed her breathing and tried to relax, knowing however that she would never have any peace of mind until the child was safe. It was all up to her now – the way it should be, for it was because of her the child was in danger. Clenching her hands together to stop them shaking Agnes was suddenly thankful her journey was going to be a relatively long one. It would give her time to think.

Ted and Sadie heard the commotion before they had even turned the corner that led into the block of flats. Exchanging fearful glances they both quickened their step. At first they couldn't see anything for the crowds of people milling around the courtyard, then, one of Sadie's neighbours caught sight of her and hurried forward.

'Oh, Gawd, Sadie, love. Yer'll never guess what's 'appened. Poor Lil's been done in, an' little Charlie's been bashed round the 'ead an' all. And we can't find your Molly, she . . .'

Sadie pushed the woman aside, her heart thumping with fear. With Ted behind her, she pulled at the people swarming around the door of the first-floor flat, then stopped dead in her tracks at the sight that confronted her. With a muffled scream she leapt forward.

258

'Lil! Lil! Oh, God! Please ... please, don't be dead ...' Dropping to her knees, she gently cradled her friend's head in her lap. 'Come on, Lil, mate. It's me, Sadie. Come on, yer silly cow, stop pissing about ... Lil ... Lil ...'

Her vision blurred as tears rained down her face, then two small bodies were tugging at her, their childish shrills of fear penetrating Sadie's own grief. Her arms going out automatically she pulled the two stricken boys to her, holding them tightly against her heaving chest.

Over all the din came the sound of police whistles, and someone in the crowd shouted that the ambulance cart was on the way, but to the deeply shocked Sadie, the sounds all seemed to blur together in a confusion of unintelligible noises. Raising her head she looked over the boys' heads and saw Ted Parker staring down at her. Then he too seemed to jump and dance before her eyes. Holding Billy and Charlie tight, she lowered her gaze and gently rocked the two youngsters back and forth, not knowing if she was comforting them or herself in the instinctive gesture.

There was a question she wanted to ask the boys, a question that was screaming around inside her head, but couldn't bring herself to say the words, for fear of what the answer might be.

Clutching the boys tight, her eyes clouded over as she looked around the familiar faces. Some she only knew by sight, others she didn't recognise, but the only face she wanted to see, longed to see, wasn't there.

CHAPTER TWENTY

'I don't bloody well believe it. I mean, how the fucking hell can anyone just walk in off the street and stab a woman, a pregnant woman at that, knock one kid unconscious and make off with another one in broad daylight, and no one see anything? I could understand it if it had happened at night, but Gawd Almighty, in the middle of the day? And where's all the nosy neighbours when yer need them?' Ted stormed. 'That bloke must lead a charmed life, that's all I can say . . . Bastard!'

'Calm down, Ted. We're doing everything we can . . .'

'Oh, yeah. Like what?' Ted cut in angrily. 'Yer said the same thing when the kid first went missing, an' yer've done bleeding sod all, as far as I can see.'

The policeman's mouth tightened. 'Now that's enough, Ted. I know you're upset so I'll let that slide. But you know full bloody well me and the rest of the

nick have been working our bloody guts out trying
to find that kid. And we're not getting paid any overtime for it, either.'

Ted stared back into the angry face and let his gaze
drop. Shaking his head from side to side he nipped
on his bottom lip before replying quietly, 'Yeah, I
know, Officer, I know.' Running a hand through his
thick hair he said, 'But I was so close. So bloody close.
If I'd only been ten minutes earlier I might have been
in time to stop that maniac. Then Molly would be
where she belongs, with her brother, and that poor
cow wouldn't've been knifed, an' . . .'

The constable laid a comforting hand on Ted's
shoulder. 'I understand, mate . . . It's a right bloody
mess, ain't it?'

John Smith sighed tiredly. Since the Masters girl had
gone missing he'd hardly had a decent night's sleep.
Added to his daily workload he'd taken Agnes Handly
under his wing as well. The other men had laughed
at him, saying they'd begrudge looking after that old
trout in the line of work, but to waste his own time?
Well, they'd said, rather him than them. But the
seasoned policeman had just smiled and carried on
with his work quietly, refusing to be drawn into any
conflict with his colleagues. And even if they didn't
understand, or share his ideals, they respected the
bulky man and kept their counsel.

Now, as of one-thirty this afternoon, 27 May 1898,
the whole of the Metropolitan Police force was on full
alert. There was no talk about overtime now, paid or
otherwise. There was a madman on the loose, but the
criminal they were looking for was far worse than any

madman, for this particular one was a child molester the lowest of the low. A man who brought shame on his own sex, for no one was more reviled than a man who sought out innocent children to pander to his sick, perverted sexual desires, and the sooner he was caught and locked up the better for every decent person alive. Every policeman in London was drafted onto the streets, knocking on doors, pulling in every pervert known to them. But all to no avail. A couple of Sadie North's neighbours had come forward giving a description of the smartly dressed man seen entering Lily Knight's flat, but apart from that, they had no more information to give. Now, two hours later, the entire police force were out pounding the streets looking for the man known as Kenneth Stokes, alias Wells, and his accomplice, Agnes Handly. John Smith had tried to tell his superiors that Agnes Handly was as much a victim as anyone, but no one would listen and the constable knew better than to pursue that line. Though it would have been helpful if he could find Agnes. She might know more than she thought, but like the elusive Stokes, Agnes was nowhere to be found. Though not for a second did John Smith imagine she was with the man they sought. For he firmly believed that unfortunate wretch was more sinned against than sinning.

'Look, I'm sorry, mate.' Ted was talking again, his face tired and drawn, more from worry than lack of sleep. Also he was experiencing a great feeling of deflation. As he had said to the policeman, he'd been so near to finding Micky's sister. He remembered the journey to Sadie North's home, and how he had imagined seeing Micky's face when he returned his sister to him. Never for a moment had Ted envisaged the horrific scene that had greeted him instead. The woman, Lily Knight, was now in hospital fighting for her life, unaware her baby, brought into the world prematurely by the vicious attack on its mother, was dead. Sadie North was at her friend's bedside with the two Knight boys whom she had taken under her wing for the time being.

Then there was Micky.

Micky, once so full of life, so full of hope for the future, even nursing a crush on Ellen, and thinking nobody noticed. Now he was over at the bakery, crying his eyes out in her arms. In his hour of need he had reverted to childhood and in Ellen he saw only a mother figure, someone to cling to. She was the first person he had asked for when Ted had returned with his grim news. Ted had been apprehensive about taking the boy over to the bakery, but Arthur, give him his due, had welcomed Micky in with open arms, even offering to keep him for as long as he wanted to stay. And that had been suspicious in itself. But any business he had with Arthur and Ellen would have to wait for now. They had a lifetime in front of them – unlike Micky's sister if they didn't find her soon. He knew the police were doing everything they could but he was still angry at the lack of progress and despite his better judgement he couldn't resist having another dig.

'I ain't 'aving a go at you, Johnny, but it doesn't look as if the rest of the law's exactly breaking its neck trying ter find the kid. I mean, like I said before, I could understand him getting away if it'd been night, but how the 'ell could he walk the streets with the kid without someone noticing? He must 'ave taken a cab. If I was a copper, that would 'ave been the first thing I'd've done – question the cab drivers. Or maybe he had a carriage waiting? But however he got away he had ter be out on the streets for a while, and the kid would've called fer help, wouldn't she?'

Like Ted, the constable was also tired and frustrated and his patience, held under control through years of experience, finally snapped.

'Now you listen to me, mouth almighty. You haven't got a clue about what's going on. And I don't have to justify myself or the rest of the force to you or anyone else, but I will anyway, if only to shut you up. For your information almost every man wearing a uniform has a daughter or niece and they'd be on the warpath even if they weren't officers of the law. That's what's the matter with people like you. You seem to think policemen are a breed apart from the rest of the human race. Well, they're not. They're just like any other man, with feelings and anger. They cry and laugh just like you, but because they wear a uniform people imagine they're above human feelings. And another thing, don't call me Johnny. It's "Officer" to you, mate. As it happens we've already spoken to most of the cab drivers near the location of the flats, and one of the drivers remembers a man carrying a little girl. He thought she was asleep. As for her calling out? Huh! You don't know anything about children either, do you? Just imagine if you were eight years old and had just seen a friend stabbed and covered in blood. It must have been like a nightmare to her. Then the man she's petrified of is suddenly there. Do you really think she'd have called for help? She must have been terrified of making a sound in case the man hurt her. Though the poor little cow didn't even have the choice, seeing as she was unconscious. One more crack about the police and you'll feel the weight of my hand, no matter how big you are. And it won't be the first time, will it?'

At the sudden change in the constable's voice Ted jumped. Then, as long-ago memories resurfaced he smiled sheepishly. 'Yeah, I remember.' His lean frame relaxed for the first time that afternoon. 'How old was I? Twelve, thirteen? You caught me nicking an apple off a fruit stall up Mare Street. I didn't even 'ave a chance ter take a bite outta it, did I? Gawd, but yer gave me a fright when you grabbed me by the scruff of the neck. I'd already had a good look up and down the road before I got up the nerve to pinch that apple, an' I didn't see you. And when you suddenly appeared, I thought you was some sort of magician. I can still see it now. All me mates were watching, 'cos they'd dared me to do it, but they soon legged it when you showed up. But I knew wherever they was hiding they'd still be watching, so I put on a front, pretending I wasn't scared. Gawd! I was so cocky, wasn't I? Giving you a load of lip, till yer grabbed me by the ear and marched me down the length of the market. Then yer asked if I'd rather 'ave a clip round the ear, or be taken 'ome to me mum an' tell her what I'd done. Well! I didn't 'ave much of a choice, did I? 'Cos I was more frightened of me mum than you. Then I spotted me mates hiding behind the wall of the church. Well! I couldn't let them see how scared I was, so I put on me swagger and told you to go ahead and clout me.' As the memory became clearer Ted slapped his knee in mirth. 'I didn't know what'd hit me. I thought me head was gonna fall off. I wasn't so cocky then, was I? That clout sent me cross-eyed and bandy-legged. Me eyes were rolling, I could've sworn I heard bells ringing, an' I staggered 'ome looking and walking like a half wit with me mates following 'aving a good laugh at my expense.'

As the memory came flooding back Ted threw back his head and laughed uproariously.

Listening to Ted's infectious laughter John felt his own lips beginning to twitch and within seconds the two men were rolling with mirth. It was just what they both needed after the trauma of the last couple of hours. They were still laughing when a loud knock interrupted their merriment. Immediately the laughter stopped as if turned off by a tap. Exchanging apprehensive glances the constable was the first to move. Throwing the front door open he saw two of his colleagues standing on the doorstep.

'Well, what's happened?' he said over-loudly, his nerves causing a hardness in his voice.

The elder of the policemen raised his eyebrows before answering. 'We've got the cab driver that took a man and little girl to a house near Epping Forest. Inspector Lewis has already left, but we thought you deserved to know what's happening, especially after all the hard work you've put into finding the kid.'

Standing behind John Smith Ted couldn't help but notice the deference in the officer's tone, nor the way both men were looking to the older policeman for guidance, even though they were all of the same rank.

His blunt features tight with repressed anger the constable cursed quietly. 'Well, that's no surprise, is it? It's always the same. We work our arses off while he sits behind his desk shuffling papers, bawling out us lowly constables when things go wrong, but he's first in the queue if there's any glory to be had. Any excuse to get his picture in the papers, lazy bastard!'

Again the waiting officers exchanged startled glances. For as long as they'd known the middle-aged officer they had never even heard him raise his voice, let alone act in this manner. But if anything his outburst only increased their respect for voicing what the rest of the station thought of their inspector.

Reaching for his helmet from the hall table John said to Ted, 'Looks like we've finally had some luck, and about time too. Let's just hope it doesn't turn out to be a wild goose chase. Anyway, I'll let you know everything as soon as I get back.'

The words, although kindly spoken, were nonetheless a dismissal, and Ted wasn't used to being treated in such a fashion. His lips tightening he retorted, 'If yer think I'm just gonna wait here twiddling me thumbs when you know where that filthy swine is hiding, you've got another think coming. If yer won't let me come with yer then I'll find out where he is on me own.'

Knowing Ted wasn't the type to make empty threats John sighed. Turning to the waiting two men he said, 'Wait a minute, will you? I just want a quick word with Ted.'

Closing the door slightly so the curious men couldn't overhear the conversation, he faced Ted squarely. 'Look, mate, I understand how you must be feeling. There's no one wants to catch that piece of vermin more than me, but I can't let you come with us, you must know that. My inspector would have my head on a plate if I brought a civilian along with us.'

His face grim Ted reached behind the constable and threw the door wide open. 'Don't let me keep you, your mates are waiting fer you, and I've got business to see to meself.'

Knowing it was useless to argue further John Smith took his leave.

Within minutes Ted was striding down the street, making his way to the high street situated near the building where Sadie North lived. But once there he was bitterly disappointed, for the cabbie who had taken Stokes and Molly on their journey was nowhere to be found. Frustrated, angry, and reluctant to face Micky without some concrete news, Ted pounded the pavements for nearly half an hour before plucking up the courage to face the young man who had become so dear to him.

Arthur turned the closed sign on the bakery door, sighing with a mixture of tiredness and relief that another day of curious strangers and listening to sly innuendoes was over, at least until tomorrow, when the whole sordid experience would start all over again. And all because they were hoping to see the infamous Agnes Handly, supposed partner in crime of Kenneth

Stokes. It made Arthur wonder at the stupidity of some people. Surely they realised Agnes wasn't going to return to her job, not with the entire police force trying to track down her whereabouts. Then again, there was no accounting for people's peculiarities. His only consolation was that today was early closing.

But his ordeal wasn't over yet. He raised his eyes. There was a time, not so long ago, when this had been his favourite part of the day. Then he would climb the stairs, a smile on his face, to the rooms above to be greeted by a cheerful Ellen and a hot meal waiting for him. And as they ate he and Ellen would talk about the day's events, with Ellen recounting some amusing tale concerning some of their more awkward customers. But not any longer. Oh, his dinner would still be waiting for him, but he would have to eat his meal alone, for Ellen no longer sat at the table with him. She was civil to him, as she would be to any stranger. There wasn't even the opportunity to sit down to resolve their differences, no chance for him to try to explain what had made him act the way he had that night – not with Micky Masters temporarily in residence. Then there was Ted Parker dropping in at any hour of the day or night as if he owned the place.

Yet by far the worst part for Arthur was the way Ellen's face lit up like a beacon whenever Ted walked into the room. And it wasn't only Ellen who came to life on seeing Ted; Micky too would run to him, clinging onto the charismatic man, gathering strength from Ted's presence, while he, Arthur was left alone and ignored as if he wasn't even in the room. And each time Arthur witnessed the obvious attraction between his wife and the local market trader, a man half Arthur's age, his stomach would churn with fear. He was living on a knife's edge, expecting Ellen to announce she was leaving him, and there would be nothing he could do to stop her. But if it came to that, he wasn't about to make it easy for her and Ted Parker. He'd never agree to a divorce.

Yet he remembered vividly that night when John Smith had deposited Agnes on him, and she'd confronted him about his relationship with Ellen, insinuating he was as bad as the man who had abducted Molly Masters. But the ultimate shame was finding Ellen and Ted standing in the doorway. Nor could he forget the triumphant, gloating look on Ted Parker's face. If he'd been a man of Ted's calibre he would have stood his ground and faced him down. But no, not him. Instead he had grabbed the whisky decanter and scuttled away like a frightened rabbit into the bedroom. Even with the door closed, he could hear Ted telling Ellen their marriage was a sham, and as he'd listened Arthur's self-esteem had hit rock bottom. He'd felt like a nobody, somebody who was worthless, useless and practically non-existent.

He hadn't planned what had happened that night. He had forced himself on Ellen. He still couldn't comprehend how he could have committed such a despicable act. He'd wanted so badly to feel like a proper man, and also to make their marriage a proper one in every respect. Yet never in a million years would he have made love to Ellen if he hadn't been so full of anger and drink. Even so, he'd hoped Ellen would forgive him eventually. But instead of putting a halt to the flourishing relationship between Ellen and Ted, he had driven her further into his rival's arms.

'You all right, Arthur?'

Arthur jumped at the sound of Nora Parker's voice. Plastering a smile on his face he replied heartily, 'Yeah, I'm fine thanks, Nora. And thanks also for helping out in the shop, I really appreciate it. Here.' Opening the till, he handed Nora half a sovereign for her work of the last few days.

Nora took the money. 'Thanks, Arthur. It's nice being back at work. I mean Ted doesn't keep me short, but there's nothing so rewarding as earning yer own money. D'yer want me back tomorrow? Only I'll 'ave plenty of time ter spare now Micky's moved in here. I know it's only a temporary arrangement, but in the meantime I'm available ter help out if yer want me.'

'That'll be very helpful, Nora. I was thinking of hiring someone to run the shop now Agnes has scarpered and Ellen's preoccupied with young Micky. So yes please, Nora. It'll be a godsend with you in charge of the shop and the takings. It's comforting to know there's someone I can trust.'

As Nora reached the door she hesitated, wondering if she should say something to ease Arthur's mind. But what? Everyone, including herself, had predicted that the marriage wouldn't last. But never had she imagined it would be her son who would ultimately blow Arthur's world apart. There were a hundred things she wanted to say, but the words stuck in her throat. Instead she patted Arthur's arm affectionately saying, ''Bye, Arthur, I'll see yer in the morning.'

''Bye, Nora, and thanks again.'

271

After he had locked up Arthur spent another fifteen minutes doing mundane jobs in the shop, leaving it until the last minute before he would have to go upstairs and face Ellen. With nothing left to do he made his way up the stairs, his feet dragging as he mounted the steps, wondering with dread what kind of reception he would receive.

'You're late. I've had to put your dinner back in the oven to keep warm. Sit down and I'll get it for you.'

As Arthur waited for his meal he reflected sorrowfully that Ellen hadn't even asked why he was late; as he feared, she was no longer interested in his life.

Tucking into his dinner he looked to where Ellen was sitting by the fireplace embroidering a linen handkerchief, something she had never been interested in before. In fact she had taken up numerous new hobbies, and Arthur knew they were merely a diversion so she wouldn't have to talk to him any more than was absolutely necessary. But Arthur wasn't going to give up on his marriage without a fight, however feeble his attempts were.

As he spooned a forkful of shepherd's pie into his mouth he asked casually, 'Where's Micky? He hasn't gone out wandering the streets again, has he?'

Without looking up Ellen replied, 'No, he's in bed. He was nearly hysterical after hearing the latest news so I sent for the doctor. He gave Micky something to make him sleep. Hopefully he's stay asleep until morning. He's absolutely exhausted in mind and body.'

'Oh, well, that's something, I suppose. Where is he by the way? I presume you've put him in the box room.'

This time Ellen looked up at her husband. With a coolness in her voice she said, 'No, he's sleeping in our . . . I mean my bed. I did think of putting him in the spare room, but if I had, there'd be nowhere for you to sleep. Unless you were hoping to share my bed again, and let me tell you, Arthur, that is never going to happen. Of course if you want your bed back, then I'll move into the box room with Micky. It'll be a tight squeeze, but I'll be able to sleep nights without worrying you'll take it into your mind to try it on again.'

Suddenly Arthur lost his appetite. Pushing his plate away he meet Ellen's gaze and, with a voice filled with emotion he said, 'Please, Ellen, won't you ever forgive me for that night? I mean, be fair. In the two years we've been married I've never ever bothered you in that way. Besides, even if I was over rough, by law I had every right to make love to my wife . . .'

Ellen's head jerked up as Arthur's words hit her with the force of a physical blow. Her voice dripping with scorn she said, 'Why don't we call it by its proper name – rape! Because that's what you did to me, Arthur. You raped me, violated my body like a dog rutting a bitch in heat, and with the same selfish indifference to my feelings.'

Seeing the look of disgust on her face, Arthur felt the blood rush to his cheeks. But this time, instead of trying to appease Ellen, he felt a surge of anger wash over him, and before the voice of reason could stop him he turned viciously on his wife.

'I don't suppose you'd have objected if it'd been Ted Parker, would you? Oh, no. Not on your life you wouldn't. D'you really think I don't know what's going on between you two? How far has it gone? Was I really the first one to bed you . . .'

Before he could say anything more, Ellen was standing in front of him, her face filled with fury, her arm raised. Caught unaware Arthur never got the chance to dodge the powerful blow Ellen landed on his face. Reeling back in shock Arthur could only stare in amazement at the woman gazing at him with hate-filled eyes. There was no resemblance to the Ellen he had known since birth, and her next words confirmed his worst fears.

'Get out of my sight, Arthur. I don't know you any more, and I don't even want to try. We're finished. The only reason I've stayed these past two weeks was because I wanted to be sure there weren't any reper-cussions from that night. And this morning I found out there weren't, so there's nothing to keep me with you. Get out, Arthur, just go; I can't stand even being in the same room as you.'

And Arthur, his brief, angry outburst squashed the moment Ellen had retaliated, turned, and almost ran from the room.

CHAPTER TWENTY-ONE

As Arthur stormed out into the street he collided with Ted who was obviously heading for the place he had just left. As their bodies touched, Arthur felt Ted's hard, muscle-toned physique against his own flabby frame, and this only served to remind him once again of his inadequacies. For a moment Arthur felt a surge of rage against this man, against all the people who looked on him with derision or pity, but most of all he raged against God. All his life Arthur had strived to be a good man, a decent human being, wanting only to be liked and respected, but no matter how hard he had tried, somehow he'd always failed. And now he couldn't lie to himself any longer. There would always be two types of men in the world. Men like him, and men like Ted Parker. And the Ted Parkers of this world always got what they wanted, leaving their crumbs to men like him. The worst part of the scenario was that men like Arthur would always be grateful for their leavings.

'You all right, Arthur, mate?' Ted was staring at him, a puzzled look on his face.

Composing himself Arthur fought to control himself. He'd lost Ellen, that much was plain, but that didn't mean he was going to stand meekly by and let Ted Parker take his wife without some sort of fight. Even if he lost everything, he could still retain his dignity. Pulling himself up to his fullest height, Arthur replied tersely, 'Of course I'm all right. Why shouldn't I be?'

Ted shrugged his shoulders. There was clearly something troubling Arthur, and it was probably due to him. Still, he wasn't going to be a hypocrite and pretend to be a concerned friend at this late stage. 'All right, I was only asking.' Jerking his head towards the closed bakery he asked briskly, 'Is it all right if I go up ter see Micky?'

Arthur stared at him coldly. 'Why ask me? You'll do what you want regardless of what I say. I mean, it's only my home, though you'd never know it the way you come and go as you please.' Bobbing his head he added, 'Well! What are you waiting for? It's not as if you don't know the way, is it?'

Ted's eyebrows arched in surprise at the baker's manner then said dryly, 'Yeah! I know me way right enough. Cheers, Arthur.' He turned on his heel then stopped. 'Will I see yer later?'

Arthur uttered a mirthless snort of laughter. 'Oh, I'll be back, Ted. I don't know what time, it all depends on how long I stay in the pub. If I'm enjoying myself I might stay until closing time. On the other hand if I get bored I could be back home within the hour. But

I don't suppose it'll bother you either way, unless of course you'd like to spend some time alone with Micky.'

Now there was an unmistakable sneer in Arthur's tone. But Ted, impatient to share his news with Ellen, simply turned his back on Arthur and began to walk round to the back door that led to the rooms above the bakery. Arthur watched his rival enter his home, his hands forming into balled fists at his side, furious that he had been dismissed so casually especially as he'd thought he had handled Ted with a dignified show of strength. Oh! How he would have loved to run after the tall, athletic figure and beat him to the ground, recognising with despair that he was incapable of such an act. His shoulders slumped, he walked towards the nearest pub.

'Ted!' Ellen cried with genuine pleasure.

Resisting the impulse to pull her into his arms and rain passionate kisses over her lovely face, Ted had to content himself with a gentle hug and a chaste kiss on her cheek.

'Have you any more news, Ted?' She hovered by his side, her face and manner showing her anxiety. They were in the living room now, and, ignoring Ellen's query, Ted asked, 'Where's Micky?' His eyes roamed around the room, expecting the youngster to suddenly appear.

'The doctor gave him some sleeping powders. He said Micky shouldn't wake up until morning, but he left me some more, just in case.' Taking Ted's hand Ellen led him to the settee and pulled him down beside

her onto the soft cushions and laid her head agains
his shoulder. 'You mustn't blame yourself for wha
happened. There was no way you could have knowr
that odious man had already found out Molly's where
abouts.'

Ted gently touched her lips with his fingers. 'Shush
love. There's something I've gotta tell yer ... Oh! By
the way, I bumped into Arthur on me way in. He wa:
in a funny mood. You two 'ad a row?'

Ellen kept her face averted. 'No, of course not.
think all this business with Micky and his sister i:
getting him down. He doesn't like any deviation from
his routine.'

Ted snorted. 'Huh! Well, he's gonna 'ave ter get usec
to things changing, isn't he? ... All right, all right
don't get yerself agitated,' he said quickly as he fel
Ellen begin to fidget awkwardly in the circle of hi.
arm. 'I ain't gonna say anything till young Molly':
been found. After all ...' He planted a kiss on the to
of her shiny hair. 'We've got all the time in the world
ain't we?'

Relaxing again Ellen murmured, 'You said you hac
something to tell me.'

Ted clapped his hand to his forehead. 'Gawd!
nearly forgot why I came round, except for th
obvious.' He grinned affectionately, the smile wavering
as he remembered the reason for his visit. 'The thing
is, love, the coppers 'ave found the cabbie who pickec
up Stokes and Molly; that's to say, he picked up a mar
and girl fitting the descriptions. The time factor fits ar
all.' Ellen was now sitting upright, her eyes bright witl
renewed hope, leaving Ted to wonder if he had don

the right thing in telling Ellen before Molly had been found, but it was too late. 'Now look, love, don't go getting yer 'opes up just yet.'

'But like you've just said, it looks promising. How did you find out?'

'Johnny Smith was at my place when two of his mates called with the news. Apparently their inspector had already left for the address the cabbie gave them about half an hour before Johnny found out. Anyway, I wanted ter go with 'em but he wasn't 'aving any of that. 'Course I wasn't best pleased, so I went ter the cab rank meself and asked around, but the bloke I was after wasn't there. His mates weren't sure if he was still down at the station or off on another fare. So I thought I'd pop round ter keep yer up ter date, then go back an' see if he's back yet. If he ain't, I'll find out where he lives and go round. I hope I won't 'ave ter wait that long though. With a bit of luck the coppers 'ave already found the pair of 'em, and are on their way back home right this minute.'

Neither of them heard the bedroom door open until a weak voice whispered, 'I wanna come with yer.'

Startled, Ellen and Ted jumped apart.

'Micky, what on earth are you doing out of bed?' Ellen exclaimed in alarm.

Then Ted was hurrying towards the pale young boy, just catching him as his legs gave way beneath him.

'The only place you're going is back ter bed, mate,' he said firmly as he swept the frail figure up into his arms.

'No, I ain't. I'm coming with yer, an' yer can't stop me,' Micky protested in a pitifully weak voice.

'Don't be daft, yer silly bugger, yer can hardly stand let alone walk, and I ain't got time ter carry yer.' Looking at the tears beginning to form in the boy's eyes Ted's voice softened. Taking him into the bedroom he lowered him gently onto the bed then sat down on the side. 'Look, mate, I know yer've 'eard it all before, but this time there's a real chance of finding Molly. But I ain't gonna lie ter yer. You ain't stupid, so I ain't gonna treat yer like a kid. Like I said, there's a good chance the police are already on their way back with your sister, but then again this Stokes is a wily bastard. He's been getting away with the same sort of thing fer years. We've just gotta pray that this time he's finally run outta luck. And I know yer want ter be there when he's found, but you must know yer just ain't up ter it. Even if I was ter help yer, you'd only slow me down.'

Ellen stood by the door, her hand held against her throat. 'Ted's right, Micky. You're much too weak to go with him. But as soon as he knows anything, he'll come straight here, won't you, Ted?' Her eyes fixed on the solemn-faced man.

Ted held her gaze for a moment before turning his attention back to the agitated form laid out on the bed. ''Course I will.' Taking hold of Micky's hand he said, 'I'm gonna ask yer a question, Micky, an' I want a straight answer, all right?'

Micky's head nodded listlessly.

'Right then. Do you trust me?'

''Course I do.' The answer came back without hesitation.

'Good! Then yer know I'll do everything in my power to find Molly an' bring her back to you.'

280

Micky's eyes blinked rapidly as he fought to stay awake. 'I know yer will, Ted. But . . . but I'm so frightened, Ted. Even if yer do find her, what if that man's already . . .' He gulped loudly, unable to utter the words that had filled his mind since Molly had vanished.

Ted bowed his head and gripped the small hand tighter. 'I know, mate, I know. But we've gotta look on the bright side. At least up till this morning Molly was safe, an' that bloke will be too busy hiding from the law ter think of anything else, and as I said ter Ellen, they've got a good chance of catching 'im.' Turning his head he said to Ellen, 'Make him a cup of cocoa, will yer, love, it'll help settle him.'

Grateful for something to do, Ellen hurried off. She was pouring hot milk into a mug when Ted entered the kitchen.

'Put another one of those powders the doctor gave him into his drink.'

Ellen, her gaze anxious, said, 'I can't, Ted. The doctor said he was only to have one dose every four hours, and it's only been a couple of hours since he—'

Ted interrupted impatiently, 'Yeah, I know. He also said the medicine would probably knock him out till the morning, an' he was wrong about that. Anyway, it can't do him any harm, can it?' Seeing the doubt in Ellen's eyes he pressed home his point. 'Look, the poor little sod's doing his best ter stay awake, frightened ter close his eyes 'cos he feels guilty being tucked up safe while his sister's out there somewhere with a madman. I'm only thinking of Micky, and what's best fer him. So you tell me, d'yer think it's better fer him

281

ter toss an' turn all night, his mind filled with pictures too horrific ter imagine, or give 'im another sleeping powder ter knock 'im out, an' give his mind a bit of peace, at least till tomorrow?'

Against her better judgement Ellen had to admit Ted's logic made sense. Reaching into a drawer she took out another of the sleeping draughts the doctor had left and poured it into the hot cocoa. Giving it one final stir she held it out to Ted saying, 'You give it to him, Ted. I can't face him just now. I know I'm being a coward, but I'm afraid if I go into that room I'll break down, and that's the last thing he needs right now.'

'Don't be too hard on yerself, darlin'. If it wasn't fer you, he'd be in a worse state than he is right now.' Putting his hand out he touched her face lovingly. 'I'll take this into him, then be on me way.'

But it was another fifteen minutes before Ted left them. In spite of his hurry to be out doing something, Ted hadn't the heart to leave the boy until he was sure the medicine had taken effect and Micky was fast asleep.

For Ellen there was no such escape. The only thing she could so was sit by Micky's bedside and pray. She never imagined she would be able to sleep at such a time, but if she didn't know how fatigued she was, her mind and body did. Within an hour of Ted's departure, she too was afforded the luxury of sleep.

CHAPTER TWENTY-TWO

'What an almighty cock-up. When I get my hands on that lying cabbie, he'll wish he'd never been born. Sending me on a wild goose chase, a man of my standing. He's made a laughing stock of me, that's what he's done.'

Inspector William Lewis, his hands clasped behind his back, paced up and down in front of the house he'd been sent to, his fleshy face almost purple with rage. A dozen officers stood awkwardly a few feet away, their heads lowered for fear their inspector would see the glee in their eyes at witnessing the posturing man brought low. But what was really the icing on the cake was the waiting journalists, summoned by Inspector Lewis himself to capture his triumph when he arrested the known child molester and kidnapper. He'd also requested a photographer to be present at his moment of glory, but his plans of becoming a hero had gone badly wrong. For the house

he had ordered his men to break into by kicking in
the front door, so as not to give Kenneth Stokes any
chance of escaping, had been the worst decision he'd
ever made in his twenty years in the police force. For
the said house was owned by the local magistrate, and
that distinguished man, outraged by the onslaught on
his home, not to mention the intrusion on his privacy,
was in no mood to listen to reason. Instead he had
threatened to make a formal complaint to Inspector
Lewis' superiors.

His head swinging from side to side, looking for
someone to vent his rage on, his eyes alighted on the
small group of journalists and the two photographers,
both of whom had already taken a number of pictures,
unknown to the livid senior officer. Flinging out his
arm to his assembled men Lewis thundered to no one
in particular, 'Get rid of these vultures. I want them
out of here. Do you hear me? Get them away from
here – now!'

A group of uniformed men began to advance on the
newspaper men, but they needn't have bothered. The
men from the newspapers had already gathered
enough information and pictures for a good story for
tomorrow's newspapers. Grinning broadly, for they
too disliked the glory-hunting inspector as much as
his own men did, they began to depart, watched by
the waiting officers who were enviously wishing they
could leave too. They'd been hanging around for over
half an hour, and all because their inspector was too
proud to admit defeat, hoping instead that something,
anything might happen to save his face.

Then, from their ranks, a solitary man stepped

forward and approached the furious man. As if one, they held their breath in admiration as John Smith planted himself firmly, and without fear, in front of his superior and said clearly, 'Could I have a word, Sir?'

The plain-clothes man looked up sharply, his eyes narrowing as he saw who dared to confront him. Of course, John Smith. They had joined the force in the same year, but there the similarity ended. He, William Lewis, had always intended to rise in the ranks, whereas John Smith had been content to remain out on the street as a lowly constable. Yet Lewis knew that PC Smith could have made it to the top if he'd wanted to, for he was an intelligent man, and a bloody good copper to boot. With this in mind the inspector motioned John further back from his men. He was anxious to hear what Smith had to say, for whatever it was it would be something worth listening to, and he certainly hadn't come up with any other plans despite furiously racking his brains. Even so, he didn't want his men to hear what Smith had to say. There was still time to save face if Smith could come up with a good idea. If he had, he, Lewis, would find some way to take the credit, so it was imperative their conversation was not overheard.

Rocking back on his heels he gave the impression he was doing John Smith a favour by listening to him, but despite his best efforts, PC Smith knew the man too well to be either deceived or impressed.

'Well, come on, man, if you've got something to say then spit it out,' he barked.

Unaffected by the man's tone John said in a calm,

clear voice, 'I think we should search the forest, Sir It's obvious Stokes deliberately gave the cabbie the wrong address. He must have known we'd question all the hackney cab drivers and this was most likely his way of throwing us off the scent and thumbing his nose at us into the bargain.'

Lewis tipped his trilby hat further back on his head and said shortly, 'I've already worked that much out for myself, Constable. In spite of what you and the rest of the men think of me, I'm not entirely stupid So if you've nothing further to say, I suggest . . .'

Not at all intimidated by his superior John Smith continued. 'It's my opinion Stokes knows this particular area. Look at the facts. He hires a cab and gives the driver the address of the local magistrate. Maybe that was just a coincidence, but I don't think so. Like I said, he's trying to rub our noses in it, and what better way than to humiliate us by leading us to that particular house. Look around you, Sir.' John waved his arm towards the surrounding area. 'There's only eight houses in all, and we've spoken to every home owner. Every one of them is either a respectable businessman or professional person, that's only to be expected in a place like this. Yet the address we were given was the biggest and most expensive one, owned by a man who could make life very difficult for us if he has a mind to do so. Like I said, it might just be a coincidence, but it's the sort of prank Stokes would play, and if that's the case, then like I said, he must be familiar with the area. Shall I go on, Sir?'

Lewis struggled with his pride before indicating with a nod of his head that John Smith should continue.

'All right then. We know he doesn't live in any of these houses, so I think he has a hideaway somewhere in the forest. Think about it, Sir. It's the only possible solution. He was definitely dropped off here, he was on foot, with a child and no apparent transport, yet nobody saw him. He couldn't vanish into thin air, so he must be nearby somewhere.

'And the only place he could be is in the forest. Don't forget, Sir, we've never been able to find out where he lives. Every time we've picked him up with a child, it's always been in some seedy boarding house or hotel. And as despicable as Stokes is, he's no fool. He's had years to find or even build a place to bring his victims to without fear of being found, and what better place to hide than in Epping Forest.'

Inspector Lewis nipped nervously on his bottom lip. What Smith said made sense. But if he was right, it would take more than his handful of officers to find Stokes' hideout. It would take considerable manpower to search the vast expanse of Epping Forest, not to mention the time factor. Even with a hundred officers it might take days, maybe even longer. As Smith said, Stokes was no fool. An image of Kenneth Stokes' smug, sneering, mocking face floated before his eyes and his face hardened.

'All right, Smith, we'll try it your way.' Taking a gold hunter from his inside pocket he flipped open the case. 'It's nearly four now, that leaves us a good four hours if the light holds, but we're going to need more men.' Clicking the fob watch closed he continued. 'Send one of the men back for more officers, and by that I mean every man available, on duty or off. It'll mean leaving the streets empty for the rest of the afternoon, but I reckon the good people of the East End will be able to fend for themselves until nightfall.'

'Right you are, Sir.' John Smith touched the tip of his helmet as a salute. 'I'll see to it straight away. And, Sir . . .'

'Yes?' The word seemed to explode from Lewis's lips as he tried to keep a tight rein on his rising temper. It galled him to have to ask for help from one of his men; it was doubly galling to take advice from this particular constable. But he was wise enough to know that if anyone could find Stokes and the Masters child, that man was John Smith.

Undaunted, John said, 'Even if we round up all the shift we're still going to be short of manpower. We need to call in Scotland Yard for additional help, but we won't be able to manage that today. In the meantime I think we should ask for volunteers to help in the search. Feelings are running high in the East End, and I doubt we'd have any trouble in finding men to help us.'

His lips pursed tight, Lewis gave a curt nod of his head, cursing himself for not thinking of Smith's suggestion himself. It was the perfect and most logical solution to his immediate problem of the shortage of men.

Stirring himself to action Lewis strode towards his waiting officers, then stood to one side as Constable Smith instructed the men as to the course of action.

As the men began to enter the forest the sound of an approaching carriage caught the inspector's attention. Thinking it was more reporters arriving he walked forward, holding his arm up to stop the hackney carriage going any further. His face grim he yanked open the carriage door, ready to give the intruders short shrift, but he didn't get the chance to speak before a tall, rugged-looking man leapt down.

'Thanks, mate. There yer go,' he said tossing half a crown up to the cab driver. 'Hang about a minute, will yer, mate? Just till I see what's happening.'

'Righto, guv,' the driver answered happily, not wanting to leave the scene of the unfolding drama.

'Just a minute, where do you think you're going?'

Ted glanced down at the hand gripping his arm, then looked coldly at the man barring his way. 'If you want ter use that hand in the next couple of weeks I'd take it off me arm if I was you.'

Lewis bridled visibly. He'd had enough humiliation for one day without some nosy sightseer giving him grief. Assuming his superior demeanour he barked, 'Don't take that tone with me, mister. My name is Inspector Lewis, and there is a police investigation going on here. So you can just get back in that cab and . . .'

Ted shook off the offending arm with ease. 'I don't care if you're the bleedin' pope. This is a public place, and I've got as much right here as you have.'

The two men faced each other, neither one of them prepared to give way, then Ted's head whipped round as he heard his name being called.

'Ted, am I glad to see you!' John Smith appeared, his presence diffusing the situation. Ignoring the hostile atmosphere he clapped Ted on the shoulder. 'We think Stokes is hiding somewhere in the forest.

I've already sent one of the men back to get more help, so you can take his place.' Conscious of his inspector's growing wrath John introduced Ted. 'This is Ted Parker, Sir. He's sort of guardian to Micky Masters, the brother of the child Stokes has abducted.' Then turning to Ted he said, 'We've been expecting more journalists and the inspector is the only man with the authority to stop them entering the forest.' The blatant lie uttered in a respectful tone did much to soothe his inspector's anger while giving the man a loophole to redeem himself, a chance that the man seized gratefully.

Clearing his throat Lewis said, 'I'm sorry, Mr Parker. As Constable Smith said, I thought you were another reporter. I apologise for my earlier actions.' The words sounded as if they were being ground out, as they indeed were, but he knew that men like Ted Parker weren't easily intimidated, if at all.

But Ted had already forgotten the surly man's presence. 'You're joking, ain't yer? Bleeding 'ell, Johnny, it'd take an army to search that place. You sure he's in there?'

This time the constable didn't take Ted to task for calling him by name. There were much more important issues at stake. 'No, we're not sure, but it's the only lead we've got. Look, let's get going, I'll fill you in as we go.'

'Just a minute, Constable.' The authoritative voice stopped both men in their tracks. 'I'm going to take Mr Parker's carriage back to the station. I should have gone sooner instead of sending an inexperienced officer. I'll be of more use there than here. I'm leaving you in charge in my absence, Smith. Don't let me down.'

Striving to keep a straight face John replied, 'I'll do my best, Sir.'

Both men waited until Lewis had driven away, then John said in an uncharacteristic manner, 'Arsehole.'

Coming from the usually staid officer, the word caused Ted to forget the urgency of the moment. Throwing back his head he gave a huge burst of laughter, and John, his lips twitching, joined in as together they walked into the vast forest of Epping.

Dusk was falling when two market porters, willing volunteers in the search for Molly Masters, stumbled upon an old hut, almost obscured by a clump of trees. Obeying the instructions they had been given not to try and apprehend Stokes without police back up the men shouted for attention, trying desperately to curb the overwhelming temptation to ignore the police order and kick the door in themselves, and waited for the police to arrive. They didn't have long to wait. Within minutes, two uniformed officers came crashing through the undergrowth and, without any preliminaries, put their shoulders to the door, aided by the excited men who had first stumbled on the hut.

With the combined weight of the four men the door flew open, its hinges shattered by the onslaught as the men crashed into the hut, falling over themselves by the sheer number of their bodies. They were stumbling to their feet when more men, uniformed and civilians alike, converged on the hut, their faces lit up exuberantly. But their joy was short-lived, for although it was clear the two-room hut had recently been used, it was now uninhabited. And the disappointment of the men, who had been combing the forest for hours, after putting in a full day's work, was so great they could have wept. As word spread through the densely shrouded woods, the euphoria that had gripped the search party quickly evaporated as they realised that once again the lunatic they had been hunting had eluded them, and, with the deepening dusk, they knew they could do no more this night.

'That's that, then,' Ted said tiredly. Like the other men, he too felt like crying with disappointment and frustration. But Ted had more reason than the rest of the men to feel such devastating numbness in his body, for this was the second time in one day when his hopes of finding Molly Masters alive and well had been dashed to the ground.

'Come on, Ted. There's nothing more any of us can do today. Let's go home and get some sleep. We're going to need as much rest as we can get, because we're going to be back here at first light tomorrow morning. And by then we'll have more officers, and probably more volunteers too once the word spreads. It won't be just us now: Scotland Yard will be quick to get in on the act, and the top brass will send every available man up here.'

John Smith led Ted away from the hut, his face drawn with fatigue. Like every man in the search party he had been on his feet since dawn. He should have gone off duty hours ago, but when the life of a child was at stake, time became immaterial. Looking around him in the fading light he said earnestly, 'He's still here somewhere, I know he is, I can feel it. He must have put a lot of time and trouble in getting that hut fit to live in; he'd even put a padlock on the front door to prevent anyone from going in. He must have left in a hurry, because he didn't have time to put the lock in place.'

'You don't know fer sure that hut's got anything ter do with Stokes,' Ted said wearily. 'For all we know it could belong ter some gamekeeper, or . . .'

'Nah!' John cut in sharply. 'It's Stokes, I know it is. And if he's got one hiding place in here, what's to say he hasn't got another one? I know this bloke, Ted, he's clever. He's been at this game for over twenty years, and in all that time we've only managed to put him away twice. But this time it's gonna be different. We'll get the bastard, Ted, I swear it, by all that's holy and good in this world, I swear we'll get him, and when we do, I promise he'll never hurt another child again.'

A junior officer approached John, beckoning him to one side. Ted looked on absently as the two men spoke in whispers. Then John was back by Ted's side.

'Inspector Lewis has just sent word that the Knight woman's dead – and her baby. So it's murder now. And no amount of fancy lawyers are going to get him out of this mess, not this time. It's the hangman's noose for Kenneth Stokes, and nobody deserves it more than that evil bastard.'

Ted swung his head from side to side in anguish, the guilt almost tearing him apart. Now he had two more lives on his conscience. He should have acted quicker, instead of poncing about trying to find someone to look after his stall. Those precious minutes could have prevented the tragic events.

'Don't take it so hard, Ted. I know how you feel but there's nothing you could have done. The bes thing we can do now is go home, get some rest, and come back in the morning.'

But Ted didn't budge. He couldn't face going back home without Molly, couldn't bear to see the look o desolation in Micky's eyes when he knew that he, Ted had failed him again.

'You go, John ... Officer, I'm staying. I noticed a pub on me way 'ere. It ain't far, I'll get a room fer the night.' Raising his head he stared hard at the man by his side. 'I can't go 'ome; not yet, not without Molly D'yer understand, I can't go 'ome, not till we find her I just can't.'

Knowing it was futile to argue with the distraugh man, and too bone-weary to try, John patted Ted or the back. 'You do what you feel you must, Ted. I'n off home to my wife and bed. I'll see you in the morning. Oh, and I'll get someone to stop by the bakery. Ellen will be worried if you don't show up Take care, Ted. Goodnight.'

Ted, unable to move, remained leaning against on of the hundreds of oak trees that populated the forest He could have stayed there all night, but his minc alerted him to the fact that if he didn't move soor he might well have to spend the night, and suddenly that idea didn't seem so appealing. Following the las of the demoralised men back to the road, Ted walkec to the pub he had noticed earlier and booked a roon for the night.

Two hours and several pints of beer later he starec

up at the ceiling and rubbed his eyes. They felt as if they were filled with sand and grit. He desperately needed sleep, if only for a few hours, but every time he closed his eyes he saw Micky's white, pleading face.

'I'll find her, mate. I promise I'll find her, and bring her back ter yer. Trust me, Micky . . . Please God! Let me find her. Let her live, God. She's only a little kid. Don't let that madman hurt her. Please, God, keep her safe till I find her.'

His prayer seemed to echo and hang in the empty air, mocking and taunting him. Choking back a sob he turned his head into the pillow and closed his eyes.

CHAPTER TWENTY-THREE

An owl hooted in the dark causing a small huddled figure to jump in alarm. Her heart beating rapidly Agnes tried valiantly to control her rising fear. Nothing had turned out as she had planned; everything that could go wrong had gone wrong. Now she was trapped in what she could only describe as a living nightmare. Every sound, even the smallest rustle in the long grass was intensified in the eerie silence of the night, conjuring up frightening images to a woman already teetering on hysteria.

Stifling a scream Agnes tried to focus on the circumstances that had brought her to this predicament.

Somehow, in the busy traffic, her carriage had overtaken the one Kenneth and the child were travelling in. So it was that she arrived at the destination five minutes before the second hackney cab. Ordering the driver to stop before the carriage reached the house, Agnes had quickly alighted, paid the fare, and scurried into the woods, intending to watch Kenneth arrive and make sure he was safely inside the house before raising the alarm. She'd already decided not to carry out her original plan of trying to rescue the little girl herself. It had been a comforting thought and one she had relished, herself hailed as a heroine, her picture in the papers, the exoneration of her blackened name, but most important of all, the safety of the child Kenneth now had in his clutches. But she had reluctantly realised that such an act was beyond her capabilities, and one only found in the penny novels she was so fond of reading. No! The safest and most realistic course of action was to wait until he was home and feeling safe, then raise the alarm at one of the nearby houses.

She couldn't believe her eyes when Kenneth, clutching a silent, fair-haired girl by the hand, had waited until the cab had departed, then, looking left and right, he had scooped the girl up into his arms and headed for the forest. He had passed within feet of her, and Agnes hadn't realised she had stopped breathing until a loud burst of air was expelled from her lungs. It hadn't been just the fear of Kenneth spotting her that had left her breathless, it had been the sheer audacity of him. It was true the area was sparsely populated – she had counted only eight houses – but still, somebody could have seen him enter the forest with the girl.

And for the next few minutes she had braced herself for a shout from one of the householders, challenging him, but no such sound came, and Agnes realised that it was down to her to save the Masters girl. For if she left to seek help, Kenneth could vanish deep into the forest, a place he seemed familiar with judging by the ease and confidence he displayed. He appeared to know exactly where he was going.

It was a good half hour before she had seen the hut, and she would never have found it on her own. Neither would anyone else.

Kenneth had chosen his hiding place well.

The hut was situated amidst a clump of trees far away from the dozens of paths and open spaces used by the public. She'd watched as he'd unlocked the padlock, opened the door, and pushed the girl inside, but not before Agnes had caught a glimpse of terror in the child's eyes. Not once had she uttered a sound until Kenneth prodded her in the back, then had come a soft moan, a pitiful sound that had wrenched at Agnes' heart.

She had experienced a rush of anger, a quick burst of courage, but the feelings were shortlived, much to her shame. And so she had waited and done nothing, telling herself that if she heard the girl cry out or scream then she would put her own safety to one side and start screaming herself. But the child had remained silent, and Agnes had stayed where she was, trying to work out what to do for the best. Her life had been uneventful until she had met Kenneth, so she had never had the opportunity to test her courage. Like most people she had daydreamed about performing an heroic act, like pushing a child out of the way of a runaway carriage, thus saving it from the hooves of wild horses, unheeding of her own safety. She had also fantasised about running into a burning building to help people trapped inside, and the subsequent adulation that followed any act of heroism. She had truly believed that in the right circumstances she would forget her own fears and jump in to help without stopping to think of her own safety.

Now that time had come and she had found herself wanting. She had been forced to examine what she was really made of, and that knowledge brought her head low; the sense of guilt and shame was overwhelming. But not even the deepest sense of self-loathing could spark her into action. The minutes had ticked away while she struggled with her inner self, trying to dredge up some courage to do something, anything, rather than just stand here helpless while God only knew what horrors that evil bastard was inflicting on a helpless child.

Then had come salvation in the form of the search party.

Before she knew it the forest was crawling with coppers and volunteers. Her first instinct was one of relief. She had been on the verge of calling attention to herself when instinct stopped her as she realised what it would look like if she was found here, only feet away from the place Kenneth had the child hidden. They would think she was in it with Kenneth; they already thought it. Nobody would believe the truth, and looking at the whole sordid business from their view she couldn't say she blamed them. So she had stayed where she was, frightened to move for fear of attracting attention. Then those two men had stumbled on the hut and raised the alarm, and she had slipped away, hiding among the trees, hoping no one would see her, all the while sending up a prayer of thanks that Kenneth Wells, as she knew him, would at last be caught, and the Masters girl freed from her terrifying experience.

She couldn't believe her eyes when the hut door had been broken down and there was no sign of Kenneth or the child. Her mouth agape, she had stood rooted to the spot, thinking she was going out of her mind.

Long after the men had left she had remained hidden. With the light fading rapidly the men had searched on until it was too dark to continue. But they would be back. She had heard John Smith's voice, and had been tempted to call out to him. He alone would have believed her, she trusted him, but again she had hesitated too long. For the next voice she recognised had been that of Ted Parker, and she knew only too well what he thought of her. It had been fortunate that all eyes had been focused on the hut, for if not then surely someone would have spotted her, even in the fading light. It was at that moment she had realised what her options were. If she called out the volunteers might see her first and turn on her; and from what she'd seen and heard, those men far outnumbered the police. But if she stayed quiet she would be left alone in the forest all night, and the very notion of that prospect terrified her. She was still trying to summon up the courage to call out to John for help when she'd heard him tell Ted the news about the Knight woman and her unborn baby. But it wasn't the shocking news of the murder of the pregnant woman that had stilled her tongue, it was the tone in John's voice, a tone deep with anger and hate – it could have been a stranger talking, for if she hadn't known for sure it was John, she wouldn't have recognised his voice. And for the first time her faith in the kindly policeman faltered. Maybe now he too would turn against her, and she was startled to find how deeply hurtful that idea was. So she had stayed quiet.

Now she was stranded until morning, afraid to close her eyes in case some animal crept up on her in the dark. Afraid too of dreaming, for surely in her dreams she would see the child, hear her silent screams for help.

She didn't know she was crying until she felt the salty water trickle over her dry lips.

Then a light had come on in the hut.

Kenneth Stokes was elated. At last he had Molly Masters just where he wanted her, locked away from the outside world where no one could disturb them. Never had he wanted a child as badly as he had wanted Molly, and the more obstacles that had been placed in his way, the more he had wanted her, not least because he had got one over on everyone who had tried to stand in his way. Especially that smug bastard John Smith. After such a long, frustrating wait, he was in no great hurry to put his mark on the golden-haired girl. Instead he savoured the moment, alternating between taunting the child and whispering vile words of what he intended to do with her. Mercifully she was so traumatised by the unexpected abduction and seeing Mrs Knight lying covered in blood, his words had disintregated into mere, unintelligible sounds that floated over her dulled senses.

However, his initial euphoria was shortlived.

At first he thought his mind was playing tricks on him, until he'd peered out of the window. He didn't know how he had been tracked down so fast, but he had prepared for such an emergency. Scooping Molly out of the chair, he leant down, pulled back a strip of carpet, inserted his finger into a hole in the wooden floor beneath and yanked open a trap door. Within minutes he was safely hidden in the basement below, the carpet-covered trap door shut tight. He had no worries of being discovered, for who would think of looking for a basement under an old hut in the forest?

After being released from his last imprisonment he had thought long and hard about the time he had spent behind bars. The experience hadn't been a pleasant one, for even amongst thieves and murderers, men like him were treated as the lowest form of life. He had endured countless beatings, often within sight of the so-called prison guards, supposedly there to guard against such incidents, who had turned a blind eye to his sufferings, often delivering a blow or punch themselves. Even now, years later, he could still remember the degradation, the pain, suffering and fear he had been forced to endure. There had even been times he had genuinely been afraid for his life.

One thing he knew: he would never, ever go back into prison again. But nor had he considered giving up his pursuit of children for his own depraved purposes. There then had remained the problem of where he could take his victims without fear of discovery. Then, one afternoon, when he had been out walking aimlessly in the forest he had stumbled, quite by accident, upon the hut. On closer inspection he had found the two-room hut deserted, and by the squalor and disarray of the place it was obvious it had been unoccupied for some time. He could only assume that the dilapidated hut had once been home to a gamekeeper. And in the owner's absence it seemed that numerous tramps had availed themselves of the opportunity of having a roof over their heads.

During the time it had lain empty the door had been broken down, the windows smashed, and the wooden floor littered with empty beer bottles. But far worse, above the stale smell of beer, tobacco and rotting food, was the overpowering stench of human waste. Whoever had occupied the hut had obviously used it as a toilet. Kenneth, fastidious by nature, had been appalled at the way some people lived. Even animals didn't live in their own filth. Then he had heard a scurrying noise and jumped as two large rats emerged from the fire grate, their wicked black eyes staring at him fearlessly. He had retreated from the hut, a linen handkerchief covering his face.

He had hurried away, fearful of catching something, and returned to the hotel he had been staying at. Yet the memory of his find wouldn't go away. It hadn't taken him long to see the possibilities of the abandoned hut. Because of its location, the likelihood of someone chancing on it was almost negligible. Take him for example. He'd been walking in the forest for years, usually on the look out for unsupervised children, and he had never seen the hut until that day. As the germ of the idea grew in Kenneth's mind, so did his excitement.

He did not relish the task of cleaning the hut, although he knew he had no choice but to undertake the unpleasant task himself. He had enough money to hire builders and cleaners, but he couldn't take the risk of anybody knowing about the hut. The first thing he had done was to padlock the door and board up the window to prevent any passing tramp from entering what he now looked upon as his private property. Once the hut had been made secure, he'd had to start on the interior. On the first three visits to his new hideaway he had flinched at its appalling state and returned to his comfortable hotel, unable to tackle the gruesome task. Again he'd been strongly tempted to find someone willing to do the job for him, which wouldn't have been hard, providing the pay was good enough.

Weeks came and went, during which time he couldn't get his mind off the hut, his thoughts alternating between being eager to put his plans into motion to make the hut habitable, and repelled by the filthy conditions he would have to tackle to make it so. The longer he put it off the more anxious he became that someone else might chance on the hut, see the new padlock, find it empty, and become curious enough to make enquiries. That thought had been enough to galvanise him into action. Once he had taken up residence he would soon find some plausible reason for his being there, if anyone should stumble upon his new home and ask questions. Not that he was worried. If he'd been a tramp it would be a different matter, but not many people questioned a man of obvious wealth and refinement.

For someone as fastidious as himself the task of cleaning up other people's mess had been a living nightmare. On two occasions he had been physically sick, then, as the days passed he had stayed longer on each visit until he had become desensitised to the squalor. One blessing was that the previous legal owner had taken his furniture with him, leaving only a stained, flea-ridden mattress, a table and two hard-backed chairs, all the worse for wear, but easy enough to get rid of. It would have been difficult if he'd had to dispose of two fully furnished rooms.

The table and chairs had been chopped up and distributed in the forest, the mattress, which could have crawled out of its own accord, he had dumped as far away from the hut as possible. Then he had brought in furniture to replace the items he'd destroyed. The procedure had been simple enough. He'd hired a horse and carriage, loaded the furniture into the covered vehicle and ridden into the forest. No one had taken any notice of him, for gentlemen riding in the forest weren't an uncommon sight. Still, he'd kept a watchful eye out before entering the denser part of the forest.

The clean up of the hut had taken him the best part of a fortnight as he couldn't bear to be inside for more than a couple of hours at a time. He had left the floors until last, intending to scrub the wooden floor before laying some remnants of carpet. Because, he had told himself, if he planned to spend some considerable time in this place, he might as well have some creature comforts. It was then he had made the startling discovery. Hidden under a thick, hessian mat was a brass handle set in a square section of the floor. His heart beating with growing excitement he had pulled on the brass ring, lifting it up with bated breath. Bracing himself for what he might find, and with a gas lamp held in a shaking hand he had descended the rungs of the ladder, some of which were badly rotten causing him to stumble several times. Safely jumping off the last step he had swept the lamp around the basement, hardly daring to believe his luck. Like the two rooms above, the basement needed a good clean, but elated by his find, he didn't even flinch at the prospect of further work.

It had taken another few weeks to transport more furniture, for he didn't want to arouse any suspicion if by chance someone noticed his frequent trips into the forest, but it had been worth it. Every minute he had spent getting the hut habitable, every piece of filth he'd had to handle, had all been worth it.

He had been just thinking about his good fortune when he'd heard the commotion in the wood. Glancing at Molly he had seen a spark of life creep into her eyes and he had grinned.

'Don't go getting your hopes up, my sweet Molly, dear. They're not going to find you; no one's ever going to find you.'

Grabbing her he put a hand over her mouth, just in case she plucked up the courage to scream, and ran with her into the second room. Within a few minutes he had the trap door open, clambered down the repaired ladder and thrown her unceremoniously onto a mattress before scrambling back up the ladder to secure the trap door. It was an exercise he had practised countless times. He had replaced the brass ring with a hole he had drilled into the wooden floor, blocking it with the plug of wood he had removed from the same place. All he had to do when he wanted to use the basement was lift the carpet, push the plug out, and with his finger pull up the door. Once inside he simply put the plug back in place to fill the hole. He had also nailed a piece of carpet to the edges of the trap door so that when he closed it from below, the carpet concealed any sign of the trap door. It was highly unlikely anyone would ever even think of looking for a trap door in the simple hut, but Kenneth had learned never to take any unnecessary chances. He had no idea who had built the basement, or for what purpose, nor did he care.

Bound and now gagged, Molly could only listen to the sound of heavy footsteps and men's voices, her tormented mind flitting from hope to despair. Then there was silence, and the last remnant of hope died. When he was sure the last of the men had left, and safe in the knowledge that Molly was helpless, Kenneth had taken the opportunity of a couple of hours' sleep; it had been a long, fraught day, and his hand was stinging from where that old slag had used a knife on him. When he had woken he had listened intently, still cautious. When he was satisfied it was all clear he had advanced on the sleeping child, an evil smile curving his lips. But he recoiled in disgust at the stench of urine and faeces emanating from the still form. Maddened with rage he viciously kicked the chair, knocking both child and chair backwards. Molly awoke seconds before she landed on the floor with a sickening thud.

'You bitch, you filthy bitch.' The nasty man was glaring down at her, his face twisted with anger. 'You did it on purpose, didn't you? Thought you were being clever, didn't you? Well you're not getting off that easily.' Wrinkling his nose he ripped the gag from her mouth, untied the rope holding her to the chair and snarled, 'You stink like a sewer, you . . .'

Eyes wide with fear Molly whimpered, 'I'm sorry, Mister, I couldn't 'elp it. I . . . I tried ter . . . ter 'old it, honest, I did but . . . but I could . . . couldn't . . .'

'Shut up, just shut your mouth and do as you're told.'

Terrified into silence Molly did as she was bid, her small heart beating inside her breast like a trapped bird.

'Get up that ladder, and be quick. Go on, do as you're told, or by God you'll pay dearly. And take the lamp, I've got my hands full.'

Her legs stiff from being bound so long, Molly stumbled then quickly regained her balance, her fear outweighing her pain.

Keeping his distance Kenneth followed her up the ladder, the handkerchief still held to his nose. In his other hand he carried a suitcase. Once upstairs he pointed towards a small chest of drawers hissing, 'There's a bowl of water and soap on there. Get yourself cleaned up, then wash those filthy clothes, and be quick about it.' Opening the suitcase he took out a long, white nightdress and threw it at her feet. 'When you're finished put that on . . . Well! Get moving.'

Molly's feet almost left the floor in a hurry to do as she was told.

While he waited Kenneth picked up a wicker chair and flopped into it, his face cold as he stared at the mess the search party had made. The furniture had all been knocked over and the floor was covered with muddy footprints. Then he winced. Looking down at his hand he saw blood seeping through the makeshift bandage. Cursing, he carefully pulled the bandage off, his lips tightening as he saw the cut was still bleeding, indicating that his injury was worse than he had first imagined. For the first time, Kenneth felt a jolt of alarm. He had taken great care to clean the wound, covering it with a strip of linen he had torn off one of the dresses he had bought for Molly; he liked his children to look nice. But at this moment Molly was the furthest from his mind. The only person he could think about at present was himself. Pulling the lamp nearer he scrutinised his injury, and what he saw frightened him, for the wound was not only bleeding, but the pain was beginning to cause him great discomfort. Again he cursed the woman who had attacked him.

Thinking hard he went over his options. Obviously he needed proper medical care, but the nearest hospital was miles away. Then he smiled. Of course, there was an old retired doctor living nearby. He had met him on several occasions during his visits to the forest. With time on his hands the elderly doctor often took long walks in the forest, as did many people. They had only exchanged pleasantries on those

meetings, even though the doctor had tried to engage
Kenneth in long conversations. Kenneth, on the other
hand, had kept their meetings as brief as possible
talking long enough not to arouse suspicion as to his
frequent excursions into the forest, but pleasant
enough to not arouse any suspicions. Now he was
glad he had made the effort. Looking at his fob watch
he saw it was nearly eleven and frowned. He hadn'
realised he had slept that long. The old boy would
probably be in bed by now. Still, he could always
knock and concoct some tale as to his predicament.

Looking at Molly he pondered what to do about the
girl. Obviously he couldn't take her with him. He
would have to tie her up again, though he doubted
she would attempt to escape. She'd be too frightened
to venture out into the darkness on her own.

'You nearly ready?' he shouted impatiently.

Molly, who was desperately trying to get herself
cleaned up, afraid of making the man more angry
quickly completed her ablutions, put the wet clothes
on the floor in the corner and pulled on the night
dress he had given her. Her lips trembling, she walked
towards him.

Kenneth stared at her hungrily, then another sharp
pain brought his mind back to his immediate needs.

'Now, listen to me. I've got to go out, but I'll be
watching this place, so don't go getting any ideas, do
you hear me?'

Molly nodded dumbly, too scared to move, let alone
try and find her way through the black night into the
forest.

'Now, I'm going to trust you. You come and sit down

and you stay there until I get back.' Warily approaching him, Molly let herself be lowered into the wicker chair. 'Don't forget, I'll be watching. If you so much as put your head outside the door, I'll see you.'

Keeping his eyes on the pitiful figure, Kenneth inspected the door, cursing loudly as he realised it had been torn off its hinges then propped back into place, the padlock dangling uselessly on its chain. It would be a long time before he could repair the damage. He would have to wait until he was sure the police had given up interest in the hut, and that could be a long time. In the meanwhile he had the basement, and that was all he cared about.

He thought again about tying the child up, then dismissed the idea. She was already rendered helpless by her fear of him, and what he would do if she dared disobey him. And that form of intimidation was far more binding than any rope.

Picking up the lamp he went towards the door, and was startled when the child cried out, 'Don't leave me in the dark, Mister. I'll be good, honest, I will . . . just do— don't leave me in the dark.'

Grinning cruelly, he bent over the terrified little girl. 'You've been a bad girl, Molly. Fouling yourself as you did. And bad girls have to be punished. Don't make it worse by talking back to me. All right?'

The fair head bobbed, then dropped onto her chest.

Kenneth hesitated. This was how he liked them best. Mentally beaten into submission, willing to do anything to keep him happy. Then he moved towards the door. She would be even more compliant by the time he returned.

Propping up the door as best he could from the outside Kenneth hurried through the forest, anxious to get his wound seen to – and even more anxious to get back to the waiting child.

Left alone in the darkness Molly didn't move. It was as if her limbs, even the very core of her being, had been frozen. Her tortured mind however was still free to feel, to fear, and to pray.

'Please, Micky, come and get me. Or Sadie, why haven't you come for me? I'm so scared. Please, someone, help me. Come and get me, please come and get me before the bad man comes back.'

CHAPTER TWENTY-FOUR

Agnes watched in disbelief as she heard and saw Kenneth leave the hut. It was impossible, she told herself. She'd seen with her own eyes the police and members of the search party enter the hut and find it empty; she hadn't believed the evidence of her own eyes then either. Blinking rapidly she clutched at her throat. Was she losing her mind? What other explanation could there be? After all, it was only a small wooden shack. The police couldn't have failed to spot them if Kenneth and the child had been in there. But she'd seen them go in, of that she was sure. She shook her head as if to clear it. She was desperately tired, both mentally and physically. Was she mad? There was only one way to find out, and that was to search the hut herself.

She waited until the light from the gas lamp Kenneth was carrying had faded, then, taking a deep breath, she gingerly pushed the broken door with one hand while holding it upright with the other, and peered in. The room was pitch black, the only light was a thin stream from the moon, but it wasn't enough to enable her to see into the shack. Feeling a little foolish, and on edge in case Kenneth was lurking somewhere in the woods, she called out softly, 'Molly? Molly, are yer in there, love?'

Silence greeted her. Then she heard a movement and, encouraged by the sound she called again, 'Molly? You there, mate? Don't be frightened, I've come ter take yer back 'ome.'

The sound came again, and this time Agnes looked in the direction of the source. Realising she would have to enter the hut Agnes moved the door away from the entrance, propping it up against the inner wall. With the door removed, the thin stream of light from the full moon dimly illuminated the interior. It was very faint, but it was enough to see the shadowy figure of a small form hunched up in a ball in a chair.

'Molly?' Agnes whispered. 'It's all right, love. I ain't gonna hurt yer,' she repeated, realising the child was probably too frightened to answer. 'Don't be scared, Molly, I'm 'ere ter 'elp yer.'

The huddled form sprang to life and ran towards her. Even in the dim light Agnes saw the elfin face light up with relief at the sight of her, and swallowed hard. She couldn't remember the last time anyone had been so pleased to see her. Then reality set in, and with it the fear came flooding back. There was no time for pleasantries. Kenneth could be playing a cruel trick on the child, pretending to leave and then return, hoping to catch her out in some minor misdemeanour. It was just the sort of thing he was capable of.

'Come on, love. There's no time for talking, we've gotta get outta 'ere before that wicked bas— man comes back. Quickly now . . . Molly! Are yer listening ter me?'

But Molly, her initial joy over and terrified into submission by her abductor, afraid this lady was a friend of his, trying to trick her, stayed where she was. Reading her mind, and knowing time was of the essence, Agnes sprang forward and grabbed the child by the hand, pulling her across the small space of floor. Within minutes they were in the forest and Molly stopped struggling and gripped Agnes' hand tightly for fear the lady would let go of her and leave her alone in the frightening darkness of the forest.

With only the watery light of the moon to guide them the pair stumbled blindly through the woods until Agnes decided they were far enough away from the hut to stop and rest. Gasping for breath she squeezed the tiny hand holding hers so trustingly now and said, 'It's all right, love, I think we're safe enough now. But we ain't gonna be able to find our way outta this place till morning. 'Ere, let's sit down and 'ave a rest and a natter.'

Sinking onto the damp grass, the child cuddled by her side, Agnes talked rapidly, trying to put the girl's mind at ease. 'I know your name, but yer don't know mine, so I'll introduce meself. My name's Agnes, I know yer brother Micky . . .'

Instantly she felt the child's hand attempt to pull

away from hers, and with a sinking heart she realised why. Keeping her voice light she continued, 'Oh, I know what Micky's said about me. That I was a miserable old cow that was always 'aving a go at 'im, am I right?' The small hand stilled, encouraging Agnes to go on. 'He was right an' all. I am a miserable old cow, but I ain't wicked, not like that nasty man. And when yer went missing I tried me best ter 'elp find yer. That's why I'm 'ere. I followed Kenn— that man what snatched yer,' she quickly corrected herself. It wouldn't do to let the child know that she knew him by name. 'What we'll do is cuddle up ter keep warm, and wait fer morning, 'cos we'll only get lost if we try ter find our way out in the dark. Oh, I can't wait ter see Micky's face when he sees yer . . .'

The girl jumped in her arms. 'Micky's alive? He ain't dead then?'

Pulling her closer Agnes swallowed the lump that had formed in her throat. ''Course he ain't dead, yer silly thing. Why, he's been out walking the streets since yer went missing, half outta 'is mind he's been with worry. He's been staying with Ted Parker an' his mum. I expect he's told yer all about them, ain't he?'

Agnes felt Molly's head nod against her shoulder and her slim frame slump with relief at the news her brother was alive and well.

For a time there was silence between them, then, Molly, her voice low and trembling whispered, 'What about Mrs Knight, Sadie's friend? The . . . the bad man hurt her. She . . . she was lying on . . . on the floor and there was . . . was blo— blood all over her. She's gonna be al— all right, ain't she?'

Agnes tightened her hold on the shivering girl and leant her chin on the blonde head. She'd overheard John Smith telling Ted the woman was dead, and Stokes was now wanted for murder, but she couldn't tell the child that, not after what she'd been through. As the thought entered her mind Agnes' stomach lurched. Had she been in time? Kenneth had had the girl alone for hours. Dear God! If he'd harmed Molly while she'd been hiding, thinking only of her own skin, she'd never forgive herself. She had to ask, but she'd have to go careful.

Clearing her throat she said, 'I don't know, love, we'll 'ave ter wait and find out.' Again silence descended on them as Agnes tried to work out how to phase the question she had to ask. Keeping her voice casual she asked, 'That nasty man. Did . . . did he do anything to yer? I mean did he hurt yer?'

She waited with bated breath for the girl to answer.

'No . . . Well, he frightened me, and . . . and he said he was gonna 'urt me if I didn't do like he told me. And he was really angry 'cos I . . . I messed meself. But I couldn't 'elp it . . .' Her voice trailed off tiredly.

'So he never sort of . . . yer know, did anything yer didn't like . . .'

Stifling a yawn, Molly answered softly, ''Course he did. He took me away from Micky and Sadie. An' I wanna go back ter me brother, then we can all live together.'

In the darkness Agnes breathed a sigh of relief. She felt as if a great weight had been lifted from her shoulders. At last, after all these years, she had finally done something right. As for Micky and Molly going to live with this Sadie character, whoever she was. Well! Ted Parker would have something to say about that – and Ellen too for that matter.

'Tell yer what, love. You try and get some sleep, yer ain't got nothing ter worry about now. I'll look after yer, I promise.'

There was no answer. The girl, feeling safe in Agnes' arms, had already fallen asleep. Carefully taking off her shawl, Agnes wrapped it around the scantily clad child. Without the woollen garment Agnes shivered, but she welcomed the coldness of the night. It would help to keep her awake.

Kenneth had only walked for ten minutes before he changed his mind about seeking out the doctor's help. The pain in his hand had momentarily clouded his judgement. Then he remembered the search party would be back at first light, and even though they had already questioned everyone in the vicinity, there was no knowing if they would do the same tomorrow. In spite of the throbbing of his hand he couldn't take the chance of the police asking questions again. And if they knocked on the retired doctor's door and he told them about a man visiting him with a cut hand, the game would be up. Cursing his stupidity he quickly turned on his heel and headed back to the hut, the gas lamp illuminating his path. It was only a cut, another few hours wasn't going to make any difference. As long as he kept it clean, it should heal by itself in a few days. In the meantime he had much more pleasant pursuits to look forward to. His face illuminated by the lamp was one of pure evil.

His hand forgotten now, he quickened his pace. As he approached the hut he saw at once that the door, which he had closed, was now gone leaving the hut wide open. With a loud cry that bordered on a scream he ran forward, only to come to a dead stop. He didn't have to look round the two-room abode to know that Molly, that little bitch, had run off. Like a madman he paced the room, pulling at his hair in rage and disbelief. None of his previous children had ever had the courage to disobey him. He had held them prisoners, not only by physical force, but by mental intimidation. Who would have thought that Molly Masters, that terrified, cowed little chit of a girl, would have the nerve to disobey him? Unable to sit still he continued to pace back and forth around the confined space, his features contorted with rage.

Gradually his anger abated, his steps slowing as he began to think more rationally. What was he worried about? She couldn't get very far, could she? Right now she was probably lost, stumbling around in the dark, terrified out of her wits. He would lay bets that she would welcome even his presence in her predicament. All he had to do was wait until about five. The search party wouldn't be back until six, six-thirty at the latest. She couldn't be more than a fifteen-minute walk away, and by five she'd be asleep with exhaustion. He knew the forest like the back of his hand; he'd find her long before anyone else turned up. Satisfied in his mind he hadn't lost her, he settled back in the chair, a smirk on his lips.

'Just you wait, you little cow. You'll pay dearly for putting me to all this trouble, you wait and see.'

Agnes awoke with a start, unable to believe she'd fallen asleep. Dawn was just beginning to break, and with it their last chance to escape from the forest and the man who had turned her world upside down, and nearly ruined Molly Masters' into the bargain. Gently shaking the child awake Agnes said softly, 'Come on, love. Time to get going.'

Molly woke instantly, her body stiffening, then relaxing as she realised she was safe.

'That's a good girl.' Agnes, already on her feet, helped Molly to hers. 'Now listen, love, I ain't got a clue where we are, so we'll just 'ave ter walk round till the police come back. We might get lucky and find our way ter the road, but I wouldn't like ter bet on it. What we've gotta do is keep quiet. No talking or making any more noise than we 'ave to, 'cos that man is gonna be looking fer yer. Now, now . . .' Agnes gave the little girl's shoulders a reassuring hug, as Molly jerked violently at the mention of the 'nasty man'. 'He ain't gonna get yer, I won't let 'im. Besides, he doesn't know I'm with yer, does he? He thinks you're on yer own. So he's gonna be cocky, ain't he? Well, the laugh's gonna be on him. Now let's get going, and remember . . .' She gave a conspirational wink, 'Keep quiet, and yer ears open, and before yer know it, this place'll be crawling with coppers.'

'All right, lady,' Molly whispered. 'An' then I'll see

Micky and Sadie, an' Mrs Knight and Billy and Charlie. They're me friends; I'll be quiet now.' She smiled up at Agnes and squeezed her hand.

Agnes' heart missed a beat at Molly's words, but now wasn't the time to tell the child the truth. Instead she gripped the tiny hand tighter and began to creep slowly through the forest.

Sadie sat by Lily's bedside, her warm fingers clasped around the cold hand of her friend. She had been sitting in the same spot for hours. Her eyes, red from crying, were dry now, but the pain inside her wouldn't go away. Because of her, Lily, her only friend, was dead, and her children left on their own.

Her body, stiff from sitting in the same position for so long, now moved as a hand came to rest gently on her shoulder.

'Why don't you go home, love? There's nothing you can do here. You'll make yourself ill. You've had nothing to eat or drink since you came in and . . .' The nurse's words trailed off as Sadie turned and looked up at her and the anguish mirrored in the red-rimmed eyes caused the nurse to lower her gaze. She had been a nurse for over twenty years and been through the same sad ordeal more times than she could remember, but it never got any easier to deal with someone who had lost someone close. Be it a mother, brother, husband or wife, or in this case, a dear friend, the pain experienced by the people left behind to grieve never ceased to create a feeling of inadequacy inside her.

Like a woman twice her age Sadie rose unsteadily

to her feet. Brushing the kindly nurse gently to one side she said solemnly, 'Thank you fer all yer kindness, Nurse. I appreciate it, even though I never said so at the time. I'll be off now, I've gotta see ter Lily's boys like I promised.'

The nurse looked at the tired woman with sympathy. 'Don't do anything rash, dear. I know you promised to take care of your friend's children, but I've witnessed many a deathbed promise, and while the person concerned genuinely means to keep that promise, it isn't always possible to keep that vow made under the most distressing of circumstances. So don't feel too bad if you change your mind. Taking on two children, especially children who are no relation to you, could be very difficult.'

At the nurse's words, Sadie sprang into life. 'Thanks fer the advice, Nurse, but Lily was me friend. More ter the point, she's dead because of me. That's something I'm gonna 'ave ter live with fer the rest of me life. The least I can do is ter look after 'er boys, I owe her that much. Besides, I never make a promise I can't keep.' Gathering up her strength she continued firmly, 'Now then, where's the boys? Or should I say my boys, 'cos that's what they are now.'

The nurse stepped to one side, her expression worried. 'It might not be that simple, dear. You can't just take them, you know. You'll have to go through the authorities.' Seeing the look of anger flash over Sadie's face, the nurse, who was used to irate patients and their families, continued in a calm voice. 'It's no good you looking at me like that, I don't make the rules. If you were a relative it would be a different matter entirely.' She paused, a conspiratorial expression coming into her eyes. 'Then again, you could be their aunt for all anyone knows, or a cousin perhaps. If that's so, then the authorities will be only too pleased to wash their hands of them. There are enough homeless children roaming the streets as it is. I'm sure they would be only too pleased to be spared the time and expense of placing them in the workhouse. You'd have to fill in a form, of course, stating your relationship to the children, but that's merely a formality. The authorities rarely check up on the relevant documents, they're much too busy elsewhere.' Arching her eyebrows the nurse gazed expectantly at Sadie.

Immediately picking up on the nurse's meaning Sadie bristled. 'Well, of course I'm their auntie. I wouldn't saddle meself with two kids if I didn't 'ave to, would I? You give me that form ter fill in then take me to me nephews, wherever you've put them ... Only ...'

'Yes, dear?'

A wave of embarrassment swept over Sadie, then she shook off the feeling angrily. This was no time for false pride. Her chin thrust out defiantly she said tersely, 'I can't read or write. Well, not properly.'

The nurse's face relaxed. 'Oh, is that all? You come with me, dear, and we'll fill in the form together, if that's all right with you?'

Sadie nodded, a wave of gratitude flooding through her tired body and with it a sudden burst of fresh emotion. As she went to follow the uniformed figure she said in a shaking voice and on the point of tears,

"Ang on a minute, Nurse. Could . . . could I 'ave a bit of time with me mate? Just . . . just ter say good—goodbye properly.'

When the nurse left the ward Sadie stood for a few minutes before approaching her friend for the last time. Leaning over the still figure, the wrapped bundle of her dead baby placed in her lifeless arms, Sadie kissed Lily on the forehead, and with that simple act fresh tears spilled from her reddened eyes.

'Goodbye, mate. I'm gonna miss yer. But I'll take care of your boys, like I promised. I probably won't be as good a mum like you was, Lil, but . . . but I'll do me best. Oh, Lil . . . Lil. I'm so . . . so sorry. Pl—please, please, Lil, forgive me. I loved yer, yer soppy cow. Only . . . only I didn't realise it till . . . till now.'

Her body began to shake with renewed grief, and though it was genuine, there was a thread of guilt tormenting her. She would keep her word to her dead friend, but she felt no affection for the Knight boys. To her they were just two scruffy kids who happened to belong to her friend. The only child she wanted, had ever wanted was Molly. Now she was gone for ever. For even if found, and Sadie prayed fervently she would be, for the alternative was unthinkable, she would never be able to keep her. If . . . no! Not if, she silently corrected herself, *when* she was found, she would be returned to her brother and would live with him and the Parkers, while she would be left with two grief-stricken, bewildered boys of whom she knew absolutely nothing. With tears blinding her vision she felt an arm go round her shoulder and let herself be led from the room. Sobbing uncontrollably her mind kept repeating over and over again, 'Oh, Molly. My sweet, sweet Molly. Be safe, my angel. Wherever you are, please be safe. I don't care if I can't have you with me like I wanted, as long as you're safe.'

CHAPTER TWENTY-FIVE

'Arthur, where have you been all night?' Ellen stood in the doorway of the bedroom tying her red dressing gown tighter around her waist, her long hair falling loosely around her face and shoulders.

The sight of her brought an ache of pain and loneliness in Arthur such as he'd never felt. He had stayed at the Hope and Anchor until closing time, something he had never done before.

But no matter how much he had drunk, his mind had remained clear. After leaving the pub he had wandered the streets for hours trying to convince himself that he and Ellen would somehow weather the storm that had entered their lives in the shape of Ted Parker. During those dark hours he had done a lot of soul searching, and he hadn't liked what he'd seen. But he had tried to convince himself that he had always acted out of chivalry. Now, seeing her looking so young, so fresh, a flash of clarity came to him. Ellen didn't belong to him – she never had and never would. Agnes had been right when she'd accused him of marrying the young girl for his own selfish reasons, instead of adopting her, as any decent man with true honourable intentions would have done. But whatever happened in the future he would still have the memories of the time they had spent together. They had been the happiest days of his life and he would treasure them always. Now he had to undo the harm he had caused and let Ellen go while she still had some affection for him. The fact that he had already lost her was clear, but despite that awful night when he had forced himself on her, a memory that had tormented him day and night, Ellen might still stay with him out of kindness and some sort of misguided loyalty – she was that kind of woman, a rarity in this day and age. But, oh God! It would be the hardest thing he'd ever had to do in his life. Afraid his habitual weakness would let him down, he began his rehearsed words before he changed his mind.

Clearing his throat gruffly he began buttoning up his coat again, careful to avoid Ellen's searching stare. 'I'm joining the search party for young Molly. It was the talk of the pub last night, and made me realise how selfish I've been. I should have been thinking of the missing child, instead of my own feelings – but then that's what I've always done, think about myself.' Keeping his face averted he continued. 'Oh, I never did it deliberately, but nevertheless I did. I've been a selfish beggar, but it's not too late to rectify the harm I've done, especially to you ... No, don't, Ellen, let me finish,' he said quickly as he heard the rustle of

327

her slippered feet approaching. 'This is hard enough as it is. I'm afraid that if I look at you, I'll change my mind, so just stay quiet and listen, please.'

He sensed rather than saw Ellen stop in her tracks, but she was near enough for him to smell the subtle perfume she always wore, and it was nearly the undoing of him. Buttoning and unbuttoning his coat, his fingers shaking with nerves he said, 'I should never have married you, Ellen. It wasn't fair on you. The plain truth is, I took advantage of a vulnerable, innocent young girl. I even convinced myself I was acting like some kind of knight in shining armour.' He gave a nervous laugh. 'Can you imagine a more ludicrous image? Agnes saw right through me, and my selfish motives, and she was right.' He shook his head slowly as his guilty conscience continued to torment him.

'She's another one I hurt. I never intended to, but I did. It's like I've been wearing blinkers for most of my life, but walking the streets at night, alone, with no distractions, it was as if those blinkers were suddenly lifted, and I saw myself as if for the first time. Oh, I don't mean my weakness and lack of gumption, I've always known that. Maybe that was part of my reason for wanting to make you my wife. I thought people might look on me with some respect for marrying a young, pretty girl. But I was wrong again. They were laughing at me behind my back all the time. Probably making bets on how long it would be before you came to your senses and walked out on me. Well, I can't right the wrong I did Agnes, but I can you.' Now he did look at Ellen. She was standing as still as a statue, her hands holding the neck of her dressing gown together. 'I heard what Ted Parker said that night, about you being able to get an annulment on the grounds that the marriage hadn't been consummated, and he was right, though I wouldn't have thought he would know of such legal matters. But that's beside the point. We can't do anything about it now, not while Micky's sister is still missing, but once she's found, we can start putting the wheels in motion to getting the marriage annulled.'

As his words sank in Ellen stammered, 'But . . . but, Arthur, that isn't true, we . . .'

Raising his hand Arthur said quietly. 'What happened that night is between you and me, and I for one certainly don't want my despicable action becoming public knowledge. I know there's been gossip, started no doubt by Agnes, but like I said, only we know the real truth. So what do you say, Ellen? I'm giving you the opportunity to leave me, I'm letting you go, love. But you'd better make your mind up quickly, because . . . I don't know if I'm strong enough to . . . to . . .'

In spite of his valiant efforts to stay in control, his voice cracked and tears stung the back of his eyes. Desperate not to let Ellen see his distress he made for the door. Swallowing hard he said huskily, 'I'd best be off. The search party is gathering outside Hackney police station at six o'clock, I don't want to miss them. I don't know what time I'll be back. Perhaps it would be better if the shop remains closed today. I'm sure people will understand why. Goodbye, Ellen.'

Before Ellen could speak Arthur was gone. Her legs shaking, Ellen sank down gratefully onto the first chair she came to, her mind hardly daring to believe what her ears had heard. She was free. It was what she had wanted since the first time she had realised she was in love with Ted, so why wasn't she feeling any joy? Why did she feel like crying instead? Lifting her eyes to the closed door she whispered, 'Oh, Arthur. Poor, poor Arthur. I'm sorry.'

Yet even as she spoke the words, a feeling of relief and elation flooded over her. Soon she would be a free woman. The pathway to a life with Ted had been cleared. But how could she feel these emotions when young Molly was still missing? Her mind in turmoil, she crept into the bedroom and looked in on the sleeping boy. The extra sleeping draught had done the trick. Carefully she climbed onto the double bed and put her arm around the thin shoulders affectionately. Laying her head against Micky's back she closed her eyes and hugged the young boy with all the fierce, protective love a mother would feel for a son.

Creeping as silently as possible Agnes led Molly through the mass of trees that seemed to close in on them no matter which way they went. Agnes had been sure she would remember the way she had come in once the dawn broke, but she was wrong. She was hopelessly lost, but on no account must the child know they were probably going round in circles. Every so often Agnes would stop and give the little girl a reassuring cuddle, as much for her own benefit as for the child's. Grimly Agnes listened in hope for the sound of raised voices and trampling feet, but there was nothing apart from the birds twittering and the occasional rustle of a small animal scrambling through the undergrowth. At first both woman and child had jumped at the slightest sound, but now, after nearly an hour, they had become used to the noises of the forest. Stopping for a rest Agnes leant against one of the many oak trees that populated the woods keeping Molly tight by her side. If only she had some way to tell the time. It seemed to have been light for well over an hour now, and still there was no sight or sound of the search party. Surely they'd be here soon. She couldn't keep going on the way they had been. For all she knew they might be heading further into the forest, rather than out of it. The best thing would be to stay where they were and wait to be rescued.

Besides, the child was nearly dead on her feet. Not that she had complained, the poor little love. There weren't many children of her age who could be so brave in the circumstances, not after what she had been through. A rush of affection flowed through Agnes as she looked down at the pretty, heart-shaped face – a feeling that was quickly replaced by guilt as she remembered that it was she who had helped that evil bastard get his hands on her. Then her head came up defiantly as she tried to justify herself. All right, so she had been stupid enough to play into Kenneth's hands, but he himself had been thwarted by the intervention of the woman called Sadie, the woman Molly had spoken about during their seemingly endless trek.

Agnes could still feel Kenneth's hands round her throat when he'd discovered the child gone, thinking she had had some part in the removal of his intended prey. Sinking down onto the grass, she cradled Molly in her lap, her thoughts turning to the other woman Molly had spoken of with affection, Lily Knight, the woman Kenneth had murdered, together with her unborn baby. Her only comfort now was the knowledge that, as John Smith had said, the man she had known as Kenneth Wells would hang for his crimes.

In spite of her thoughts she remained alert for any unusual sounds, but as time passed and with it the undoubted arrival of the search party got closer, Agnes began to relax a little. So when she heard a rustle she didn't stir, thinking it to be yet another wild animal running about in its natural habitat – until Molly let out a high, piercing scream. Too late Agnes tried to rise, only to be knocked down by a heavy clenched fist to her forehead. Stunned she lay still, unable to move, her vision blinded momentarily by the cruel blow. But she could still hear, and the words, spoken by the familiar and now hated voice, chilled her to the very bones of her body.

'You stupid, ignorant old hag. Did you really think you could get the better of me?' He let out a laugh that to Agnes' fuddled mind sounded on the verge of hysteria. 'I should have known the kid wouldn't have the nerve to make a run for it without help. But I never thought it would be you. Did you really think you'd get one over on me? Better people than you have tried to outwit me and failed. I've been caught, oh, yes, I'll grant you that, but there was never enough evidence to keep me in jail for long. But those days are over. They'll never catch me again.' He was so close Agnes could smell his sour breath. 'And I'll tell you why, seeing as you won't be able to pass on the information, because I'm going to kill you, just like I killed that other slag who tried to keep me from my Molly.' He let out a high-pitched laugh. 'You know what's so funny, Agnes? Well, I'll tell you. Molly and me were in that hut all along. I heard the so-called search party break down the door, all full of themselves thinking they'd cornered me, and what did they find? Nothing, absolutely nothing. And this is the best part. You listening, you pathetic old cow?'

Agnes' head was beginning to clear but she remained inert, biding her time, hoping to lure Kenneth into a false sense of security. For if he thought she was incapable of movement there was a chance, a slim chance, but a chance all the same, that she might be able to catch him unaware, long enough to let Molly escape. Her heart leapt in fright as she realised she hadn't heard any sound from Molly since that awful scream. But Kenneth was still talking.

'They didn't find me because I was underneath the hut in the basement. Yeah, that's right, that run-down old hut actually has a basement. But no one will ever find it. Who would think of looking for it in a dilapidated old hut? I don't know how it came to be there, perhaps the hut was built over it, but who cares? I only found it by chance, and I've hidden it well. And now, my pitiful old friend, it's time to say goodbye. Time's getting on, and I don't intend to be out in the open when the good people of the East End and the coppers start arriving.'

Agnes was fully conscious now, still dizzy, but alert to the situation. Opening her eyes she saw the madness in his eyes, eyes that widened in shock as

Agnes grabbed hold of his coat and screamed at the top of her voice, 'Run, Molly. Run . . . run, sweetheart.'

Taken off guard, Kenneth relaxed his hold on Molly, but the terrified child remained rooted to the spot, as she had on seeing Lily Knight's blood-soaked body.

Then Agnes screamed again, 'Molly, love. Run . . . Please, run . . . run.'

And this time Molly did as she was bid. Stumbling and running blindly she ran sobbing, not knowing where she was going, expecting the nasty man to catch her at any minute.

Seeing Molly run gave Agnes a strength she didn't know she possessed, a strength brought about by sheer desperation and a desire to save the life of a child she hardly knew. As she continued to wrestle with Stokes, she saw out of the corner of her eye that his right hand was bandaged and bloodstained, and the sight gave her fresh hope.

So that was why she had managed to hold him at bay for so long: he had the use of only one hand. Twisting and turning she managed to bring up her knee, ramming it with all her remaining strength into his groin. As her knee found its mark, Kenneth let out a scream of pain and rage, but Agnes wasn't finished yet. As Stokes reeled back, she grabbed his injured hand and savagely ground it into the dirt beneath the grass. Almost out of his head with pain Kenneth lashed out with his good hand, catching Agnes a crushing blow under her chin. Her head jolted back before crashing onto a large, sharp stone.

Kenneth watched as Agnes' body jerked once then lay still.

Cursing and doubled up in pain he was about to make sure she was dead when he heard shouts and the pounding of men's boots approaching. Still racked with pain he gave Agnes' inert body one last savage kick before heading back to the hut, and safety. He knew Molly was now lost to him for ever, but there were plenty more Mollys in the world. He doubted she would tell anyone about the basement. Even if she did, who would believe her? They'd likely put any such tale down to childish hysteria, particularly when they didn't find it. At the very worst the police might search the hut again, but it would be a perfunctory procedure. And the only other person who knew was Agnes, and he was sure she wouldn't be doing any talking. A groan of pain burst from his lips as he staggered back to the hut. Ten minutes later he was safely settled down in the basement, confident his hideout would never be discovered.

The pain in his groin was easing, but his hand was throbbing badly. Glancing down at the dried blood and dirt that streaked the bandage he cursed profusely. That old cow had reopened the wound, and rubbed dirt into it. Well, she wouldn't be doing any more harm now, would she? His glee was shortlived as he prised the linen cloth away from the wound, for it had stuck deep. It was just as well he had furnished the basement with creature comforts. Finding a bottle of brandy he took a deep swallow, then another to dull the pain before redressing the wound. Scrutinising the injury closely he sighed with relief. It looked clean, and it had stopped bleeding.

A loud noise brought his head upwards. So they were back, were they? Well, let them search the hut as long as they liked, he could stay down here for days, weeks even, if the worst came to the worst. He had enough food and drink to last him that long. Taking the brandy bottle with him he lay down on the double mattress and raised the bottle. 'Cheers, lads. You work your arses off. I'm quite comfortable where I am,' he said mockingly before finishing off the remainder of the brandy and falling into a deep sleep.

Molly heard the men as they entered the forest. Following the sounds of the deep voices she stumbled across Agnes. Sobbing with relief at finding the nice lady she threw herself across the still body crying, 'Wake up, lady. The policemen are here. Wake up, lady, please, wake up.'

She was still trying to stir Agnes when Ted and John, followed closely by four other men, came across them. With a loud shout of triumph Ted bounded forward, scooping Molly up into his arms, holding the dishevelled, small body tight against his chest. Then he looked down at Agnes, his lips curling in disgust. Rounding on John he snarled, 'I told yer she was in on it, but yer wouldn't 'ave it, would yer?'

Before John could answer, Ted, still holding Molly protectively with one arm, stooped and grabbed the inert figure with his free hand.

'Come on, yer wicked old bitch. Get up and face the music.' When the figure stayed silent Ted pulled at her arm roughly. 'Stop messing about, yer ain't fooling no one . . .' Then he staggered back as the fragile figure in his arms began to beat at his face and neck with clenched fists.

'Stop it! Leave her alone. She ain't done nothing wrong. She saved me from the nasty man. She's a nice lady, she is, she is. An' she's me friend. The nasty man found us, an' . . . an' he tried ter 'urt her like he 'urt Mrs Knight. But she hit him an' told me ter run, so . . . so I did. Then I 'eard yer coming, just like she said yer would. Only the nasty man must 'ave 'urt her bad, 'cos she won't wake up . . . she won't wake up . . .' She broke off sobbing and threw her arms tight around Ted's neck crying, 'Make 'er wake up, Mister. Make 'er better, please, make 'er better.'

Ted looked helplessly at John Smith, and the uniformed man was quick to notice the look was threaded heavily with guilt.

'You get her out of here, I'll send one of the men for an ambulance cart. Because in case you haven't noticed, Agnes is badly injured.' His voice was heavy with sarcasm, which wasn't lost on Ted.

Nodding dumbly he pressed his face against the blonde head nestled on his shoulder. 'Yeah, all right.' He went to walk away then stopped. Looking to where Johnny was now kneeling beside Agnes he said, 'I'm sorry. Yer was right all along, I . . .'

John didn't even look up as he barked, 'Just get the child away from here.' Then, ignoring Ted, he shouted to the waiting men, 'Spread out. He can't be far away.' Instantly the men sprang into action, their faces beaming with relief that the child had been found. As Ted walked towards the edge of the forest to where police wagons were waiting, he heard a resounding cheer echo through the forest as word quickly spread that the little girl had been found safe, and every man he passed patted him on the back or shoulder.

Ted acknowledged the men's camaraderie and walked on. The only thing on his mind was to get Molly back to her brother as soon as possible. But mixed with his elation at finding Molly there was a deep feeling of guilt for the contemptible way he had treated Agnes.

He was nearing the roadway when he came face to face with Arthur. 'Thank God!' cried Arthur. Then he smiled at Ted. 'Take her home, Ted. Ellen's waiting for you, for you both. I'll stay here and help in the search to find Stokes.' Then he did something Ted wasn't expecting: Arthur put out his hand in friend-ship, and Ted took it.

They gripped hands tightly and looked deep into each other's eyes – and what Ted saw there said more than any words could.

Then Arthur was gone, marching into the forest with three other men. Ted watched until they disappeared from view before taking Molly to one of the waiting police wagons.

CHAPTER TWENTY-SIX

As the police wagon made its way back to Hackney more and more people began to come out of their homes to watch its progress, proving beyond question the unequalled validity of the East End grapevine. And the reception they received couldn't have been more tumultuous than if the Queen herself was riding amongst them. Ted and the constable driving the wagon found themselves the heroes of the hour, and, despite their best efforts, neither man could stop his wide, soppy grin. Molly, on the other hand, seemed oblivious of the attention she was receiving; the only thought in her mind was seeing her brother again. Despite Ted's assurances that Micky was waiting for her, Molly wouldn't believe it until she saw him with her own eyes. Being possessed of a kind nature she couldn't help but think of the two ladies who had tried to help her and been hurt in the process, but her prime concern was to see Micky. To hear his voice again, even if he started to tease her, or even shout at her, although Micky had rarely shouted at her. When the wagon stopped outside a bakery she looked up at Ted, puzzled.

'Why we stopping 'ere, Mister? The lady . . . I mean Agnes, said Micky was staying with you an' yer mum. You don't live 'ere.' Squirming in Ted's grasp Molly cried in alarm, 'Yer've been lying ter me, ain't yer? And that old lady what 'elped me get away from the nasty man. Yer've both been lying ter me. Something's 'appened ter him, ain't it? That's why 'e didn't come back fer me that night, 'cos he couldn't . . .'

Ted easily caught hold of the flailing arms, saying warmly, 'We ain't been lying ter yer, love, honest. He was staying with me and Mum, but then he decided he wanted ter be with Ellen, you know, the lady that Micky used ter work fer?'

But Molly was no longer listening or struggling. Instead her eyes as wide as saucers stared past him to the alley that ran down the back of the bakery. Then, with an ear-splitting scream that caused Ted to flinch, she shouted, 'Micky!'

Ted's head swivelled on his shoulders as he followed her line of sight, and there, looking incongruous and pitiful, clothed in one of Ted's nightshirts that hung down to the boy's ankles, stood Micky, a look of disbelief on his face, as he stared back at the girl he had thought he'd never see again. Beside him, her hand on his shoulder, stood a smiling Ellen, looking as though she was trying her hardest not to let her emotions get the better of her. But, like Ted and the young constable, she couldn't stop the trembling of her lips, nor the tears of joy that were slowly rolling down her cheeks.

Then Micky was half running, half stumbling, as he ran to his sister. Molly had already jumped down from the wagon and ran, her little legs pumping furiously as she raced towards her brother's outstretched arms.

'Molly . . . Oh, Moll, I thought yer was dead.' Micky's voice shook as Molly propelled herself into his arms, the impact of her body catching the still drowsy Micky off balance. But Molly hung onto his neck for dear life, and down the two of them went, then lay on the bumpy, cold cobbles, holding each other tight, afraid to let go for fear that someone or something would separate them again.

More people were still spilling out onto the streets, mainly the women, for their menfolk were out with the search party, and on each of their faces was the relief and joy that only a mother could feel for the safe return of a child, any child. The young constable who had driven Molly and Ted home saw the crowd begin to gather and quickly took control.

'I think we should get 'em indoors, Sir.' Jerking his head towards the groups of women heading their way he said, 'They mean well, but under the circumstances it'd be better if the children could spend some time alone together before facing . . .'

His words were rudely cut off as a man wearing an overcoat, already busily scribbling on a large pad of paper, tried to pass them, but the constable blocked his path. 'Now, now, Sir. Leave the youngsters in peace, they've been through enough without being pestered by you lot.'

341

But the journalist wasn't to be put off so easily. Here was the story of a lifetime, and he was determined to get first-hand information and interviews before any of his rivals turned up.

'Come on, mate. Just a few words with the kids. It ain't often stories like these 'ave an 'appy ending.'

'I said no, and I mean no. You'll have plenty of time later to get your story. Right now they need a doctor not a nosy reporter badgering them with a load of questions . . . Hey, you there.'

A loud bang and puff of smoke caught the constable's attention. Muttering angrily he headed towards the man about to take another photograph of the children still locked together on the ground. It was a poignant sight, and one that would earn the photographer a good deal of money. He was preparing to take another one when the uniformed man blocked his path.

With the policeman's attention diverted elsewhere the reporter grinned and started towards the alley.

'No yer don't, mate.' Ted swung the man around pushing him backwards.

'Now, 'ang on a minute,' the man protested, then stopped as he stared into Ted's face. It was the face of a man not be trifled with, and the reporter knew when he was beaten. Besides, his associate had already taken a photo of the Masters children, while he himself would write the headline above it, plus a story to accompany it. He had been one of the first journalists to cover the story of the missing girl and the murder of Lily Knight, so he had more than enough information to warrant the front page of his newspaper

Throwing up his hands in defeat he grinned good naturedly. 'All right, all right. No need ter get stroppy.' Tipping his hat to the back of his head he said, 'I know when I've met me match. You'd better hurry up and get the pair of 'em indoors before the rest of the bloodhounds turn up. They're front-page news at the moment, the pair of 'em, an' yer can't keep 'em all away – as big as you are,' he laughed.

Ted smiled back. 'Don't bet on it,' he said then he was striding down the alley to the three people that needed him most at this time; two of whom he already loved, and the third . . . Ted gave a mental shrug. He didn't think he'd have much trouble in learning to love Molly Masters.

Bending down he lifted both children into his arms with ease. Then with a loving glance at Ellen he followed her indoors, kicking the door behind them with his foot, and the sound of the door closing gave him the feeling of security. Soon, very soon, their privacy would be invaded. It was only to be expected. The doctor had already been sent for. But until he arrived Ted had the children and Ellen all to himself. And he was going to make the most of that time.

For the next five days Agnes drifted in and out of consciousness, thus preventing the police from questioning her as to the whereabouts of Kenneth Stokes. The exhaustive search of Epping Forest had proved fruitless. It seemed as if the hunted man had disappeared from the face of the earth.

The only other person who might have helped them was the child, Molly Masters, but she too had had little information to help them find the man who had abducted her. It had been left to John Smith to tackle the delicate task of questioning the little girl, much to the chagrin of his inspector who had already had his nose put out of joint when the case had been taken over by Scotland Yard.

In the presence of a doctor, John had tried to get Molly to tell him where Kenneth Stokes had taken her but each of his questions had been met with a stone wall. It was as if events from the time she had been taken from Lily Knight's house until Agnes had led her to safety had been blanked from her mind. The doctor had explained to John that such cases where a child was concerned was perfectly normal. The trauma Molly had been through had left a profound and lasting effect on the little girl. The doctor had gone on to say that in his experience some people, both adult and children, had recalled unpleasant memories given time, while others never had – it all depended on the individual concerned.

Which didn't help the police at all.

At the moment the Masters children were staying at Ted's house, with Nora Parker fiercely guarding the children from prying eyes and nosy reporters, of which there were an abundance.

There was also a heavy presence of newspapermen gathered outside the Hackney hospital where Agnes still lay unconscious from the savage attack on her by Stokes.

The police were on guard outside the private room in which Agnes lay. One of the few people allowed in to sit with her was Ted Parker. It was on the fifth day as he sat by her bedside, the guilt about the way he had treated her still heavy on his mind, when her eyes opened.

Seeing Ted by her bed, Agnes' eyes widened in fear, and this alone caused Ted's stomach to churn in shame. Quick to put her mind at ease he caught hold of the frail hand lying outside the starched sheets and said gently, 'It's all right, Agnes. I ain't gonna hurt yer. I was wrong about yer, and I feel ashamed of meself when I think of the times I've gone fer yer. Johnny Smith kept telling me yer wouldn't 'ave anything ter do with the likes of Stokes, but I wouldn't listen. I should 'ave, 'cos he was right. Yer saved Molly from that pervert, an' nearly got yerself killed doing it.'

Agnes felt the tenderness in Ted's touch and voice and relaxed. She tried to speak but her lips felt as if they were glued together. With a weak movement of her head she looked at the pitcher of water on the locker by her bed. Ted saw her distress and instantly poured the liquid into a glass. Lifting Agnes' head from the pillows he held the glass to her dried, cracked lips.

Gulping eagerly at the cool water Agnes spluttered and coughed, the action causing her to screw up her eyes in pain. Ted laid her back on the pillow, his face taking on a look of genuine concern.

''Ang on, Agnes, I'll get a nurse or doctor. They've been waiting fer yer to come round.'

Agnes caught at Ted's hand.

'No, wait a minute,' she croaked painfully. 'Yer said Mo— Molly's all right?'

345

'Yeah, she's fine, Agnes. And it's all thanks ter you, yer . . .'

Impatiently Agnes squeezed Ted's hand, motioning him to be quiet.

Quickly picking up on her signal he sat down again and said earnestly, 'What is it, Agnes? You trying ter tell me something?'

Agnes nodded her head gingerly. Looking towards the closed door then back to Ted's anxious face she whispered, "Ave they found 'im?'

She didn't have to name who she was referring to. Alert now, Ted moved closer to the bed. 'No, they ain't. It's like he's vanished into thin air. But you know something, don't yer, Agnes?'

Agnes's eyes fluttered and closed, and for a heart-stopping moment Ted thought she'd fallen back into unconsciousness. Then she spoke, but her voice was so weak Ted had to lean his ear against her mouth to hear what she was trying so hard to convey.

'The hut, Ted. He's hiding in the hut.'

Deeply disappointed, Ted drew his head back, gently stroking her hand. 'Nah! They've looked there, Agnes. If he was there, he ain't now.'

Again Agnes became agitated, her grip on Ted's hand tightening.

"Ere, don't go upsetting yerself, love. It ain't your fault, yer . . .'

Desperate to make herself heard Agnes motioned for Ted to come closer. Again laying his ear against her mouth he listened, humouring her as she spoke disjointedly. Then he sat bolt upright as her words sank in.

'A basement! Nah, there can't be. The coppers would've found it by now if there was one. They've had the place upside down, they . . .'

'No, it's there . . . he . . . he told me.' Agnes swallowed painfully. 'More water, please, Ted.'

Ted moved like lightning to get the water. If Agnes was telling the truth it would explain a lot of things. But more important still, if Stokes was hiding in a basement beneath the hut in the forest, he wanted to be the one to find him.

Her thirst quenched, Agnes tried once more to make Ted believe her. 'Thanks, Ted.' Her claw-like hand gripped his, and Ted didn't flinch at her touch, as he would have in the past. 'Listen . . . I ain't . . . ain't going off me 'ead. He thought he was gonna kill me, otherwise he'd never 'ave let me in on his little secret. You go there, Ted. You go and look. Don't . . . don't tell the law . . . just go and see if he's still there.' Her eyes nearly closed, her grip on his hand loosening, she pleaded, 'Yer know what I mean, Ted?'

Ted nodded grimly. Yes! He understood all right.

Leaning over her he did something he never thought he would: he kissed Agnes on the forehead, and the gesture was made with true affection and gratitude.

At that moment the doctor entered the room followed by John Smith. 'The policeman on guard said he thought he heard voices. Has she come round?'

Ted stood up, his hand still holding Agnes'. 'Yeah, she did. But she didn't make much sense. Still, it's a good sign, ain't it?' The hand in his relaxed as Agnes, drifting back into sleep, realised Ted had understood her message.

John looked Ted straight in the eye. 'You sure she didn't say anything – like where we could find Stokes?'

Ted shook his head. 'Nah! Sorry, Officer. Like I said, she didn't make much sense. I couldn't understand what she was trying ter say.' Adopting a casual manner he grinned saying, 'Anyway I gotta get off, I've got a business ter run – see ya.'

John Smith watched Ted go, a quizzical look in his eyes. Then he shrugged. If Ted was up to something, as an officer of the law maybe it was best he didn't know about it.

Kenneth Stokes lay on the mattress, his face and body contorted in agony, leaving him as helpless as a newborn baby. Yet despite the pain and fever that racked his body, his mind remained crystal clear, trying desperately to understand what was happening to him.

He remembered cleaning and changing his bandage, and drinking a bottle of brandy while listening to the heavy boots pounding above him. He had fallen asleep and woken up to find his injured hand formed into a rigid clench he had no control over. When he had tried to rise from the mattress he had felt unwell accompanied by fleeting pains in his back. Putting the symptoms down to the likelihood his wound had become infected, he had struggled to change the dressing, but even that relatively simple task had proved difficult. He didn't know if he had passed out or simply fallen asleep afterwards, but when he awoke he found himself drenched in sweat.

Reaching for a jug of water he'd put by his side he tried to sit up but found each movement tortuous. But he truly became alarmed when, after managing to pour himself a drink, he found it difficult to swallow. He had slept again, his only notion of time being his fob watch, and even this was denied him as he couldn't control his good hand to light the lamp on the table by his bed. Still, he put his illness down to a severe cold, made worse by the infection in his hand.

But on the fourth day he awoke to find his jaw, which had begun to feel stiff, had worsened to such an extent that his teeth were clenched together so tightly he could barely open his mouth. Then the spasms had started, and Stokes could lie to himself no longer. He'd always prided himself on being an intellectual man, a man who had continued to further his education even after he'd left the hallowed halls of Eton. One of his favourite pastimes was reading up on medical matters, a knowledge that had often come into use when trying to inveigle his way into the homes of ignorant parents, who were only too pleased to have a nice, generous doctor who seemed happy to help their sick children for no recompense. Now that knowledge was striking terror into the very fibre of his being.

Lockjaw.

Another spasm struck, causing the upper part of his body to arch painfully, quickly accompanied by a sudden increased pressure on his clenched teeth. When it was over Kenneth lay back sweating in pain and fear. He knew another spasm could kill him, and there was nothing he could do to help himself.

Damn that slut. If she had handed over Molly, non
of this would have happened. It wasn't him that had
picked up the knife. He'd had no choice but to protec
himself and had been stabbed in the process. Eve
then he might have been all right if that other old ha
hadn't rubbed the wounded hand in the dirt. Th
flimsy bandage hadn't been thick enough to stop th
dirt from penetrating through the inadequate cover
ing. That's what had done it, he was sure. Damn then
both to hell.

Then he heard footsteps overhead, and a spark o
hope leapt into his eyes. He no longer cared if he wa
caught. He had enough money to buy the best lawyers
If by some miracle the Knight woman was still alive
he could plead self-defence, and the same went fo
Agnes Handly. Oh! What did it matter? As long as h
was found and received medical attention.

There was still time – surely there was still time!

But would whoever was in the hut find the tra
door? The fear came flooding back. No one woul
ever find him unless they knew where to look, he'
made sure of that. Then he heard the unmistakabl
sound of the trap door opening.

Ted walked slowly around the small hut, his shar
eyes fixed firmly on the wooden floor. He had looke
under the three rugs and the wide strip of carpet i
the largest room, but had found nothing. Now h
was beginning to wonder if Agnes' mind had bee
turned by the experience she had gone through. Ye
she had seemed so sure. Sinking down onto a chai
he thought carefully. He'd bet that Agnes' mind wa

as sane as his, and if that was the case then somewhere in these small rooms a trap door lay hidden. His eyes fixed on the floor, he stared again at the strip of carpet. He'd already looked under it once, but knowing the man Stokes, he would be careful to make sure his secret hideaway wouldn't be easily found, if there was one. Getting down on his knees he looked again under the carpet, sighing and feeling he was wasting his time in going over the same ground, but he was here now and he might as well be thorough. It was tacked down in each corner but the carpet was loose and easy to look under. This time Ted ran his hand over the floorboards beneath but found nothing out of the ordinary. Leaning back on his heels Ted nipped at his bottom lip in disappointment. Nothing, absolutely nothing.

He was about to leave when he remembered Agnes' words, the desperate look in her eyes, and the surprisingly firm grip on his hand when the doctor and John Smith had entered the room. Muttering 'Oh, the hell with it,' he got down on his knees. If he had to crawl over the entire floor on his hands and knees and look at every floorboard, then that's what he would do: he owed Agnes that much. For a start he'd have that carpet up. There was nothing under it, he'd already checked, but it wouldn't do any harm to have a closer look. Not having any tool to take out the nails that were holding the carpet in place, he pulled at the rough material with both hands and was rewarded with a sudden tearing of the frayed material. Pulling the carpet back he looked at the wooden flooring. With the floor bare, Ted ran his hand again over the

351

surface the wood, not expecting to find anything bu
feeling impelled to do his best before returning tc
Agnes. Running his hand in the opposite directior
he felt a slight, almost imperceptible groove in the
flooring.

Telling himself not to get his hopes up, nonetheles:
Ted couldn't stop a growing feeling of excitemen
mounting. On closer inspection he saw what lookec
like a wooden plug blocking a circular hole. Hardl
daring to breathe Ted poked the plug with his finge
then leant back as the plug fell away to reveal a hole
His excitement mounting Ted hooked his finge
through the hole and pulled, then fell back as a larg
square of the flooring gave way. Ted had to restrair
himself from shouting his glee out loud. Even though
it was light outside, the area below the hut wa;
cloaked in darkness.

Getting to his feet Ted quickly found a gas lamp
then there followed a frustrating search for somethin;
to light it with. Then he found a box of matches ir
the empty grate. Gingerly descending the ladder Tec
started to wonder what he was getting so excitec
about. All right, so he'd found out where Stokes hac
kept Molly, and maybe others, but it was obvious by
the darkness that the man he was looking for had lon;
gone. His initial euphoria subsiding, Ted continuec
further down, then he let out a muffled shout as ar
overpowering stench hit his nostrils.

'Bleeding 'ell!' He stopped halfway down the
ladder, undecided whether or not to investigate
further, then he heard a peculiar sound coming fron
below. The unfamiliar noise reminded Ted of ar

animal grunting, and without thinking he made his way down to the bottom of the ladder. Holding his jacket over his nose Ted waved the lamp around the gloomy underground room, noting the items of furniture here were of much better quality than that above. He turned, the lamp lighting up the room, then gasped out loud as the light centred on the mattress, and the grotesque figure lying on it. Surprised and shocked, Ted inched nearer the bed, holding the lamp high so he could see better. And what he saw appalled him.

The man lay in obvious agony, his torso raised from the mattress, his head at an unnatural angle. But it was his face that shocked Ted the most, in particular the lips that were stretched wide over clenched teeth, giving the appearance of a mirthless, unnatural grin.

As if in a trance Ted approached the contorted body, his own face solemn. The stench was emanating from the incapacitated man, but such was Ted's shock at finding him here, he no longer noticed the rank, unpleasant smell.

'Are you Stokes?' Ted spoke in a clipped, brusque voice, even though he already knew the answer, if only by the quality of the man's clothing, now fouled but still that of a man of means. Besides, who else could it be? But he had to be sure.

With apparent agony the man tried to speak through his rigid, clenched teeth. 'Yeees . . . He— help me. Pl— please . . .'

Ted remained still, his face expressionless and Kenneth felt a moment of relief. Someone had found him. It didn't matter what the law would do to him, at least he'd be alive. Then he looked up into the stranger's eyes, and what he saw reflected there killed any hope of redemption.

Ted lowered the lamp and pulled a chair nearer the double bed and sat down. 'So you're the scum that snatched young Molly, an' Gawd knows 'ow many other poor little cows. Not ter mention murdering Lily Knight an' her unborn baby, just so yer could get yer 'ands on an innocent little girl. An' yer really think I'm gonna 'elp yer? You must be fucking mad.' Ted rose abruptly. Standing over the man he had grown to hate, Ted was about to speak further when Stokes' body went into another, more violent spasm, the suddenness causing Ted to stagger away from the twitching form. He waited until the spasm was over then, for the last time, looked down at the man who had caused so much pain and misery and said in a voice filled with deep loathing, 'Die, you bastard. And die hard, 'cos it's no more than a piece of filth like you deserves.'

Then he turned and climbed back up the ladder, aware that Stokes' eyes were following him with silent pleading. But Ted didn't hesitate. Stepping off the last rung of the ladder he closed the trap door, pulled the ripped carpet back into place, turned out the lamp and left the hut.

He never looked back.

Left once again in the darkness Kenneth knew he was going to die. Yet not for one moment did he think to ask forgiveness for his dreadful sins. For in his eyes, he had done nothing wrong. Another spasm attacked his weakened body, the first of many before he finally died, choking on his own tongue. And his death was exactly that which Ted had wished on him. For Kenneth Stokes took a long time to die.

CHAPTER TWENTY-SEVEN

The children were asleep. Ted had left reluctantly, by Ellen's wishes, leaving her alone with Arthur and the children. It was ten o'clock and Ellen could hardly believe all that had happened during the last five days. Cautiously she lifted the net curtain and peered down into the street, then quickly let the curtain drop.

'Still out there, are they, love?' Arthur had entered the room with two mugs of cocoa in his hands.

Ellen smiled tiredly. 'Just a few. Journalists, I expect. I feel sorry for them in a way. After all, they are only trying to make a living.' Taking one of the mugs she added, 'I don't think I'll need any rocking tonight. I'm so tired I can hardly keep my eyes open.'

Arthur grunted in reply. 'Me neither. It's a pity we couldn't find that pervert though. For all we know he might have snatched some other child while we were chasing round in circles in the forest. God! I hope not. Mind you, it was a miracle the hut was found at all, the way it was situated. Johnny reckons Stokes must have mingled with the search party. There's no other way he could have got out of those woods because, don't forget, only Johnny and a few of the older police officers know what Stokes looks like. I don't blame the police for calling off the search. It was obvious after the third day that the man was long gone. At least we got Molly back, and in time, according to the doctor, so that's something to be thankful for.'

Ellen smiled over the top of her mug. 'Yes, indeed that is something to be thankful for. To be honest I'd begun to think the worst, but Micky never gave up hope.'

An awkward silence descended on them until Arthur coughed and said, 'We should talk about the future, Ellen. I know you're worried about hurting me, but I brought it on myself, and now it's time to make amends.'

'Really, Arthur, there's no rush. It's barely been a week since Molly was found, and we've hardly had time to catch our breath.'

Arthur shook his head and, in a resigned voice, said, 'The longer we put things off, the harder it's going to be. Ted's already becoming impatient, and I can't say as I blame him. By the way . . .' He paused uncomfortably, shifting in his chair before continuing. 'I expect you've told Ted about that night, not that I'm blaming you, I'd just like to know when to expect a thrashing.'

Her face flushed, Ellen replied quietly, 'I told him

we'd been together once, but that we'd both known
it was a mistake, and decided to carry on as we had
before, in a platonic relationship. Ted agreed that that
part of our marriage would be best left between the
three of us, so you needn't worry on that score.'

Arthur gave a nervous laugh. 'Well, that's a relief
I must say. Now look, Ellen, I know you're tired, we
both are, but as I said before, we need to talk. I've
been thinking a lot these past few days and I've come
to a decision.' Reaching out he took hold of her hand
'I'm leaving the East End . . . No, don't stop me,' he
added as Ellen made to speak. 'Like I said, I've had
a lot of time to think things over and I believe it's
best for all of us if I leave.' Looking into Ellen's
shocked face Arthur saw something else mirrored in
her eyes – relief. Arthur lowered his gaze for a
moment so that Ellen wouldn't see the pain his
words were costing him. A brisk note entered his
voice as he went on. 'What I propose to do is leave
you the business, and set up somewhere else.'
Fumbling in his pocket he brought out a crumpled
letter. 'This came a couple of days ago. I would have
told you, but with all the commotion going on, it
went completely out of my head.' Unfolding the
paper he said, 'It's from Mr Bradley, you remember,
the couple we met in Southend,' he said as Ellen
looked puzzled.

'Oh, oh yes, of course, I remember. What does he
have to say? Not bad news I hope?'

'No, no, far from it. He wrote that he and his wife
were sorry we had to cut our holiday short, and he's
invited us down to stay with them in Chislehurst,

when it's convenient. I didn't pay it much attention
at first, but now it would be the perfect answer. It will
give me the chance to get away. I've already written
back explaining the situation and now I'm waiting for
a reply. Of course they may take back the invitation
when they realise it'll only be me for company.' He
laughed self-consciously. 'But I hope not. I was planning to go away, but I wasn't relishing the notion of
going somewhere strange by myself.'

He fell silent and his silence brought a wash of guilt
over Ellen. But before she could say anything Arthur
got up abruptly. 'To be brutally honest, the fact is I
just haven't the gumption to stay around once you
and Ted become common knowledge. I've been the
butt of too many jokes in my life, and I'm tired of
them. I know it will look like I'm running away, which
I am, but I'd rather they all had a good laugh at my
expense when I'm well out of earshot. At least then
I'll be able to salvage a bit of pride.'

Ellen didn't know what to say. All Arthur had said
made sense, but it wasn't fair to expect him to leave
his business and home when in essence he'd done
nothing wrong. Yet it would solve a lot of worries if
Arthur was no longer around. The selfish notion
bowed Ellen's head in shame.

'I'll give it a week, then, if I don't hear from the
Bradleys, I'll make alternative arrangements.' Arthur
was speaking again, almost rambling, to cover the
awkwardness between them. 'In the meantime I'll go
on sleeping in the spare room, speaking of which . . .'
He yawned loudly. 'I think I'll retire now, I have to
be up early in the morning. I have my customers to

think of, though I'd appreciate it if you kept my plans to yourself, and Ted of course. Then, when the time comes, I'll just slip away quietly. You'll have to take on another baker of course. Bill Cummons would be only too happy to be offered the job, and he did do a good job while we were away on holiday; that's if you want to carry on with the business. I hope you do, it's been in the family a long time. Anyway, good night, love, see you in the morning.' Stopping outside the spare room he said quietly, 'You know, Ellen, I may not have all the qualities of a man like Ted Parker, but I'm a bloody good baker.'

Ellen didn't reply, her throat was too full. Putting out the lamp she crept into her bedroom and climbed in beside Molly; Micky was sleeping on a bedroll on the floor. Since they had been reunited, they hadn't let each other out of their sight for any longer than necessary. By mutual agreement it had been decided that the children should move back in with Ellen; and though Nora had protested at first, for she had grown used to having the children with her, she had been relieved at heart. At her age she had become set in her ways, and having two children under her feet was beginning to take its toll, though not for the world would she have admitted it.

Snuggling up against Molly's warm body Ellen stared at the far wall thinking over what Arthur had proposed. If she had any loyalty at all she'd at least try and talk him out of his plans, but she wasn't going to. She would keep quiet and let Arthur go, because that's what she wanted; but she'd never have a moment's peace or experience true joy until she knew for certain that Arthur was settled and happy, and for a man of her husband's character, that could take a very long time.

The hospital room was eerily quiet, with only the swishing of the nurses' uniforms as they passed by on their way to and from the main ward. At this time of night, with most of the patients asleep, it was a peaceful place to be, a safe place that induced a feeling of security.

'I'd better be on me way, Agnes, before the Sister realises I'm still 'ere and kicks me out on me ear.' Ted patted the thin hand. 'I'll be back tomorrow.'

Agnes, trying hard to keep awake, squeezed his hand. 'You sure he's dead, Ted? I mean yer not just telling me that ter make me feel better, 'cos I'd rather know the truth.'

Ted kept hold of her fingers, replying grimly, 'Yeah, he's dead all right. If not right now, then he will be soon. No one's gonna find 'im where he is. Even if some tramp comes across the hut, whoever it is ain't gonna be looking fer a trap door in a run-down hut, are they? And Stokes ain't in no condition ter call out fer 'elp. Nah, he's a goner, so yer just rest an' get yerself better.'

In a hoarse whisper Agnes wheezed, 'An' yer don't . . . don't feel guilty . . . fer leaving 'im ter die, I mean?'

A muscle in Ted's face twitched but his voice was deadly calm as he answered. 'No, I don't. Any more than I'd regret having a rabid dog put down, though I think I'd show the dog some pity. They ain't got no control over what nature made them.' Smoothing

361

down the covers of the bed he lingered for a minute before asking, 'Agnes, will yer tell me something? It's about Arthur and Ellen. You know what went on there better than anyone else, an' I was wondering like if . . .'

Agnes' fingers scratched at the sheets in agitation. 'Don't take . . . any notice of what I said . . . about Arthur . . . forcing 'imself on Ellen. It . . . it ain't true. I was . . . just . . . just being spiteful, that's all. Just . . . just a spiteful old . . . old woman . . .'

Ted's lean frame relaxed at her words. He had heard the rumours, but had been too afraid of tackling Ellen about them for fear of what her answer would be. He hadn't trusted himself not to give Arthur a good beating if the rumours had contained any truth. Now he was glad he'd kept his own counsel, because if he hadn't, maybe Arthur wouldn't be as accommodating as he was being. Ellen had explained what had happened, but he had wanted to hear it from Agnes, just to be sure. And he had to admit it took a different kind of courage for a man to admit he had lived and slept with an attractive young woman for over two years, and never had any physical contact with her, especially when it wasn't true. Arthur could have made it hard for them to start a new life together. He could have insisted on dragging Ellen through a public divorce, but, whatever his reasons, he was making it easy for them, and for that Ted owed him a debt of gratitude. That's not to say he wasn't disappointed that Arthur had been with Ellen first, but it had happened, and in all fairness to the man, he had been married at the time. Anyway, it was a subject

362

he didn't want to dwell on. It was in the past; he had the future to look to now. A future with Ellen, Micky and Molly. He might have to wait a while, but it would be worth it in the end.

CHAPTER TWENTY-EIGHT

It was Christmas Day and the rooms above the bakery were full to bursting. Ellen and Ted had decided to have their Christmas dinner here rather than at Ted's house, which hadn't pleased Nora Parker at first, until Ellen had asked if the older woman would help her prepare and cook the large meal, professing to be out of her depth at cooking for such a large gathering. Now, as Nora basted the enormous turkey, she thought, not for the first time, that it was the strangest Christmas dinner she'd ever been to. Putting the bird back into the oven Nora wiped the sweat from her face and took a large gulp of sherry as she mentally counted the number of people she was catering for, just to make sure she hadn't left anyone out. There was Sadie and the two boys, Ellen, Ted, and Micky and Molly, plus herself and John Smith. A look of sadness flitted over her face as she recalled the memory of poor Sarah Smith. Just a bad cold, John had told her when she'd enquired after his wife. But the cold had turned into pneumonia. Within a few days Sarah was dead, leaving John shocked and grief-stricken at the suddenness with which his beloved wife had been taken from him.

That had been over two months ago, but John still hadn't come to terms with his bereavement. It had taken her, Ted and Ellen to persuade the solemn man to have his Christmas dinner with them instead of sitting alone in an empty house brooding. Taking a few steps from the kitchen she peered into the sitting room where the table was already set for the festive occasion.

'Need any 'elp, Nora?' Sadie North, dressed in a simple blue blouse and black skirt, looked at Nora hopefully. Nora understood exactly how Sadie felt and her mood softened towards the former prostitute. She and Sadie hadn't exactly hit it off at first, but were now friends, due to their association with Molly. Sadie and the Knight boys had visited frequently since Molly had come to live with her brother and Ellen, but this was the first time she and the boys had been invited to what was essentially a family occasion, and it was obvious Sadie was feeling a bit awkward.

'Yeah, thanks, Sadie, I could do with an extra pair of 'ands.' Sadie gratefully followed Nora back into the kitchen. ''Ere yer go, love, get that down yer,' Nora said gaily, handing Sadie a glass of sherry.

'Cheers, Nora.' Sadie took the drink gratefully. 'What d'yer want me ter do?'

Waving her hand in the air Nora said, 'Nothing,

thanks. I just thought you was looking a bit left outta it.'

Sadie leant her buttocks against the table. 'Is it that obvious?'

Nora laughed. 'Don't worry, mate, I don't think anyone else has noticed, 'specially the two lovebirds.' She nodded towards the other room where Ted and Ellen were standing together, smiling like doting parents as the four children played with the toys they had received for Christmas.

Following Nora's glance Sadie asked hesitantly, ''As there been any news of Arthur . . . I mean, about getting the annulment? 'Cos Ellen and Ted can't get married till it's all sorted. It must be hard fer you, I mean, with your Ted living at your 'ouse one minute, and here the next. It must be confusing fer the kids an' all.'

'Nah.' Nora waved her hand airily, the sherry beginning to take its toll. 'Kids tend ter take things at face value. They're much easier at dealing with changes in their lives just as long as they feel safe. Anyway, according ter Ellen it won't be too long now. They're just waiting fer the solicitors, that's probably what's 'olding everything up. Mind you, just between the two of us, I think the reason it's taking so long is 'cos Arthur's been dragging his feet, at least he was till he met the widowed sister of that Bradley woman. Like I said, up till a couple of months ago Arthur kept stalling every time Ellen wrote ter him, making up any excuse to delay signing the final papers. Now suddenly he's doing all he can ter hurry up the whole business. Of course he's making out he's doing it fer

Ellen's sake, but I've known Arthur since he was in short trousers.

He's the type of bloke that can't cope on his own. First he depended on 'is dad, then when he died he latched onto Agnes. I don't know the whys and where-fores of how he dumped Agnes, but I do know he started to spend more and more time with Ellen's parents after Ellen was born. From that time on he became besotted with Ellen. Yer see what I mean about him not being capable of living alone. Ellen and her parents became like a sort of family ter him. Now he's taken up with this widowed woman he's got someone else to look after him. I wouldn't be at all surprised if he announced he was getting married again, once the annulment has been finalised.

My Ted's already been ter the solicitors. Gave them a right rollicking he did, but them sort ain't easily frightened. Most likely they're making as much money as they can outta the whole thing while they still can. Gawd knows how long it'd take if they was trying ter get a divorce. Most likely be too long in the tooth to care,' she ended on a raucous laugh, then put her hand to her mouth in dismay. 'Bleeding 'ell, I'll be pissed if I 'ave any more. 'Ere, 'elp me get this turkey outta the oven, before it dries up.'

Ted and Ellen looked up at the sound of loud laughter coming from the kitchen.

'Sounds like Mum's been at the sherry again,' Ted grinned widely, his arm tightening around Ellen's waist. 'You all right fer a drink, Johnny?'

John Smith glanced up absently, his thoughts wandering to a time when he and Sarah had shared

367

many a Christmas together. Jolted out of his reverie, John put on a brave face for the young couple's benefit, though he was already regretting accepting their kind offer. Now he was here, he mustn't put a damper on the proceedings.

'Thanks Ted, I'll have another beer, please.'

While Ted fetched the beer, Ellen sat down on the arm of John's chair, saying gently, 'You must miss your wife terribly. I just want you to know that we won't be offended if you want to leave early, though it would be wonderful if you could stay for the day.'

John patted Ellen's hand affectionately. 'You're a lovely girl, Ellen. Ted's a lucky man, and so am I for having such good friends. It's a pity Agnes couldn't be with us, though I can understand why she wanted to get away, poor soul.' A look of sadness clouded his eyes. 'All her life Agnes wanted to be popular, to feel important, much the same as Arthur did. Then when she achieved that aim she couldn't handle it. It must have been very hard for her to suddenly find herself the centre of attraction. You would have thought she'd have gloried in having her name splashed all over the newspaper, and people who'd previously poked fun at her suddenly swarming round her, wanting to be her friend.

There's an old saying that goes, "Beware of what you wish for, 'cos it might come true." And that's what happened to Agnes. All that she wished for came too late. That's why she went away, she couldn't handle being in the limelight. But I think the real reason she upped sticks was because she didn't think she deserved the praise and fame that came after she'd put her life on the line to save Molly, because she still blamed herself for her part in the whole sordid episode.'

He fell silent, and Ellen waited, sure the solemn man had more to say, and she was right.

Toying with his empty glass John looked up at Ellen and asked, 'I don't suppose you know where she is, only I can't bear to think of her in some strange hotel or boarding house all alone on Christmas day.'

Ellen shook her head. 'No, I don't, Johnny, I wish I did. If we knew where she was Ted would have gone to fetch her home. The last we heard from her she wrote to say she was having a nice time and would be back soon – that was nearly a month ago.'

'What you two looking so gloomy about?' Ted handed John another beer. 'It's Christmas, everyone's happy at Christmas.'

John took the bottle of beer gratefully, hoping the alcohol would help cheer him into the festive proceedings.

'We were just talking about Agnes, and how we'd hoped she would have come back in time for Christmas,' Ellen answered.

The smile on Ted's lips wavered at the mention of Agnes. He most of all wished she could have shared the special occasion with them. He still hadn't shaken off the guilt for the awful way he had treated her, and he had a feeling he never would.

He was saved from further self-recrimination by his mother's voice calling loudly, 'Come on, you lot. Get yerselves up ter the table. Ellen, if yer could fetch the vegetables, Ted can start carving.'

Nora and Sadie were carrying a large platter upon

which rested the golden browned turkey and a large portion of roast potatoes. Putting the heavy tray onto the table Nora said, 'It's a good job Ted brought over the extra chairs, else some of us would've had to have our dinner standing up.'

Ellen had just finished saying grace, a ritual that was greeted with muffled glee by the Knight boys, until they were given a quick clout to the backs of their heads by an embarrassed Sadie, when they heard a loud knock on the back door.

'Good Lord, who could that be?' Ellen had risen to her feet.

'Sit down. I'll go and see who it is.' Ted pushed her gently back onto her chair. 'Don't start without me, will yer?'

Bounding down the stairs, he saw a large white envelope lying on the mat, and pulled open the door. There, on the doorstep were several gaily wrapped parcels. His head swinging from left to right he saw a figure walking quickly away and called out, 'Hey, Agnes, where yer going, yer silly cow?'

Agnes stopped in her tracks and turned to face Ted. 'I'm sorry, Ted. I didn't mean ter spoil yer Christmas dinner, only I just got back and I wanted ter leave the presents fer the kids.'

Ted caught at her arm and pulled her into the house, along with the parcels. 'Get inside, fer Gawd's sake, before we freeze ter death. Anyway, why didn't yer let us know you was back home? Yer know we would 'ave wanted yer with us at Christmas. I don't know why yer went away in the first place.'

With much pushing and prodding, Ted propelled the embarrassed woman up the stairs. Pushing open the door he shouted merrily, 'Look who I found lurking outside.'

A great cry of pleasure went up as the assembled group saw who it was. But it was Molly who ran into Agnes' arms. 'Oh, I'm glad yer came, Agnes. It wouldn't 'ave been the same without you, would it, Micky?'

Her face flushed, Agnes looked around the room, a sudden warmth spreading through her chilled body. She had been afraid she wouldn't have been welcomed, especially on a day primarily reserved for family. But she saw now she had been wrong. She hadn't been intruding. All these people were genuinely pleased to see her. It was an experience she wasn't used to, and she had to swallow the lump in her throat before answering, 'Yer sure I ain't disturbing yer?'

Ellen started towards her, but it was John who pulled up the one remaining chair and placed it beside him. 'Here you go, old girl. You sit with me.'

Her legs unsteady, Agnes sat down as Ellen said grace once again for the benefit of the late visitor. With the formalities over, Ted began carving the turkey, while Nora and Sadie made sure the children had enough vegetables on their plates, much to their disgust. But before the assembled group could start on the tantalising meal Ted rose to his feet. Looking around the table to make sure everyone had a drink he raised his glass.

'Merry Christmas, everyone. To friends and family,

all together on the best day of the year.' His eyes swept around the table, but it was Agnes his eyes lingered on as if he were speaking to her alone. And that kindly gesture created in Agnes a feeling of belonging – a feeling of being loved, and for a moment she feared she would break down. Then she felt a strong hand grip hers and looked up into John's face and the moment passed.

There was a tinkle of glasses touching, then a resounding 'Merry Christmas' filled the room before the hungry group began their meal.